ISSUES IN AMERICAN SOCIETY

ISSUES IN AMERICAN SOCIETY

Joseph Boskin

BOSTON UNIVERSITY

GENERAL EDITOR

Glencoe Publishing Co., Inc.

ENCINO, CALIFORNIA

dedication

teachers & dreamers & prodders: they moved my mind
into areas i never imagined:

melvin bernstein *who constantly questioned life's precepts*
erwin palmer *who understood the poetry of imagination*
kermit kuntz *who weaved history's complex tale*
david noble *who danced with ideas*
david ruja *who knew the difference between the "it" and "i"*
vladimir de lissivoy *who understood only too well the*
  wanting curiosity

Copyright © 1978 by Glencoe Publishing Co., Inc.

Glencoe Publishing Co., Inc.
17337 Ventura Boulevard
Encino, California 91316
Collier Macmillan Canada, Ltd.

Library of Congress Catalog Card Number: N76-4016

First printing 1978

ISBN 0-02-472330-4

CONTENTS

vii PREFACE

ix INTRODUCTION: THE HISTORICAL MOMENT IS NOW

xiv PART 1: ETHICAL QUESTS

3 *Chapter 1:* Because We Are Human Beings: On Ethical Impulses and Ethical Dilemmas *M. J. Lunine*

30 PART 2: TRADITIONAL KNOTS

33 *Chapter 2:* The Essential American Soul: Violent *Joseph Boskin*
53 *Chapter 3:* It Is Always the Woman Who Is Raped *Deena Metzger*
65 *Chapter 4:* Woman Talk: The Conversation and Various Asides on Woman's Culture, Water Coolers, W.C.s, and Children *Deena Metzger*
85 *Chapter 5:* *Day Work:* A Short Play and an Afterword *Floyd Barbour*
105 *Chapter 6:* "The poor always ye have with you" *Fred T. Arnstein*
133 *Chapter 7:* The Problem of Prisons *David F. Greenberg*

158 PART 3: TROUBLED DWELLINGS

161 *Chapter 8:* The State of Urban Society *Robert J. Ross*
183 *Chapter 9:* The Future Suburbs: The Closing Frontier *Jay Ostrower*

206 PART 4: INSTITUTIONAL DIMENSIONS

209 *Chapter 10:* The Custom-Made Family Blues *Roslyn L. Feldberg and Janet A. Kohen*
233 *Chapter 11:* Laboring in Contemporary America: Can we whistle while we work? *Joseph Boskin*
249 *Chapter 12:* Education for Justice and Freedom: The Economic Dimension *Paul Nash*
275 *Chapter 13:* How to Grow Old and Poor in an Affluent Society *Robert N. Butler*
295 *Chapter 14:* Scratching Our Revolutionary Itch: How Advertising Absorbs the Imagery and Slogans of Radicalism *David Kunzle*

316 PART 5: AN ALTERNATIVE

319 *Chapter 15:* The Mysterious Flavor of Cultural Radicalism *Robert A. Rosenstone*

331 CONTRIBUTORS

PREFACE

No society is without its serious problems. But to acknowledge and confront them is quite another matter. The core of difference between groups and nations is precisely in this area. One of the basic distinctions between a closed and an open society is that the latter is willing to admit its faults and to act to correct them. An open society recognizes that to bury or suppress its problems is to provide the groundwork for disruptive conflict and violence.

A hallmark of American society has been its introspective nature, its desire to probe beneath the surface in order to ascertain whether its vaunted ideals are being translated into reality. Often they are not. Numerous social and political programs have been devised over the years to remedy these failures. But all too often these programs have been either only half-hearted attempts or too shallow, barely touching the essentials of the problem. Especially in recent years, an "instant" approach too frequently has been taken to complex and troublesome issues, and so the problems continue to exist.

This work is an expression of the various types of issues and problems that confront American society. Some are tenacious difficulties, and others are newer issues. Regardless of its type or nature, however, no social problem stands alone. Each affects others, creates secondary problems elsewhere, and even solutions can lead to further ills.

The thrust of these articles, then, is towards a wholistic approach to social problems. Because all problems and solutions are entwined, we are forced to consider solutions which will affect the overall structure of society. Merely to tinker in one area at the exclusion of others is to create a patchwork of bandaids which will come off at the first rain. And so this book poses hard questions for us: what are the minimum and maximum policies which will enable us to bring about viable solutions to the problems that vex us? how will we go about producing such solutions?

who should participate in these discussions and debates? shall we leave the decisions to persons elected to political office?

This book poses further questions, suggests others, and demands still more. And therein lies the challenge: to formulate effective programs to deal with these issues and problems — and by so doing, to develop a society that is responsive to its inhabitants and meets the basic needs of all.

J. B.
Boston, Massachusetts
May 1977

INTRODUCTION: THE HISTORICAL MOMENT IS NOW

Norman Cousins, longtime editor of one of the most influential literary journals in the country, stated it succinctly in the mid-seventies:

> The most serious problem confronting the nation is not inflation or the energy shortage or dwindling resources or the danger of war in the Middle East. The most serious problem right now is that the American people are psychologically depleted and are not primed for innovation.
>
> Where does new hope begin?[1]

Considering the enormous vitality of the nineteen-sixties, with their intense challenges, demands for basic change, accent on *now*, and sense of power, Norman Cousins's question was both remarkable and frightening. How long has it been that way: the cold cynicism and hard anger, vaulting escapism and inner withdrawal, dismaying disappointment, halting expectations, and wavering directions that characterize contemporary American society? And how long will it remain that way? At a Washington Journalism Center conference in January 1976, economics professor Sar Levitan told the assembly that his statistics had failed him. They measured the nation's quantities, he noted, but were unable to deal with the elusive qualities of life. In frustration, Levitan reached for a green plastic pitcher, poured some water into a glass, peered out at the audience and quietly said, "You can focus on the half-full or the half-empty, and this is the age of focusing on the half-empty."

Levitan's view was shared by nearly all of the fifteen speakers who addressed the topic of the quality of American life. A psychiatrist, Murray Bowen, summed up the mood: "American society is an anxious mess." Pointing to a national malaise, Bowen groped for a historical meaning to the fierce crosscurrents he saw operating in America and concluded: "We are approaching the end of being able to continue our way of life on earth."[2]

Sam Bass Warner, in an address before an audience celebrating the Bicentennial, was more direct. "We are now a cancerous nation, ever dividing and subdividing into thousands of institutions public and private." Most of those institutions, he had noted on another occasion, "have been shorn of their legitimacy."[3]

The sixties proudly and insistently challenged American values and institutions, calling for a reordering of historical direction. The people who analyzed the complexity of society, who peered into hidden areas, exposed, and prodded, clearly operated from a set purpose. Strengthened by a philosophical and political knowledge of what ought to be, the activists sought to develop a caring culture, one in which the values of cooperation, peace, inner harmony, sharing, and abundance would prevail.

But their hopes were only partially realized. The system proved to be too formidable, too stolidly entrenched, too resistant to change. Those with power were able to conduct an enervating war in Southeast Asia and to seriously undermine the counterculture's antiwar movement and other programs. Although the antiwar forces were eventually able to effect withdrawal from Vietnam—and prevent Lyndon Johnson from running for reelection in 1968—they were unable to withstand the assault against themselves. As the record sadly demonstrates, the diverse movements of the sixties—feminist, ethnic, environmental, student, vegetarian—were all under surveillance, their ranks planted with informers, their telephones implanted with listening devices, their actions plotted, and their objectives decried and publicly distorted. The law-enforcement agencies on the local and federal levels constantly committed unlawful actions in their tenacious desire to prevent political change.

Gradually, these assaults upon the constitutional and moral foundation of society were exposed. In a startling series of revelations, it was disclosed that President Richard Nixon, elected by the largest popular majority in American electoral history, not only had conspired to establish a secret intelligence apparatus responsible only to himself, but had flagrantly lied about its operation and his role in it. He became the first president to resign, his action coming just before impeachment proceedings were about to begin in the House of Representatives. The man he had twice selected to serve as vice president, Spiro Agnew, had resigned from his post the previous year because of alleged criminal activities. "Watergate," the name of an office and residential complex in Washington where the bugged and infiltrated Democratic Party headquarters were located in 1972, became the symbol of the corruption. Many other persons involved in the Watergate affair were indicted and went to jail.

In a remarkable way, despite the disclosures and admissions of guilt, the persons involved with Vietnam and Watergate prevailed. The enormity of the crimes associated with Watergate did not exclude these people from the comforts of privileged prisons, lenient sentences, and financial profit. Many wrote books, travelled the lecture circuit, appeared on television, and were rewarded with celebrity status.

The war in Southeast Asia had other negative effects. President Lyndon Johnson, intent on fighting a war and simultaneously furthering his Great Society programs, stretched the financial resources of the nation. The massive war led to a massive recession. The economy was wrenched and disrupted. Millions lost their jobs, prices soared, governmental agencies cut welfare programs to the sick, aged, indigent, and jobless, and fears intensified. The capitalist system, always sensitive to the slightest influence, changed in two different directions. What economists had predicted would never occur, occurred. The country was confronted with both recession *and* inflation and the attendant unemployment and increasing costs. The thrust of the sixties had been shared abundance; the accent of the seventies was unshared scarcity. The sixties promoted communalism and equality; the seventies, a return to individualism and survival. As sociologist Robert Ross noted, Frank Sinatra's highly popular song "I Did It My Way" was America's national anthem.

How quickly the mood turned around. It went from optimism to despair and disillusionment; from a note of power to helplessness. The situation in the seventies evoked an old Depression song about being down and not liking it one whit:

> *I'm goin' down this road feelin' bad;*
> *I'm goin' down this road feelin' bad;*
> *I'm goin' down this road feelin' bad, Lord God,*
> *Cause I ain't goin' be treated thisaway.*
>
> *My kids need three meals a day;*
> *My kids need three meals a day;*
> *My kids need three meals a day, Lord God,*
> *And I ain't goin' be treated thisaway.*
>
> *I'm goin' where the climate suits my clothes;*
> *I'm goin' where the climate suits my clothes;*
> *I'm goin' where the climate suits my clothes, Lord God,*
> *And I ain't goin' be treated thisaway.*
>
> *These two-dollar shoes hurt my feet;*
> *These two-dollar shoes hurt my feet;*
> *These two-dollar shoes hurt my feet, Lord God,*
> *And I ain't goin' be treated thisaway.*

The alternating fluctuation of expectation and disillusionment characteristic of the sixties and seventies, however, is not an uncommon historical pattern. America's economic system is so constructed that it allows for wrenching swings both in people's socioeconomic situations and outlook on life. Despite these polar swings, until recently an optimistic attitude and philosophy prevailed. Philosopher Robert L. Heilbroner in *The Future as History* noted that optimism as a philosophy of life, as an attitude toward history, is "an enduring trait of national character" and "it could almost be called exclusively American."[4]

The events of the seventies, however, have assaulted the foundations of that philosophy. Confident expectations have not been met by compatible experience; rather, the opposite has proven to be the case. Polls taken during the seventies indicate that a substantial number of people perceive that the deep difficulties confronting society—material shortages, polluted environment, corrupt officials, racial tensions, urban decay, individual and group violence, bewildering bureaucracies, powerful multinational conglomerates, hustling businessmen, insensitive institutions—will not easily be solved. They will be an integral part of the landscape for many years to come. Moreover, in many instances the American public expects these problems to be permanent. Daily existence will become harsher, despite the loud denials of politicians.

Compounding the situation is the general failure of the media, and particularly of the most significant educational development of our technological age—television—to create a climate of rationality. The gap between image and reality has appreciably narrowed, obscuring and detracting from important issues. The visual media are being used both consciously and subliminally to prevent hard analysis of the system.

It remains, therefore, for the print media to deal with the crucial issues and problems of our time. This book attempts to place the current situation into historical perspective, analyze the nature of the issues, and present certain concrete alternatives. The volume will focus upon particular facets of the issues, but will relate them to the larger socioeconomic system. This work is not directed toward identifying social *problems*, for these subjects are publicly acknowledged areas of concern. Awareness of a problem is a crucial step in the development of public concern; this book deals with what are already social *issues*. It is around issues that positions are taken and around which forces organize to block or push forward major decisions. Social issues indicate dysfunctions of the structure of society.

Moreover, the articles in the volume arise from and express a profound concern. It is always difficult to know just how serious issues are; closeness to a situation sometimes produces myopia or exaggeration. But these issues are too deeply enmeshed in the social fabric to be lightly dismissed. It is essential to remember Pogo's discovery as he sought his detractors: "We have met the enemy," he announced, "and they is us."

Heilbroner sagely expressed it in other terms:

When we estrange ourselves from history we do not enlarge, we diminish ourselves, even as individuals. We subtract from our lives one meaning which they do in fact possess, whether we recognize it or not. We cannot help living in history. We can only fail to be aware of it.[5]

The historical moment calls for involvement.

1. Norman Cousins, "Confidence in U.S. Key to Our Future," *Boston Globe*, 5 **NOTES** January 1975.

2. Nick King, "Gauging the Quality of Life," *Boston Globe*, 18 January 1976.

3. Sam Bass Warner, Jr., ed., "The Two Revolutions," in *The American Experiment: Perspectives on 200 Years* (Boston: Houghton Mifflin Co., 1976), p. 13; "Perfection, Pastoralism and Public Policy," *Faculty Seminar on the Humanities and Public Policy*, Duke University, 13 January 1976, p. 2.

4. Robert L. Heilbroner, *The Future as History* (New York: Harper & Brothers, 1959), p. 17.

5. Ibid., p. 209.

SURVEY SHOWS SPANKING COMMON IN NATION'S SCHOOLS

(New York) The spanking of disruptive students is still widely practiced in the nation's public schools despite opposition from some parents and educators, an Associated Press survey shows.

Educators in Arizona, Connecticut, Florida, Georgia, Hawaii, Maine, Minnesota, Nevada, New Mexico, North Carolina, North Dakota, Ohio, Pennsylvania, South Carolina, Tennessee, Texas, and Wyoming say they still resort to spanking. It is used primarily in the elementary grades and junior high school, and the officials say it's done with discretion and only when all else fails.

[*Richard Burke, AP*, Boston Globe, *16 January 1976.*]

SEMINAR FOR IBM SECURITY OFFICERS URGES NETWORK FOR SPYING ON RADICALS

(Berkeley, Calif.) Nineteen IBM security officers earlier this month attended a seminar on combating terrorism which called for establishment of an intelligence network to spy on radical groups, the firm said last week.

[*Mike Silverman, AP*, Boston Globe, *14 November 1974.*]

A MAN MUST DO WHAT HE MUST DO—JUST DON'T GET CAUGHT

(Los Angeles) They will be businessmen, sitting down to fill out their income tax statements in front of the world Sunday afternoon at the Rose Bowl in Pasadena. They will be jaywalkers in full stride. They will be sleight-of-hand automobile and storm-door salesmen in full wheel and deal.

If the Super Bowl is supposed to best reflect the United States of America—brassy, overblown, wealthy, violent, and whatever—shouldn't the people playing in it reflect the average American? Why shouldn't they all be cheating?

"What's cheating?" Oakland Raider guard Gene Upshaw asked yesterday under the warm California sun. "You only cheat if you're caught. In our society, cheating is encouraged. Where have you been living? Cheating is the American way of life."

"Everybody cheats," Minnesota Viking defensive tackle Alan Page said. "On a percentage basis, I'd say 100 percent of all pro football players cheat sometimes."

[*Leigh Montville*, Boston Globe, *6 January 1977.*]

WHEN *the institutional trappings are removed, the rhetoric and bombast pushed aside, at bottom democratic societies rest upon faith in the social contract. Each individual, operating from understanding, compassion and responsibility, elects to create and participate in a society which reflects individual rights and democratic ideals. Along the way, each individual is required to reevaluate and rethink his or her position in relation to the direction and institutional framework of society. When it appears that basic values are being eroded or cannot be attained, it becomes necessary to reorder the way society functions.*

But what if the system has become rigidly fixed, unresponsive to its intrinsic values and to people's desires? What if the system no longer aims for the essential democratic values and even hampers their development?

If one word could describe the events of contemporary American society, that word would be corrupt. *The moral foundation of the country seems to have rotted away, making the dilemma of our times an ethical one. The problem is not just the corruption of the oil companies' passing millions of dollars to politicians, or of a vice president's taking illegal money in an unmarked envelope in the basement of the White House, or even of police organizations' and military groups' spying on those deemed suspect: it is all of these acts, but much more. The system is no longer responsible or responsive, because those in power, those who make policy and determine direction, represent powerful institutions that undermine the social contract.*

There are, of course, many persons in important posts who are responsible and concerned, but they have considerable difficulty maintaining themselves against those who would keep the corrupt status quo. A government contract administrator, for example, notices skullduggery in industrial-military spending, an "overrun" of two billion dollars, and mentions it to his superiors. Nothing is done. Eventually the administrator testifies before a congressional subcommittee and for his efforts is fired from his supposedly protected civil service position. There is some squawking about this action, but not much. The administrator is forced to spend his time and money fighting for his financial life. This example can be witnessed too many times in contemporary America.

The article in this section explores various aspects of the ethical problem. In "Because We Are Human Beings," M. J. Lunine movingly presents three personal episodes in contemporary America which reflect conflicts over values and issues. The article reinforces Bob Kuttner's challenging statement in The Village Voice *(quoted in* Harper's, *September 1973, p. 8), a thought which is crucial to our time: "If the system is entirely corrupt and the major forms of corruption institutionalized and licit, then the social contract is dead."*

ETHICAL QUESTS

1 | BECAUSE WE ARE HUMAN BEINGS:

On Ethical Impulses and Ethical Dilemmas

M. J. LUNINE

The biggest problem facing them—before I approached them—was how much popcorn and punch to have for a group that could number anywhere from forty to one hundred. That evening the public library was to have its Christmas program (public library—Christmas: is that constitutional? No problem: no known non-Christians around to worry or wonder about).

"Could I please leave this attaché case of books and papers behind your counter, while I go out for lunch?" I amiably asked the two librarians. In the process of writing this chapter I had been sorting out notes, documents, sources, thoughts, memories, and feelings in a corner of the children's section—the largest part of the library—and I had decided it would be presumptuous to leave my things spread across the low, broad table.

As I handed the heavy case across the counter, the person who took it from me looked at my stranger's face, weighed the object and the situation, and nervously said to her partner, "Say, you don't think there's a bomb in here, do you?" "I hope not," the partner replied, more poignantly than humorously. And I was speechless.

Palm Desert, California, where this incident occurred, is a monument of and to a class society. Superannuated, perennial adolescents live out joyless lives of unimaginative affluence and programmed hedonism while being served and serviced by an underclass conditioned to be more awed than outraged, more envious than resentful.

Is Palm Desert an aberration from American realities? Is it an abortion of America's possibilities? Is it the apotheosis of those possibilities? Or is it, somehow, all three?

What is this country becoming after its two hundredth birthday? What matters to us: what do we value? what do we believe in? *Is* there an "us"—or are there simply fragments of persons inside clusters of people? How ought human beings to live in this small world moving into the twenty-first century? And even if we know what we want, have we any choice, any chance of influencing or changing the institutions of a centralized, postindustrial society with a garrison-state mentality and a multinational, monopolistic economy?

Must violence be as American as popcorn and punch at Christmas programs in public libraries? Or do we have it within our individual and collective (organizable) will and capability to create—not to re-create—a decent and just society as part of a humane and sane world?

On these ethical and political matters, in the crucial job of raising these questions again and again, this country's best teachers have been its students. For the past fifteen years, articulate, active, nonviolent students have been our major source of conscience and compassion, and of self-effacing conviction and courage. In the midst of materialism, racism, and belligerent nationalism, they have spoken out and acted for human values, for equality, and for peace. As I wrote in an open letter to President Nixon on May 4, 1973, with such students primarily in mind:

> Future historians will note that the trustees of personal liberty and social justice during these obscene times were precisely those whom you and yours have calumniated. Future historians will note that the true patriots of these obscene times were those who protested racism cloaked in Law and Order, poverty cloaked in Free Enterprise, pollution cloaked in Progress, and wanton war cloaked in National Interest.

Colleges and universities during the fifteen-year period from Vietnam to Watergate have been this society's barometer—and occasionally its compass. This is as it should be in a society that would be open, pluralistic, experimental, self-correcting, and dependent on the rule of reason tempered by love.

This examination of the ethical dilemma of American society focuses and builds on the recent history, current situation, and future prospects of college students' social expression and involvement. For it is students who have moved this country—or tried—by asking those questions worthy of human beings and good societies and by seeking and sometimes providing answers. And it is the academy that has not only conserved and handed down accumulated knowledge, useful techniques, and seasoned values but also provided the arena for discussed and practiced change. The academy remains a rational society's best institutional source of conscience and criticism.

This chapter has four intentions: (1) to give the reader through three case studies a sense of fundamental ethical issues and struggles as experienced by actual, though in some instances now dead, individuals in specific academic institutions over the period 1960–1975; (2) to observe the apparent decline and possible death of student dissent, protest, and proposal of any possibilities of real change in America for the better; (3) to suggest that there really survive both continuity of conscience and effort and a possibility, therefore, of peaceful, real change; and (4) to consider the ethical dilemma posed by such continuity and possibility.

Long before America's involvement in Southeast Asia and Watergate became part of the national experience (and grist for the mill of a celebration of the intrinsic virtue and durability of our national system), pockets of faculty and students were seeking and discussing not merely new sets of facts, but new ways of observing, analyzing, and facing up to the realities of a revolutionary age of enormous power concentration and manipulation, and of horrendous nuclear and population explosions.

These people said that the dynamic realities of the world were poverty, hunger, disease, illiteracy, and joylessness, combined with the unprecedented thrust of people everywhere toward identity and individual dignity—not a new holy war between superpowers for mythical ideological purity and illusory world primacy. They tried to keep alive the awareness that mankind has the power and the weakness to destroy itself in a nuclear holocaust. They pointed out that the gap in the quality and quantity of life between the poor nations and the rich nations continues to get larger. They argued that the "communist world" was neither monolithic nor purely evil, and that the "free world" similarly was neither unified nor in all its parts subject to the constitutional rule of law and dedicated to liberty, justice, and a decent life for all.

Both teachers and students came to see that the United States itself was already in a period of fundamental, far-reaching, perhaps revolutionary change and had to be understood from this perspective. We were being challenged by our own ideals; individual, institutional, systemic, prejudiced exploitation of racial "minorities," of female people, of poor people, of old people, of migratory workers, of culturally or behaviorally "different" people began to be understood as, of all things, un-American. We were conceding that this richest nation of all time has incredible, intolerable, institutionalized poverty amidst, because of, and for the sake of plenty. We were experiencing overt changes in the structure of our national government and in the process of decision making. We saw the ascent of the executive branch and the erosion of checks and balances by the Congress, the press, and the people; the increasing use and misuse of surveillance, secrecy, and official violent crime at home and abroad in the name of our national interest and honor; and the growing tendency to substitute such garrison state values as orthodoxy, conformity, and obedience for the open society values of diversity, dissent, and trust in the democratic process. We sensed we were on the brink of—or already part of—a technological revolution which was changing the way we work, live, and try to order our individual and collective lives, a revolution resisted by the moralisms and the mythology of a preindustrial economy in an agrarian society. Especially in the colleges and universities we were feeling the shock waves of a knowledge (or at least an information) explosion, and we were simultaneously thrilled and bemused by the multiplicity of things to try to understand, by the obsolescence of information, and by the rise in stature and authority of experts and specialists. We were viewing, assessing, and frequently participating in a clash of cultures, generations, and ethical systems. It was (and is) a revolution in the arts, the media, language, and reason itself—with an absence of consensus on the meaning of decency, the meaning of patriotism, even the meaning of meaning.

In the 1960s, in our courses, articles, books, and campus and community forums and speeches, we unfortunately had intimations of how and why within fifteen years there would be the "escalation" of Vietnam, the public phenomenon of a Watergate, and the at-last-acknowledged abuses of responsibility, law, and human decency by the FBI, CIA, and IRS.

We talked about the absence of consensus in the United States on such crucial fundamentals as freedom and dissent (civil liberties) and human dignity and social justice (civil rights). We decried a new and complicated form of isolationism: greater involvement around the world, a decreasing appreciation of the realities of the world, and a decreasing ability to relate to most of the people of the world. We sensed a loss of nerve and of humor in our country, epitomized by those who tried to ban Plato (a "homosexual") in Texas; Robin Hood (a "Communist") in Indiana; and thinking (the John Birch Society, among others) anywhere. We diagnosed a national increase in anxiety, leading either to hostility and the need for devil theories, scapegoats, and targets or to self- or media-induced complacency, leading to apathy, hedonism, and withdrawal. We observed a growth of fear: fear of ideas, of criticism, of reform, and of change, with an inability to confront the tragic complexity of personal, national, and international events. In short, we (perhaps superfluously) proclaimed that the United States was an intellectually and emotionally underdeveloped nation.

During this period of national and worldwide change, higher education itself was undergoing radical transformations, sometimes the effect of, and sometimes an influence on, the other changes already mentioned. In general, for higher education the proliferation of institutions, programs, and purposes was accompanied by the disintegration of shared values, priorities, activities, and goals. Colleges and universities, especially state universities, were caught at the vortex of social, economic, and political pressures as they opened their doors to previously excluded groups of students and experienced the ups and downs of uncertain financial support from all levels of government, from foundations, and from the often-aligned military, space, and industrial research interests. A confusion, if not a cacophony, of notions arose as to what a university should be and should do; who should teach what to whom for what purpose, and with how much regard for personal development and social change?

We were concerned that, ironically, higher education was resulting in a growing disintegration of the educational experience and of the person experiencing it; an increasing disconnection of information (facts) from knowledge (understanding) and wisdom (awareness of purposes and ends) contributing to a corrupting separation of public behavior from personal values.

Students articulated and demonstrated the need for colleges and universities to practice what they teach about the dignity of each individual, the efficacy of reason, the importance of due process and equal rights, the necessity of beauty and creativity, and the ethical and organic relationship of education to society's institutions.

We asked, and we continue to ask: How can we educate people capable of comprehending and responding creatively to an age of profound change with its proliferation of ideas and events? What style, spirit, and substance of education (formal and informal, collegiate and lifelong) can we devise that will nurture the development of individuals who respect themselves and others and in whom there is a harmony of private belief and public action?

The reader should try to interpret the following three case studies in terms of the environment of the past fifteen years, an environment of revolutionary changes internationally and domestically, of great growth and great confusion in higher education, of marvelous individual searches and efforts, and of monstrous institutional seizures and reactions.

II

One student who respected himself and others and lived a life that harmonized his private beliefs with his public statements and actions was John C. Farrell. During his junior year, in 1962, as editor in chief of the University of Colorado's *Colorado Daily*, John received the Overseas Press Club Award for the best editorials dealing with foreign affairs in United States college journalism. His greatest service for those of us then at the University of Colorado (and indeed throughout and beyond the state of Colorado), however, was his tough-minded analysis of domestic civil liberties issues such as free speech, the right of dissent, academic freedom, and due process and his spirited advocacy of often unpopular, though always decent and democratic, positions.

It was a time of innocence even for involved liberals. It was before whites were treated like blacks—in Chicago, in Washington, and at Kent State; it was before we destroyed a part of the world to save it. But the issues revolved around the fundamental, precious ethic of civil liberty: individual rights of conscience, speech, dissent, and assembly; a free society's dependence on criticism and debate; and procedural, "negative" freedom from government interference and restraint. John Farrell examined and defended those rights to the edification and benefit of thousands in a way very few other collegiate or professional editors have.

Of course, he was controversial. He was attacked by major and minor Colorado newspapers, criticized by individual students and student groups, accused of complicity in a conspiracy by a prominent faculty member, and castigated by the American Legion. But he persisted and he prevailed, as the following excerpts from his writings, together with some comments of mine, suggest. He helped move this country and helped us understand better what this country might be.

A review of the major stories in a single issue of the *Colorado Daily* (May 10, 1962) provides an insight into the mood of not only one public university but actually much of the national literate community of that time. The contention aroused by the issues, the course of the events described, and the atmosphere of concern and conflict were all being analyzed and often influenced by John Farrell.

The banner read: "ASUC [student senate] Asks HUAC [House Committee on Un-American Activities] Abolition." The main headline for the lead story was: "Rozek Charges Plot—Nine to Testify in District Court." Inside the paper was a report about University President Quigg Newton's asking the American Legion to drop "unsubstantiated charges" and defending the freedom of certain students and university employees. And on the now-famous editorial and letters page was an editorial by Farrell entitled "Um Yum," dealing puckishly with charges that the *Daily* was not taking the Spring Weekend festivities and frivolities seriously.

The campus appearance of Senator Barry Goldwater prompted some controversial behavior several days before the event by members of the Young People's Socialist League. An extraordinary seventeen-minute-long introduction of Goldwater in the form of a castigation of YPSL by CU Professor Edward J. Rozek stimulated an immediate and continuing controversy about whose rights, reputations, and liberties had been abused or curtailed, with the result that three faculty members, three students, and three administrative officials were charged with conspiracy to stifle academic freedom on campus. A complicated, classic case. Conspiracy was not proved. But the university and the state learned much about the nature of individual freedom, of serious universities, and of society's efforts to be open.

The student senate's HUAC resolution stated:

> Dissent is necessary, as Supreme Court Justice William O. Douglas argues, for the full development of a free and democratic society. For such a society in which open intellectual inquiry will be developed, in which members of the academic community will be invited to criticize and debate, in which the meaning of "American" will not be dogmatically imposed, the HUAC must be abolished.
>
> Therefore, be it resolved: That the ASUC believes in the inherent right of the individual in a free and open society to express without fear of recrimina-

tion any opinion which is neither libelous nor slanderous nor constitutes conspiracy or incitement to commit a concrete criminal act,

And, that the ASUC believes the HUAC is restricting both academic freedom and intellectual inquiry,

And, that the ASUC deplores the HUAC's continuous assault against the academic community (such as the recent subpoenaing of students at Los Angeles),

And, that the ASUC therefore urges the abolition of the HUAC.

A sad footnote to this story and the history of our recent past is that the student senator who introduced the resolution, Allen Nossaman (the previous editor in chief of the *Colorado Daily*), found it necessary to warn his colleagues before they voted "that a vote for the proposal might mean that they would later be called Communists for their action." Incidentally, the vote was six to four in favor, with two abstentions.[1]

President Newton's reported remarks were splendid. "I will not interfere with the right of faculty members or students to speak their minds honestly, whether what they say is popular or unpopular. I will not act on the basis of unsubstantiated rumor. And I will not destroy the things the University stands for in order to appease careless and poorly informed critics."[2]

John Farrell in his editorial this same day wrote: "Rather than rebut these unfounded charges [that we sneered at the traditional Homecoming festivities, leered at the traditional Miss CU festivities, and jeered at the traditional CU Days festivities] with tedious argument, or recite the CU Days Pledge of Allegiance to the effect that the traditional Um Yum Breakfast is better than Quaker Puffed Wheat, we will instead utilize this space for a message on the meaning of CU Days, the current event in the festivity cycle."[3]

Farrell always wrote with precision and passion and humor. On March 5, 1962, Denver's *Rocky Mountain News* columnist Pasquale Marranzino attacked the "shameful display of bad behavior" of YPSL during the Rozek-Goldwater event. He suggested that the organization "should be thrown off the campus until the affiliate can gain some adult posture or learn some manners. Each member should be publicly identified and their parents should be informed of their behavior." He concluded: "I know the great liberals—especially the juveniles on the *Colorado Daily*, the campus newspaper—will cry bitter tears over these suggestions. I know I am interfering with free speech and constitutional rights and all that bunk."

John's editorial response the next day: "The *News* is usually a mite more subliminal in suggesting that the First Amendment is bunk; it's rare that we have such a forthright statement of that paper's political philosophy as the judicious Marranzino has given us in his most recent constitutional opinion. All that bunk, eh, Pocky?"

After the Leyden-Chiles-Wickersham American Legion Post No. 1 of Denver passed a resolution asking that the University investigate YPSL and "any and all other un-American activities, groups and individuals connected with the University," John Farrell commented in a long editorial, "Marching Up To Boulder":

> The American Legion is to politics what a drum and bugle corps is to a parade—noisy, unsophisticated, and a lot of fun.
>
> But sometimes the strident voice of the Legion, like the shrill toot of a horn, can get on your nerves. In its latest attempt to make a political comment, the voice of the Legion rises to an unnerving pitch to proclaim that un-American activities are in full sway at the University with tacit administrative approval. . . .
>
> The resolution was prompted by the now-celebrated visit of Sen. Barry Goldwater. It asserted that YPSL violated the senator's "constitutional rights and the dignity of his office" by heckling. "The officers and those in authority at the University of Colorado have done nothing to correct the situation and leave the unfortunate impression that the Young People's Socialist League was right in this disgraceful demonstration," the resolution states.
>
> First the facts. YPSL did not violate the senator's constitutional rights. They did not try to prevent Goldwater from exercising his constitutional right of free speech. Rather, they criticized his ideas and protested a preferential seating plan used by the campus Young Republicans at a public meeting where the hall was paid for not by the YR's, but by a state university. . . .
>
> So if it's un-American to be a pesky proponent of your point of view (which in YPSL's case is democratic socialism—anti-Communist as well as antireactionary), then YPSL is un-American. . . .
>
> The point here was best made a few years ago by Supreme Court Chief Justice Earl Warren who said: "Who can define the meaning of un-American?"
>
> Well, we're not sure if the First Amendment permits a definition of un-American; but if one is to be attempted, the American Legion is not the group to do it. Like the mustard-flavored belch of a Legionnaire enjoying a Fourth of July picnic, the definition would be humorous but not precise.[4]

The Overseas Press Club Award was deserved by Farrell; he did write about international affairs in addition to and in the process of writing about domestic matters. But he understood before most of his contemporaries that no human or social issue is only domestic or only foreign.

When he introduced the *Daily's* new weekly supplement, "The Gadfly," in an editorial, Farrell showed his sense of the interrelatedness of events and problems and of the organic unity of all people—the source of his undying belief in the possibility of understanding and controlling events. "We will attempt to produce a magazine that will arouse student interest and concern about social issues that we must understand and work toward resolving because we are human beings. . . . Students who become provoked by the 'Gadfly' will seek out other newspapers, magazines, and journals to become better informed about the world and its inmates. Perhaps they might use this knowledge to in some small way make the world a better place in which to live."

Perhaps John's most significant editorial statement was his piece on the appearance and the meaning of Senator Goldwater and "Goldwaterism." This piece reveals his political discernment, his philosophical acuity, his historical perspective, his social predilections, and his ethical sensibilities. It also prophesies where he would put his life—though he had no way of knowing it then—and the direction of many of his fellow young Americans' struggles and efforts.

A QUESTION, BARRY

Today's speech by Sen. Barry Goldwater should be of historical interest to some, while inspiring nostalgia in those old enough to remember Chautauqua meetings.

Everyone should attend his speech, not to hear the next president of the United States—elections are won in the big cities, not in resorts—but to hear an echo of the thundering hoofbeat political philosophy of Social Darwinism, the creed best expressed in the Gospel according to Carnegie. Seventy-five years after the Social Darwinians had been disposed of by reformers from Henry George to Teddy Roosevelt, the same arguments turn up today shrouded in the homespun lingo of Rugged Individual Goldwater.

For after all, the homilies of Goldwater are the same as those expounded by William Graham Sumner and Herbert Spencer to justify the gorging of wealth that this country witnessed in the last half of the nineteenth century by the "robber barons" from Rockefeller to Morgan.

For these men, aggrandizement of wealth was proof that they were fit to survive. The Social Darwinians used Darwin's biological concept of the "survival of the fittest" to argue that government's intervention in behalf of the common man, who was being exploited by the wealthy, would constitute interference with nature's processes. In short, Social Darwinism explained to the satisfaction of the gentry of that day why they should suffer no pangs of conscience for the natural process of the rich getting richer and the poor getting poorer.

Goldwater's philosophy is identical. His "rugged individuals" demonstrate their claim to success and happiness in the competition of the marketplace. For the government to concern itself with the needs of the society's downtrodden at the expense of curtailing the sometimes voracious appetite of the Rugged Individual is not only un-natural, but un-American.

What the Social Darwinians overlooked is the same fact that their political progeny, Barry Goldwater, fails to recognize today. A man's ability and gumption are not the only factors in determining his success.

Perhaps the best way to illustrate this fact is to pose a question for Sen. Goldwater to answer this afternoon: Had you, Sen. Goldwater, been born a Negro in the squalid slums of Savannah, Georgia, or in the oppressive poverty of a peasant's hut in Brazil, do you think you would be here today proclaiming the merits of the Rugged Individual?

What became of John Farrell? He married Beverly Curry in June of 1962, and graduated a year later to go on to earn master's degrees in history at Colorado and in international relations at Columbia. He was an assistant editor at the Stanford University Press and at the age of twenty-six editor in chief of Columbia University's *Journal of International*

Affairs. By 1968, in addition to doing graduate work at Columbia, he had edited and written introductions for two volumes of essays, *Image and Reality in World Politics* and *Theory and Reality in International Relations*. In October 1970 he began his Ph.D. work with Louis Hartz in the American Civilization Program at Harvard.

Before joining the Latin American program of the Ford Foundation, John's experience also included being the speech writer and press secretary for a congressional candidate from Colorado, serving as a foreign service officer in Ecuador for a United States government he knew and asserted was engaged in an immoral war in Indochina, and working for two years in Washington as legislative assistant to congressman Al Lowenstein of New York. While in Quito, John and Beverly adopted Pia; a second daughter, Kerry, was born just before their arrival in Bogota in June, 1972.

Ten years after John had speculated about the chances for any kind of decent life for one born "in the oppressive poverty of a peasant's hut in Brazil," he found himself in Colombia helping establish a Research Center for the Defense of Public Interests. The center had begun working on environmental issues that directly affected the interests of the poor, helping a fishermen's cooperative protest factories' dumping waste and killing fish on the Magdalena River and protesting the use of dangerous pesticides that allegedly had caused birth defects among farm families.

It made sense that John was doing this work, helping solve human problems in his country, the world. In the opening pages of his doctoral dissertation, John had written: "Individual men, endowed by nature with a sense of fraternity, are able to consider and sometimes even to prefer the interests of others to their own."

It made no apparent sense that John's marvelous heart failed in June, 1975. He was 34.

The story of John Farrell—and of countless other students, faculty, and townspeople in Boulder and across the country—is an episode in the continuing struggle to define and defend the constitutional rights, the civil liberties, of free individuals. Coming into clearer and more central focus during the mid-sixties was another dimension of the struggle: the fight for the civil (human) rights of a decent life—dignity, equality, good housing, education, employment, full participation in and protection by society.

John had anticipated this shift of focus in his editorial comments about "The Gadfly" and about Goldwater's insensitivity to the plight of the poor. He had also addressed the issue of human rights in an editorial (May 1, 1962) about the Voting Rights Bill controversy:

> The Southern senators are filibustering with good cause. If the Negro gets the vote he will undoubtedly use it to retire from Congress those many segregationists who impair our democratic image, both to our own citizens who suffer under the primitive systems of segregation, and to people around the world who question our right to pose as the land of the free as long as

this system exists. . . . Members of the conservative coalition in the Senate see nothing wrong with using the weary states' rights doctrine as a justification for preserving individual rights—the right of white individuals to discriminate against black ones.

III

On January 7, 1964, at 10:20 A.M., about sixty civil rights demonstrators—mostly black and mostly young—left the First (black) Baptist Church of Nashville and headed downtown to peacefully picket two cafeterias (the B & W and Cross-Keys) for the right of black people to eat there. We were well-organized and instructed to be careful of street lights and of other people's and our own safety.

At 10:25 A.M., we passed in front of the War Memorial Building, singing: "Everybody wants freedom, everybody wants freedom, everybody wants freedom, free-dom, free-dom." We were walking slowly enough for me to note the giant, fine words inscribed on the front of the monumental building: "America Is Privileged To Spend Her Blood And Her Might For The Principles That Gave Her Birth And Happiness And The Peace Which She Has Treasured."

We passed in front of the Chamber of Commerce Building at 10:30 A.M. The American flag was waving briskly. We were singing "We shall overcome . . . some-day . . . some-day." Two policemen were efficiently directing traffic. Two bystanders, well-dressed white businessmen, took it all in. One said to the other, "We ain't come very far since the Civil War." Two less well-dressed white men were sitting, with heads drooping, on the end of the Chamber of Commerce patio. "That's just like a bunch of niggers. They ought to be in school. I'm paying taxes for their schools," one said loudly. "Gonna be a lot of ignorant niggers," his companion commented.

By 10:40 A.M., our group rendezvoused with another contingent of marchers, who were singing as they joined us, "I'm so glad we're fighting for our rights." At a nearby parking lot a white attendant remarked to his buddy, "A few of 'em are gonna cross the wrong person. And somebody's gonna get hurt." "I'll be there when the season opens up," the buddy wisecracked.

We had been circling in front of the entrance of the B & W Cafeteria, singing "I'm so glad . . ." for about fifteen or twenty minutes when, at 11:15 A.M., a gang of young, white toughs obviously out for a fight showed up. "They ain't going in here, Daddy," one of them called out.

At 11:22 A.M., two policemen came and separated the demonstrators from the antidemonstrators. The two groups faced each other, and waited. A tall, well-dressed white lady remarked quite audibly, "They ought to get some scalding hot water," pointing to the windows four stories above. Another well-dressed white woman began handing out hate literature to the white toughs. They skimmed it for a moment and then, in response to the resumed singing of the demonstrators, broke out in a chorus of "Dixie."

By now more police had appeared. Demonstrators were trying to maintain their positions in the circle in front of the restaurant. Some pushing and scuffling was beginning. The police were studiously polite to both sides, but one could notice some back-of-the-hand giggling and occasional fraternal nudging.

Two black soldiers, nattily dressed in the uniform of an airborne division, came by and kept walking. "I think I'll go back to Panama," one said. Two young, white ladies in their twenties joined the crowd. "They're just little kids." "They don't know what they're fighting for."

The singing had changed to a locomotive cheer: "Give me an F—F! Give me an R—R! . . . What does it spell—Freedom! Again—Freedom!! Louder—Freedom!!!"

Some delegates from Memphis to a convention in Nashville stopped to observe and comment: "It's all Communist-inspired." "In Russia they'd put 'em in front of a firing squad." "I got a bunch of bloodhounds. I'd like to turn 'em loose and have 'em run through 'em."

The police chief arrived and issued a courteous appeal for no violence. He put his hand gently on the shoulder of a black teenage girl, who reacted almost hysterically, "Don't you put your hands on me!" A white tough proclaimed, "More fun than I've had in a long time."

The two young, white women exchanged more comments. "I don't know which group is worse." "It's a darn shame—white people and colored people."

More singing, more pushing, some grabbing and punching. "Give me an F . . . ." Suddenly and loudly, sirens: at 12:40 P.M., four fire engines, sirens screaming, roared into the street area in front of the B & W. The whites in the crowd roared back in approval. I wondered: is this a show of force—not by the police, but by other official, uniformed, equipped forces of the city—to disperse the demonstrators? (The fire engines had responded to a false alarm, was the later, official explanation.)

The police chief made the final comment, as everyone dispersed: "They have just as much right to stand on the sidewalk as we have. But if 9,000 sightseers wouldn't watch them, they'd stop it."

But sightseers or not, "they" didn't stop—for a long time.

This one incident of many gives the reader some feel of the struggle for civil rights in the sixties. It also raises many of the issues and complexities—psychological, sociological, economic, political, and, of course, racial—of life in the United States at that time.

Many blacks and some whites carried on the struggle, forcing the country—for a while, at least—to look at itself more seriously and critically than it had in the previous hundred years. "Black power," in all its manifestations, forced us to face squarely certain philosophical and ethical questions about human rights and human misery, social injustice, economic inequities, and political imbalance. There were also the pragmatic questions, Who *has* power in the United States? How and why is this power employed? Who makes the important decisions in "our" system and by what means? What are the effects of these decisions? And can anyone do anything about them?

Our discussions in the mid-sixties (as later in the mid-seventies) about the crisis in American values, focused on the epicenter of the earthquake: the turbulent area of the struggle for human rights, the painful effort to make America be in her practice what she had pretended to be in her rhetoric. "I am here to talk about the focal point of the crisis in American values," I would begin lectures and panel discussions in Tennessee, Massachusetts, New Mexico, Washington, and Ohio, "the cluster of responses to our national flaws and failures that is black power. Black power must be understood as a response to an intolerable situation that shows no signs of being corrected by our present economic and

United Press International

political systems and by the prevailing religious and social ethics of American civilization."

There is no single conceptual or operational definition of black power. It has many dimensions.

Black power is inarticulate groans of anguish; obscene shouts of defiance; frightening acts of mindless and of calculated violence; demagogic statements of racial chauvinism, colored Marxism, and pseudo-intellectualism.

It is also useful works of rigorous scholarship and documented research; precious creations of beauty and meaning; and important interpretations of the racial struggle in the United States as a functional part of the worldwide fight for freedom for oppressed peoples.

Moreover, it is an indictment of American ideology as vacuous, if not false; of the prevailing Christian ethic as self-deceptive, if not deceitful; and of the American political system as unrepresentative, unresponsive, irresponsible, irrational, and racist. Black power represents a dissatisfaction with civil rights laws and their implementation for being superficial, slow, and neocolonialist, and with the American economic system for being exploitative, manipulative, irresponsible, and racist.

Black power also is an indictment of the "American way of life" as materialistic, hedonistic, neurotic, inhumane, hypocritical, shallow, and racist; an indictment of America as an overgrown child, unwilling to face realities and unable to solve her problems, lacking the values, the ideas, the institutions, the techniques, the imagination, and the will to really even try.

What I am calling black power—this complex cluster of anguish and yearning, of hate and hope, of violence and beauty, of speechless outrage and articulate proposals, of protests and programs—can also be a coherent, if sometimes vague, ideology involving goals and tactics.

Black students in the 1960s understood the two basic needs of black power as an ideology and program: self-respect and self-determination. It was they who took the lead in defining themselves as black and in helping create this sense of identity, pride, and commitment in large numbers of poor and ignorant blacks as well as their more affluent and smug brothers and sisters.

While many of the most articulate black students were humanistic and hopeful, not all blacks in the colleges and universities were optimistic. The mood of many young black people shifted, especially after the killing of Dr. Martin Luther King., Jr., in Memphis in April 1968. Deeper doubt and greater ambivalence than ever seemed to be troubling many young black people.

Outstanding among the more deeply critical students at Fisk University was Donald L. Graham, known to his fellow students, because of his extraordinary artistic talents, as "Dante." Dante would leave school, give serious thought to leaving society, but finally, in Joycean fashion, forge in the smithy of his soul—out of his passionate feeling, incisive analysis, and lively, growing artistry—poetry that would catch, as black novelist and essayist John Oliver Killens would suggest, "the many-sided moods of black America today, especially *young black America*."

One of the most revealing selections from Graham's *Black Song* (published in Nashville, November 21, 1966) is a poem that, as Killens says in his introduction to the slender, powerful volume, "is calmly devastating and states the mood of thousands of black young men who stand today at the western ridge."

> *the west ridge is menthol-cool*
>
> *the west ridge is an old ridge -*
> *a cold dying place,*
> *tired waves swirl beneath*
> *the green torch lady*
> *and death rides the stark gray water - birds*
>
> *down by the river a cross burns*
> *in perverted truth -*
> *spreading its inverted light;*
> *casting ragged shadows.*
> *as cladded men dance jim crow jigs*
> *amidst children standing*
> *like small tents.*
>
> *the grain has withered on its stalks -*
> *and drooped with the oleanders -*
> *in a mush - brown - wet - rot*
> *pale bodies writhe in ecstasy -*
> *unmindful of the blood - caked - mud upon their skins -*
> *while their bastard children cower in corners -*
> *and pray for purity to the nadinola gods -*
>
> *the sands are shifting*
> *the wind is cold today and*
> *there's likely to be hell tomorrow for*
> *the green lady holds only embers*
>
> *all around, brothers are balled*
> *like ebony chains*
> *whispering truths in a black hue*
> *the black exodus is on . . .*
> *we are going to "step-all the way up" and out of*
> *this menthol scented lie . . . .*
> *the cry - "uhuru"* [5]

Graham's disciplined fury suggests a dismal future: large numbers of Americans estranged, alienated, and ready for violence and revolution, this in turn producing a reaction of massive suppression of the black militancy and also of whatever chance our society might have had to face and solve her crucial problems.

Graham/Dante himself actually returned to Fisk to finish his academic work, later pursuing graduate studies while continuing to develop and publish his poetry. He returned to Fisk in 1969 to teach writing, and became known as a serious teacher with high standards. He remained angry, but angry, as Killens put it, "with an artistic vengeance, meaning that his artistry was equal to his righteous indignation." During his second year of teaching, growing more and more as a teacher and as an artist, Dante (together with another young faculty member, a teacher of business administration who wrote and loved poetry) was killed in an automobile accident. He was 25. He left a pregnant wife and some angry-loving poems.

The proposition is very simple. Black America's problems symbolize the problems of our entire nation, problems that epitomize the crisis in American values:

Each individual's problems of personal identity, human dignity, purpose and meaning in life; of being free to define and authenticate one's own life; of being able to make it as far as one's ability dictates.

Society's problems of providing a decent standard of living for all; of solving the old curse of poverty and inequality in a new age of automation and megalopolis; of constructing a truly representative, responsible, and humane government; of producing a truly just system of laws equally enforced and equitably adjudicated.

The world's problem of applying human intelligence and sympathy to the solution of man-made problems.

The preceding analysis of black power during the 1960s was based on the personalities, expressions, and activities of particular black students, teachers, writers, and artists during that time. That we are at present in a period of apparent peace and quiet does not diminish its significance or alter the objective realities of the conditions that gave rise to black power movements. By 1967 I had realized that the black American (ironically enough) is the prototypical American: he or she typifies America's economic, political, social, and ethical problems (and the imperative need for America to solve them) better than any other American can. By May, 1970, I realized that especially in times of tension, conflict, and repression, the plight of the least powerful members of a society also is prophetic of that society's direction as a whole.

IV

I was both surprised and incredulous when a black woman student told me in May of 1968 that the National Guard, which was carrying on "practice maneuvers" in north Nashville just off the Tennessee State and

Fisk campuses, was moving in "to destroy us physically, as they've destroyed our identity. . . . There's no possibility of communication or of reconciliation."

I had been deeply touched but intellectually unpersuaded by some black students' invitation to my wife and me to join them in one of the more strongly built Fisk dormitories, where paramedical supplies and skills were available.

Two years later, National Guardsmen would kill four and wound nine white students, and hundreds of survivors for several years after would be organizing paramedical and paralegal services and facilities on the campus of Kent State University in Kent, Ohio, U.S.A.

Two years later, a decade and maybe an age of hopeful protest and proposals would come to an end at Kent State. Two years later, the two thrusts of the ethical impulse of the sixties would converge: the cause of individual civil liberties—conscience, speech, dissent, assembly—and the cause of the most basic civil right—life—would meet in a death embrace on the common at Kent State. And after the gun smoke had cleared, we would see that white, middle-class students had been niggerized and an American public university and town Vietnamized.

Of course, Kent State, like Watergate a little later, served only to support and substantiate what black folk had been saying all along, observed Professor Gloria Joseph of Hampshire College. She felt that black people had long been on the receiving end of the repressive tactics of those in power, but that only when repression was felt by white America did it become a problem, and that only then did people become concerned about a rising trend towards fascism.

It is true, Dr. John P. Adams of the Board of Christian Social Concerns of the United Methodist Church has written, that "such abuses of authority often take place in the United States—in certain cities and in contacts between the police and minority citizens particularly—but they are usually without witnesses and rarely photographed. At Kent State there were hundreds of witnesses, and prize-winning photographs depict the entire event. . . . That event is a graphic example—perhaps the clearest and most classic illustration—of the irresponsible and unlawful use of firearms by a government agency against its own citizens. . . . Consequently, the Kent event must not be allowed to fade into the past until the real truth is known about the shooting and until responsibility for it is determined."[6]

In 1977, more than seven years after these unprecedented events— the killing of four and the wounding of nine; the closing down of a major university for two months; the closing down by veritable martial law of an American city for nearly a week; the bringing in of a special Grand Jury report that excoriated and indicted the victims, a report later expunged by order of a federal court; the carrying on at the university, town, state, national, and international levels of the controversy over what crime and what punishment; the investigating and reporting by the university, state police, FBI, American Association of University Professors, American Civil Liberties Union, Scranton Commission, and others; the fruitless striving by the parents of the victims to secure justice through both criminal and civil litigation proceedings—the real truth was yet to be known about the shooting, and responsibility was yet to be determined.

In late August of 1975, sensitive editorial writers in major Ohio newspapers could still write: "The Kent State tragedy is as close as we are likely to come to a social natural disaster. That does not mean it has to be shrugged off or that its possible repetition, like the killing eruption of a long-dormant volcano, has to be contemplated fatalistically. It means that the protection against such horror is less in holding a few token persons legally to blame than in a broad recognition by the public that its own interests rest with meeting even severe political provocation with re-straint, decency, and a keen respect for the opinions and the lives of all members of the community." (*Dayton Daily News*, 29 August 1975). "What happened [at Kent State]," wrote the *Cleveland Plain Dealer* the same day, "is one of the most shocking and troubling events of this decade, and it should not be thought of ever with complacency."

V

Commentators—scholarly, journalistic, political, polemical, old and young, left and right, inside and outside the academy—all have been astounded (most, happily so) by the rapid demise of the curious, precious combination of understanding, anger, compassion, impatience, con-science, and sense of possibility that propelled the ethical impulse of the 1960s and that suffered a perhaps mortal wound at Kent State on May 4, 1970.

In solemn and forlorn anticipation of the fifth anniversary of that event, an editor of the *Daily Kent Stater*, Keith Sinzinger, found:

> Allison Krause is gone. Jeff Miller is gone. Sandy Scheur is gone. Bill Schroeder is gone. . . . Awareness is gone. Activism is gone.
>
> The real question becomes why we, as "survivors" of the May 4 tragedy, have allowed this change of values, this realignment of priorities, this departure from the memory of the past to come about.
>
> Are the issues gone?
>
> The face of America has changed. Nixon is gone. Agnew is gone. Mitchell is gone. The draft is gone.
>
> The world has changed. Thieu is gone. Vietnam is liberated. Cambodia is liberated. U.S. imperialism has been defeated in Southeast Asia.
>
> Yet, it seems sentiment left us long before the issues, long before Nixon's resignation or the surrender of South Vietnam.
>
> The May 4 shootings shocked America—into numbness. The killings of students did not stop. Jackson State. Southern University.

But the youth of America was left more than numb—they became disillusioned, frustrated, fearful, and apolitical. The loss of idealism grew with each year, each new batch of students farther removed from the painful memory.

Preoccupation with drugs, alcohol, social life, or other nonpolitical activity has drawn many students away from the issues. Others have turned inward to more esoteric discoveries or academic work.

Most have accepted the system. The few who are active attempt to work through it complacently, with little thought of challenging its authority, ethics or ideals. . . .

Radicalism is gone. Enthusiasm is gone. Excitement is gone. Support is gone.

What is left?

Despite the indifference or ignorance of KSU students concerning the events of May 4 and its aftermath, the spirit and memory of that day will never leave the campus. It places a special mark on every KSU student—past, present and future—associating us with a historical event, a national tragedy which turned the tide of America and shook its youth from the foundation of idealism.[7]

Earlier that year, in a special *New Republic* supplement called "This Fractured Democracy," Yale history professor C. Van Woodward revealed and repeated his astonishment at "the sudden subsidence of the radical flame of the '60s. . . . rarely in history has publicized activism been replaced so rapidly by apparent apathy, strident dissent by silence. . . . the American youth rebellion of the 1960s . . . received a vast amount of attention while it was in progress, but extremely little since the radical phase suddenly ended."

In addition to this notion of sudden, rapid termination, Professor Woodward asserts that what occurred was a veritable "collapse of the political activists in 1970." Reviewing and summarizing various kinds of hypotheses that attempt to explain or at least interpret the "collapse," he writes: "Framed for the most part in expectation of an enduring movement or one of intensifying activism, dissent, radicalism, and protest, the long-range theories of interpretation and explanation are caught short by an unexpected and unexplained silence and cessation."[8]

Perhaps a critic more sympathetic to the need for major social change and to the efforts to bring it about in the 1960s is Irving Howe. In the same issue of *The New Republic* Howe discusses the "disintegration" of the movement he apparently (and I think incorrectly) identifies only with the New Left. "For the third time in the twentieth century," he writes, "a radical movement in America had taken on a mass character and seemed close to becoming a powerful force. Then, in a twinkling, it vanished."[9]

Woodward's and Howe's observations gain support from "hard" and "soft" data—from statistical reports stemming from systematic surveys and from testaments of various significant persons. Referring to his 1974 nationwide survey of 190,000 freshmen at 364 two-year and four-year colleges and universities, Professor Alexander W. Astin of UCLA emphasizes that more caution and convervatism are evident in fresh-men's political, social, and academic views. "Almost none of the attitudinal items in the survey could be interpreted as a liberalizing of views, and this was certainly not true of the other eight surveys," Professor Astin is quoted as saying, in Beverly T. Watkins' article "Freshman Thinking" in *The Chronicle of Higher Education* (January 13, 1975). "Although one might have expected the events of Watergate and the political climate that led to a Democratic landslide election last year to prompt a move toward the political left or at least a defection from the political right," Ms. Watkins writes, "Mr. Astin notes [that] there was a move toward the political center by students from the left and an apparent move away from politics in general. . . . Fewer freshmen included among their important life goals "keeping up with political affairs" (42.4 percent in 1973; 36.6 percent in 1974) or "influencing the political structure" (14.6 percent in 1973; 13.5 percent in 1974)."

Both establishment and antiestablishment political and ideological activists proclaim a new age of small causes. A former young speech writer for presidents Nixon and Ford and vice presidents Ford and Agnew—"I went to work for Agnew because he personified for me 'the old American verities' "—John R. Coyne, Jr., in the *New York Times* of August 24, 1975, writes: "I know I'll never again set off in search of that cause larger than self."

Essentially the same sentiment was expressed in the *New York Times Magazine* nearly two years earlier (28 October 1973) by one of the erstwhile "white prep-and-Ivy-educated males, [Columbia] class of '70, who were born to power but looked prime to reject it." James S. Kunen, author of *The Strawberry Statement*, wrote an essay "on what my friends are doing these days, to see if it's true that, after shutting down campuses five years ago, they're entering establishment careers—what we used to call 'selling out.' "

Kunen's major concern is that he has met himself at last and that he is his parents. "There is one cause for which I can conceive of risking my life—The Passing of Trucks. I do it constantly. Still, one thing bothers me, especially when I pass hitchhikers without picking them up: Have I become one of the people I used to be against? . . . The question is: will we, despite the hallucinations and barricades in our backgrounds, become indistinguishable from our parents?"

By the mid-seventies one could read press-service feature stories with such titles as, "Where Radicals Raged, Streakers Stride" (UPS, *Dayton Daily News*, 11 March 1975). The typical lead paragraph was: "Five years ago, the nation's college campuses were hotbeds of political dissent. Today, student radicals have dropped into obscurity and only the clomp-clomp of an occasional sneaker-clad streaker disturbs the halls of academia."

Whether because of the successful intimidation of the Kent State shootings, the end of the draft and the belated military withdrawal from

Southeast Asia, the impact of recession, inflation, and a tight job market, or the corrosive effects on spirits, minds, and bodies of assassinations, corruption, and essentially unchecked power, the ethical activists are silent and withdrawn.

"I've made my peace," young faculty members concede. "I've gone private," black intellectuals tell me—and show me. "I'm tired," one of the most deeply engaged and keenly analytical Kent State professors admits, "no more tilting at windmills." "I've spent my time in Washington and in the Middle East; I'm settling back into Boulder," says one of the articulate and uncompromising student civil libertarians of the early sixties. (And he runs for and is elected to the city council.)

"We've lowered our sights," a bright education major from North Dakota tells me during a conference attended by five hundred students, faculty members, and administrators from all over the country. "We've turned our attention into ourselves. We're practical now." This conference was able to discuss, for three days and nights in large and small groups, "The Impact on Higher Education of the 'Troubled Economy': on Universities' Budgets, Priorities, and Programs; on Faculty Members' Loads, Morale, and Careers; on Students' Concerns, Activities, and Aspirations," without ever seriously considering matters of food, energy, war, racism, poverty, individual freedom, or social justice.

I could write a letter to 1,200 directors of university and college honors programs in the fall of 1973, asking the following quite rhetorical questions:

> What matters to students now? What are they interested in now—and later—and do they think about the later? Has their mood shifted from one of a sense of outrage to one of a sense of futility? Have they turned from protest and activism to serious studiousness? If so, what are they studying—and for what purpose? Are they silent again? apolitical? resigned? cynical? And what matters to the faculty—are they simply exhausted by nearly a decade of unprecedented tension, stress, conflict, and violence on campus? Have they returned to traditional academic interests and roles? And what of the institutions themselves: has the pendulum moved from innovation and reform to rigidity and a legitimacy verging on docility? Have the post–Kent State and Jackson State impulses for liberalization of curricula, structure, and procedure and for the humanization of roles subsided and died?

By implication and extension, one must ask: Has the ethical impulse for social change—for personal freedom and human rights—subsided and died?

VI

John Farrell is dead—even a giant heart can break. Dante is dead—his poet's soul would relish the living metaphor created by his Camusian death in an automobile accident. Allison, Bill, Jeff, and Sandy are dead—victims of demagoguery, savagery, and the triumph of the garrison state. The period is dead. Its ethical impulse is not dead.

As usual the angle of vision of its black critics and reconstructors is the most pertinent and valuable for the United States to consider. On November 12, 1975, not the echo but the continuation of the ethical impulse rang clear and plain in middle-American Miami University's Millett Auditorium in Oxford, Ohio. While a local and national anti-Senate Bill #1 (the Criminal Justice Codification Act of 1975) campaign was being carried on for the sake of individual freedom and the guarantee of due process of law (the "negative" civil liberties that must pervade the processes of a decent society), the speech this night by Lerone Bennett, Jr., historian, writer, and *Ebony* editor, was a call for the substantiation of those civil and human rights that must be a "positive," living reality for all people in a decent society.

Bennett appealed to his small, largely black audience to commemorate the Bicentennial by creating a human and rational environment for all people. Continuing the moral tradition of Gandhi and King, he said that no human can be safe or free in this country until all humans are safe and free in this country. It is self-evident, he maintained, that an oppressed people will not lend themselves to a ritual that legitimizes their own oppression.

Bennett stressed the need for a further definition of freedom—not only the abstract and negative "natural rights of abstract man" (which concept, for the Founding Fathers, excluded blacks, women, the poor, and American Indians) but also positive and concrete rights for "real people" (food, shelter, education, work). We should create a new declaration of independence, a national action plan to heal our wounds and our divisions, and solve the problems of the aged, unify our people, provide work for all and put an end to discrimination.

Bennett indicted American historiography as being not only racist and parochial but also ignorant of the history of poor white people; American education as being reactionary and racist in its caution and defensiveness and its failure to develop white as well as black minds; and American ideology and mythology as being hypocritical in their crying over welfare for the poor but applauding subsidies for the powerful.

Graham's vision of the United States as "an old ridge—a cold dying place" was revised by Bennett's seeing two roads before us at this point of no return: "We can become a Democracy for the first time. Or we can become the Fourth Reich. This is our choice on the eve of our two hundredth birthday."

Finally, Bennett called for both individual responsible action and organized institutional change—and in so doing he revealed once again the basic duality and dilemma of our ethical struggle for personal freedom and social justice:

We all must assume our personal responsibilities existentially . . . be prepared and productive. Everyone must do what he or she must do. . . . We must begin and complete the Second Revolution by conquering small enemies—doing day by day where we are. . . . We're in a lull period in this country. A general lull—reflected in the student population. We must speak to the fact—where are we today, why, what can we do about it. . . . One thing: every individual ought to consider himself or herself mandated to do something to bring about some improvement—don't wait for leaders. . . . Let's change the way people act—not their hearts—we do this by changing institutions, especially the economic situation of black people. Other changes will come—and make it possible for poor whites to feel secure.

And let's realize we're probably engaged in a very long struggle. We in the sixties and seventies underestimated what we were up against. We thought we had the cat—it would all be over soon. We need to understand the kind of struggle we're engaged in. It might take a generation—the rest of our lives—of hard, long, unglamorous struggle.[10]

We are in a lull period now. The struggle will be hard, long, unglamorous. And even if we know what we want, have we any chance of influencing the institutions of a power-centered, postindustrial society in a multinational corporate-garrison economy? The problems and needs persist and grow. The ethical impulse persists, too: for, as John Farrell understood, some people are able to consider and sometimes even to prefer the interests of others to their own. Moreover, we are learning, slowly, painfully, that the interests of others are ultimately our own.

But our very efforts suffer from the dilemma of theoretical simplicity and practical difficulty. When Lerone Bennett, Jr. calls for both small, individual effort and systemic, institutional change, he might be asking for the incompatible, if not for the impossible. When he urges each of us to "conquer small enemies—doing every day where we are," he is recommending something that is on a human scale, manageable and quite attractive. But what of the causes larger than self? What of the larger view necessary for the analysis that must precede and inform institutional change? What of the larger vision of a decent society?

Is conquering small enemies, working for small causes, going private, making peace, the way to change the system? Can one retreat to one's private activity and at the same time relate to, understand, and work for social change? "Is it possible," Irving Howe asks, "for people of the left to be both 'in' and 'out' of the world they would transform, sharing with their fellows all the seemingly small concerns of the moment yet continuing to assert a basic social criticism?"[11]

In this personal history and commentary of what I have called the ethical impulse of the sixties, I have tried to indicate the increasing complexity of an American ethic: an ethic partly of protest, which is individual, personal, and skeptical, and partly of proposal, which is collective, social, and substantive; an ethic partly of process, which depends on diversity, debate, and suspended judgment, and partly of substance, which requires organization, agreement, and commitment—in short, both an individualistic and a social ethic.

Both dimensions of this ethic are precious and compelling. Are they compatible? If they are not compatible, we are faced with a dilemma that could be devastating.

The necessary ethical synthesis will require individual will but collective action; personal conviction but organizational loyalty; means whose decency is the same as the decency of the ends; nonviolence but utterly serious involvement; intellectual leadership but genuine respect for, and alliance with, all groups. It will take, in short, a synthesis of the civil liberties ethic of individual freedom and the civil rights ethic of social responsibility.

But how optimistic this discussion is! It assumes that we do indeed have it within our individual and collective will and capability to create a decent and just society as part of a humane and sane world. What if that voice of the black power chorus is correct, the voice that says America is an overgrown child, unwilling to face realities and unable to solve her problems, lacking the values, the ideas, the institutions, the techniques, the imagination, and the will to really even try? What if this America is systemically corrupt: a culture of personal impotence within a structure of irresponsible concentrated power?

Conservative writer John R. Coyne, Jr., says that "perhaps we can still pull it out. If we can find a way to reestablish the proper relationship between students and teachers, between representatives and the people they represent, between ideas and action, philosophy and politics, values and life—then we might make it. But it's getting late."[12]

Liberal analyst Anthony Lewis, in the *New York Times* and *The New Republic* in the spring of 1975, considers the causes and consequences of thirty years of American involvement in Southeast Asia, and somehow remains hopeful. "Well, I am an optimist; I think Americans can learn, and have learned from the tragedy of Indochina. We know much more now about the danger of concentrated executive power—especially when it is exercised in secrecy and deception, so that there can be no effective political check. . . . Finally, the American public, a very large part of it, has learned that imposing our social and political assumptions on people of a sharply different culture will not work; and that is a tremendous change."[13] The American feeling now, Lewis believes, "should be one of release, not despair. For if we understand what has happened in Vietnam, we shall know it did not represent American ideals. We went wrong because we strayed from openness, realism, humanity. We can regain our ideals and our confidence. But understanding comes first."[14]

"We need to understand the kind of struggle we're engaged in," Lerone Bennett said. "It might take a generation—the rest of our lives—of hard, long, unglamorous struggle."

In his individual way, during his short life, John Farrell wrote: "We will attempt to . . . arouse student interest and concern about social issues that we must understand and work toward resolving because we are human beings."

If the original premise of this essay is reasonably valid—that our two ethical strains are increasingly incompatible—solutions or remedies are not easy to come by. To proclaim that the solution requires a synthesis of the civil liberties ethic of individual freedom and the civil rights ethic of social responsibility is to say nothing and everything. How do we actually achieve such a synthesis?

By "reestablishing proper relationships between students and teachers, between representatives and the people they represent, between ideas and action, philosophy and politics, values and life," suggests a conservative, John R. Coyne, Jr. But how are such "proper" relationships to be reestablished—or, better, established?

"By learning from experience and regaining our ideals, confidence, and a proper course of action on the basis of understanding," a liberal, Anthony Lewis, asserts. But who will be the teachers?

By understanding "the kind of struggle we're engaged in," Lerone Bennett, Jr., says. "It might take a generation—the rest of our lives—of hard, long, unglamorous struggle." But can such a struggle remain nonviolent?

As did John Farrell, the author of this essay continues to believe—not despite but because of his analysis—that people can be educated to be both critical and creative, analytical and imaginative, active and reflective, practical and generous, individualistic and social.

The question is, what other kinds of institutional changes are required for such an education to be possible?

SOLUTIONS

A decade and maybe an age of hopeful protest and proposal came to an end at Kent State University on May 4, 1970. The two thrusts of the ethical impulse of the 1960s converged there that day. The cause of individual civil liberties—conscience, speech, dissent, assembly—and the cause of the most basic civil right—life—met in a death embrace on the common at Kent State.

This essay examines the ethical impulse of the 1960s by means of three case studies of the ideas, actions, and fates of its most important possessors, portrayors, and purveyors: university students.

Against the background of a summary analysis of revolutionary changes in world, national, and institutional environments, representative students are shown to have moved this country—or tried to—toward becoming a more decent and serious society.

SUMMARY

Has the ethical impulse for social change—for personal freedom and human rights—subsided and died? Many critics and observers think so. This writer disagrees: for while the conditions, problems, and needs behind it persist and grow, the ethical impulse persists, too.

But there is also a persistent ethical dilemma: how does one pursue and practice individual liberty and at the same time participate in and contribute to a society and world of conflicting demands and pressing human needs?

Does the United States have an ethic at once precious, compelling, and impossible? Have we an American ethic with two incompatible dimensions: a semi-ethic of protest, which is individual, personal, and skeptical, and a semi-ethic of proposal, which is collective, social, and substantive? Is there a semi-ethic of process, which depends on diversity, debate, and suspended judgment, and a semi-ethic of substance, which requires organization, agreement, and commitment—an individualistic and a social ethic?

The essay ends on a note perhaps more hopeful than warranted by the analysis it provides.

NOTES

1. "ASUC Blasts HUAC," *Colorado Daily*, 10 May 1962, pp. 1, 7.

2. "Newton Asks Legion to Drop 'Unsubstantiation Charges,'" *Colorado Daily*, 10 May 1962, p. 8.

3. Editorial, *Colorado Daily*, 10 May 1962, p. 4.

4. Lead editorial, *Colorado Daily*, 6 March 1962, p. 4.

5. D. L. Graham, "the west ridge is menthol-cool," in "selections from BLACK SONG," 21 November 1966, Nashville, Tenn.

6. John P. Adams, "Kent State: Why the Church?" *American Report*, 12 November 1971, pp. 22-S, 24-S.

7. Keith Sinzinger, "All Is Gone Since 1970; Silence Prevails," *Daily Kent Stater*, 2 May 1975, p. 5.

8. C. Vann Woodward, "What Became of the 1960's?" *The New Republic*, 9 November 1974, pp. 18–25.

9. Irving Howe, "Historical Memory, Political Visions," *The New Republic*, 9 November 1974, pp. 25–28.

10. Lerone Bennet, Jr., "Dangers and Opportunities," public lecture, Miami University, Oxford, Ohio, 12 November 1975.

11. Howe, "Historical Memory," p. 27.

12. John R. Coyne, Jr., "Post-Berkeley, Post-Agnew, Post-Nixon Blues," *New York Times*, 24 August 1975, p. 19-E.

13. Anthony Lewis, "Hubris, National and Personal," *The New Republic*, 3 May 1975, p. 19.

14. Anthony Lewis, "Vietnam: 30 Years of War," *Cincinnati Enquirer*.

1 Why does the author focus on the efforts of students, and of particular students, in trying to describe and summarize the civil liberties and civil rights protest movements of the past two decades?

2 What does the author mean by saying that the two thrusts of the ethical impulse of the sixties converged at Kent State on May 4, 1970?

3 How does the author define and assess black power and relate this to the subject of ethical impulses and ethical dilemmas?

4 Do you agree or disagree with the author's suggestion that the black perspective on American society is the clearest and most useful angle of vision?

5 Summarize—with examples from this chapter or from your own experiences—the conflicts each individual faces in working out his or her personal philosophy of individual happiness and social concern.

6 What does the author seem to be suggesting an individual can or should do?

7 Do you share John Farrell's view of what it means to be a human being?

8 Is the author optimistic about the possibility of peaceful social change in the United States?

The Declaration of Independence

The Constitution of the United States of America

Bentley, Eric, ed. *Thirty Years of Treason: Excerpts from Hearings before the House Committee on Un-American Activities, 1938–1968.* New York: Viking Press, 1971.

Carmichael, Stokley, and Hamilton, Charles V. *Black Power: The Politics of Liberation in America.* New York: Random House, 1967.

Davies, Peter. *The Truth about Kent State: A Challenge to the American Conscience.* New York: Farrar, Straus & Giroux, 1973.

Hellman, Lillian. *Scoundrel Time.* Boston: Little, Brown, 1976.

King, Martin Luther, Jr. *Where Do We Go from Here: Chaos or Community.* New York: Harper & Row, 1967.

Michener, James A. *Kent State.* New York: Random House, 1971.

Sale, Kirkpatrick. *SDS: Ten Years toward a Revolution.* New York: Random House, 1974.

Zinn, Howard. *SNCC, The New Abolitionists.* Boston: Beacon Press, 1964.

TEXAS POLICE AREN'T CHARGED FOR RAIDING WRONG APARTMENT

(Plainview, Tex.) No disciplinary action will be taken against officers who broke through the door of an apartment with a sledgehammer and terrorized three occupants before discovering they had raided the wrong address, police said.

Lt. Jimmy Davis, head of the Amarillo Metro Squad, said correct procedures were followed in the abortive narcotics raid.

"Absolutely not," Davis said in dismissing disciplinary action. "As far as I know, no one's done anything wrong except make a mistake."

[*UPI*, Boston Globe, *21 March 1976.*]

NOW SOCKS IT TO OHIO STORE

(Cleveland) J. Watren Harris, board chairman of the May Co. Department Stores, says a shipment of men's socks called offensive by the Ohio Chapter of the National Organization of Women has been removed from the company's stores.

The socks bore the slogan: "Help stamp out rape. Say yes."

Harris said the socks came in with another order and store personnel had not known they were there. He said standing orders for buyers to avoid controversial merchandise have been reemphasized.

During a weekend meeting about two hundred delegates to the state NOW meeting demonstrated at May's downtown store after learning the socks were for sale there.

[*UPI*, Boston Globe, *24 November 1976.*]

STUDY FINDS POOR UNAIDED IN COURT

(Washington, D.C.) A Justice Department study reported today that there had been only "token" compliance with the landmark Supreme Court ruling in 1972 that required the appointment of a lawyer to represent any indigent defendant who faced a possible jail term.

"The Sixth Amendment right to counsel is an empty one for many defendants," the study said.

[*Lesley Oelsner*, New York Times, *15 November 1975.*]

DEATH PENALTY DEBATE MIRRORS MOOD OF PUBLIC

(Washington, D.C.) If Harold Hughes and a handful of his Senate colleagues had their way, all death sentences would be carried out on prime-time television.

In a gentle satire on the futility of capital punishment as a deterrent to crime, Sen. Hughes (D-Iowa) tried in vain to amend a bill reinstating the death penalty. His amendment would have required that executions be covered on radio and TV in a way "to assure the widest possible exposure to the public."

[*David Heas, Knight News Service,* Boston Globe, *24 March 1974*]

REFLECTING *societal ambivalence if not outright lack of concern, certain social issues have affected the sociopolitical scene for hundreds of years. The topics analyzed in this section—violence, racism, poverty and the condition of women and prisons—indicate that despite protest and reform over the years, substantial change is still needed to rectify unjust situations. That they continue to exist is added proof that the system has not been able, or is unwilling, to deal with inequality. Joseph Boskin, in "The Essential American Soul: Violent," notes that violence has always been an integral part of the socioeconomic system, that violence is utilized as a means of maintaining power over dissidents, and that violent techniques cannot be redirected or minimized until the system itself is altered.*

Deena Metzger's experience of assault in "It Is Always The Woman Who is Raped" indicts us all for not doing more to prevent such violence. In "Woman Talk" she discusses conversation as a symbolic and significant means of communication.

In Day Work Floyd Barbour uses a play to present dramatically the intricate nuances of attitudes and fears between whites and blacks, and in an afterword writes movingly of his experiences and expectations. Fred Arnstein's "the Poor always ye have with you" is a direct and unusual challenge to the reader to deal with his own attitudes towards poverty. And Daniel Greenberg, in "The Problem of Prisons," openly calls for "the abolition of prisons" as the only solution to the contemporary counterpart of slavery.

TRADITIONAL KNOTS

2 | THE ESSENTIAL AMERICAN SOUL: VIOLENT

> *But you have there the myth of the essential white America. All the other stuff, the love, the democracy, the floundering into lust, is a sort of by-play. The essential American soul is hard, isolate, stoic, and a killer. It has never yet melted.*
>
> D. H. *Lawrence,* Studies in Classic American Literature *(1923)*

Graffiti—quiet, furious writings on bathroom stalls, brick walls, fences, subway trains, trolley stations, the sides of buildings, in fact almost everywhere a literate culture can express itself anonymously but knowingly—graffiti reflected the conflict in American society in the late sixties and early seventies. In downtown Boston in 1969, at the four corners of the historic Commons, near the site of the Boston Massacre and the rally two centuries later of over 100,000 persons protesting against the violence in Cambodia and at Kent State and Jackson State, city officials placed four large, movable blank walls where people could try their creative graffiti impulses. One summer in the early 1970s, at one of the busiest walls, there appeared a question which expressed the exasperation of coping with conditions: "Is there any intelligent life on earth?" A few days later came the answer: "Yes, but I'm only here for a short visit."

Words mirror the concerns of a people. From the mid-sixties through the seventies, the terms "crime" and "violence," "law and order," "police" and "pigs," "mugging" and "bugging," "killings," "riots," and "commission" assailed the senses through the media at an overwhelming rate. The nation was engulfed by talk of disequilibrium, by discussion of and anxiety about being attacked, raped, mugged, robbed, ripped off,

33

and reduced to lifelessness. The index guides and catalogs in our libraries pointed to the burgeoning conflict and violence, and to the growing fascination with them. Before 1960, there was no separate category for the subject "Violence" in the *Reader's Guide to Periodical Literature*, the main index which lists all of the articles published in the country. In the March, 1963–February, 1965 edition of the *Guide*, the topic appeared for the first time, replacing "Force," which had been used for over sixty years. There had always been a separate entry which covered acts of "Crime" and it is interesting to note that violence was categorized under this heading. Occasionally, acts of violence were also included in the "Force" listing.

Concurrent with the advent of "Violence" as a distinct topic in the mid-sixties, there also appeared a plethora of articles in such diverse magazines as the *Nation, McCalls,* and *Ladies Home Journal*. A decade later, the *Guide* had an extensive listing of articles under "Violence" and referred the reader to related categories, including "Terrorism." The titles of these pieces are a study in collective anxiety: "America as a Gun Culture," "America, the Violent," "Chemistry of Violence," "Violence Around Us," "We're Teaching Our Children that Violence Is Fun: Closer Look at Toys," "Tooth and Claw," "Nobody Ever Learned Anything from Violence Except How to Duck," and one which was rather jolting in its implications, the "War on Violence."

The term "Commission" must also be identified as a significant aspect of this concern. The government has utilized commissions as a means of ascertaining the nature and intensity of social and political issues for over a hundred years, particularly in the twentieth century. But within a single decade, four major presidential commissions focused on the subjects of crime, conflict, and violence: the President's Commission on the Assassination of John Kennedy (Warren Commission); the President's Commission on Law Enforcement and the Administration of Justice (Katzenbach Commission); the National Advisory Commission on the Causes and Prevention of Violence (Eisenhower Commission); and the National Advisory Commission on Civil Disorders (Kerner Commission). In addition, there were bodies which dealt with such related issues as marijuana, and municipal and state bodies which concentrated on specific episodes, such as the Governor's Commission on the Los Angeles Riot, 1966 (McCone Commission). The result was the expenditure of millions of dollars and the publication of hundreds of volumes of testimony and social science analyses, followed by the audible silence of governmental inaction. Only an extremely wealthy and frightened nation could have spent so much money, energy, and time in such endeavors. And only a nation entrapped could have paid so little attention to their analyses and suggestions for change. Crime, conflict, and violence provoked such intellectual and emotional anguish that, like Job—who was perfect and upright, fearing God and eschewing evil—the nation appeared to cry out, "Why has thou set me as a mark against thee, so that I am a burden to myself?"

II

Mass media reflected and intensified the anxiety of the period. Although television networks have always used the themes of conflict and violence as a basic format—in the early years they focused on cowboys and crime—the degree and nature of violence increased in the late sixties and seventies. The crime serials and police stories became the setting for violence of all sorts, as many bizarre forms of criminality were dramatized. The unusual accent on crime and police in the movies and television represented an important change in entertainment. In replacing the western theme as the cultural "folk drama," investigators and detectives such as "Kojak," "Mannix," "Barnaby Jones," "Baretta," "Ironside," "Cannon," "Harry O," and "Columbo" became the counterparts of the rugged cowboy, while the western law-and-order men were superseded by the urban law-and-order men and women of "Naked City," "Dragnet," "The Rookies," "Police Woman," "Police Story," "Emergency," "Mod Squad," "Barney Miller," "The Streets of San Francisco," "Starsky and Hutch," "Hawaii Five-O" and "S.W.A.T."

The fusion of the relationship between West(ern) and east could be seen in the television series "McCloud." Sam McCloud, an earthy, intuitive sheriff from Colorado, worked with the New York Police Department and frequently upset the bureaucratic procedures of the department. His actions often led to the solution of baffling crimes. However, "McCloud" represented a halfway individual. It was the eastern policeman who gradually inherited the traditional style of western individualism.

Cinematic plots were television themes writ larger and gorier. Films made by whites or blacks about ethnic communities, such as *Shaft* and *Superfly*, were done with intimate views of vice and corruption, sadism and degradation. The level of violence was stupendous in the two epic films which dealt with the Mafia, *The Godfather* and *The Godfather, Part II*, in which the Corleone family struggled to maintain their position and extend their power, thus succeeding within our economic system. Violence between the generations was carefully and brutally etched in the film *Joe*. And in Sam Peckinpah's films, particularly *The Wild Bunch* and *Straw Dogs*, violence was portrayed as an innate aspect of human behavior. *Dr. Strangelove* and *Seven Days in May* detailed the coming of thermonuclear war.

In both the cinema and television shows, the accent was on the physical reality of violence. Gaping gunshot wounds, splattered bodies, spurting blood, and pain were graphically portrayed. More important, however, was the way in which violence was validated by all sides. The line between the representatives of "good" and "bad" was constantly blurred, since each group tended to use similar if not identical means to cope with and/or demolish the other. In fact, the sordidness of their work, of the way they led their lives, was elevated into a symbolic representation of society itself. Society was pictured as being, simply and directly, *violent*.

Twenty years earlier, in an article entitled "Trigger Mortis," Marya Mannes had predicted with concern that in the seventies a strange mutation would occur in the hands of newborn children: all the curled fingers normal to babies would continue to be in the proper places, save that the index finger of the right hand would be higher than the others and bent as though holding a revolver.

Not only was there a multitude of visual presentations of conflict and violence (and of articles and books analyzing and deploring these tendencies), but at a certain point articles appeared stating that people should accept the reality of its continuing existence. A story in the *Boston Globe* on December 3, 1972, declared that "violence is becoming a way of life in the nation's cities." Two weeks later *Newsweek* magazine made "Living With Crime, U.S.A." its featured story of the week. "Crime's grip on American today," the article correctly noted, "is both a reality and a state of mind."

> Few citizens actually die of fear, but its chilling effects have become part of the daily life for millions in and around the nation's cities. While some statistics suggest that crime itself may actually be levelling off, the fear of crime seems to be escalating into a fortress mentality that alters the way people see themselves and the way they live their lives.[1]

Two years after this article a movie appeared which suggested that people should recognize the ugliness of the situation, but refuse to accept it passively. In the film *Death Wish*, a middle-class New York architect, played by craggy-faced Charles Bronson, rejects helplessness when the police are unable to find the three men who killed his wife and raped his daughter in their apartment. After travelling to Tucson and acquiring bits of western lore, the architect returns to the city and becomes the first urban vigilante. Within a short time, partly due to the media, his shooting of would-be muggers leads to a marked decrease in the incidence of mugging. The police recognize his importance and refuse to arrest him even after his identity is learned. Rather, he is permitted to "leave town by sundown" and continue his practice in Chicago. The "eastern" folk drama was thus carried to another level.

The exposed state of violence in society was reflected in art as well, a medium hitherto thought by most Americans to be reserved for more gentle pastimes. The relationship between violence and art, however, was not a new phenomenon; it possessed a powerful tradition. Art critic Harold Rosenberg in the late sixties observed of this connection:

> Violence in American art goes back a long way and appears mostly in popular art forms, particularly farce; in vaudeville acts, burlesque shows (with pratfalls and people socking each other with rubber bladders) and in various kinds of mechanical situations like Rube Goldberg cartoons. This is an old tradition in America. And it goes back to the Mississippi boatman and American frontier humor which was a humor of violence.[2]

The sudden awareness of the degree of violence in the visual and plastic arts made more cogent Richard Hofstadter's statement that "the rediscovery of our violence will undoubtedly be one of the more important intellectual legacies of the 1960s."[3] The medium of art, one of the sharpest of mirrors, provided a social commentary in which violence became central to the message as well as to the form of the art work. Artists and sculptors depicted the violence of modern war, racial conflict, social and environmental pollution, technological power, and personal anguish. The subject was explored in a series of exhibitions. In 1969 in Chicago, the Museum of Contemporary Art organized a show titled "Violence in Recent American Art." But in London and New York, "The Destruction in Arts Symposiums" held in 1966 and 1968 isolated the element of destruction in new art forms and attempted to discover any links with destruction in society.

While painters and sculptors were elevating violence into an art form, frightened people were attempting to cope with what they regarded as dangers to their bodies and possessions. By the mid-seventies, the accent was on self-protection, with various governmental and public agencies suggesting possible self-defense techniques. Solutions to such dangerous situations as attack or robbery ranged from individual action such as karate training to group protection by private policemen. Across the land alarm systems attached to the sides of houses or wired into police stations were ready to howl at any unwarranted entry. Double- and triple-locking devices on doors in apartments and houses in urban areas became commonplace; windows were attached to alarms or permanently sealed. Gun purchases soared. Women were exhorted to carry small, handy mace containers or sharp objects to ward off attackers. Instructions on how to protect oneself appeared in newspapers and magazines. More complex issues received heavy publicity. The cover feature story in *Time* magazine on June 20, 1975, centered on "Crime: Why—and What To Do?" In a fourteen-page article—considerably longer than most stories which appeared in the magazine—*Time* analyzed the causes and nature of increased crime and called for various pragmatic and legal changes. The tone of the article reflected a general uneasiness towards the subject: crime was an expression of larger, more intricate socioeconomic problems which would continue to affect the stability of society.

Given the state of general apprehension and the ceaseless statistics indicating rises in violence, it is not surprising that so much attention was suddenly directed toward the subject. But at the same time, the situation raises basic questions about the nature and history of violence: what factors in the American experience nurtured violence? Has the propensity for violence increased, or has the awareness of and sensitivity to violence, as well as the fear of internal dislocation, escalated?

III

Any study of American history requires a study of various types of violence and their relationship to political, economic, and social developments. Richard Hofstadter has defined acts of violence as those "which kill or injure persons or do significant damage to property."[4] From the earliest period of colonization, the North American hemisphere has been the scene of many forms of violence, committed either by the native inhabitants or by the newcomers. Indeed, most contemporary forms of violence can be traced back to the early experiences of the initial settlement of America. "American Violence," Richard M. Brown has cogently observed in his book *American Violence*, "antedates the American nation. Most of the major types of our violent activity were well established before we gained independence from Great Britain."[5]

Not only the forms of American violence but the patterns as well were present early in the nation's history, fused with the manipulation of land, political development, and the creation of institutions. Violence has been an integral part of the American cultural fabric and thus cannot be separated from events, attitudes, or expectations. Perhaps what has been most unusual about the history of violence in the United States is the enormous gap between the reality of its existence and the general failure or refusal to accept that reality. Consequently, what appears to be a unique increase in crime and violence in contemporary America is actually intimately related to the affairs of the past three centuries. Some forms of violence have disappeared, their usage transformed or eliminated. The vigilante committee, for example, no longer conducts "necktie parties." Lynchings of blacks—once a mainstay in the southern repertoire—are now a rarity. Other types of repression, such as violent religious persecution, have been significantly modified.

Patterns of violence cut through American history like the Mississippi River through the center of our country. The creation of the nation was the result of a prolonged military struggle and even the problem of sovereignty was eventually settled in one of the bloodiest civil wars in recent Western history. Long before the Constitution established the mechanism of government, the arrival of the Western European produced innumerable wars over crucial issues such as land usage and ownership.

The settlement of the country was largely accomplished through starkly violent means. Armed conflict over land occurred between whites and Indians, between cattlemen and farmers, and among members of these groups. Religious clashes, political repression, labor-management struggles, political assassinations, industrial sabotage, "cutthroat" competition, and racial mob actions created a tradition of violence studded with individual crimes of the most gruesome type. Nor was violence geographically restricted. Urban violence has a long past, dating back to the Boston uprising against Governor Andros in 1689, the New York Slave Conspiracy of 1712, the Draft Riots of the 1860s, and innumerable antiforeign, antiblack mob actions throughout the centuries. Indeed, the high degree of violence would indicate that its use as a problem-solving technique—whether social, political, or economic—has been a fully accepted, institutionalized policy.

Once the government was launched, moreover, the policy of expansion inaugurated a series of conflicts and wars with England, Mexico, Russia, Spain, and Canada. In the nineteenth and twentieth centuries, America's imperialistic thrust led to heavy involvement in the Pacific and Southeast Asia. The creation of the American overseas empire, similar to the establishment of its domestic empire, was accomplished with incredible swiftness and force.

There is another crucial aspect of violence which, though not often associated with it, directly contributes to its extent. This is the violence emanating from "force." "Acts of force," wrote Hofstadter, "are those which prevent the normal free action or movement of other persons, or which inhibit them through the threat of violence."[6] Although the line between violence and force is a blurred one, there is a significant relationship between the two. "The two are confused, and certainly the relation between them is often intimate, but the distinction is necessary not only for our own clarity but because it has come to have such tactical and moral importance to authorities and dissidents alike."[7]

Whether termed the power elite, ruling class, or establishment, those who formulate policies and control the decision-making process use force to maintain their power. Force may be nonviolent (not employing physical abuse), but its impact is based upon the possibility, if not probability, of violence. George Jackson, one of the Soledad Brothers who served ten years in prison for a seventy-dollar robbery, became acutely aware of the relationship between force and violence. "Politics," he wrote shortly before his highly suspect death at the hands of prison guards in 1972, "is violence." Jackson was critical of the nonviolent techniques of Dr. Martin Luther King: "It may serve our purpose to claim nonviolence, but we must never delude ourselves into thinking that we can seize power from a position of weakness. . . . Nonviolence must constantly demonstrate the effects of its implied opposite"[8]

It is possible to trace the pattern of establishment "force" which has resulted in a climate conducive to violence. One can see a consistent pattern of control, repression, intimidation, and death, a pattern first emerging in the actions against the western Pennsylvania farmers during the Whiskey Rebellion of the 1790s. The Justice Department's actions against the Black Panthers in the 1960s only confirmed a tradition whose history included the use of the Pinkerton Agency by industrialists against labor organizers, the use of spies to conduct clandestine actions against so-called Un-American or subversive persons who desired social and/or political change, and the relationship between police enforcement agencies and such local community vigilante groups as the Ku Klux Klan.

Since America began, government has used its agencies to incarcerate, harass, or put in jeopardy those deemed politically undesirable. George Jackson was just one of many individuals who was systematically placed in "solitary confinement"; the twentieth-century list extends back to anarchist Emma Goldman, and includes such radicals as "Big Bill" Haywood of the Industrial Workers of the World, socialist Eugene V. Debs, Sacco and Vanzetti, the Holywood Ten, the Berrigan brothers and the Gainesville Nine in the 1960s, W. E. B. Du Bois, Paul Robeson, and countless thousands of pacifists, conscientious objectors, birth-control advocates, and others whose philosophies were in opposition to governmental policies or to the capitalist system.

A second aspect of force, less obvious but nonetheless insidiously destructive, was characterized by Dr. Martin Luther King's telling phrase, "legalized injustice." Institutionalized slavery and racism, "Jim Crow," peonage, the slum ghetto, welfare and poor laws, institutionalized sexism, segregated school systems, lopsided tax laws—in short, inequitable, discriminatory systems which produce frustrated expectations and hence anger and hostility—result in an internal violence.

"Once established," Newton Garver rightly observes, "such systems may require relatively little overt violence" to maintain them.[9] And precisely because so little is required to maintain discriminatory systems, it is extremely difficult to alter their structure or eliminate them entirely. Over a period of time an internal violence, a violence of petty but brutal acts by the victims against one another, develops. Psychologist Kenneth Clark concluded that there was more violence in a single day of normal life in Harlem than there was in any day of the Harlem uprising in 1964.

But the reactions of people trapped within the system are not always directed inwardly. Because of their institutionalized powerlessness, minorities are often forced to use violent techniques to protest their predicament or to alter their situation. Bacon's Rebellion in the 1680s, slave retaliations and revolts, Coxey's Army of 1894, labor strikes and protests, urban racial uprisings, the Bonus March of 1932, hunger riots, student movements of the 1930s and 1960s, antiwar protests, rent strikes, farmer boycotts, and countless other individual acts attest to the energies of the lower classes to assert themselves. The frequent upsurge of the powerless emanates from what Ronald Segal in *The Americans: A Conflict of Creed and Reality* has termed "the tie between disappointment and violence"—that is, the enormous frustration and anger resulting from society's failure to provide the means to achieve the expectations it has engendered.

Imposed and responsive violence have entwined time and again, producing a cyclical pattern of internal and external explosions, obscuring the line between causes and responsibilities. The initiators of violence are often overshadowed by the horror of the event. Yet, it can be demonstrated that those in power have the ability and the means to minimize violence and significantly alter its direction and intensity by developing policies which would produce a modicum of harmony. But this has not occurred. Rather, the power elite has railed against the victims and punished them. Those who have been discriminated against, who attempt to protest or change their situations, are pronounced the culprits. As Segal has perceptively stated: "Every American government has sought to invalidate the tie between disappointment and violence, at least where its own aspirations have not been involved; has denounced violence as an improper and pointless means of effecting change."[10]

At times, particularly in recent history, the power elite often praised the broadening of liberties through the destruction of its internal and external "enemies." Hence the treatment of socialists, communists, anarchists, pacifists, utopianists, and others as "un-American." The most recent expression of this perverse idea, however, was provided during the Vietnam War by an Air Force officer after he had participated in eliminating an entire South Vietnamese village: "In order to liberate the village," he explained, "we had to destroy it."

To rationalize them and forestall negative responses to them, violent actions have often been couched in honey-coated niceties, obtuse phrases, or misleading descriptions. The invasion of Cambodia by American forces under the orders of President Nixon was called an "incursion." Against the planeless North Vietnamese, the American military conducted not illegal bombing missions but "protective reaction strikes."

The result has been a serious gap between image and reality, between intention and objective. Thus, in the January 1, 1973, issue of *Newsweek*, the magazine informed readers that James R. Schlesinger was appointed Director of the Central Intelligence Agency, one of the country's most secret agencies. (The CIA later came under heavy attack for conducting assassination plots against foreign leaders and for illegally spying on domestic leaders, among other unethical acts.) Although the agency could in no way be regarded as a contributor to the entertainment media, *Newsweek*'s headline about the appointment was written as a half-joke: "The CIA's New Super Spook." The archetypal cartoon spook, "Casper the Ghost," was a wispy, good-natured, frolicking supernatural being. Schlesinger, the newly appointed director, was shown wearing a white shirt and a tie, with pipe extending from a firm mouth, and was described as a "tweedy economist" who represented the "passing of control from an old crew of World War II cloak-and-dagger professionals to a new breed of cost-conscious systems managers who promise more spook for the buck." It was reassuring that the CIA, whose budget is known to very few Congresspersons and virtually no citizens, was practicing economy at a time of financial hardship; but were people to believe that the new head of the CIA would no longer engage in the violent activities which comprised its most fundamental techniques? Schlesinger when chairman of the Atomic Energy Commission had taken his family to watch the five-megaton nuclear explosion on Amchitka Island in 1972 after an outcry across the land for its cessation. When queried about the safety of his family so close to the explosion's epicenter, Schlesinger lightly replied: "My wife is delighted to get away . . . and it's fun for the kids."

IV

What are the sources of violence, which initiate but also perpetuate its flow? From the beginning, American society has been wedded to acquisitiveness through competitive struggle. "All are constantly seeking to acquire property, power, and reputation" wrote the French observer Alexis de Tocqueville in the 1830s in his classic work, *Democracy in America*.[11] By adopting the accumulation of property as the measuring rod of individual worth, Americans ensured the use of violence, a technique for accumulating property. As Richard Segal bluntly put it, "the gospel of money was a gospel of violence,"[12] a statement which echoed de Tocqueville, who observed, "I know of no country, indeed, where the love of money has taken stronger hold on the affections of men, and where a profounder contempt is expressed for the theory of the permanent equality of property."[13] More recently, poet Louis Untermeyer, who published fifty-six anthologies of poetry—ranging from books for scholars to Golden Books for children to collections of erotic ribaldry—and who influenced generations of poets, adivsed prospective writers on his ninetieth birthday to "write out of love, write out of instinct, write out of reason. But always for money."[14]

The American mode, then, essentially has been competition over cooperation, individualism over community, and force over accommodation. Achievement was counted not in terms of inner worth, but in relation to ownership, and ownership was measured by comparison with others. The value of competing and of besting others in the scramble for scarce goods and a viable position within the social structure prevailed. As Vincent Lombardi, one of the most revered football coaches, stated quite succinctly: "Winning isn't everything, it's the only thing."

Thus, means have always been subservient to the ends in the drive for property, status, and power; violence has always been acceptable because it proved the worth of the struggle; the mass media reflected violence and became a technique of its perpetuation; and violence became as revered as the objectives it was intended to secure. These messages were not lost on those socialized to the system, the young and the immigrants who poured into the country. Both groups quickly assimilated the lesson: competition means strength and brings material rewards and worth; cooperation intimates weakness and fosters waste and poverty. "Nice guys," said Leo Durocher, the aggressive baseball coach, "finish last."

Augmenting these values was the physical nature of the country. The wilderness provided the challenge, a never-ending struggle to prove self-sufficiency, to gain mastery of nature, to produce and reap. Indeed, the extravagance of nature helped to set everyone on a path of conquest. Symbolizing the struggle were the farmer and the cowboy, the one using hard work to conquer the soil, the other using grit to capture the land. In time, the cowboy became the sole representative of the fight, whose symbol was his gun.

Guns have always had a magical power in American culture. The failure of Congress to pass significant gun restrictions reflects not only the power of the National Rifle Association but also an attachment, conscious or subconscious, to the weapon. Contemporary Boy Scout literature is full of pictures of high-powered weapons. *Boy's Life*, the organization's monthly publication, carried a picture of a .22 air rifle described as "far and away the most potent in its class," "expertly crafted," and providing "indoor family shooting fun" in its December, 1972, issue. That this was a common advertisement could be seen from the other twenty-six weapons advertised, all praised for their beauty, power, and accuracy.

One gun in particular has come to have special meaning in the contemporary period. The handgun—used by more murderers in the United States than all other weapons combined—has become the ubiquitous weapon, our ultimate equalizer. Sales figures of the gun point up its significance. In 1972, for instance, retail pistol and revolver sales throughout the country totalled $75.6 million, an increase of 59.4 percent over 1968. Almost the same amount—$76.1 million—was spent on all types of baseball goods during the same year. [15]

The emphasis upon competition to achieve property and status—"a place in the American sun"—has produced an enormous disparity between the unlimited ideals of society and its limited willingness to allow

Bill Owens

all groups to attain these ideals. Throughout American history, but particularly in the twentieth centry, expectations have been thwarted. Despite astounding industrial progress through the years—America's share of the world's industrial production leaped from obscurity at the beginning of the nineteenth century to 20 percent by 1860 and over 40 percent by 1913—the number of poor in the country remains extremely high. In his important study *Wealth and Power in America*, Gabriel Kolko has estimated that "the richest tenth receives 30 percent of the annual money income, as in 1961; or 14 percent of the nation owns 68 percent of the new wealth, as in 1962." The lower half of the population receives only one-quarter of the national personal income. One-third of the population lives under the poverty level. Even with the burgeoning industrial capacity, production, automation, and computerization of the past fifty years, "the basic distribution of income and wealth in the United States is essentially the same now as it was in 1939, or even 1909."[16]

The lopsided nature of the economic structure has been graphically demonstrated: over a fifteen-year period, from 1960 to 1975, the top five hundred corporations in the United States increased their share of all manufacturing and mining assets from fifty to seventy percent. Furthermore, their power and influence extended internationally. The largest automobile manufacturing concern in the world, General Motors, had an operating revenue in 1975 exceeding those of all but a dozen nations; it possessed 127 plants in the United States and 43 abroad. Despite the depression of the seventies, corporate profits increased considerably, as did corporate influence over prices and supply. Despite high levels of unemployment, which reached fifteen percent in some states of the nation, executive salaries rarely diminished.

The chasm between the upper and less privileged classes, between the white and nonwhite segments, has always produced tensions resulting in internal and external violence. On one level, in the scramble for limited jobs, whites have fought, killed, and blocked blacks; blacks have found themselves the "last to be hired, the first to be fired" and forced to scab; women have taken positions well below their qualifications and for less pay than men receive; other working-class groups have been relegated to menial, unskilled positions, and all have suffered from an economic system which is constantly erratic, disruptive, demeaning, and demanding. On another level, anger and bitterness at the harshness of their situation have provoked these less privileged classes to violent outbursts against the system.

V

Economic dislocations produce wrenched lives and aspirations. And since the bulk of the population either resides in massive urban areas or earns a living in city-related jobs, the increase in violence in the metropolitan communities has often been dramatic, if not overwhelming. Deprivation clearly triggers survival instincts.

In the 1970s, the incidence of personal crimes, gang warfare, bank robberies, and other acts of violence skyrocketed. One young bank robber in New York, who held ten persons hostage for eight hours after being trapped by the police, explained why his target was a bank: "I was completely broke, man. I walked in here with two cents in my pocket. When I get broke I do crazy things."[17]

The protection of property in economically difficult times becomes an overwhelming concern which often leads to strange and dangerous consequences. Each year thousands of children and adults die violent deaths as handguns, shotguns, and rifles are discharged, the barrels directed against innocent members of the family or friends. Store owners resort to bizarre means to prevent burglaries. In a small city in Texas, a welding-shop owner who lost several thousand dollars in equipment brought in Larry, Leroy, Leon, and Cleo to guard his store. The names belonged to rattlesnakes that had not been fed for months. The owner explained that he was scared of the snakes and sympathetically posted a sign in the window warning patrons about the snakes, who were secreted in certain places—waiting.

Perhaps the clearest reflection of the high degree of urban violence—with the most dangerous implications for the future—is to be found in the behavior of younger persons. Arrests in the seven- to nineteen-year-old bracket for such felonious crimes as rape, assault, and robbery soared in the decade of the seventies. Children and teenagers with guns and knives are quite different from adult criminals; they are more unpredictable, given to panic or sudden fits of rage. Younger persons apparently do not fear the consequences of their actions and often seem callous and unfeeling, exhibiting no remorse or guilt. Operating in gangs of three or more, the younger age groups seek out elderly or defenseless persons, seeking easy money or convertible goods. In 1975, gangs of high-school students and other teenagers terrorized riders on the San Francisco transit system practically every night. The attacks occurred during the nonrush hours and were spontaneously and loosely planned; nevertheless, they employed specific techniques. Groups of youths—often going to or from school—gathered at a transit stop. They ignored cars that were filled, selecting only those with few passengers or those carrying older women. Victims were often extremely reluctant to identify the teenagers who robbed them, behavior reflecting their intense fear of retaliation and doubt that the police could protect them.

Violence is not only an urban but overwhelmingly a lower-class phenomenon. Low-income neighborhoods often show a violent-crime rate many times higher than neighborhoods where incomes are two or three times higher. But the causes are obvious, and tragic in their implications. Lower-class groups are trapped in their environments and thus strike at those closest to them; middle- and upper-income groups have enough flexibility to direct their frustrations in ways either hidden or more acceptable.

Despite the violence of minority actions in the cities from the mid-sixties to the early seventies, relatively few programs were developed to alleviate the profound socioeconomic causes which produced the uprisings and revolts. Those programs which were initiated by Congress and the cities were of short duration. President Lyndon Johnson, eager to fight a war in Southeast Asia, totally ignored the recommendations of the President's Commission on Civil Disorders, which called for a massive infusion of federal funds into the cities. President Nixon spoke of a "new federalism" in apportioning governmental funds, but he was opposed to poverty programs, legal assistance programs—indeed, to any aid which might give the smallest degree of power to lower-class and minority groups—and was generally unsympathetic to the problems of the cities.

Consequently, the historical and pragmatic factors which first provoked violence—scarcity, racism, inequities, competition, unemployment, acquisitiveness—continue to plague American society. There is a saying that "all societies get the crime they deserve." A similar equation can be drawn about the prevailing nature and intensity of violence. Its existence is a reflection of a society which, though fearful of its consequences, feels that violence in some degree works in a productive way; or which possesses a fatalistic attitude toward its power and complexity; or which refuses to acknowledge that the system makes us brothers and sisters in acts of inhumanity.

Violence, then, is endemic to the system. Only because of a powerful, nonviolent civil rights movement during the fifties and sixties, a largely nonviolent student protest movement during the sixties, and the rise of a counterculture which emphasized cooperation, communalism, and redistribution of goods was the essential history of and emphasis on violence in American culture challenged. H. Rap Brown, the black militant who claimed that "violence is necessary and it's as American as cherry pie," understood that life for Americans in the streets, factories, schools, countryside, and overseas is harsh and unrelenting. Violence is never far removed from the details of daily existence.

SOLUTIONS

There are two discernible ways of treating the nature and degree of violence in American Society. One involves the ways in which people harm each other; the other touches upon traditions and traditional ways of problem solving.

First, it *is* possible to reduce the amount and kinds of physical harm perpetrated on a daily basis in the nation. Violent measures can and should be discouraged and perhaps eliminated. All weapons, especially guns, must be outlawed; the possible exception is weapons possessed by law enforcement agencies, and even in this case the weapons should be nonlethal. Where animal hunting is deemed ecologically sound, a system of gun rentals could be established and all weapons returned after the hunt. This solution would be opposed by many, in particular by the National Rifle Association, who argue that "guns don't kill, people do." But year after year the statistics demonstrate that most maiming and killings are the result of handguns—the money spent annually on guns alone almost equals the cash outlay for baseball equipment.

Into this category of deadly weapons falls the automobile. Undoubtedly one of the most powerful instruments people use to hurt one another (either unintentionally or deliberately), the automobile has been the cause of too many arguments that have resulted in death. Is it asking too much to demand stricter driver's tests and a more consistent enforcement of traffic laws? Otherwise, how is it possible to pare down the extraordinary amount of "innocent" mayhem which exists on the streets and highways of the nation?

Second, our historical penchant for violence as a means of achieving national and personal goals—as a problem-solving technique—has reached the point where a national examination and debate is necessary. The recent escalation of violence on all socioeconomic levels and in virtually all urban and rural communities has forced scholars, religious figures, business persons, and even some politicians to examine the intriguing relationship of violence to historical development and traditions, and to analyze the degree to which violence has become a seemingly automatic personal and national response to problems. And as more becomes known about violence and its effect on the stability of our institutions and ourselves, it becomes imperative that society engage in a discussion of its continuing consequences.

Changes in attitudes towards violence and in violent behavior will be difficult, if not impossible, to attain. Nevertheless, as violent acts increase and expand into presently nonviolent areas, and as attitudes towards the use of violence harden, it becomes essential to attempt attitudinal and behavioral modification. Otherwise, Thomas Hobbes's concise description of a society without security becomes a reality:

> In such condition, there is no place for industry: because the fruit thereof is uncertain, and consequently no culture of the earth, . . . no account of time, no arts, no letters, no society, and which is worst of all, continual fear, and danger of violent death; and the life of man solitary, poor, nasty, brutish and short.[18]

"The rediscovery of our violence," wrote historian Richard Hofstadter at the end of the decade, "will undoubtedly be one of the more important intellectual legacies of the 1960s." The harsh events of the 1960s and seventies refocused attention on the nature and patterns of violence in American culture. As the intensity of violence increased, so did intellectual and political concerns. Consequently, two major presidential commissions—the National Advisory Commission on Civil Disorders and the National Commission on the Causes and Prevention of Violence —a number of smaller commissions, and a host of historical, psychological, and sociological studies have delved into the relationship of violence to the American past and into the ways in which violence is used to resolve conflict.

The incidents of the past decades have dramatically demonstrated that violence is an integral part of the American character. On one level, its major expression and perpetuation is at the hands of the decision makers in our society; on another level, its use reflects the basic American values of competition and acquisition. In a society dominated by the concept of scarcity and the consequent division into classes by wealth, the need of all to survive and accumulate goods releases powerful hostilities. As one scholar bluntly put it, "the gospel of money is a gospel of violence." The result is a culture in which acquisition is a primary value, and in which H. Rap Brown's comment that "violence is necessary and it's as American as cherry pie" is quoted often.

The patterns of violence clearly antedate the making of the nation itself and have been an attendant part of the expansion of the country across the North American continent and into other parts of the world. Violence thus cannot be disassociated from the development of the nation or from the ways in which people live and make a living.

The varieties of American violence run from the individual to the group and include virtually every type of behavior known in other societies. Perhaps the major American form of violence is the "vigilante" committee or group, which has existed almost from the nation's birth, flourishing in eastern as well as western communities. With the exception of genocide, the United States has witnessed all forms of violence.

Conversely, it might be noted that given the diversity of American society, it is remarkable that the country does not suffer from a higher degree of violence. Most people adhere to the law and support it as the primary foundation of society.

Yet because of this very diversity the United States does experience great spasms of violence. It is vulnerable to violence as few other cultures are and for that reason must be deeply sensitive to the manner, function, and degree of violence. When persons kill one another over a parking space or because of a dented fender, it is clear that a serious situation exists. That little or nothing is being done at the local or national levels is indeed frightening.

QUESTIONS

1 Define "conflict" and "violence." Is this the first time in your education that this subject has been presented and discussed? To what extent has it been included in your textbooks and course materials?

2 What is meant by the term "force," and what is its relationship to "violence"? How is force used by authority to maintain and structure society?

3 What has been your experience with violent events? Describe the circumstances and your involvement.

4 What have been the main patterns of conflict and violence in the United States? In your neighborhood? How are they similar and dissimilar?

5 What is the relationship between violence and the mass media? Would the lessening of violence in the mass media decrease the amount or types of violence in society?

6 What types of conflict and violence exist in your educational institution? Are they harmful or beneficial to learning?

7 What is meant by "legitimate" conflict and violence?

8 Would you want a society without violence? Without conflict? If you had the opportunity, how would you structure an institution, community, or society to minimize or eliminate conflict and violence?

READINGS Brown, Richard M. *Strain of Violence: Historical Studies of American Violence and Vigilantism.* New York: Oxford University Press, 1975.

Clark, Kenneth. *Dark Ghetto.* New York: Harper & Row, 1969.

Connery, Robert. *Urban Riots.* New York: Vintage, 1968.

Graham, Hugh D., and Gurr, Ted R., eds. *Violence in America.* New York: Signet, 1969.

Hofstadter, Richard, and Wallace, Michael, eds. *American Violence: A Documentary History.* New York: A. A. Knopf, 1970.

Report of the National Commission on Civil Disorders. New York: Bantam Books, 1968.

To Establish Justice, to Insure Domestic Tranquility: The Final Report of the National Commission on the Causes and Prevention of Violence. New York: Bantam Books, 1970.

Slater, Philip. *The Pursuit of Loneliness.* Boston: Beacon Press, 1970.

1. *Newsweek*, 18 December 1972, p. 31.

2. Harold Rosenberg, "Rosenberg on Violence in Art and Other Matters," *Arts Canada*, February 1969, p. 32.

3. Richard Hofstadter and Michael Wallace, *American Violence: A Documentary History* (New York: Vintage, 1971), p. 3.

4. Ibid., p. 9.

5. Richard M. Brown, ed., *American Violence* (Englewood Cliffs, N.J.: Prentice-Hall, 1970), p. 1.

6. Hofstadter and Wallace, *American Violence: A Documentary History*, p. 9.

7. Ibid.

8. George Jackson, *Soledad Brother: Prison Letters of George Jackson* (New York: Bantam Books, 1970), pp. 165–66.

9. Thomas Rose, ed., *Violence in America* (New York: Random House, 1969), p. 12.

10. Ronald Segal, *The Americans: A Conflict of Creed and Reality* (New York: Bantam Books, 1968), p. 4.

11. Alexis de Tocqueville, *Democracy in America*, Vol. 2, ed. Phillips Bradley (New York: Vintage), p. 256.

12. Segal, *The Americans*, p. 20.

13. de Tocqueville, *Democracy in America*, p. 270.

14. Michael Knight, "Untermeyer at 90: An Anthology of Living," *New York Times*, 30 September 1975.

15. Nathan Cobb, "Booming Handgun Business Soars to Record $75 Million," *Boston Globe*, 3 June 1973.

16. Gabriel Kolko, *Wealth and Power in America* (New York: Praeger, 1966).

17. "Hostages Freed After Police Capture New York City Bank Bandit," *Boston Globe*, 7 October 1975.

18. Thomas Hobbes, *Leviathan*, pt. 1, ch. 13.

3 | IT IS ALWAYS THE WOMAN WHO IS RAPED*

DEENA METZGER

Rape is an aggressive act against women as woman. The rapist is educated to his behavior by his society, and rape is the extreme manifestation of approved activities in which one segment of society dominates another. Rape is a ritual of power.

There are at least two ways of knowing. One is intellectual and the other is experiential. With which voice shall I speak to you? After rape there is a terrible silence. Then, if one is fortunate, one begins to learn to speak again. Why is the silence so terrible and so profound? What is the meaning of the crime that has been acted out: Why are its effects so dire?

Rape is the most common of the violent crimes. As the incidence of rape increases and we focus our attention on understanding the rapist—learning almost nothing of the victims—we continue the social patterns that perpetuate the crime.

Literature, art, and myth are full of images of rapes that are approved, even canonized. We distinguish the crime on the street from "The Rape of the Sabine Women," yet the painting by Poussin is informed by the same values that produce the street crime. Rape is the assault of a man on a woman, but it is also the symbolic enactment of social and cultural attitudes. On one level, perhaps unconscious, it is a gross and extreme form of social regulation by which woman is brutally stripped of her humanity and confronted with her definition as a nonperson, a function.

These attitudes are not peculiar to the rapist. The rapist is not an eccentric but an extremist acting out the being and nonbeing scenario that is basic to American society. In this scenario, the rapist uses power to

*Published in the *American Journal of Psychiatry* 133:4
(April 1976), pp. 405–08.

confront the egalitarian aspect of sexuality—community. That the act that physically and symbolically indicates communion should be so often distorted into combat is not ironic but tragic, undermining essential relationships. Rape asserts only combat, brutalizing the communal aspect of sexuality, destroying meaning, relationship, and person, creating a universe of emptiness and ontological terror. There is no distinction between the male social intent and the private female response. A woman who is raped understands her condition with metaphysical clarity.

Rape is mythically asserted, artistically glorified, historically condoned, and symbolically urged in the media and in advertising. Persephone is a classic example of the rape victim. Persephone has been promised by Zeus to Hades. Her primary definition is property. The earth opens, Hades carries her within, imprisoning her in hell; she is isolated. Her mother, Demeter, mourns her, leaves Olympus, and in her grief withholds spring. Neither Zeus nor Hades is condemned. Male power is glorified, while Demeter, condemned for withholding, is reluctantly placated. Persephone is returned; spring comes. However, Persephone, having eaten pomegranate seeds while in hell, must return to Hades every year. Thus Persephone is responsible for winter. The victim bears the burden and guilt of the crime that has been perpetrated against her.

We can translate this myth into contemporary experience. A man commits a crime against a woman. The authorities ask her, "Why were you walking alone? What were you wearing? What did you say? Are you a virgin? Did you pull down the shades?" Three basic attitudes of power are involved here: 1) to be weak is a crime deserving punishment; 2) the weak are accomplices in the crimes against them, and 3) the victim has committed the crime.

The stories of Persephone, Leda, and Europa are early mythic tales that teach rape as a learned cultural activity. The rights of men over women, the attitude underlying all cases of rape, were translated later into the droit du seigneur, the "giving" of the bride in marriage, the rites and rights of the marriage bed. These social customs reinforced the idea of woman as property, to be entered and used for man's purposes: woman as function.

A function is not a person. Rape is one manifestation of society's intent to depersonalize woman. It separates the woman from her humanity. Reduced instantly from person to object, property, flesh, vessel, the woman is immediately separated from anyone or anything that can comfort her. The basic experience of rape is isolation. Humanity depends on community, and the effect of rape is to destroy simultaneously the sense of community and the sense of person. Demeter and Persephone are separated because there is no comfort Demeter can give. Persephone is alone and empty. After I was raped, I knew that women were vessels, shells that could be emptied, flesh and bone frames without centers or substances. Women were moons shining only with reflected light, dead planets.

Because women's assertion of self conflicts with social and cultural patterns and with role and biology, the loss of self after rape is grave. Rape is the instant proof of unalterable conditions, the erosion of years of work. Contemporary feminism has only begun to change this condition. The very unique interest of women in autobiography is a sign of the difficulty women have with identity. Where men always have asked, "What is the meaning of my life?" women are beginning to simply ask, "Do I have a life?" The effect of rape is the same whether the victim is a young girl, virgin, mother, or old woman. Rape is a crime against the person, not against the hymen.

My experience and that of the women I know tells me there is no treatment for rape other than community. Therapy or consciousness raising can be helpful as long as no "cure" for a "condition" or "disease" is implied. Rape is loss. Like death, it is best treated with a period of mourning and grief. We should develop social ceremonies for rape, rituals, that, like funerals and wakes, would allow the mourners to recover the spirits that the rapist, like death, steals. The social community is the appropriate center for the restoration of spirit, but the rape victim is usually shamed into silence and/or self-imposed isolation.

In some ways, rape is never erased. Years later, even the word "rape" or the shadow of a familiar face can cause unexplained pain. The raped woman often cannot bear to be touched. Isolation is her condition. Touched, she knows she cannot feel; touched, she remains untouched. She is incarcerated in Hades. Her mother is outside and cannot hear her.

After I was raped, I had intercourse with my husband as a ritual gesture. (I had learned as a child to get back on my bike after falling, lest I never mount again.) Intercourse was easy. It didn't matter. I was an abandoned house. Vacated. Anyone or anything could enter.

Later I went through the ritual of talking to people. It always seemed as if I were talking through glass or under water. I could never tell my mother; she couldn't bear the pain. Others, it seemed to me, drew away. I could not bear to be alone, but in company I felt abandoned, estranged. For months I looked to my husband for comfort he could or would not give. A year later, we began a divorce.

I felt endangered everywhere. Every noise startled me. Every leaf was camouflage for an assassin. For months a friend of mine described searching the faces on the street as if to ask, "Are you the one?"

Revenge became an obsession. My husband was a party to this; vengeance would relieve his feeling of impotence. We spent days searching the streets in a mythic ritual. He was looking for power. I was looking for self. If a crime had been committed, then perhaps there had been a victim and a victim is a person; perhaps I would find myself.

Rape is usually the assault by the stranger, the unknown asserting his perceived socially, culturally, politically, and God-given rights. In earlier times rape was more frequently enacted by familiars. The woman who was shared, given, offered, dedicated was in effect raped; to be entered without permission, invitation, or desire is to be raped. Today most rapes are forced entrance by a stranger. The stranger is anyone. Simply a hand emerging from the shadows. Being anyone, the rapist is everyone. He asserts that the woman does not belong to herself. She is there for his use, his pleasure. She is nothing in herself.

The rapist acts for the society, concretizing certain ideas through his behavior. He is often marginally integrated into the society, and rape is the way he affiliates himself, if not through the act, then through the attitudes. Through rape he asserts power and possession in a common, violent, and spontaneous action. By choosing to assert himself against woman and her body, he—like church, state, schools, advertisers, and the media—is simply asserting certain rights and prerogatives over woman, using her for his own purposes. He is translating cultural thoughts into action.

The rapist is any man against any woman, Some form of anonymity is essential. He acts against the woman who happens to walk down the street, happens to be stranded, happens to be alone. It is an act not against someone but against anyone. Chance is an essential element. It reinforces the nonperson status of the victim, who is attacked at the moment of her nonbeing, in the shadows, alone, in silence, nameless; the rapist forces the identity of nonperson indelibly upon her. Whoever she had previously assumed herself to be, after the rape she is nothing: a body, a thing.

Yet rape is an assault on one's most private being. At her core, woman has a deep biological sense of herself, created through the cycles of blood and ovulation, through the pattern of puberty, menstruation, pregnancy, lactation, and menopause. This identity is enhanced by the cultural and symbolic values that the woman's body represents. It is this essence that is also violated: what she is and what she means. Finally, rape is a crime that gives the criminal pleasure. Not only is the victim possessed as by a demon, but she hears the demon laughing. She is used against herself. The groan of pleasure makes her feel despicable. Even before she is accused by police, parents, physicians, interrogators, she experiences herself as complicitor. Self-hate reinforces her person-lessness.

Perhaps for these reasons, there are almost no stories of rape written by women. Leda is assaulted by a "feathered glory." A magnificent bull kidnaps Europa. Daphne, pursued by Apollo, becomes a laurel, but Apollo is not deformed. Woman is one of the expected spoils of war. Cassandra is not the only one who speaks and cannot be heard; there have been millions.

Because rape is an act of power that male society will not undermine, the woman is defiled. Perhaps less consistently than at other times, the victim is isolated or isolates herself; she enters a psychic quarantine as if she were contaminated, diseased, scarred. Although today women do not automatically lose their social and economic value through rape, they are

devalued through accusations of seduction. The woman is suspect while the man is protected. Society asserts he is ill, marginal, or falsely accused. Men protect his rights and worry that the accusation may be false or the evidence contrived. The rapist is protected because he is themselves. The issue is always power. Rape, like the immaculate conception, becomes an act without an actor—the immaculate defilement.

The nonperson status of women is maintained in various ways, all of which seem to focus on sexuality. Symbolically, woman is the door, the opening, the entrance that must be sealed, protected. In one sense, according to Octavio Paz, woman is the essential violated one; she is the wound, the entered, *La Malinche, La Chingada*.[1] Her condition is one of violation, and it is against identification with such openness that man arms and armors himself. When man himself is entered and violated he is, according to Jean Genet, used as a woman, womanized, degraded.

Yet society simultaneously asserts that woman is the not-yet-entered, the innocent. The virgin is the unknown. To have intercourse is to know and be known. Sexuality is therefore knowledge, and woman is often insulated from this knowledge. That is part of the pattern of power and powerlessness, of being and nonbeing. To be without knowledge is to be nothing. For we are what we know. Woman at her best (as virgin) is thus nothing. Traditional heroines or women of power are grandmothers beyond sexuality, like Golda Meir, or virgins, like Mary, Joan of Arc, Elizabeth the Virgin Queen. The combined image of power and knowledge (sexuality) is terrifying: ogress, witch, Medusa, Clytemnestra, Medea—something to be destroyed.

The rapist acts against the societal injunction to protect the innocence of woman. He acts against the protection of woman, he denies the fortress of the private house. In so doing, he acts on the myth that for woman one error is fatal. Men, like the prodigal son, are capable of change, growth, learning. Women, for whom definition is finite, are confined within a single fall. Therefore the rapist has absolute power; he can destroy identity with a single act.

The raped young woman goes from nonbeing to Nonbeing—to not being at all. Rape is the act by which woman is known without knowing anything herself, the means by which knowledge and therefore presence is bypassed and nonbeing (innocence), which was tentative or temporary, becomes permanent. Raped, the woman becomes known, manifest, without gaining the identity that comes from knowledge. The only knowledge she gains is the knowledge of her lack of self.

With the exception of a few remarkable and brave women writers, including Doris Lessing, Simone de Beauvoir, Anaïs Nin, Kate Millet, and Colette, contemporary and historic literature (which reflects and creates social values and attitudes) asserts the nonbeing of women. From D. H. Lawrence's *Plumed Serpent* and *The Man Who Died*, to Henry Miller's *Tropic of Cancer*, Norman Mailer's *An American Dream*, and Erica Jong's *Fear of Flying*, nonbeing is the definitive condition of woman. And rape, which the film critic Arthur Knight recognizes as a "film cliché," is the act that confirms this nonbeing.

The literary, mythic, and historic attitudes toward rape are still with us. The charge against Joan Little for the murder of the rapist jailer who assaulted her in 1975 is the classic case of the victim accused of the crime. It is as if simple defenselessness, isolation of woman in itself, invites attack. The circle is complete. Men isolate women and then accuse that isolation. Rape is socially seen as response rather than provocation—it is the desperate male response to a powerlessness that is confirmed for him by the specter of female identity. Similarly, when [in 1975] Inez Garcia acted as a person against her attacker, she was the one charged. Worse than the image of an attacked woman is an image of a woman counterattacking. Here, the contradiction of nonbeing creates panic.

In a society such as ours, where the fantasy of power is a constant stimulus and Superman, John Wayne, James Bond, and Kissinger are cultural heroes, while powerlessness and alienation are the reality, it is inevitable that rape occurs frequently. Males denied power in their daily lives find means to act as if they had it. Women are the obvious victims because male society still defines them as powerless, functional nonpersons. Providing men with the feeling of power has been considered to be one of woman's duties.

In 1968 I was raped at gunpoint. Later, lying naked on the floor, I could only whisper over and over again, "One doesn't treat people like this." I had had only a momentary glimpse of the rapist, a stranger. From my brief description, a police artist drew a face identical to a photo I later identified in police records. This man, who was on parole, had been incarcerated for rape. His parole officer called him for questioning but concluded on the basis of an alibi that he had been too far from the scene of the crime.

The first fictional account I wrote of the rape (in an unpublished novel titled "Flying With a Rock") was couched in fantasy. I described the rape of a madwoman. I was still maddened by the assault and could only develop a character who had lost all sense of herself. Four years later I wrote a more accurate version, which describes a woman both overpowered and divested of her power.[2] Her last words are "I cannot." She is emptied out. I decided to make this public in order to break some of the silence and isolation which reinforces the personlessness of women. The private voice in the public sphere confirms our common experience through which we begin to assert ourselves. Unlike my character, now, I can.

From

SKIN / SHADOWS / SILENCE
A LOVE LETTER
IN THE FORM OF A NOVEL[3]

It is afternoon. You've heard this story before. This is the story I will tell twice and then again. It does not empty easily. This story has left a scar and the scar needs to be cut out. This story will be told again.

It is afternoon. I am alone. In an office. It is afternoon. I am alone. In an office. It is afternoon. I am alone.

There is a knock at the door. Or the sound of the door opening in the outer office. Or a knock and the sound of a door opening in the outer office this afternoon. I am alone. Thinking of things one thinks when one is alone in the afternoon. Almost a daydream. Allowed to think. Why should I be startled by a knock at my door or the sound of another door opening. Why should I hear the door or even interrupt my thoughts which are so pleasant this quiet afternoon. All the work is done.

Why bother to turn my head when I hear the floor creak? My thoughts are so pleasant, nothing can interrupt them. This is my time to muse. A rare afternoon alone. All the work is done.

Probably it is not a knock at the door that I hear and do not respond to. Probably it is the sound of a door opening quietly and of soft footprints across the floor. Or maybe it is the sound of a knock, a tentative tap to see if I am in. But it is a quiet afternoon and all the work is done and I am in to no one but myself, so I do not answer the door. Probably there is no sound. It is not that I refuse to be interrupted but that my dreams are so intense that I hear nothing, not the initial knock on the outer door (if indeed there was a knock—probably there was no knock), nor the sound of the lock turning, nor the cautious feet across the floor, nor the cautious turning of the lock to my inner office and the stealthy opening of the door, nor the hand raised against me. Nothing. It is afternoon and I hear nothing, suspect nothing, till the gun is pressed against my head and the hand muzzles my mouth.

"Say nothing," he whispers.

It is a gun which is against my head. There is a man holding it. I cannot see him. But I do not think I know him. He ties an unclean and wrinkled handkerchief across my mouth. I close my eyes because I am afraid to know him. Simultaneously I keep them open in order to see this man. But I think I can see nothing.

"Take your clothes off," he says. Everything he says is in a strained and I assume disguised voice. Perhaps he is someone I know. Which is more awful—an anonymous assault by a stranger or by a friend?

My hands are shaking and he is laughing. I am struggling to obey. My feet are shaking also.

I can only see his feet. I have told you before about his scuffed black shoes which look like those with steel linings in the toes. They are laced with frayed black laces. His socks are white. Dirty white. His feet are wide. I suspect his legs are hairy and that the hairs are damp.

It is afternoon. A quiet afternoon. No one is about.

No one is knocking at the door. "Take off your clothes," he says. My body is shaking. The dress peels from me like skin, a heap of feathers disordered, plucked live from the skin, a mound of fresh leather in a corner. And the animal is still alive! And the deer stretches denuded flanks, twitching. I can see the blood run across the hooves.

I am naked. He is wearing clothes. I do not wish to see his legs hairy at the ankle bone. I cannot bear to see his clothes against my skin. I am naked. He is fully clothed.

I remember nothing. I will remember nothing. I tell you this without hearing my own voice. I tell you this again and again so I will never remember it. I remember how naked I am next to his clothed legs in order to forget everything.

Handprints on my back. Indelible markings. In later mirrors it seems my back grows away from his hands. An announcement in reversal. In recoil.

An invasion. A tree opening to fire. And a black hollow from which no twig can emerge again. Perhaps it is a gun penetrating me and orgasm will be a round of bullets. Pain is a relief. I cherish it as a distraction from knowing. I am an enemy country. Destroy me with fire. But there is no distraction. The cloth rubs against my legs. There is a gun resting on my shoulder. I do not forget that death is the voyeur at this encounter.

Turning. Turning. The flesh of the spitted deer crackles against the fire. I *want to reach for a knife to carve myself into morsels, to divide into portions, to carve a slit downwards from my navel to my spine.*

There is a circle of steel against my ear.

I have told this before. It is afternoon, a quiet afternoon, and the taste of my own meat smeared on unknown flesh is in my mouth. I choke upon it. It is afternoon. I do not know what is thrust in my mouth. What banquet is this? What severed leg? What joint? What goat, deer, bone? I wish blood were dripping down my throat now. How long can I hold his sperm in my mouth without swallowing?

It is afternoon. I have told you this before. It is a quiet afternoon. I do not hear the sound of someone knocking at my door.

I try to say, "Come in." I would like someone to help me from the floor. I need a pillow under my head. Wrap me in a blanket. Turn the lights out.

It is early evening. It is night. It is tomorrow. I would like someone to help me up from the floor. I cannot say, "Come in," to the knock on the door. I cannot yell for help. I need to be wrapped in a blanket. I need a pillow under my head. And a nightdress. And a cover of white cloth.

Everything is quiet. My body is numb. I feel nothing. My body is numb. It is early evening.

There is a knock on the door. I cannot hear the knock at the door. I cannot say, "Come in." I need . . .

There is a knock at the door. I cannot say . . . I . . .

There is a knock . . . I can not . . . I . . .

I can not . . .

. . .

SUMMARY

Our sexually polarized society often attacks women in the most intimate way—by denying selfhood through rape. That society condones this brutal experience is evidenced by its long history in fact, in mythology, in literature, in art, and currently in the advertising and entertainment media.

The psychological distress caused by the act of rape is far greater than any physical suffering. When a woman is raped she is in effect told that she is nothing but a receptacle, that she is nothing in herself. And when a man rapes he is in effect acting out the privileges that society implicitly says are his. Rape is always political, a means by which women can be kept in their place and a tactic against which women *must* unite.

Indeed, the extent to which rape is tolerated in American society indicates the degree to which this country remains uncivilized. Not only women, but also men must work for a humanistic community of equals to replace the sexually polarized one that still exists. Degradation of *any* type, directed against *any* group or individual must be eliminated; the eradication of rape as a social and political institution is a necessary step toward this goal.

NOTES

1. *La Malinche* refers to the mistress of Cortez, the Indian woman through whom the invasion occurred: "The Mexican people have not forgiven *La Malinche* for her betrayal. She embodies the open, the *chingado*, to our closed, stoic, impassive Indians. . . . The *Chingada* is the Mother forcibly opened, violated, or deceived. . . . This passivity, open to the outside world, causes her to lose her identity . . . she is no one; she disappears into nothingness; she is Nothingness. And yet she is the cruel incarnation of the feminine condition." Octavio Paz, *The Labyrinth of Solitude*, trans. Lysander Kemp (New York: Grove Press, 1961), pp. 85–86.

2. See Deena Metzger, *Skin: Shadows/SILENCE: A Love Letter in the Form of a Novel* (Reno, Nevada: West Coast Poetry Review, 1975).

3. Ibid.

QUESTIONS

1 Can a man be raped?

2 Do you think the rape of women will ever cease? Why?

3 The criminal justice system has traditionally held the testimony of the rape victim to be suspect (even though actual instruction to juries to view victim's testimony with a "grain of salt" is now forbidden). Why is the rape victim so often seen as at least an accessory to the crime against herself?

4 How is rape usually depicted in films and novels? Why do you think this is so?

5 Can a woman be raped by her husband?

6 Why do you suppose the crime of rape is on the rise?

Metzger, Deena. *Skin: Shadows/SILENCE: A Love Letter in the Form of a Novel.* Reno, Nevada: West Coast Poetry Review, 1975.

Paz, Octavio. *The Labyrinth of Solitude,* trans. Lysander Kemp. New York: Grove Press, 1961.

LeJeune/Stockmarket, Los Angeles

The value of this paper derives from the labor, thought, and experience of many women. I wish to thank Barbara Myerhoff, Sheila de Bretteville, and Jane Rosenzweig, in particular, and to acknowledge all the others with whom I have talked for their contributions to this work. We are so much each other it is no longer possible to know which ideas are whose. I prefer to think of this work as a chorus of voices, as in writing it I feel that I am drawing upon and giving to the common pool which is our common lives.

"Woman Talk" was presented at the National Conference on Popular Culture at Milwaukee, Wisconsin, in 1974.

4 | WOMAN TALK

The Conversation and Various Asides on Woman's Culture, Water Coolers, W.C.s, and Children

DEENA METZGER

Woman has always been associated with the dark, with the unknown. It has been in society's interest to consider women unknowable. This "mystery" was one device to keep women from power. Separated from the "light" of the dominant society, we have maintained a culture of our own, expressed in our forms, though frequently transmitted (as is the case with other oppressed cultures) in uncodified ways. Often our communication is nonverbal, implied rather than overt, inferred from behavior, intuition, gesture, and touch, so that the substance of our talk is in the environment of language rather than in the words themselves. Not taught in schools, not included in curricula or official publications, our culture is communicated mother to daughter, and through sisters, grandmothers and friends. Given the ephemeral nature of this communication, it may seem surprising that woman's culture incorporates certain universal elements which have been maintained against the influence and effect of the dominant culture within which or against which it exists. This is because women everywhere and seemingly in all history not only share a common biology but are socialized into similar roles and are similarly oppressed.

In western society, and particularly in the United States, women are charged with being the guardians of certain values necessary to the survival of humanity, though ironically these values undermine and challenge the antihuman thrust of contemporary industrial, technological, and political life. In middle-class society, this contradiction is mitigated through the relegation of women to the home, in order to isolate them from the public sphere and to prevent these humanistic attitudes from entering and influencing public life. A policy of containment. When isolation is unenforceable, other means are necessary to neutralize women's culture. The standards of public behavior become clear and rigid so that those women participating in the world do so only through profound alteration of their selves.

Further the values which they retain are regarded as trivial, dubbed "female," so that they lose their power to influence others. Certain values—survival values—persist only in isolation, circumscribed within the home, the female domain.

Woman's culture is the complex expression of women's sensibility, knowledge, values, and rituals, and of the attitudes which result from the interaction of role, biology, historical conditions, and memory. Our culture differs markedly from the dominant culture, something we have always known. It is this difference which Virginia Woolf referred to when she asked: "How can we enter the professions . . . and yet remain civilized human beings?"[1] Or when she wrote "If you are going to make the same incomes from the same professions that these men make, you will have to accept the same conditions that they accept . . . you will have to perform some duties that are very barbarous."[2] For Virginia Woolf, the dominant culture with its emphasis upon aggression, competition, rank, and power was alien. In contrast, woman's culture develops structures which are essentially nonhierarchical, intimate, and cooperative. These qualities are evident in the range of women's activities and work, from art making to car pooling, from politics to conversation.

The tone with which women address each other when they are alone, the conversations women have with other women, are models of woman's culture. My goal here is to make that conversation public, to make it known, to make it accessible, to honor it so that the forms need not remain underground, so that women can begin to emerge from the private sphere and so that men and women can become whole through access to, and participation in all modes of being.

A conversation between women is a very special act. Women know this. A conversation between women is different from a conversation between men, is different from conversations between men and women, and is different from conversations which take place under the auspices or influence of the dominant culture. To understand what occurs within a conversation between women is to understand both that woman's culture exists and that it is subversive: that woman's talk is wonderfully dangerous to the dominant society. The spontaneous casual interchange between women reaffirms values which atrophy in public life, while the organized conversation of women, such as one encounters in consciousness raising groups (CR), clearly and properly threatens the existing social, political, economic, and psychological order.

Woman's conversation is an interchange of language, silence, gesture, and touch which informs and connects. Camaraderie is as important as data. Seemingly simple exchanges as well as sophisticated theoretical or analytical discussions serve several different needs. When women speak to each other the sentence functions both to communicate information and to establish intimate connection between them. In conversation as in other activities within the female domain (CR, car pooling, collective child care, play groups, feminist programs), the focus is upon the relationship; the practical aim of the activity rarely (in contrast to public life) takes precedence over human interaction. Whereas in the business world the human element is considered a nuisance, in women's activities that element is honored. Here nonverbal gestures, touch, the meetings of the eyes, enhance the intensity of the conversation and are a language in themselves. Moreover, women tend to search for the common denominator, for an area of shared and meaningful experience. Women so often talk about what have been depicted as "women's things" because they are more interested in the feeling of community than in abstract talk; they appreciate these events of daily life because they are the common denominator of everyone's experience and the basis of all human relationships. Additionally, these "trivial" matters are in fact the "stuff of life," at once the simple and the symbolic—what sustains us.

> Her parties! That was it! her parties! Both of them criticised her very unfairly for her parties . . . She could not imagine Peter or Richard taking the trouble to give a party for no reason whatever.
> But to go deeper, beneath what people said (and these judgments, how superficial, how fragmentary they are!) in her mind now, what did it mean to her, this thing she called life? Oh, it was very queer. Here was So-and-so in South Kensington; someone up in Bayswater; and somebody else, say in Mayfair. And she felt quite continuously a sense of their existence; and she felt what a waste; and she felt what a pity; and she felt if only they could be brought together; so she did it. And it was an offering; to combine, to create; but to whom? . . .
> An offering for the sake of offering, perhaps. Anyhow it was her gift.[3]

Women's discussion, whether it be of dinner parties, recipes, work, politics, science, or art, is something more than talk. Men in this society seem to feel the need to be separate, different from, superior to each other; women tend to search for what brings them together rather than what sets them apart.

Women introducing themselves to each other tend to avoid professional definitions, preferring to offer statements about their lives rather than their careers, offering some bit of information which can create an intimate experience. Men in our society tend to define themselves by what they have accomplished or are doing in the public world. They are carpenters or doctors, "working on . . .", while women, particularly since CR, often introduce themselves in terms of their personal struggles, openly communicating a current internal dilemma. Women, not having the same urge to present a facade of power, will frequently say, "I've just divorced" or "I'm trying to get my life together" as a means of introduction. Men tend to communicate rank, accomplishment, fixed position or specific information; women are as apt to communicate failure, loss, disappointment, struggle—not something accomplished but something to be resolved, not only the public but the private as well.

At a recent national conference I met beforehand with women panelists, each a professional woman distinguished in her field. Though we were all strangers to one another, within moments of our meeting we were engaged in a lively discussion of research and family, politics and personal life, the talk punctuated by the acknowledged pleasure of being together. However, when preparing to enter the conference room we all (consciously, though with some humor) put on rank like a uniform, suppressing our emotions, our private lives, manifesting only those few behaviors appropriate to being "Dr. X" or "Dr. Y."

Because women's conversations blur the distinction between public and private, any interchange which is wholly abstract or objective, removed from personal reality, is experienced as incomplete; subjectivity and personal interaction are required for wholeness. Men talking about themselves deliberately limit their talk to a narrow focus, exchanging only that impersonal data, those facts and ideas which will establish a public definition of self. Women pursue a broader, less focused conversation, in which giving information is not primary. In the exchange of ideas, a working environment is created. Women are willing to reveal the raw materials of their lives in order to explore together. Women's conversations may have a more "unfinished" tone because women begin with the unknown as often as with the known. If men's conversations reveal, women's conversations explore.

Men tend to talk about what is unique about themselves, to exchange choice bits of information. They are likely to guide the conversation to their area of expertise and hence of power or prestige—"Do you know who's going to win the series?"; "The real economic interests which run this country are . . ."; "My study reveals that poverty in the United States . . . ." Their statements are complete in themselves. Mini-presentations. Lectures. Panel discussions, at best. Women are more likely to concern themselves with the person they are speaking with: What do you want to know? What do you need from me?

Men more commonly tell jokes or make puns. Jokes are complete verbal events which evoke laughter but rarely commentary. An appropriate response to a joke is another joke. Parallel play. The pun, similarly, is verbal punctuation. It stops the conversation. Its nature is to interrupt, inhibit response or continuity. The desired facial response to a pun is the dropped jaw, the acknowledgement of the interruption, the sudden appearance of a psychological wall.

Women do not commonly invoke such forms, preferring other forms which are more responsive. "You know how it is" is a common phrase inviting identification and laughter, often bitter. Similarly, the tendency of some women to raise rather than lower their voices at the end of sentences does not imply uncertainty so much as invitation, willingness to negotiate or even accommodate, a desire for response and interaction. The sentence takes the form of a question in order to invite an answer.

These qualities found in women's conversation and other activities are becoming visible as women come to know themselves and to develop the courage and determination to express their own values and sensibilities, rather than continuing to conform to old alien forms. Sometimes women organize deliberately to incorporate certain forms and values. The structure of CR is not accidental. It is a conscious form developed specifically to provide integrity between method and goal. The procedures which regulate CR themselves create an egalitarian model for the society women hope will develop. According to Juliet Mitchell:

> CR is the reinterpretation of a Chinese revolutionary practice of "speaking bitterness," a reinterpretation made by middle-class women in place of Chinese peasants and in a country riddled by psychotherapeutic practices. These peasants, subdued by violent coercion and abject poverty, took a step out of thinking their fate was natural by articulating it. The first symptom of oppression is the repression of words; the state of suffering is so total and so assumed that it is not known to be there. "Speaking bitterness" is the bringing to consciousness of the virtually unconscious oppression; one person's realization of an injustice brings to mind other injustices for the whole group."[4]

In the process of "sharing bitterness," each woman is given equal time to speak or to be silent. Each woman has a turn, and value

William McNally

judgments are discouraged. CR usually occurs in a leaderless group where topics are mutually decided upon and where each woman knows she will be listened to and given support and respect.

The egalitarian circle of CR finds its analogue in other female activities—abstractly in the nonhierarchical structures of feminist organizations; visually in much of women's art; and in the form and imagery of women's literature, as in Virginia Woolf's *To The Lighthouse*. Each woman has her moment of light in CR, as each aspect of experience, significant or ordinary, is illuminated in turn by the sweep of the beam of light. Such diverse writers as Virginia Woolf, Anaïs Nin, Gertrude Stein, and Colette all avoid the established, traditional plot which develops towards a climax, preferring rhythms, cycles, attention to detail, an interest in the impermanent, and the significance of the ordinary, of that which is common to us all. Literature, quilts (the combined bits and pieces of ordinary history) and conversations repeat each in their own way the egalitarian, collective, nonjudgmental structure of CR. The expressions are different, the forms and values are similar. Woman's work is often nonauthoritarian, cyclical, repetitive, cooperative, and complex. It is a weaving together of the individual and the collective, the personal and the public, the intimate and the universal.

Now—as in the past when feminist movements were strong—we are cognizant that a woman's culture exists which crosses class, economic, national, and racial lines. When women become more conscious of themselves, they relinquish the dominant culture's habit of distinguishing discrete units, preferring to affirm commonality. Women's movements have generally been international, focusing upon similarities rather than differences. At the height of the Vietnam War, a delegation of women from North Vietnam asserted at a conference in Canada: "We [women] are the fourth world." During that conference the following emerged in a manifesto:

> A female culture exists. It is a culture that is subordinated and under male culture's colonial imperialist rule all over the world. Underneath the surface of every national, ethnic, or racial culture is the split between the two primary cultures of the world—the female culture and the male culture.[5]

Woman's culture develops from the positive and negative aspects of our lives, and from the common aspects of role, biology, and oppression. The idea of woman's culture arises from the identification of forms and patterns which underlie women's activities and expression. It must be understood that the identification of woman's culture is a joyous experience because so often in this society we have been isolated from each other. The new conversation among women, the new intimacy, the identification of our common experience, is an act which destroys the terrible loneliness which has so often been the lot of women. The meaning of the community of women can only be understood in the context of our historical separation from each other through the nuclear family and the organization of industrial and technological life. Virginia Woolf's words are a powerful reminder: "Our real lives are our common lives."[6]

Woman's culture is expressed through woman's talk. We rarely build monuments. What we build together is often as impermanent and as essential as language itself. Our conversational forms are repetitive and open-ended. Like "woman's work," relationship requires constant attention; it is never "done." One can find continuing patterns but not conclusions. Our lives exist most often in the flux of the everyday.

I choose to look at woman's conversation because it is devalued, rarely appreciated, because its structure and purpose are unknown, because it is unique and ubiquitous, because it is available to and practiced by most women, is spontaneous but organized, because it contains all the patterns of other women's activities, and because it is beautiful.

The way women talk to each other is the way they are. Their conversation is an integral and organized response to the way they experience the world. Similarly, the world's response to woman's conversation is like its response to women in general. The anxiety which the dominant culture experiences when women get together (reflected in the unremitting ridicule of women's groups, organizations, and auxiliaries) parallels the anxiety revealed in the constant ridicule of woman's talk.

The fear of women is twofold: mythic/historic and contemporary. Today woman's talk represents to the dominant culture the challenge of an antagonistic culture's sensibility. Even a balanced coexistence of both cultures implies radical change.

Woman's talk is the means by which woman's culture is actualized, because it reinforces and maintains cultural characteristics. Arising from the culture, it vitalizes it and projects it.

The underlying goal of almost any woman's activity is to create intimacy, relationships, and then community. But a special aspect of much of woman's talk is to create *communitas*—that special state of being when the connections between people are very intensely experienced. The dynamic of *communitas* is that one's sense of self is heightened directly through one's perception of identity with another. Perhaps one can say that *communitas* is the experience of community, is the moment in which the complete connection between human beings is realized. The moment of *communitas* is almost always associated with excitement and joy. And now among women it is often accompanied by the sense of group power. Within conversation women do not pursue or rarely pursue *communitas* to the point of ecstasy. Ecstasy serves to overwhelm and therefore to transport the woman outside herself; the goal of much conversation between women is to locate, but not to transcend, their identities. The ultimate goal is connection.

Because of the potential for community and *communitas* in woman's talk, it is now common to see women coming together to talk, expectantly and purposefully. One knows, one anticipates, that something important is going to happen. One readies herself as for a ritual occasion or a ceremony. And as in the case of rituals or ceremonies, one knows that the richness of the event derives not only from the activity and its symbolism but from the satisfaction of multiple needs.

From childhood I remember the intense and then inexplicable excitement surrounding slumber parties—the secret and delicious confessions in the dark, the intoxicating presence of one's special friends. Later I was taught to set this aside as part of an infantile past. Now perhaps we can look at it again, as we must look at other "inanities": the coffee *klatsch*, the Tupperware party, the bridal and baby showers, the luncheon, the card party, and most curious of all, the compulsion women retain from girlhood to accompany one another to the bathroom.

As children, the bathroom was for many of us the only place where we could have privacy with one another, so many of us not having had the "room of one's own" which Virginia Woolf insisted was necessary. For young girls the bathroom is the place of secrets, of discussion of the "mysteries" of our bodies which until very recently were considered taboo, unknowable even to ourselves. Discovering and exploring our shared biology creates an easy camaraderie which is extended to other women at the dressmaker's, the beauty parlor, the health club and the powder room. The women's bathroom is still often the only woman space in a public building, and women retreat there together in order to be able to talk of their own things in their own voices.

I recently discovered how international this habit is when traveling in Latin America. I was doing research and much of my time was spent in formal, official conversations in which there was rarely, if ever, any reference to the personal, the private, or to daily life. One evening during dinner I went to the bathroom and was not surprised to see that the three other women at the table followed me. In the "powder room," which even here was the familiar lounge-sitting room, we spontaneously seated ourselves in a circle and entered an open conversation free of political and governmental inhibitions and proscriptions, sharing our lives, work, and families. In the course of the half-hour we spent—indeed, we were reluctant to return to the more formal dinner party—other women, strangers who entered, joined us. I realized then that the classic "withdrawal" of men in the nineteenth century for brandy and cigars must have been received by the women with relief. In retrospect that half-hour I spent was one of the richest and most valuable experiences of my stay, for it was the only time I could be sure of honest communication. Women seek those experiences which are levelers and which destroy imposed, artificial solitude and isolation.

The community of women and the conversations which sustain it exist in every class, despite the dominant culture's insistence that class differences supersede personal experience and that women are jealous of and competitive towards one another. Jealousy is an artificial construct designed by men to create distrust among women and to maintain themselves at the center of interest and activity. Similarly the trivialization of "woman talk" is an attempt to deflect women from the realization that conversation among women easily crosses class lines, because it is a response to the common female experience. The community of women, sisterhood, challenges all the arbitrary distinctions, the assumptions of class and rank, which are postulated essentially to maintain status, privilege, and power. Woman-to-woman talk is different from boss to worker, jailer to prisoner, doctor to patient, adult to child. In woman-to-woman talk, equality is postulated.

While CR is most common among white middle-class women, it is clear that the phenomenon is spreading from young, political, university women to housewives, secretaries, and high school students—essentially unpoliticized women. More and more women are coming together regularly in their places of employment or education and in their neighborhoods. Without identifying the activity as CR, they talk about their lives in new ways and adopt many of the structures and goals of the organized CR groups. CR is a collective form directed toward helping individual women liberate themselves in the context of the liberation of all women. Women's personal and collective history is investigated in an atmosphere of emotional support. The intimacy of the group derives from the combination of talk, touch, caring, and analysis within a nonhierarchical setting.

A consistent element of woman's conversation seems to be the appreciation of the communality of woman's experience and an increasingly insistent urge to preserve its positive aspects while rebelling against the common oppression. This enables women to cross barriers of race, culture, nationalism, and lately (ironically most difficult in America), of age. The recent interest of American women in their grandmothers and historic forebears reflects positive self-images and new alliances.

Simply listening to the words exchanged in a conversation among women does not reveal what it is about. In the most ordinary interchanges, women combine content with comfort, negotiating very complex interactions in seemingly simple ways. As Phyllis Chesler writes in *Women and Madness:*

> Two women talking often seem to be reciting monologues at each other, neither really listening to (or "judging") what the other is saying. Two personal confessions, two sets of feelings, seem to be paralleling one another, rather "mindlessly," and without "going anywhere." In fact, what the women are doing—or where they are "going" is toward some kind of emotional resolution and comfort. . . . A very special prescience is at work here. On its most ordinary level it affords women a measure of emotional reality and a kind of comfort that they cannot find with men—and that men do not have with each other. On its highest level, it constitutes the basic tools of art and psychic awareness.[7]

Comfort is provided physically as well as intellectually. The new knowledge about our bodies and our lives allows us to be increasingly easy with one another physically: stroking, holding hands, hugging are codes of understanding and nurturance. Face-to-face conversation becomes important and more and and more frequently women make special appointments to get together to talk.

Historically, women's conversation, the spoken and written words, the camaraderie in the kitchen as well as the letters, diaries and journals, have been methods by which women sustained one another, and maintained sanity in the face of their oppression. Isolation from public life and from one another, as well as total devaluation of their existence and activities, has had dire results. The history of women's literature, for example, is the history of madness. Margery Kempe, Virginia Woolf, Charlotte Perkins Gillman, Emily Dickinson, Sylvia Plath, Anne Sexton—all have testified in their lives or work to the ravages of this separation.

Looking at the effects of isolation in another culture provides a perspective to help us understand its effect upon women today. Writing of the Athenian *polis*, Hannah Arendt says:

> The principal characteristic of the tyrant was that he deprived the citizen of access to the public realm, where he could show himself, see and be seen, hear and be heard, that he prohibited the *agoreuein* and *politeuein*, confined the citizens to the privacy of their households . . . According to the Greeks, to be banished to the privacy of household life was tantamount to being deprived of the specifically human potentialities of life.[8]

Today, woman's conversation relieves this situation, but should not be mistaken for a therapy which inhibits action by adjusting woman to her situation. To the contrary, these organized conversations lead toward action.

Comfort is an element of conversation, but it does not suppress pain. Rather, it provides a place where pain can be analyzed and acted upon. Initially, this may create even greater anxiety: having once internalized the authority of the dominant culture, women find it difficult to rid themselves of it. The earlier, false security of personal problems requiring personal solutions is no longer viable. While demanding social change, CR also provides the understanding and support needed to create a new interaction between the individual and her environment. This is the major goal of CR.

The form of woman's conversation provides a model for women's extension in the world, showing that it is possible to incorporate into public life the values traditionally relegated to women. These values speak to the human need for play, nurturance, and fantasy; they insist upon the coincidence of our intellectual, emotional, and physical lives. Woman's conversation challenges arbitrary distinctions, too often maintained by language itself. Women are saying that the distinction between public and private, affective and practical, is false.

Woman in Western society became the custodian of values inherited from preindustrial society, the guardian of creative and collective interaction which could not survive the distortions of industrial society and the profit motive. It is now accepted among anthropologists that woman the forager, as opposed to man the hunter, was the inventor of agriculture, the one who made possible the neolithic revolution, based upon a dependable food supply. Woman burdened (and blessed) with children did not have man's mobility and remained in the compound with other women where collectively they fished, farmed, domesticated animals and plants, and invented spinning, weaving, pottery, basketry, and the decorative arts. Woman is continually identified with earth, growth, cyclical life, fecundity, and animals. She is Nature herself, the nature which man seeks to subdue and erase.

Man pursued pottery and agriculture when they produced surplus value, after the pottery wheel was invented and after the plow replaced the hoe and slash-and-burn agriculture. Man displays anxiety toward woman and nature. He is able to interact even with his fellow men only from a position of power and control, when each is in his place. His interest has been in those weapons and tools which allow him to survive independent of others. Man pursued many formerly collective activities when he could do them alone.

The women in so-called primitive cultures who have recently rejected running water and washing machines have not done so because they are too stupid to see their practical advantage, nor out of a stubborn and irrational conservatism, but rather because they perceived the inevitable erosion of community life with the elimination of the well and communal laundering. In the United States one can look upon the twenty-four-hour laundromats as a last vestige of collective domestic life, providing the poor or transient with the opportunity for a human exchange.

The new conversation between women develops as the contradiction increases between women's collective urges and the intrinsic, relentless alienating forces of contemporary society. As the women's movement validates an old collective history, as present experience resurrects it, the conflict between women's communal sense and the isolation to which they have been confined is intensified.

Earlier women felt constrained to learn the forms of conversation of the dominant society. Now it is easier to say: that is not my style. Women do not object to the characteristics of conventional speech: formality, impersonality, competitiveness, and the focus upon concrete data and information. They *do* object to the dominance of these forms. To create the woman's sentence (as Virginia Woolf advised) is not another act to emphasize differences, but the offering of a new form for both men and women to use. A concomitant of woman's culture is a choice of style and behavior in public life.

As we can see, the charge to preserve the values of community has not meant living in a society where those values were predominant. Whatever our own subculture, women have had to live within the

dominant society. Every movement out of the home reminds women that they have been separated from one another despite their interdependence, and that they are still aliens in the public world. Total integration into the dominant mode will not end women's estrangement from it. Women must see *their* way of life reflected in public forms of speech and behavior.

Contemporary society isolates women through the home and the nuclear family, though neither homemaking nor child rearing can be performed effectively alone. Women give each other substantial assistance, though this is unacknowledged publicly and increasingly more difficult to integrate into the structures of the dominant culture. Often the aid appears insignificant, but the proverbial cup of sugar, baby-sitting exchange, and potluck supper are real gestures, fulfilling real survival needs. In ethnic ghettos and in poor and immigrant neighborhoods the cooperation among women is vital and more evident than in middle-class neighborhoods. Mothers, daughters, and grandmothers exchange earning and child-rearing services and act out on a daily basis the fact that they cannot survive independent of one another. These gestures are not merely economic or pragmatic—there is no value in abandoning this cooperation when times are better—they represent a common stake in a common existence, and are symbolic of the community women yearn for.

When women reach conversationally for community, they are acting upon forms and values learned in the home. Community is the public manifestation of the home; it is the means by which women extend the home to one another.

The home may be defined as the place where numerous life-sustaining activities occur at once and where a variety of needs are fulfilled or attended to simultaneously. The home is the place where women learn to respond to many different needs with one action, and where it is usually necessary to regard others with a concern equal to that with which one regards oneself. It is the place where one cannot conclude any single task before beginning another. It is the place where work cannot be concretely defined. It is the place where no activity is discrete. It is the place where almost nothing ever gets done and stays done. It is the place where no single goal can be postulated, and where a complex of actions serves a variety of purposes.

One of the characteristics of home work or housework is that each action is complex and the general task of homemaking is more complex still. Nevertheless, one cannot create a hierarchy of values because all the elements are necessary. Trivial and so-called significant work demand equal time and equal attention. In the home one cannot chose among feeding, loving, working, shopping, earning, creating, cleaning, relating, imagining, playing, and baby sitting. All these operations are equally necessary. Often all are performed within a single day, even simultaneously. Everything seems to have equal value if one defines value either by urgency or time spent. When writing a speech for the United Nations or the Senate, one cannot tell a child to stop crying. There are rarely efficient, silent, unassuming secretaries at home to order the day and keep life in line. Messy, uncontainable human needs spill over onto the work, taking precedence—making a work of art is not always more urgent than making a sauce for the broccoli. That broccoli is both trivial and extraordinary, because the act which puts food on the table is both commonplace and symbolic. An act of caring and loving, it sustains life, yet it is also banal. These oppositions are the constant poles of women's lives—the association of the sacred and symbolic with the trivial and ordinary. These qualities are plaited into every aspect of women's work, including conversation. This sense of the trivial and commonplace is increased by the failure of woman's work to create surplus value, to create a commodity, to produce a profit, or to be stored anywhere but in heaven. Moreover, in her homemaking woman is seen as a user, a consumer, and a burden, which adds further to her sense of valueless-ness. Nevertheless, she is aware that her labor sustains the most fundamental processes of the race.

In the home, a woman not only does not and cannot choose among art, children, and broccoli, but she is forced to think about them simultaneously; she worries about work, art, and the world while she is cooking, and thinks about the broccoli while she is pursuing other work. Her work necessarily reflects, in form and content, this union: it is permeated with the smell of life. This is not chaos, but a perspective which becomes a form, *strudeled* instead of linear. This is the experience which allows a woman to look at her life simultaneously with awe and disgust, with nonchalance and wonder.

Even as I write this, I am also aware of other needs and demands—I suspect that all the women reading this will understand. I am thinking about my children, a novel I'm writing, dinner, teaching, my compañero, The Woman's Building, the dog, a social engagement, a grant proposal, an errand which has to be run, tasks which need to be completed, and my friends.

It is from this simultaneity of need and response that women derive the ability to pursue a conversation on many levels and many subjects, to move from children to Michelangelo, the price of milk, Virginia Woolf, a hemline, personal tragedy, general feelings, the war, politics, myth, ideas, facts, emotions, and experiences. Women do not, cannot, and should not separate these concerns. They do not segregate the personal from the public, the theoretical from the practical, the important from the trivial. Rather the conversation creates a meaningful order from these bits and fragments of everyday life. (It was exactly at this point that my son Marc entered my bedroom/study with a question. "Let me finish the sentence," I said. I continued typing until David yelled to me from another room. "Just a moment, I've got to finish a thought . . ." I answered. Then Marc said, "Your next novel should be a record of your interruptions.") It is in talk that the prosaic operations of life gain their proper meaning, and the overwhelming moments regain perspective.

These same patterns are seen in women's study programs. As women attempt to reconstruct their history, they investigate the common lives of unknown women as well as the uncommon lives of historic figures. Studying "extraordinary women" is often done to discover in their activities the texture of daily life. There is a growing interest in diaries, journals, autobiographies, in personal experience, in the art and literature of the attic as opposed to the musuem, in the life histories of one's mother and grandmother.

Woman is centered in the home and confined to it by man, who claims her, isolates her from others, but also isolates her from himself as well. Woman has always been considered dangerous because she has been made to represent those forces which man fears—nature, animality, chaos, the unconscious, blood, the dream life, the emotions. Although she comprises 51 percent of the population, woman has been defined as "the other." The characteristics with which she is "endowed" are irrelevant or threatening to the dominant culture. Woman inhabits either the home or the "other world." Man, on the other hand, lives *in* the world.

Women, we know, are defined as emotional, weak, and irrational; men as serious, strong, and rational. Emotion, play, and fantasy are confined to the home. Women do not "work." The work world is serious and complex; the home is simple and tangential. The distinction between home and work increases until it appears that any contact between the two will disrupt the work system altogether. The work world is threatened by the presence within it of women *as* women, by the values of the home, and finally by the very proximity of the home. Woman becomes the enemy twice—as the repository and personification of all man's anxieties and as the embodiment of a real threat to the system man has devised.

When woman does leave the home to enter the work world, she must do it on man's terms, which results in a further estrangement from other women as her own style and value are eroded. The kind of conversation which women manage outside the dominant culture rarely exists within it.

Isolation, a given in women's lives, is increased by progress and upward mobility. Personal and public prosperity serves to further separate home and work and to limit the behavior acceptable at each. Additionally, the physical distance between the sectors increases. The suburb is not designed to satisfy women's needs, though it has been packaged and marketed to seduce women into becoming accomplices in their own loneliness and isolation. The suburb creates distance between home and work, freeing the work space, the city, from female contamination. Just as the older doctor moves his office from the home, retires his nurse wife to card parties and charity drives, and relocates to a small office building and then to a prestigious medical complex, so the house is shifted to the suburb and the suburb itself extended miles and miles from the city center. Industry and business are cordoned off by zoning restrictions and then transplanted to industrial parks and governmental complexes. Concrete blocks are erected which do not contain children, animals, extensive greenery, or the aged. The entire institutional apparatus is grotesquely insulated from domestic life by being relocated in dead cities and artificial compounds like Brasilia. We can speculate with grim humor that the rush to the moon and other planets (which in the United States is so conspicuously accomplished without the aid of women, children, or poets) is man's final attempt to locate his work outside the home, by placing it in another world altogether.

If woman's culture is cooperative, then woman's experience in the dominant culture is against her being. Her life is a series of impossible attempts to conform to the pervasive "why can't a woman be more like a man." (How does the world look from Eliza Doolittle's perspective?) Looking at the suburb again, we can see that it is a jail subtly created through the "puffing" of false privacy and fraudulent claims of domestic self-sufficiency. The private car, the supermarket, the backyard playgrounds provide further insulation. The environs of home have become an alien territory where it is difficult to find a place to talk.

Woman's work like woman's art has always taken place at the hub of life. While it is Virginia Woolf who laments that woman has always had to write novels on the dining-room table, lacking an income and a room of her own, it is also Virginia Woolf whose heroines are centered in daily life, engaging in the "eternal conspiracy of hush and clean bottles." A special kind of conversation develops when women work together and engage collectively in the business of life. This special conversation, the historic conversation of weavers and basket makers, of home work—pursued a century ago at quilting bees and echoed today at cake sales, and in CR groups, women's work collectives, and women's centers—is a conversation which reaffirms a consciousness eroded by the current organization of daily life.

When conversation was still considered an art, woman functioned as a muse, presiding over a salon. Today it is her conversation, not Samuel Johnson's, which is valued. In the new woman-to-woman relationship it is acknowledged with pleasure (and surprise) that women are interesting, intelligent. It is becoming a cliché that women are more interesting than men. As Vivian Gornick writes in "Consciousness and Raising," "This is mainly why feminists often say that women are the most interesting people around these days, because they are experiencing a psychic invigoration of rediscovery."[9]

In a polarized culture, perhaps the water cooler, that comic image of flirtation and waste, is the bleak remnant of the complex interchange and personal interactions which were part of the normal female integration of work and life. Supplementing the lunch and coffee break (note that even language defines vital human functions as interruptions of the normal order), the water cooler is the paltry vestige of laundering at the river, the collective cultivation of land, the communal oven, the pot-bellied stove in the family store, the candy-store hangout. It is an anachronism reminding us that work and life have not always been antagonistic enterprises. The new conversation of women, like the joking at the cooler, works to correct this distortion.

In the past "woman talk" implied the frivolous exchange of inessentials. Women's gatherings were called pink teas, tea parties, hen parties, and cat sessions. At its best, woman's conversation was considered chatter and at its worst, gossip. In either case it was inconsequential. Yet is is strange that gossip was for so long devalued since, like woman's conversation, it provides a form of social interaction. While it is necessary to be aware (as Sheila Rowbotham points out) that gossip provides a powerful form of social control over the behavior of other women, yet it is also necessary to realize (as Barbara Myerhoff notes) that gossip is often a benign, personal form of social regulation. Gossip can be seen as the subculture equivalent of law, but while law is abstract and impersonal, gossip only works within the context of a personal relationship. Law is absolute; gossip negotiates.

Devaluing women's activities has been a means of social control, of maintaining women "in their place" outside public life. The use of pejoratives was once effective, but no longer. The deprecation of "woman talk" once kept us silent, but no longer. Woman talk functions despite or because of these oppressive activities.

At this point woman talk is being organized as a political vehicle for initiating revolutionary change. "Chit chat" is the means by which women begin to enter the culture—but on their own terms. In the CR group women test nonhierarchical, noncompetitive, nonelitist social relations in order to propose institutional changes. In the CR group women rediscover the collective experience and the complex view of the world which integrates the extraordinary and the day-to-day.

The new conversation among women is becoming a political act. In the past women have been defined as dangerous, their talk as disruptive. The myth is coming true.

SUMMARY

Women's conversation is a special form of communication which transmits through its form and content the intimate, cooperative, non-hierarchical values of women's culture. In the dominant culture, talk is impersonal, competitive, pragmatic, and aggressive. Women's talk is personal, responsive, and nurturing. The major function of women's conversation is to create community; therefore, woman talk avoids excessive focus upon expertise in favor of finding common ground and experience.

Consciousness Raising is the formal application of the values of women's conversation to the solution of personal and social problems. In CR, women's personal experiences, often made known for the first time, are shared, explored, and honored, so that individual women can achieve liberation in the context of the liberation of all women.

Women's talk, like other women's activities, perceptions, and experience, is devalued and trivialized in the dominant culture to oppress and isolate women. Today woman's conversation, revalued and lovingly practiced, is a way to gain respect and community. Woman talk is a political act against an oppressive society; it also offers society at large a usable form for participating in a humanizing activity which fuses the personal and the public, the intellectual and the emotional. Woman talk is an effective form with which to mitigate the dire results of a polarized and alienated society.

NOTES

1. Virginia Woolf, *Three Guineas,* paperback ed. (New York: Harcourt Brace Jovanovich, 1963), p. 75.

2. Ibid., pp. 69–70.

3. Virginia Woolf, *Mrs. Dalloway*, paperback ed. (New York: Harcourt Brace Jovanovich, 1964), pp. 183–84.

4. Juliet Mitchell, *Woman's Estate*, paperback ed. (New York: Random House, 1973), p. 62.

5. Barbara Burris (in agreement with Kathy Barry, Terry Moore, Joann Delor, Joann Parent, and Cate Stadelman), "The Fourth World Manifesto," in *Radical Feminism*, eds. Anne Koedt, Ellen Levine, and Anita Rapone (New York: Quadrangle, 1973), pp. 322–57.

6. Virginia Woolf, *A Room of One's Own*, paperback ed. (New York: Harcourt Brace Jovanovich, 1963), p. 117.

7. Phyllis Chesler, *Women and Madness*, paperback ed. (New York: Avon, 1973), p. 268.

8. Hannah Arendt, *Origins of Totalitarianism* (New York: Harcourt Brace Jovanovich, 1966).

9. Vivian Gornick, "Consciousness and Raising," in Vivian Gornick and Barbara K. Moran, eds., *Woman in Sexist Society* (New York: New American Library, 1972).

QUESTIONS

1 Why is the article entitled "Woman Talk"? What does this phrase say about stereotypes of women in our society?

2 Why is it that women confront stereotypes and discriminatory treatment? What is the historical background that leads us to this situation?

3 Do you see any similarities between the minority status of women in American society and that of other groups such as blacks? How are the difficulties both groups face similar and what are the differences?

4 Why do some women resist the idea of equality of the sexes? Do you see differences in attitudes towards male-female roles among females of different ages? What are they?

5 Do you think "woman's culture" will ever become the dominant one? Can you imagine what that might be like?

6 What does "androgynous" mean? What does "unisex" mean? Do you believe that the women's movement has anything to do with either of these terms?

7 Are any women you know actively involved in the women's movement? What are their objectives and how are they trying to reach them? Describe your personal experiences with these women.

Chesler, Phyllis. *Women & Madness*. New York: Doubleday, 1972.

Dworkin, Andrea. *Woman Hating*. New York: E. P. Dutton, 1974.

Harding, M. Esteher. *Woman's Mysteries*. New York: G. P. Putnam's Sons, 1971.

Hess, Thomas B., and Elizabeth C. Baker, eds. *Art and Sexual Politics*. New York: Macmillan, 1973.

Lessing, Doris. *The Golden Notebook*. New York: Simon & Schuster, 1962.

Miller, Jean Baker. *Toward a New Psychology of Women*. Boston: Beacon Press, 1976.

Millet, Kate. *Sexual Politics*. New York: Doubleday, 1969.

Mitchell, Juliet. *Woman's Estate*. New York: Vintage Books, 1973.

Moffat, Mary Jane, and Charlotte Painter, eds. *Revelations: Diaries of Women*. New York: Random House, 1974.

Rich, Adrienne. *Of Woman Born*. New York: W. W. Norton, 1976.

READINGS

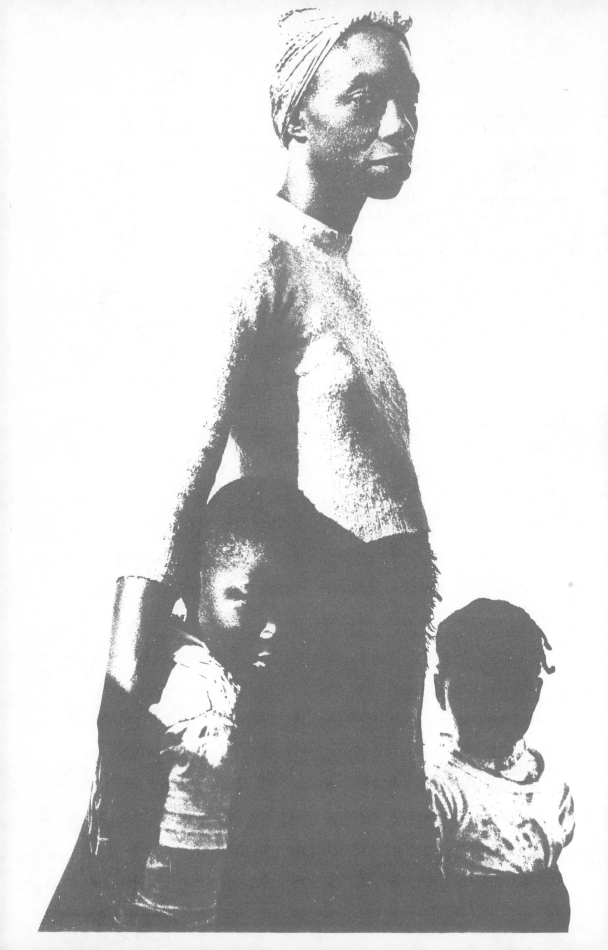

5 | DAY WORK

A Short Play and an Afterword

FLOYD BARBOUR

Characters   DORIS HARDING   *late thirties, housewife.*
HAROLD HARDING   *her husband, early forties, businessman*
MARIE   *their young, "colored" maid.*

Set   DORIS HARDING's *cheery sitting room. A wing chair is center, a hassock beside it. Windows looking out onto a cheery horizon are in left wall; telephone table by left wall. Down right is a dressing table with hairbrush on it; a bench. A closet is upstage right and a door leading to the hallway is upstage center.*

Time   *The present; morning to dark*

Place   *Suburbia*

At Rise   *The memory of a waltz plays. Closet door is open.* DORIS *can be seen foraging for something in the closet. She is wearing a frilly dressing gown. At last she finds what she is looking for: a sheer, red negligee. She takes it from closet, shutting closet door. Holding negligee,* DORIS *crosses down center where the mirror would be (where the audience is). She holds negligee to her, turns about, and dances to the waltz, a sweet waltz, a floating waltz. Then, a nervous shadow crossing her face,* DORIS *turns, drops negligee onto bench left; simulates closing music off. She crosses to wing chair. She sits, looking out into the depths of space, her wrist dangling over arm of chair.*

(Directions refer to actors' right and left.)

[*Count Five*]   HAROLD *knocks on door; pause, he enters. He is dressed in a dark suit, morning paper beneath his arm. He pauses to locate his wife; now, seeing her wrist dangling over arm of chair, he moves down towards her. He pauses behind chair.*

HAROLD   Morning, dear. [*Then, moving around, he kisses* DORIS *on cheek. And while seating himself on hassock:*] Did you sleep well?

DORIS   Do I ever?

HAROLD   [*Overlooking this*] We're going to have a natural occurrence today. . . .

DORIS   [*Suddenly, a whisper*] Where's Marie?

HAROLD   [*Unfolding newspaper*] Downstairs, in the kitchen.

DORIS   [*Anxiety rising in her voice*] Harold, I want to talk to you about her.

HAROLD   About Marie? [*Simultaneously pointing to negligee*] Say, when did you get that?

DORIS   [*Visibly hurt*] I wore it last night—you didn't even notice!

HAROLD   [*Placating*] Of course I noticed. I was just teasing, honey, baby-lamb. . . .

DORIS   Harold, please, stop.

HAROLD   [*Deep sigh; turns to newspaper*] Says here, there's going to be a natural occurence . . . an eclipse . . . .

DORIS   [*Standing left*] Harold, I want to talk to you . . . about *her.*

HAROLD   What, dear?

DORIS   [*Whisper*] You say she's in the kitchen?

HAROLD   Who?

DORIS   Marie—I want to talk to you about Marie.

HAROLD   [*Glancing up*] What about her?

DORIS   I don't know, I can't put it into words.

HAROLD   [*With patience*] Try, dear.

DORIS   [*Pacing*] I went—I went to the kitchen last night . . . I wanted to fix—I wanted to open a can of soup . . . I couldn't find the can opener. . . .

HAROLD   You couldn't what?

DORIS   I couldn't find the can opener.

HAROLD   I don't see what you . . . .

DORIS   [*Interrupting*] Don't you see? I couldn't find the can opener.

HAROLD   Well, ask Marie.

DORIS   That is what I'm talking about!

HAROLD   What?

DORIS   *That:* I have lost control, I have lost control of my own house! I won't be dependent on one of *them*!

HAROLD   You and Marie have gotten along fine.

DORIS   No, *you* and Marie have gotten along fine!

HAROLD   [*Putting his paper aside*] Okay, dear, tell me what's wrong.

DORIS   I am telling you what's wrong. [*Short pause*] I read this article . . . .

HAROLD   [*Glancing at his watch*] Oh, Doris . . . .

DORIS   Don't "oh Doris" me! Won't you listen, for once?

HAROLD   I am listening.

DORIS   No, you're not. You're thinking about escaping to your office! Yes, you are. That's what concerns you!

HAROLD   Honey, look, I'm almost late . . . .

DORIS   Then go, leaving me at her mercy!

HAROLD   [*Has stood up*] I guess I shouldn't have come in this morning.

DORIS   [*Going to him*] No, it's not that. I'm happy you came to see me. I'm always happy you come to see me. I'm sorry darling. Please sit down. Don't go just yet. Oh, I know it's difficult having a . . . nagging wife. . . .

HAROLD   Honey, look . . . .

DORIS   No, I do. I know it's difficult. I'm difficult. I don't mean to be. You must have patience, Harold. I don't mean that, you've had too much patience, but have some more, a little more . . . .

HAROLD   [*Not unkindly*] Doris, you've worked yourself into a state . . . And it's not even nine o'clock.

DORIS   [*False smile*] Yes. [*Sitting in chair*] You mentioned something . . . .

HAROLD   What?

DORIS   In the paper.

HAROLD   The eclipse?

DORIS   The eclipse.

HAROLD   Happening today, that's all.

DORIS   [*Leaning forward*] Where is she?

HAROLD   You know where she is.

DORIS [*An accusation*] She fixed *your* breakfast soon enough!

HAROLD [*Circumventing this*] You were telling me something . . . .

DORIS Yes.

HAROLD About an article.

DORIS It was nothing.

HAROLD It must have been something, to upset you so.

DORIS It didn't upset me; why do you say it did?

HAROLD I only thought . . . .

DORIS Yes, it *did* upset me.

HAROLD Well, then . . . .

DORIS No, *she* is what upset me. I told you. I went to the kitchen: I couldn't find the can opener. I went to the pantry: I couldn't find the light switch . . . .

HAROLD What were you doing in the pantry?

DORIS That is not what I'm talking about, Harold. I read this article about *them:* colored maids—no, listen. In nice homes like ours. All the maids got together one day and decided they would murder the ladies they worked for.

HAROLD Doris . . . .

DORIS Got together and decided that at a certain hour they would murder these ladies. Why not, all you husbands are away from home, most of the day, half the night. Why not slaughter poor creatures like myself? And they did. They axed these ladies to death, dismembered the bodies, and stuffed the remains in the furnace.

HAROLD [*Making a face*] Oh, Doris.

DORIS And I caught her . . . .

HAROLD Who? Marie?

DORIS Whom are we talking about? Of course, Marie. I caught her trying on one of my gowns yesterday. Standing before that mirror, trying on one of my gowns. I just stood back and watched her!

HAROLD Well, what harm could she do?

DORIS [*Almost a scream*] I don't like domestics trying on my things!

HAROLD Honey, you're the one who wanted someone in, days, to help you. What with your clubs and associations and charities. You're the one who said you had to have help with this big house.

DORIS I couldn't find the light switch in the pantry. I used to know where everything was . . . .

HAROLD Look, if it'll be any comfort to you, I'll be home early today.

DORIS Why bother? Look at you. I look at you, looking at her. Think because I'm imprisoned here, I don't know what's going on? Think I don't see? You're all the same, taking your mean pleasures wherever you can find them!

HAROLD Doris, please.

DORIS You used to call me your vesper sparrow. You don't do that anymore. You don't even ask me to turn a collar, or mend your pajamas.

HAROLD I don't wear pajamas, Doris.

DORIS [*Anguished*] Oh, Harold! I used to know where everything was. Now, I don't know where anything is. Don't you see, Harold? It's *them*. Their conspiracy!

[*A light rap on door.*]

VOICE It's me . . . .

[HAROLD *crosses to open door.* MARIE, *wearing a maid's uniform, stands in doorway with breakfast tray. She comes in: pleasant, smiling, cheerful. She moves by* HAROLD *who playfully taps her on the rear.*]

MARIE [*Crossing to* DORIS] Mornin', Miss Doris. [*She places tray on hassock.*]

HAROLD That's right, Marie, cheer Miss Doris up. She's been acting like a little girl afraid of the dark. [*Gets his paper*] I'll probably be home early this evening, Marie. Whatcha cookin' up good for me?

MARIE Whatcha like?

HAROLD You know: southern fried chicken!

MARIE You had that last night.

HAROLD But ah loves it: it sure do hit the spot.

MARIE [*Pouring coffee for* DORIS] Go on, Mr. Harold. [*Chuckles*] I brought an extra cup, Mr. Harold, 'case you want an extra cup of coffee.

HAROLD No, thank you, Marie; I'd better be going.

[HAROLD *stands watching* MARIE *pour. He is about to move off. Comes back to kiss* DORIS *goodbye.*]

HAROLD Forget all that stuff you read, honey; it just gets you upset. [*To

MARIE] They call this the great exodus: all of your people coming out here to work and all of us going into the city to work. Then at night, all of us coming back out here, and all of you going back to the city.

MARIE   [*Shrugging*] I don' mind.

HAROLD   [*Thoughtful*] Yeah; well, I'll be leaving, or I'll miss my train.

[HAROLD *exits, leaving door ajar.*]

DORIS   Would you close that door, Marie, there's a draft.

MARIE   [*Crossing to door*] Yes, ma'am.

[MARIE *gets a broom and dust cloth which were outside door. She brings them inside room, closing door.*]

MARIE   Should I do the bedrooms now?

DORIS   [*Sipping her coffee*] No, you can do that later.

MARIE   [*Straightening up; putting red negligee in closet.*] You two sure was havin' a discussion this mornin'.

DORIS   You heard us?

MARIE   [*Shakes head "no"*] Jes' grumblin's.

DORIS   What do you two talk about, when I hear you in the kitchen?

MARIE   Oh, Mr. Harold's always jokin' about somethin' or other.

DORIS   [*Inward*] It's all me. [*Looking up*] He's good to me. I've just been so, so harassed lately. At what point comes the end to our romantic dream? But then, you wouldn't understand that sort of thing. *You* people, I mean.

MARIE   No, ma'am . . . .

DORIS   He used to call me his vesper sparrow, because I used to love to sing, before I lost my urge to sing. That's what it is, Marie: loss and more loss.

MARIE   Yes, ma'am.

DORIS   How long have you been with us, Marie?

MARIE   Goin' on three months now.

DORIS   Do you like day work, Marie?

MARIE   Workin' in service is all right.

DORIS   But, do you like it?

MARIE   S'only kind of work I can get.

DORIS   Why? There're enough jobs.

MARIE   No, ma'am.

DORIS   There are. I look in the paper any day and see hundreds of jobs. You people just don't look, that's all!

MARIE   Well, I don' know . . . .

DORIS   No, you don't! You just don't try. You whine and blame us for the way the world treats you, and when we give you something, you don't know how to utilize it. Utilization, that's the key! Utilization and civilization!

MARIE   Yes, ma'am.

DORIS   Have some coffee, Marie.

MARIE   I already had some, thanks, ma'am.

DORIS   Suit yourself. [*Pause*] Mr. Harold says there's going to be an eclipse today.

MARIE   [*Dusting*] A what?

DORIS   An eclipse: that's when the day goes black at noon.

MARIE   [*A pause*] Yes, ma,am, I been here goin' on three months; and I been treated real nice too.

DORIS   That's right. Your own people trick you up here, and when you get here, they have nothing for you. You have to turn to us, and we are there for you to turn to. You always think someone is taking from you. It's *you* doing the taking, from us: our flour, our sugar, our linen.

MARIE   Yes, ma'am.

DORIS   "Yes, ma'am; no, ma'am." [*Suddenly*] Why do you people hate us so?

MARIE   Nobody hates you, Miss Doris.

DORIS   [*Having risen*] What have we ever done to you, except try to help you?

MARIE   Yes.

DORIS   Is it envy? Is that it?

MARIE   I don' envy nobody.

DORIS   That's what it is: envy. You'd love to be walking around in my gowns and dresses, wouldn't you? Go ahead, you can tell me. Go ahead. You'd love to be moving around in my white skin. Wouldn't you?

MARIE   Not me, Miss Doris.

DORIS I've seen you, I've watched you pick over my things, running your greedy fingers over my things. Think I haven't watched you? You'd love to be wearing my hats, my furs, my . . . lingerie. [*Sudden thought*] You'd love to have Mr. Harold, wouldn't you?

MARIE [*Shaking head "no"*] Huh-huh, Miss Doris, I got Jackson and he's more'n enough for me.

DORIS [*At window*] See, the world is already getting darker . . . blacker . . . a total night.

[*From this point on lighting follows the line of an eclipse.*]

MARIE [*Picking up tray*] You through with these things, Miss Doris?

DORIS Please leave those things alone. Sit down. Stop fidgeting about. [*Short pause*] What's he like?

MARIE Who?

DORIS Jackson, you know, what's he like?

MARIE Like hisself, I guess.

DORIS I suppose he's very . . . passionate?

MARIE Whatcha mean?

DORIS I've heard, you people are very . . . in bed, I mean. You're very . . . sensual . . . . Jackson. My parents had a handyman named Jackson. A very large, black man. Used to sweat a lot. We had to let him go, he used to track so much dirt through the house.

MARIE That's not *my* Jackson.

DORIS [*Center*] I've walked along streets and had your men look at me . . . . You know, in that—animal way . . . stare at me . . . . So I have to hurry along the street, almost run down the street, not to have them . . . not to have them . . . turn on me . . . .

MARIE Tsk-tsk, ain't that somethin'!

DORIS Those hot, burning eyes, staring through my clothing. Eyes, stares so hot I had to catch my breath . . . not to be singed. Animal stares, animal sounds. Like the world were a black monster ready to devour me. [*Turns*] Why do you people hate us so?!

MARIE [*Alarmed; gently*] Miss Doris . . . .

DORIS Take yourself, for instance. What have I ever done to you to make you want to murder me?

MARIE Lawd, Miss Doris, whatcha talkin' about?

DORIS   To make you want to pick up that broomstick and crush my skull in. What have I ever done to make you want to do that? I'm nice to you; and all you can think of is my death!

MARIE   No, ma'am.

DORIS   Yes, ma'am. Jackson. What noble ambition does Jackson have?

MARIE   Like what?

DORIS   What does he want to do, Marie?

MARIE   Eat and sleep, I guess. Oh, and sometimes he talks 'bout ownin' a house . . . .

DORIS   [*Abruptly*] Where's the phone, where's my phone?

MARIE   Over there, where it always is.

DORIS   As long as I know where it is!

MARIE   You wanta make a phone call, Miss Doris?

DORIS   No. Yes: you do it. Call Mrs. Grey and tell her I won't be going to the club meeting this afternoon. I've been taken ill.

MARIE   [*Going towards phone*] Yes, ma'am.

DORIS   You don't have to do it this very minute, Marie. Must you do everything immediately?! Can't you sit down?

MARIE   [*Sitting on chair*] Miss Doris, what's wrong today?

DORIS   [*Turning on her*] Well you might ask. I saw you yesterday trying on one of my gowns. I saw you. I didn't say anything, but I didn't like it.

MARIE   But you told me to try it on.

DORIS   [*Struck*] Why—I did not! I couldn't, wouldn't have . . . .

MARIE   You said yourself: "Marie, I never get a chance to wear this thing, let me see how you look in it." That's exactly what you said.

DORIS   [*Pushing breakfast tray to the side; sitting on hassock*] Yes, so I did. I'm sorry, Marie.

MARIE   You sure did say it.

DORIS   [*Quietly*] There was a song Harold always liked me to sing. [*Pause*] I've lost the tune. [*Inward*] If only our Buckey had lived. But he didn't live. Nothing lives; nothing thrives.

[*Deepening shadows.*]

MARIE   [*Crossing to place tray on dressing table*] Here, Miss Doris, let me brush your hair for ya, relax ya.

[MARIE *takes hairbrush; crosses behind* DORIS]

DORIS Yes, that's nice. You do a good job of brushing my hair, Marie; you do a good job of most things. I almost envy you; I almost envy the way you do a good job of most things.

MARIE There, see how soothin' that is?

DORIS I watched you in that gown, it was very becoming to you. I watched the way you moved in it. The way it flowed about you. It was very becoming. You're a pretty girl, Marie. You've got pretty movements when you walk; and the way the soft material flowed about you . . . I watched you . . . .

MARIE See how soothin' that is . . . .

DORIS The rooms in this house like you, Marie. They open to greet you. You move through this house the way I used to, but don't have the energy to anymore. This house fights me. Windows stick when I try to open them. Cobwebs won't budge when I try to dust them away. But you move through this house as if you always belonged here.

MARIE Yes, ma'am.

DORIS [*Taking brush from* MARIE] Let me do that. [*Brushes her own hair. Then pausing, hands brush back to* MARIE] Here, brush your own hair, Marie. Go over there and brush your own hair. [MARIE *crosses to mirror*] That's right. See how fine the bristles are. Feel how heavy it is. Silver-backed, an antique. [*Slight pause*] I read this article yesterday, an actual account. These colored girls, maids, who did day work, decided to remain in the suburbs one day, decided they would come out to the suburbs, murder the ladies they worked for, and wait until evening for the absent husbands. Then they would slaughter the husbands. What a thing, huh, Marie?

MARIE [*Brushing*] Yes, ma'am.

DORIS You see, it would be revenge. Terrible revenge.

MARIE Yes, ma'am.

DORIS Like a black plague devouring the good people.

MARIE Yes.

DORIS [*Change*] Have you ever thought how it might be to be me?

MARIE [*Turning*] Why, Miss Doris . . . .

DORIS Of course you have. What have you thought?

MARIE [*Slowly*] Well, sometime . . . .

[*Stage has darkened except for a little light.*]

DORIS Go on, tell me.

MARIE Well, sometime—when I get home . . . Mr. Harold treats ya so nice, and Jackson can be so down.

DORIS Go on.

MARIE I don' know. Well, I get home and it's so crowded and there's no place to put my things, and everybody's too tired to talk nice or do nice things.

DORIS That's when you wish you were here?

MARIE Sometime. [*Places hairbrush on table.*]

DORIS And what would you do if you were me?

MARIE I don' know. Walk around like you do. Take long hot baths and go to meetin's. I'd wear nice clothes, like you do. Go shoppin' in nice places. Eat in nice places. Never worry about bills or landlords. I'd say: "Marie, bring me them slippers."

DORIS [*Goes to closet, takes out pair of slippers; touch of the automaton in her movements*] Yes, ma'am.

[MARIE *sits on hassock as* DORIS *puts slippers on her.*]

MARIE How come you take so long to do as I say, Marie? What makes you so slow?

DORIS I'm sorry, ma'am, you know I try.

MARIE You don' try hard enough. And you know I can't stand excuses —me and my health problems. You know how we always treat you people as nice as we can. Do everythin' in our powers for you. You know it.

DORIS Yes, ma'am.

MARIE Then how come you so slow and backward?

DORIS Don't know, ma'am. I'm improving.

MARIE [*Angry*] Don' say you're improvin', you're not improvin', you're gettin' worse! And I've seen the way you've eye'd my things. Runnin' your greedy fingers over my perfume bottles. Takin' on airs when I'm not in the room.

DORIS I didn't mean to, ma'am.

MARIE What does that mean, not to mean to?! You did it, so you must have meant to!

DORIS Yes, ma'am.

MARIE "Yes, ma'am!" You're as bad as your men. I've seen them drivin' through our neighborhoods before eight in the mornin' in their shiny, white cars. The white hunters on their way from you or to you. Stoppin' their cars. Makin' their animal noises, animal motions. So low-down they don' dare hold their heads up. I've seen 'em, we've all seen them.

DORIS Let me brush your hair, ma'am. [MARIE *has seated herself on bench.* DORIS *picks up brush and begins to brush* MARIE's *hair.*] There, see how soothing that is, ma'am. See how soothing that is . . . .

MARIE Yes, I like that. That is soothin'. To my mind. [*She hums a tune.*] Mr. Harold likes that tune, Marie; he always liked that tune.

DORIS Yes, ma'am.

MARIE [*Stops humming*] I had this premonition, Marie. This unsoothin' dream. About you. About what to do with ya. About your wish not to see or have me livin' in this world. I had this unsoothin' dream.

DORIS No, ma'am.

MARIE Yes, and I have been tryin' to figure a way to get out of this bad dream. I have been tryin' to figure a way out of your lookin' at me and wantin' my things.

DORIS No, ma'am.

MARIE I have perceived a solution, Marie.

DORIS Oh.

MARIE Some ladies and me have decided there will be no club meetin' this afternoon for anyone.

DORIS Oh.

MARIE Some ladies and me have decided there will be no club meetin' ever again for anyone.

DORIS Oh.

MARIE We are concludin' all club meetin's for everyone.

DORIS [*Has crossed to phone. Picks up receiver; dials*] Hello . . . Give me Mrs. Grey, please.

MARIE [*Wrenching phone from her; interrupting*] Hello? Oh, Magnolia, this is Marie. Yes. Huh-huh. Miss Doris jes' wanted to say that she won't be comin' to no more club meetin's. Huh-huh, that's right . . . . Somethin' about an eclipse . . . . That's right . . . . Okay . . . . Good-bye.

DORIS I don't like that, I don't like that at all.

MARIE Hang this up.

DORIS   [*Places receiver in cradle*] It's gotten so dark . . . . Where are you, Marie? [MARIE *has crossed to table to pick up silver-backed hairbrush.*] Harold said he would be home early today. [*Picking up receiver again*] I'll call him to make sure. What's his number, Marie; Marie, what's his number?   [MARIE *replaces receiver in cradle.*]

DORIS   What are you doing? [*Tries to lift receiver*] What are you doing? You leave me alone, do you hear? [MARIE *pushes* DORIS *so that she falls upstage right, crawling*] Get away from me. Somebody . . . . [*She finds her way behind chair*] Somebody, help me . . . . Somebody . . . . [DORIS *tries to hang onto back of wing chair.* MARIE, *carrying silver-backed hairbrush, has followed her.*]

DORIS   [*A scream which becomes a cacophony in the darkness*] Somebody—help—me!

[*As* MARIE *is about to strike* DORIS *with brush, there is a moment before the stage goes black. Sound as of someone being beaten. Screams. Silence.*]

[*Count fifteen.*]   [*Lights come up. The memory of an African rhythm plays. The scene is almost the same as it was· at the beginning of the play. The breakfast tray has been removed.*

Closet door is open. MARIE *can be seen foraging for something in the closet. She takes out the sheer, red negligee. Holds it before her. She takes off her maid's cap and puts on negligee; crosses down center where the mirror would be (where the audience is). She holds negligee to her, turns about, moves to the African rhythm. She simulates turning music down; crosses to wing chair. She sits, looking out into the depths of space, her wrist dangling over arm of chair.*]

[*Pause.*]   [HAROLD *knocks on door, enters; evening paper beneath his arm. He pauses; moves towards chair. Stops behind chair.*]

HAROLD   Hello, Marie. [*Then, moving around, kissing* MARIE *on cheek, while seating himself on hassock and simultaneously opening newspaper*] What's for supper?

[*Blackout*]

An Afterword   There is a fallacy about winter, that everything goes silent beneath a blanket of whiteness, that all activity ceases. I sense instead a flurry of life, a world in preparation.

Day Work is about fear.

A few years ago I and a friend of mine were on our way to one of the suburbs outside Boston. We were going to hear Norman Mailer and Stokely Carmichael speak. My mission was to get Carmichael to contribute an article on black power to a book I was editing. It was early December, about six o'clock in the evening, in the late sixties. The streetcar we had taken was crowded with riders on their way home. Looking out of the window at a passing streetcar, I had a sudden shock. Nearly all the faces going into the city that evening were black; nearly all the faces coming out to the suburbs were white. I was the only black on the outbound streetcar. This image remained with me as I wrote *Day Work*.

The Mailer-Carmichael exchange took place in a large, comfortable family home. It was not uncommon in the sixties to read of whites who were afraid blacks might invade the suburbs to burn down such homes. I could never understand why this was so, since the only homes burning at that time were inner-city dwellings. I used to wonder whether whites secretly wished to have their manicured lawns trampled on, their manors burned. Were they as angry with the system as the inner-city people? I didn't know. And it is hard to get white people to talk about being white. It is this lack of knowledge which makes living in America so painful. So much of what I know of my neighbor comes from supposition. By extension, perhaps, so much of what I know of myself does too. It is like participating in a huge mirror show. I thought of this as I developed the characters in the play; and I thought of the house.

That evening, with the snow lightly falling, Carmichael discussed the concept of black power. He showed how it was important to white and black Americans. "Black power is not a recent or isolated phenomenon," he said. "It has grown out of the ferment of agitation and activity by different people and organizations in many black communities over the years."[1] The word *black* thrilled me. I thought of the fear which surrounds that word. I thought of Joyce's Gabriel Conroy observing the snow falling over Ireland; I thought of Wright's Bigger Thomas trapped in a Chicago snowstorm; I thought of the blackness of an eclipse.

I also wondered about the fear which permeates so much of our life in this country. There are many areas in Boston I cannot walk into; many areas my white counterpart cannot walk into. One of the sad things about living in America is the waste of potential human contact and understanding. We have such an opportunity to know so many different people and we don't take advantage of it. There is an Irish grandmother in South Boston right now whose wisdom could change my life for the better. There seems, however, to be a conspiracy to keep us from knowing each other.

I asked myself, what was this fear? Was it fear of a gigantic black takeover, a massive black retaliation? Was it a matter of guilt? Envy? Do we still live in the memory of slavery and its aftermath? Beneath the skin, the blood flows through arteries. Hearts beat in a similar manner. What sets the races apart like strangers on a train? When was the first time I had felt this fear?

When I was a child, my mother and I were in Washington, D.C. We had gone in out of the summer heat to a *People's* drugstore. I impetuously climbed up on a stool and ordered a Coke. Something in the way the white woman behind the counter looked at me alerted me to danger. Something in the way my mother returned the woman's look confirmed this danger. I got my Coke but we never went back to that drugstore in that then-segregated city.

Day Work is about unrequited love. Doris moves in a world which has become increasingly alien to her. She has tried to reach her husband: "I wore it last night—you didn't even notice." She has tried to placate her black help: "We treat you nice." She has finally retreated into herself, away from that house.

Unrequited love is hard to bear. The black often feels like the bastard child of American civilization. He has gone to war, fixed the pipes, cleaned the house, brought up the children, tested the vaccine, and still been denied entrance to the house. Love is proffered; little is returned.

What keeps the races apart? Is it that any innocent gesture may result in a subtle humiliation? Is it simply "the system"? I don't know. I do know a black is kept so busy confronting the immediate demands of his own situation that he has little time to relate to how others are being oppressed. I know, too, that the system is hard on a lot of people, regardless of color. Or perhaps a lot of people are hard on each other, regardless of the system.

These thoughts were with me as I worked on *Day Work*. I had read Jean Genet's *The Maids* with its dramatization of the classic class struggle. I read Frantz Fanon's *Black Skins, White Masks*. I became interested in the plight of the four personalities caught in our American dilemma: the black man; the black woman; the white man; the white woman. I read Calvin C. Hernton's *Sex and Racism in America* and Eldridge Cleaver's *Soul on Ice*. Cleaver classified the players in this political psychosexual drama as the *omnipotent administrator*; the *supermasculine menial*; the *ultrafeminine*; and the *amazon*. I felt all four were victims of a system which worked with or without them. It came to me that it might not be enough for the maid to take over the house if the system itself were not changed creatively and positively.

In *Day Work*, Harold Harding resembles Cleaver's omnipotent administrator. He hires, he fires, he defines. In short, he has power. He is, however, as much at the mercy of this power as those around him. This is what characterizes his innocence. He is innocent enough to be destructive. Harold goes off to work and returns to find the woman in the wing chair changed. His attitude towards her position does not change. Whether death awaits him or not, he is programmed for dinner.

Doris is the ultrafeminine made legendary in the writings of southern authors. She has lost more and more of what should rightfully be hers. Little by little her territory has been restricted. She blames the black woman and suspects her husband. She contrives to come back to life—a negligee, a memory—but she is thwarted by history. The fear she projects onto the world outside is but a reflection of the frustration she feels inside. Harold has ceased to be of help. Darkness is closing in. Doris senses what may be the eclipse of her true self, and she fears that she may have been the architect of her own undoing.

Marie is cast as the amazon. She runs two households; commutes daily between two worlds; probably fixes breakfast for Harold *and* Jackson; and she knows where the light switch is. Marie also knows when to say "yes, ma'am" and when to assume power. As Baldwin wrote in *The Fire Next Time:* "I have great respect for that unsung army of black men and women who trudged down back lanes and entered back doors, saying 'Yes, sir' and 'No, Ma'am' in order to acquire a new roof for the schoolhouse."[2] Marie is an observer of the proceedings between Harold and Miss Doris. She knows that being black is a discipline; it requires absolute concentration if one is to survive. Marie (whose beauty is rarely appreciated) carries the weight of both worlds on her shoulders. That she has come through so well is her legacy to American life.

Jackson, the supermasculine menial, does not appear in the play, but his presence *is* felt. He is Marie's man; an idea in Doris's mind; an obstacle in Harold's path. Jackson must plot his fate in enemy territory. We can imagine his home life, his anxieties and anger. He doesn't like having Marie work for Harold, but he doesn't have the means to allow her to do otherwise. He must cope with his image of himself as a man and with the reality of the white man. A character in another play of mine puts it this way:

> "Ya never had to do nothin' you didn't wantta do. Ya never had to talk lies cause you're hungry and can't put 'hungry' on a job blank. I mean, that'd get ya nowhere. You got the system on ya side. Got the top sewed up. I chose the bottom . . . . When I was a kid, I used to dream 'bout bringin' bread to the Poor. Spreadin' it on the ground the way rich white folks do for birds. "Folks," I'd say, "Folks, I got the message cause I got the hate! I got the need cause I got the hunger! I got the answer, cause I got the bread!" You dig?

Harold and Doris and Marie are exaggerations, needless to say, in what might be termed a black comedy. Jackson's pain I have yet to resolve.

Recently I went into an ice-cream parlor. The white man behind the counter was pleasant enough. Yet I had the distinct feeling I did not like him. He had a face which (though average) was a face I had some primordial need to dislike, even fear. What that need was, I don't know. Had I dreamed him in some dream of ropes and tar? I paid the man, left the parlor, and tried to analyze where that fear came from. Once before, in a foreign country, I had had the same gut reaction to certain white faces. The irony there, however, was that the faces were on people who could in no way be associated with my American prejudice. I had to learn to approach those faces without preconceived ideas. I had to learn that because a person looked like a sheriff on a horse did not mean he was *that* sheriff on a horse.

As I walked along, I wondered how often I encountered those white masks and how often they set up a given response. How often did they engender a sense of hate (for hate is based on fear)? Were we all terrified by differences, in a world where differences are suspect? How afraid of the white man was I? I thought of the time I had picked up the phone to call a friend. I dialed the number and realized the wires were crossed, for two white voices broke through the connection. The men were talking about the "niggers" moving into their neighborhood and what they intended to do about it. We know racism exists (it is America's prime export) but each time that racism is corroborated one dies a little. And we all suffer. I feel remorse for Bull Connor with whip in hand and for the victims of his assault. Both are uniquely American and, so, uniquely a part of my experience.

The black experience is first of all a human experience. It is the quest for one's inner space, without the sacrifice of one's integrity. One is constantly being forced to confront one's humanity. Will the taxi stop for me? Will the wife of the chairman shake hands with me? Will the woman in front of me, upon turning and seeing a black man, exhibit unconscious fear? Doris expresses dismay over being "dependent on one of *them*." What she fails to see is that we are all dependent on one another.

Audiences have questioned me about the conclusion of *Day Work*. Does Marie slaughter Harold? Why doesn't he show surprise? Have Marie and Harold concocted the whole thing? Will Jackson be along shortly? Was Doris right all along? I think there are enough seeds in this orange for the reader to unravel the mystery. Mystery is what it is all about.

There is a fallacy about winter and about social movements—that everything goes silent beneath a layer of inactivity. I sense instead a flurry of life, a world in preparation.

NOTES

1. From a speech by Stokely Carmichael, quoted in Floyd Barbour, *The Black Power Revolt* (New York: Macmillan, 1968), p. 68.

2. James Baldwin, *The Fire Next Time*, paperback ed. (New York: Dell, 1963), p. 124.

QUESTIONS

1 What is racism? How does racism inform the atmosphere of *Day Work?*

2 What is it to be black? What is it to be white?

3 How are the characters in *Day Work* locked into their individual roles?

4 Discuss Marie's life up until the action of the play: what was her childhood like; what were her family and aspirations like?

5 What is the thematic significance of the eclipse? Does it provide an effective metaphor for *Day Work?*

6 Is the role reversal between Doris and Marie believable? Explain.

7 Compare this play to works by other black playwrights. Do these works share similar themes?

8 How could interracial communication have altered the events of *Day Work?*

READINGS *Background:*

Bogle, Donald. *Toms, Coons, Mulattoes, Mammies and Bucks: An Interpretive History of Blacks in American Films.* New York: Viking Press, 1973.

Cruse, Harold. *The Crisis of the Negro Intellectual.* New York: William Morrow, 1967.

Fanon, Frantz. *The Wretched of the Earth.* New York: Grove Press, 1965.

Jahn, Janheinz. *Neo-African Literature: A History of Black Writing.* New York: Grove Press, 1969.

Jordan, Winthrop D. *White over Black.* Baltimore: Penguin Paperbacks, 1969.

Kovel, J. *White Racism: A Psychohistory.* New York: Pantheon, 1970.

Mitchell, Loften. *Black Drama.* New York: Hawthorn Books, 1967.

Yette, Samuel F. *The Choice: The Issue of Black Survival in America.* New York: Berkley Medallion Books, 1972.

Plays:

Bullins, Ed. *Five Plays.* New York: Bobbs-Merrill, 1969.

Childress, Alice, ed. *Black Scenes.* New York: Doubleday, 1971.

Hatch, James V., ed. *Black Theater USA: 45 Plays by Black Americans from 1847–1974*. New York: Free Press, 1974.

Jones, LeRoi. *Dutchman and The Slave*. New York: Apollo Editions, 1964.

Genet, Jean. *The Blacks*. New York: Grove Press, 1960.

Shakespeare, William. *Othello*. New York: Signet Classic edition, 1963.

Ward, Douglas Turner. *Two Plays: Happy Ending and Day of Absence*. New York: The Third Press, 1966.

Novels:

Baldwin, James. *Another Country*. New York: Dell, 1963.

Ellison, Ralph. *Invisible Man*. New York: New American Library, 1952.

Morrison, Toni. *Sula*. New York: Bantam Books, 1973.

Wright, Richard. *Native Son*. New York: Harper & Row, 1966.

6 | "THE POOR ALWAYS YE HAVE WITH YOU"

FRED T. ARNSTEIN

"The poor always ye have with you," says Jesus in the New Testament.[1] What shall we make of that statement? Shall we always have the poor with us? How shall we understand poverty and cope with it? This essay, although it contains information about poverty and the poor, is intended first as an invitation to you to explore your own attitudes toward poverty, perhaps to confirm them or perhaps to change them. The essay is divided into four parts. The first part suggests to you some important ideas that Americans have about poverty, and indicates some of the historical sources of these ideas. The second part deals with the extent and distribution of poverty in America. The third part explores some of the ways that poorness is actually experienced. In the fourth part, I discuss a few of the remedies that have been tried or proposed to deal with poverty.

In the mid-seventies, there was a dramatic drop in the purchasing power of most Americans, caused by unemployment for many and inflation for all. A recession, the most severe since World War II, resulted in more poor people and intensified the poverty of many who were already poor. "Property Taxes Soar in Nation" was a typical headline.[2] As the cost of living rose and jobs remained scarce, many people became concerned about poverty who had not been concerned before. Some of these people were upset not because they were in danger of poverty themselves, but resented shouldering the burden of relief or because they had humanitarian concerns. Poverty became a political issue of explosive power, as it had been during the Great Depression of the thirties, when, as during all periods of economic crisis, the government feared rioting and even revolution. During the Great Depression, President Franklin D. Roosevelt took steps to blunt the harshest edges of poverty and give the poor a sense of hope. There is no doubt that more unemployment and poverty in America will create similar problems and perhaps result in similar temporary programs from the government.

Yet it is astonishing how quickly attitudes and feelings about poverty can change. For most of the middle class in the mid-fifties poverty was not a public issue of any great importance. To be sure, there were poor people, but neither the press, the government, nor the middle class gave them much thought. The emphasis was on prosperity, which was supposed to eliminate poverty. It was widely assumed that there were not many poor people, that their numbers were probably decreasing. Anybody who was willing to join the system and work hard could share in the bounty—a home in the suburbs, a late-model car (with fins!), a television, an outdoor grill.

Then, about 1960, poverty was "discovered" amid the affluence.[3] The government, the press, many intellectuals, and much of the middle class became aware that there were many more of the poor than they had thought, and that poverty was in fact not being eliminated very quickly, if at all. The early sixties was a time for the recognition of social problems and for an "environmental" approach to solving them. It was widely assumed that people could be made better if only their conditions were improved. Thus, poverty became a public issue under the Kennedy administration, and after Kennedy's assassination, Lyndon Johnson declared war on it. (The war was not very effectively fought, however.) At the same time, the poor were discovering themselves and their own power. Movements of the poor became common, and these were often attached to demands for racial equality and justice.

Soon, however, under the Nixon administration, the war on poverty was for the most part abandoned. As an alternative strategy to the "war," Daniel Moynihan, one of Nixon's advisors, suggested a policy of "benign neglect"—that the best policy was just to leave the poor alone and let them solve their own problems.

The Nixon administration came to a sudden end with the president's resignation in August of 1974. With the disappearance of the Watergate scandal from the front pages, economic issues, which had been brewing all along, again became prominent. The federal government began to give official recognition to the fact that the economy was in a severe recession and that poverty was a growing problem. But this new recognition of poverty was different from the earlier episode of the sixties, for the new concern was as much about middle-class people who were losing jobs as about those who had always been poor.

The events I have described are probably well-known to you. But these changing attitudes towards poverty did not begin just with the fifties. Americans have an ambivalence about what poverty is and what to do about it, an ambivalence which reflects conflicting ideas about the poor that emerged during several centuries in England and were more or less duplicated in the United States.

The story is simply told. During much of the Middle Ages, poverty was not considered a major social problem. Most people were poor and their condition was considered normal.[4] Those who could not care for themselves were cared for by the community. Begging, for instance, was not only allowed but was often viewed as a semisacred activity. Indeed, members of the clergy took vows of "poverty" (and some still do today).

But this medieval way of life could not withstand the forces of nature and of emerging forms of social organization. The terrible Black Death, beginning in 1348, killed more than a third of Europe's population. It left social confusion in its wake.[5]

During the 1500s in England there was still more change. Although the proportion of poor people had not increased, the structure of society had changed enough that many of the poor became a social problem. Elizabethan society was far more urbanized than English society of the Middle Ages, and in cities the poor had a harder time getting along because the city provided less effective ways of taking care of them. Just as important, in the countryside, where the majority of the poor still lived, landowners were taking land for their own purposes and leaving poor peasants without their traditional base of support—farming, pasture land, timber, and game.[6]

It was during the sixteenth century that poverty was defined as a major "social problem," and repressive legislation was passed to deal with it. Here is an example:

> Edward VI.: A statute of the first year of his reign, 1547, ordains that if anyone refuses to work, he shall be condemned as a slave to the person who has denounced him as an idler. The master shall feed his slave on bread and water, weak broth and such refuse meat as he thinks fit. He has the right to force him to do any work, no matter how disgusting, with whip and chains. If the slave is absent a fortnight, he is condemned to slavery for life and is to be branded on forehead or back with the letter S; if he runs away thrice, he is to be executed as a felon.[7]

The century ended with the enactment of two important measures in 1597 and 1601, the Elizabethan poor laws. These were hardly humanitarian in their intent; they were intended to maintain stability and order by repressing the poor.[8]

As the seizures of land (called enclosures) continued and the population lost its traditional means of support, poverty and vagrancy became ever more pressing problems. An important new attempt to deal with the poor was made in 1795. The famous Speenhamland plan (named after the district where it was adopted), provided a minimum allowance for every person in the region. This measure was well-intentioned, but it was not a viable solution at that time. Among its various problems, the plan forced the poor to remain where they were to be eligible for relief, when the economy had already changed so much that there was no way the rural districts could adequately support their poor.[9]

The Speenhamland measures actually led to greater distress among the poor. Finally, in 1832 the policy was reversed and the poor were freed from their ties to specific localities. They were expected to fend for themselves, and only in the worst of circumstances could they receive aid. This aid, in the form of the prison-like workhouse, was designed to be so unpleasant that very few people would want to use it. The reform measures of 1832 were no doubt more closely attuned to the general economic circumstances of their time than previous measures had been, but they did not solve the problem of the poor. Left without any support, hundreds of thousands of the poor actually did seek recourse in the workhouses, horrible though they were.

Since that time, a variety of relief measures have been adopted both in England and the United States. Some are supposedly based on the humanitarianism of the Speenhamland reformers; others are based on the "hard-nosed" business sense that lay behind the measures of Elizabeth and the reforms of 1832. Some of the differences associated with these points of view are listed in the two columns of table 6-1. Before you read any further, look over the table carefully and decide where you stand on each set of statements. Make a note about which of each pair is closer to your own opinions, and see where you cannot agree with either member of a pair.

No doubt you noticed that there is a logical sequence in each of the columns, and you have probably already labeled the left-hand column *conservative* and the right-hand column *liberal*. Do you consistently agree with the statements in just one of the columns? Or are you a conservative in some respects and a liberal in others? Most people do not agree entirely with either column but fall somewhere in between, or have conflicting feelings within themselves. Our historical introduction shows that both sets of opinions are characteristic of Western European and American thinking, and that neither set has yet shown itself to be very helpful in dealing with the poverty in western societies.

It appears, in fact, that we are caught in a revolving door when it comes to solutions. First a liberal approach is taken, and then when that does not seem to be working, a more conservative line is adopted, until it in turn also fails. This observation is simple to make, but not to explain. Do we really not understand enough about poverty to know how to deal with it? Do we know enough but find ourselves hampered by political constraints from carrying out effective programs? Both the conservatives and the liberals sometimes claim that their programs would really work quite well if they were only applied energetically and consistently enough. An armchair philosopher (sitting entirely outside the chart) might remark that we fail to "cure" poverty largely because we do not know how to define it. Meanwhile the radical (4b in the table) also believes that poverty is not really the problem. Feeling he has a better conception of what the problem really is, he seeks the opportunity to implement his solution.

We shall return to these issues in the sections that follow, trying to understand better what the facts of poverty are, how we may best conceive of it, and what position we may take in trying to solve the problems of poverty.

Before we proceed, though, let us return to the table and make a few comments about it. The conservative and liberal positions presented there do not include all elements of conservatism and liberalism. (There is no attempt to do so, since liberals disagree among themselves, as do conservatives.) It is clear, however, that the conservative column shows an underlying belief that government intervention in social affairs should be limited, and based only on a promise of clear-cut returns. It is somewhat the businessman's mentality. The liberal column, on the other hand, puts more emphasis on aid for its own sake. It views the poor essentially as victims, who therefore deserve our humanitarian aid even if such aid does not change the system.

From this disagreement spring debates about which of the poor are "deserving" (of aid) and which are "undeserving." The conservative element in our thinking tells us that at least some of the poor are just lazy scoundrels, undeserving of help. The liberal element tells us that at least some of the poor are victims. The history of welfare is filled with

Table 6-1.	1a. Our society provides economic rewards for all those who are willing to work hard.	1b. Our society does not provide the opportunity for everybody to escape from poverty, even if everybody works hard.
	2a. Except for people who are physically handicapped, all the members of our society are rich or poor by their own choice.	2b. Most poor people are forced to be poor, even though they try to escape from poverty.
	3a. Poverty is basically caused by the immorality and laziness of the poor. Therefore, the poor should be punished or rehabilitated so that they will work harder. They should not be given aid.	3b. The poor are basically victims of their condition. Therefore, they should be helped to find a better condition, or to change their condition (in a peaceful way). Meanwhile it is our obligation to give them aid.
	4a. If rehabilitation or punishment doesn't help, we should just leave the poor alone, because there is nothing we can do for them.	4b. If attempts at peaceful solutions don't work, then we must change the whole system (by force if necessary).

examples of attempts to distinguish the deserving from the undeserving. Yet this is a very difficult thing to do. For example, should a mother on aid be considered undeserving of extra aid if she has another child? The conservative is likely to say "yes." He argues that the woman on aid is only being rewarded for increasing the tax burden if we give her more aid. The liberal will tend to say "no." First, he argues, the woman should have the right to bear children just as any middle-class woman does. If we assume that her poverty is not of her own making, then why should we deny her the equal opportunity to do what she probably considers her most essential job as a woman: having and raising children. Furthermore, if we deny her more aid, we are not only making her suffer, but we are taking away support from the new child (and her other children as well). Surely it is not a child's fault that its mother lives in poverty.

Which position do you hold in that example? Your humanitarianism is pitted against your self-interest as a taxpayer. But let us return again to the table and notice something else. The last statement (number 4) in each column is the most radical extension of each position. Forced to the limit, the conservative will suggest withdrawing all aid and letting the "unseen hand" of the market determine what happens to the poor. At its extreme (4a) this position takes us into a kind of Social Darwinism that says the health of society depends on allowing the "fittest" to survive and prosper and the "unfit" to perish. If the poor perish it is only proof that they were unfit to begin with.

The liberal, on the other hand, believes that the "unseen hand" of the market does not work as smoothly as it is supposed to. That is why he believes government intervention is necessary and that the poor are victims of the system. At the extreme position (3b), the liberal will suggest drastic changes in the system which result in large-scale government intervention to redistribute wealth.

But this liberal should not be confused with a true radical (4b), who feels that attempts to redistribute wealth do not change very much unless the whole organization of society is changed—in the work place, the political system, education, the family, and in people's ideas. The radical might look at table 1 and say: "The conservatives are wrong in their statement of facts. People are not rich or poor by their own choice. But the liberals are not helpful because, while they are correct in believing that the poor are victims, they do not propose solutions that will significantly alter the situation. For example, the War of Poverty, which was considered a liberal program, put a great deal of faith in educating poor children (through programs like Operation Headstart). Yet such an educational program amounts to a rehabilitation which the conservatives might advocate. How will education help people if there are not enough well-paying jobs for them? A truly vigorous liberalism should advocate large-scale redistribution of wealth at the very least; yet liberals tend to back away from this kind of intervention."

And this critique can be taken a step further. Even intervention, says the radical, implicitly accepts the notion (shared by liberals and conservatives alike) that the more you have, the better off you are. In fact, there is much more to life than how much you have. A society of rich people could be an unhappy or unjust society if those people were deprived of the things they value most, such as freedom of choice in their personal lives, the opportunity for participation in society, and the feeling of comradeship.

This critique takes us back to a fundamental question: what is poverty, and why should we worry about it?

II

You can get a sense of the importance and the difficulty of defining poverty if you try to answer this question: How would you count the poor? The question really cannot be answered until we have decided how we would know who is a poor person. Let us therefore make a temporary distinction to help our thinking. We will say that *the poor* are those with little money, those who do not have enough money to buy the amenities (housing, food, medical care, and transportation) that a middle-class American would consider minimally adequate. If this is our concept of the poor, then counting the poor becomes relatively simple. We just set some income as the dividing line between poor and the nonpoor, and then count everybody who falls below the line. To be sure, there will be disagreements about just where to draw the line, but at least in counting the poor, we have only the single measure of money to worry about.

On the other hand, we will say that *poverty* is a condition which may involve all sorts of barriers to participation in the benefits of society and in decision-making processes. Poverty, for example, often includes low education, jobs which pay little and offer no chance for advancement, political apathy or distrust, and discrimination based on race or sex. Poverty also involves not having the friendships and other social connections which help many people get ahead. It means being involved in a series of circumstances which makes advancement difficult and unlikely.

Poverty therefore is a way of life which is characterized by deprivation relative to the wealthier parts of society, and from which there is not much hope of escape. There are some poor people in every society, but poorness is a source of poverty only when a society seems able to do better for its members, yet fails. *Poverty is more than poorness.* It involves the sense that one is at the bottom, that one's poorness is degrading.

Imagine, for example, that we have drawn our income line to distinguish the poor from the nonpoor and have found a man who earns an amount slightly above that line. This man is far from wealthy, but if his friends and relatives are middle-class, he has a good chance of staying above the line. The same man, however, will be under extra handicaps if he lives in a rural area which has few medical, educational, or other facilities. He will also have extra problems if he is black in an area where blacks find it hard to find work or to live in the neighborhood they want, or if he is a member of any other group which finds itself the special target of discriminatory practices. Any of these circumstances will affect his chances of enjoying a minimal kind of middle-class existence. Perhaps most important of all, our man may have no family or friends who are any better off than he is. If that is true, then he does not have the easy access to help and credit which so often enable one to make down payments on cars or houses, to find out about better jobs when they open up, or to get advice about the best way to finance an education or open up a business. In all those unofficial ways, family and friends can be an informal source of credit and advice that help an individual make the most of his own possessions and skills. To emerge from a neighborhood or subculture where family and friends do not have these resources to offer makes "getting ahead" much more difficult.

It is entirely possible, therefore, to be in constant danger of poverty even though one is not "poor" (below the "poverty line") in terms of money. It is also quite possible to be poor without living in poverty. Students are an example of this situation. Many students are temporarily poor: they have little money. They may even be so poor that they have to go without meals and live in wretched conditions to finance their educations. Yet most of these students are not in poverty. They are fairly assured that because of their education and family background they will be able to take up respectable middle-class positions after graduation. Of course, this is not a certainty, and many a student frets with anxiety as graduation draws near, wondering whether all those years in school will "pay off." Nevertheless, a college education usually seems worth the expense and trouble, because it can lead to enlarged opportunities.

Since poverty is a complicated thing, there is no easy way to measure it. This is why the Bureau of the Census and others who give us data about these issues are content with various measures of poorness as the best and most consistent measure of poverty. Such simple measures of income can be misleading when we assume that they give us precise information about lifestyle or life chances. Census "poverty" data are only an approximate indicator, and must be interpreted with caution. Yet in our society and in the other industrialized societies poverty undoubtedly has more to do with money than with any other factor.

Poverty isn't *only* the lack of money, but is *first and foremost* a lack of money. Too many programs are based on the idea that we will cure "poverty" if we provide education, medical facilities, housing, or a hundred other amenities. If the poor received large amounts of money, poverty as we know it would be instantly eliminated. You might try to imagine such a situation, and see what the effects would be.

Now we shall look at a few facts and figures about the poor, so we can say something about the meaning and extent of poverty.

The most commonly used "poverty line," created by Mollie Orshansky for the Social Security Administration, is based on an "economy" food plan used by the Department of Agriculture.[10] This food plan was not meant to be adequate for any prolonged period of time, but was for "temporary or emergency use when funds are low." In order to develop the poverty index, the cost of the emergency food ration was multiplied by a factor of approximately three, taking some other factors into account as well. Thus in table 6-2, poverty levels (for 1973) for selected family sizes are shown. You might want to compare these levels with your own family's income. For example, if you come from a family with a father, mother, and two children under eighteen, your family was only considered in poverty if the family income was less than $4,505 per year. (If the same family lives on a farm, the poverty line is even lower.) It is clearly a very low threshold, so low that it greatly minimizes the extent of poverty in the United States. Nevertheless, it is still used by the census.

Recently, the census has produced a rather detailed analysis of the social characteristics of poor Americans from a 1973 study.[11] Assuming (as we must) that the census figures, with their low cutoff point, do give us some idea of the nature of poverty, we can draw some conclusions. The study tells us that there were about 23 million people below the poverty line. This was about 11 percent of the population. Table 6-3 summarizes some of the characteristics of this poorest part of our population. The first striking fact is that, while the majority of the very poor are white, two-fifths (42 percent) are either black or of Spanish origin. Thus,

Table 6-2 Income Thresholds at the Low-Income Level in 1973 by Sex of Head of Family, Size of Family, and Number of Related Children Under 18 Years Old, by Nonfarm Residence

SIZE OF FAMILY UNIT	NUMBER OF RELATED CHILDREN UNDER 18 YEARS OLD						
	NONE	1	2	3	4	5	6 OR MORE
NONFARM							
MALE HEAD							
1 person (unrelated indiv.):							
Under 65 years	$2,396						
65 years and over	2,153						
2 persons:							
Head under 65 years	2,996	$3,356					
Head 65 years and over	2,690	3,356					
3 persons	3,488	3,601	$3,806				
4 persons	4,598	4,666	4,505	$4,733			
5 persons	5,549	5,616	5,436	5,299	$5,413		
6 persons	6,365	6,386	6,251	6,115	5,934	$6,025	
7 or more persons	8,016	8,085	7,926	7,790	7,610	7,337	$7,270
FEMALE HEAD							
1 person (unrelated indiv.):							
Under 65 years	$2,217						
65 years and over	2,125						
2 persons:							
Head under 65 years	2,768	$3,022					
Head 65 years and over	2,656	3,022					
3 persons	3,375	3,215	$3,556				
4 persons	4,415	4,574	4,553	$4,505			
5 persons	5,299	5,459	5,436	5,391	$5,209		
6 persons	6,183	6,296	6,251	6,205	6,002	$5,819	
7 or more persons	7,767	7,881	7,858	7,790	7,587	7,429	$7,066

SOURCE: U.S. Bureau of the Census, *Characteristics of the Low-Income Population: 1973*, Current Population Reports, Series P-60, #98 (Washington, D.C.: U.S. Government Printing Office, January 1975), p. 161.

the statistics bear out what everyday observation tells us, that a dispro-portionate number of the poor belong to the darker-skinned minorities.

This fact can be interpreted in many different ways. Here is just one of them: since it is also a well-documented fact that members of these minority groups usually live in neighborhoods which are segregated from the white community, it seems likely that a member of a minority group tends to be at an extra disadvantage in escaping from poverty because the resources in his community are quite limited.[12] Many of his neighbors, family, and friends are doing no better than he is and cannot be of much help to him in finding a high-paying job, opening a restaurant, and so forth.

Table 6-3 also shows that only a small proportion (6 percent) of the poor live on farms. Most live in cities or towns. However, the popular image of decaying central cities and affluent suburbs is certainly overdrawn. Only 37 percent of the poor live in central cities. The rest are distributed in suburbs and smaller cities and towns. It is unfortunately true that people often try to ignore the problems nearest them and keep their fingers pointed at somebody else. Suburbanites tend to ignore the poverty around them and look at the central city as if it were a battle zone. This kind of attitude leads to the feeling "let the city rot, it's not our problem." You might want to look at the census figures for cities and towns you are familiar with to see how many poor people live there.

Table 6-3 also reveals a remarkable disparity in poverty among the regions of the United States. There is a common notion, based partly on

Summary of Characteristics of the Poorest U.S. Citizens, 1973			Table 6-3
	Total Number of "Low-Income" Persons	22,973,000	100%
RACE	White and Other	15,142,000	58%
	Black	7,388,000	32%
	Spanish	2,366,000	10%
LOCATION	Farm	1,283,000	6%
	Nonfarm	21,689,000	94%
	Nonmetropolitan Areas	9,214,000	40%
	Metropolitan Areas	13,759,000	60%
	Inside Central Cities	8,594,000	37%
	Outside Central Cities	5,165,000	22%
REGION	Northeast	4,207,000	18%
	North Central	4,864,000	21%
	West	3,841,000	16%
	South	10,061,000	44%
AGE	Under 14 years	7,545,000	33%
	14 to 64 years	12,074,000	53%
	65 years and over	3,354,000	15%
EDUCATION	Total	11,528,000	
(for persons	No years of school completed	397,000	3%
22 years	Elementary, total	4,849,000	42%
and over)	1 to 5 years	1,725,000	15%
	6 to 8 years	3,124,000	27%
	High School, total	4,824,000	42%
	1 to 3 years	2,283,000	20%
	4 years	2,541,000	22%
	College (1 year or more)	1,548,000	13%

Note: Table compiled from data in U.S. Bureau of the Census, *Characteristics of the Low-Income Population: 1973.* Percents are based on total of 22,973,000 poor, except for education. Percents sometimes do not total 100, due to rounding.

fact, that poor people of both races have been moving from the southern states to the North, and that the northern cities have become the main centers of poverty. In fact, while this movement has occurred and northern cities do have many poor, the South remains the poorest area of all. It contains more poor than the Northeast and North Central regions put together, even though the population of the South is much smaller than that of these two areas.

It may be true that some of the southern poor are not in the same kind of poverty as their northern counterparts. These are the poor rural people, who can supply many of their needs from their land. They have little money, but a fairly strong and and viable culture. Remember, however, that even in the South most of the poor don't live on farms. They live in the towns and cities. For most of these southern poor poorness *does* mean poverty, and this suggests several questions. Why does the South have so many poor? And how does "the southern way of life" deal with this fact? We would expect any culture with so many poor people to be organized so as to be able to control them and not feel too guilty about or ashamed of them.

When we turn to education, our common-sense notions are confirmed: poor people have relatively limited educations. As with the other facts which table 6-3 reveals, this one can be fruitfully discussed. It has been the subject of intense debate among social scientists. Does education, in itself, help people to get ahead?[13] The answer seems to be yes, but only to a limited degree. Some authors claim to have shown that it does not help at all. But if education is of limited help in economic advancement, then why are wealthier people better educated? Perhaps money allows one to get a better education. Or perhaps the same personal qualities and social circumstances that help one be affluent also help one get a better education. This is an important question because it strikes at one of the fundamental beliefs of Americans—that education is a key to financial success.

Finally, we notice that 3.4 million of the poor were elderly (over the age of 65), while another 7.5 million were children, and 3.4 million[14] were mothers of children. There is an important point to be made here. Critics of welfare programs, who claim that many of the poor are "undeserving" and should be put to work, are clearly wrong by ordinary (middle-class) American standards. It turns out—using the figures above—that roughly 62 percent are not able-bodied men, but are elderly people past the age of retirement, children whom we expect to be pursuing educations, or mothers who must often spend a good deal of their time taking care of children. It is difficult to estimate the exact percentage of the poor who are eligible to work, since some mothers can work, but we do know that working mothers are partially offset by men who are of working age but cannot work due to physical handicaps.

Anthony Downs dealt with the same issue but was able to make a more careful analysis.[15] Although he deals with an earlier year (1968) and only with the poor in metropolitan areas, his conclusions are in line with the 1973 data and they are very striking. Table 6-4 shows Downs's analysis of the urban poor. The table shows that most of the urban poor were either deliberately excluded from the work force because of age or maternal duties, were disabled, *or were employed but worked at jobs which paid so little that they remained poor.* Only 17 percent of the poor were males of working age who did not have jobs. These figures should be pondered, because they fly in the face of common American conceptions. The figures certainly do not prove that there is no welfare cheating, or "laziness," among the poor, but they do show that most of the poor in America are not expected or allowed to work at jobs which pay enough to lift them out of poverty. In other words, the large bulk of the American poor are not in a position to change their situations by themselves.

The curious reader will find the census figures an extensive source of interesting facts about the poor. All these figures make it clear that poverty is related to other "social problems."[16] Poverty is particularly pronounced among racial minorities, the aged, in the South, and in families where the father is absent. Although the significance of many of these circumstances is subject to debate, one fact is clear: most poorness cannot be alleviated by the poor themselves.

Breakdown of Poor People in Metropolitan Areas: 1968   Table 6-4

POPULATION GROUP	(THOUSANDS)	(PERCENT OF TOTAL)
Elderly (sixty-five and over)	2,353	18.3%
Children (under eighteen)	5,433	42.2
Adults in female-headed households (eighteen to sixty-four)	2,262	17.6
Adults in households headed by disabled males (eighteen to sixty-four)	392	3.0
Adults in households headed by unemployed males (eighteen to sixty-four)	903	7.0
Adults in households headed by employed males (eighteen to sixty-four)	1,528	11.9
All persons in poverty	12,871	100.0

*This group represents the households headed by males who were either unemployed or worked fewer than 40 weeks a year.

Source: Anthony Downs, *Who Are the Urban Poor?* (New York: Committee for Economic Development, 1970), p. 20.

III

This section is devoted to a discussion of the experience of poverty. Maybe you thought that I would try to describe here in vivid prose what life is like for the poor. But I will not do that. There are already many well-written accounts of the lives of the poor.[17] However, if you are willing, you can get close to the actual experience of poverty. You can start at the movies, you can go on to do volunteer work with the poor, you can even move into a poor neighborhood and get to know some of the residents. If you have never been poor, you can't expect to have the direct experience of poverty just by being near it. You will always be an outsider, and you must accept yourself as such. But you can be an informed outsider.

What I want to talk about in this section are some aspects of the experience of poverty that are not often discussed. I want to try to get at the meaning of poverty for our society as a whole. To begin, let me return to the matter we were speaking of: how close are you willing to get to poverty? Most students would very much prefer to stay away from it and "stick with their own kind." My university is located in Boston, a city of mostly poor and working-class people, with many university students. Very few of the students at Boston University come from poor backgrounds. When I suggest to my students that they do field projects in poor neighborhoods, the usual response is silence. And when I become insistent I often get comments about its being "too dangerous."

Now I do not mean to minimize the danger. It was brought home to me not long ago in a personal way. A friend of mine lives in the South End, a district of beautiful old buildings inhabited largely by the poor, but increasingly also by middle-class people who are looking for dwellings near the center of town. My friend was robbed of two dollars, then stabbed in the back. Fortunately, he is recovering now. But he will move to a safer place as soon as he can. He has had enough of the South End.

Nobody can blame my friend for wanting to move. In fact, we always thought he was tempting fate by living where he did. But what is even more depressing for me is to think about the people who live in the South End, fearing the same crime as my friend, who cannot move to a better neighborhood. Some can't move because they are black, but most can't move because they don't have the money: they are poor.

Most crimes of violence are committed by the poor against the poor. The poor commit crimes mostly in their own neighborhoods. Since most of the poor are no more criminals than you or I, they are faced with the same fears that we would have in such neighborhoods, except that they cannot escape.

It's not just crime that the poor would like to escape. Conditions in poor neighborhoods are usually not very pleasant. The housing tends to be dilapidated, since local homeowners don't have the money for expensive maintenance and absentee landlords want to make the maximum profit. City utilities aren't as efficient in poor neighborhoods because the city spends more effort for middle-class residents, who have more "clout." So the streets are dirty, the lights may not work properly, and the whole atmosphere can become chaotic. Many central-city neighborhoods look something like bombed-out areas in a war zone.

But something very interesting happens to people in this situation. They begin, first, to accept the dangerous and dilapidated conditions they live in and not to worry as much about them. And they also see that there are good things about their neighborhood. People live there, very human people, and social life goes on with tears, laughter, children, work, and all the rest. Given the not-so-nice conditions they live in, these people carve out a human existence for themselves. By necessity, it must differ from the more affluent life, but in some ways it is not less rewarding. There is a sense of genuine closeness that develops among those who share an oppressive situation, a closeness sometimes missing in the middle class.

Those who can leave, or who have never lived in such a neighborhood, tend to develop just the opposite image. They are seldom confronted with poverty close up, and when they are it is often in a particularly unpleasant setting. I always become edgy, for example, when I have to change subway trains at a station which is located in a "bad" neighborhood. The image which the nonpoor develop accentuates all those negative qualities which do exist among the poor. Dirt, garbage, and dilapidation are the superficial physical setting. Crime and violence seem to be the way of life. The poor neighborhood turns into a jungle in the mind of the outsider. Surely nobody with human sensibilities would live there. This jungle is populated by a species which looks vaguely human but actually is not human. It is a species of dangerous "animal." If you see one of these animals you try to avoid it, and if you do meet it you pretend it is human so as not to offend it.

The farther away one group of people is from another, the more easily they are able to form these stereotypes. Our images of the poor are usually tempered somewhat by the fact that we *do* interact with them, and the poor, up close, are not so different from other people. But in the absence of constant contact, it is easy—almost natural—for some stereotypes to emerge. Of course, stereotypes can be positive as well as negative. There are special reasons why the stereotype of the poor is so negative among us. You will be able to think of some of these reasons yourself, and you will have to come to your own conclusions about the truth of what I have already said.

My view is that our (I am assuming that you are not poor) opinion of the poor is based essentially upon the fear of being poor ourselves, and upon the fear that the poor understand that we are (to some extent) living as well as we do because they are poor. This may strike you as an overstatement, but to elaborate on the point I want to enlist the aid of the late-nineteenth-century American novelist, Edward Bellamy. Here is a famous passage from Bellamy's utopian novel *Looking Backward*, in which the author depicts himself as a young man of thirty who in the year 1887 is put to sleep by a mesmerist, only to awake in the year 2000 and find himself in a totally refashioned world where poverty has ceased to exist. In this passage, therefore, Bellamy is addressing the readers of the mythical year 2000:

By way of attempting to give the reader some general impression of the way people lived together in those days, and especially of the relations of the rich and poor to one another, perhaps I cannot do better than to compare society as it then was to a prodigious coach which the masses of humanity were harnessed to and dragged toilsomely along a very hilly and sandy road. The driver was hunger, and permitted no lagging, though the pace was necessarily very slow. Despite the difficulty of drawing the coach at all along so hard a road, the top was covered with passengers who never got down, even at the steepest ascents. These seats on top were very breezy and comfortable. Well up out of the dust, their occupants could enjoy the scenery at their leisure, or critically discuss the merits of the straining team. Naturally such places were in great demand and the competition for them was keen, every one seeking as the first end in life to secure a seat on the coach for himself and to leave it to his child after him. By the rule of the coach a man could leave his seat to whom he wished, but on the other hand there were many accidents by which it might at any time be wholly lost. For all that they were so easy, the seats were very insecure, and at every sudden jolt of the coach persons were slipping out of them and falling to the ground, where they were instantly compelled to take hold of the rope and help to drag the coach on which they had before ridden so pleasantly. It was naturally regarded as a terrible misfortune to lose one's seat, and the apprehension that this might happen to them or their friends was a constant cloud upon the happiness of those who rode.

But did they think only of themselves? you ask. Was not their very luxury rendered intolerable to them by comparison with the lot of their brothers and sisters in the harness, and the knowledge that their own weight added to their toil? Had they no compassion for fellow beings from whom fortune only distinguished them? Oh, yes; commiseration was frequently expressed by those who rode for those who had to pull the coach, especially when the vehicle came to a bad place in the road, as it was constantly doing, or to a particularly steep hill. At such times, the desperate straining of the team, their agonized leaping and plunging under the pitiless lashing of hunger, the many who fainted at the rope and were trampled in the mire, made a very distressing spectacle, which often called forth highly creditable displays of feeling on the top of the coach. At such times the passengers would call down encouragingly to the toilers of the rope, exhorting them to patience, and holding out hopes of possible compensation in another world for the hardness of their lot, while others contributed to buy salves and liniments for the crippled and injured. It was agreed that it was a great pity that the coach should be so hard to pull, and there was a sense of general relief when the specially bad piece of road was gotten over. This relief was not, indeed, wholly on account of the team, for there was always some danger at these bad places of a general overturn in which all would lose their seats.

It must in truth be admitted that the main effect of the spectacle of the misery of the toilers at the rope was to enhance the passengers' sense of the value of their seats upon the coach, and to cause them to hold on to them more desperately than before. If the passengers could only have felt assured that neither they nor their friends would ever fall from the top, it is probable that, beyond contributing to the funds for liniments and bandages, they would have troubled themselves extremely little about those who dragged the coach.

I am well aware that this will appear to the men and women of the twentieth century as incredible inhumanity, but there are two facts, both very curious, which partly explain it. In the first place, it was firmly and sincerely believed that there was no other way in which Society could get along, except the many pulled at the rope and the few rode, and not only this, but that no very radical improvement even was possible, either in the harness, the coach, the roadway, or the distribution of the toil. It had always been as it was, and it would always be so. It was a pity, but it could not be helped, and philosophy forbade wasting compassion on what was beyond remedy.

The other fact is yet more curious, consisting in a singular hallucination which those on the top of the coach generally shared, that they were not exactly like their brothers and sisters who pulled at the rope, but of fine clay, in some way belonging to a higher order of beings who might justly expect to be drawn. This seems unaccountable, but, as I once rode on this very coach and shared that very hallucination, I ought to be believed. The strangest thing about the hallucination was that those who had but just climbed up from the ground, before they had outgrown the marks of the rope upon their hands, began to fall under its influence. As for those whose parents and grandparents before them had been so fortunate as to keep their seats on the top, the conviction they cherished of the essential difference between their sort of humanity and the common article was absolute. The effect of such a delusion in moderating fellow feeling for the sufferings of the mass of men into a distant and philosophical compassion is obvious. To it I refer as the only extenuation I can offer for the indifference which, at the period I write of, marked my own attitude toward the misery of my brothers.[18]

Bellamy was writing during the age of the "robber barons"[19] of industry, the time of the rise of the giant corporations of today. The conditions he describes more accurately reflect his time than ours largely because society was more clearly divided then between the rich (who rode the coach) and the poor (who drew it), without the large "middle class" which we know as being neither very rich nor very poor. At that time it appeared that the average workingman might find his standard of living declining in the long run. Since then, however, living conditions for most groups in our society have seemed to improve.

Yet even if we allow for an average rise in living standards through the growth of a middle-income sector in the population, the fact remains that an extremely small proportion of the population is very rich and a quite large proportion is still poor—a fact which is particularly striking given the potential of our advanced technology. The great question today is not the opinion of the rich about the poor, but the opinion of the middle class. My own suspicion is that the middle class may be even more harsh in their opinion than the rich, because the middle class is much too close to poverty for its own comfort. There are other reasons as well. It is easier to identify with those who have a great deal of wealth and power than with those who have no wealth and very little power. And we are encouraged constantly by the advertising industry to identify ourselves with the rich.[20]

I am suggesting that poverty is one of the secret terrors which is held before us if we do not work hard and accept social rules. Nobody had to invent poverty for this purpose. Most of us are not the (nearly) carefree riders on Bellamy's coach. We ride, rather, part-way up, far enough to be out of the mud but not in a position to relax and enjoy the ride. This is particularly true for the "average worker," who resents watching his income, which is already small enough, being taxed away and given to others who are on welfare.

Poverty is the stick which, at its worst, pushes individuals into sacrificing their friends, their families, and their values to the single goal of *getting ahead.*[21] The sad, though fascinating, spectacle of the compulsive go-getter is familiar to all of us, and we probably all share his motivation to some degree. Yet we cannot despise what we are striving for. For those who are filled with anger at the way they are forced to live, the poor make a convenient target.

If Bellamy's analogy of the coach has value, it suggests that in fact the rich are the "social problem," not the poor. For the rich are the only group who seem to have the power to change the situation, and they are content to let it stay as is, with the contribution of "salves and liniments" to ease the pain. But Bellamy's vision is more profound than this, for he does not blame the rich any more than he blames the poor. He sees both as products of the same social system.

How then is the system to be changed? We shall consider some possibilities in a moment, but one of them belongs in this section. Sometimes the poor themselves try to change the system. They become angry about their condition and strike out in the belief that things really can be different. We have often seen the poor struggling in labor disputes. While labor unions today tend to look pretty much like the other large institutions of our society, they were formed in the heat of battle and with the highest hopes on the part of the workers.[22] We have also seen the poor take to the streets in organized militant protest[23] and in spontaneous riots. On the whole, these efforts by the poor to help themselves look sporadic and not very successful to the average American. I do not want to try to evaluate their actual importance, but I do want to end this section with the observation that the entire history of the modern world has been fueled by the revolts and revolutions of the poor and powerless against the rich and powerful. Even though the poor often do not benefit to the extent they should through the revolutions they fight, their desire for improvement is a constant source of hope for them and of fear for those who stand above.

Michael Sullivan

IV

"O.K., author, I agree that poverty is a problem. Now tell me what to do about it."

Do I have any answers? Actually I do have some answers, though they do not entirely satisfy me. The trouble is that even if you think my answers are logical, you might not like them. I hope to show that, no matter what answer we may choose, it will not simply "work," but will fit in with some values and work against others. No answer to poverty is merely technical. It is bound to involve ideas of what is best and most important in a society.

Before we decide on the answers we had better know what the options are. We can try, at one extreme, to change only the part of the social system we are concerned about, without changing the rest. Or, at the other extreme, we can try to change the entire system, thinking that in the process the troublesome part will also change. This is something like the different methods of treatment for a diseased organ of the body. We can send in a surgeon to operate on the malfunctioning organ. He might sew it, excise part of it, put in a mechanical device to help it along, or simply remove it from the body. On the other hand, we can treat the whole person through some combination of diet, exercise, mental therapy, and change of situation. It is easy to see that in the medical field neither answer is "correct" in every case. Some conditions are so acute that they must be treated surgically if the patient is to survive. Yet most conditions are caused by living itself. To become healthy and stay that way, you need to live right. Nobody but a surgeon will cure you of lung cancer once you have it, but the best way to avoid lung cancer and the surgeon is to stop smoking and live in the country.

So it is with poverty. The social surgeon might like a neat solution— like just getting rid of the poor. While it is true, so far as I know, that no society has ever tried systematically to kill off its poor population, that would be a solution. And you might well ask yourself why that disgusting solution has never been tried. Mankind has been capable of other acts equally horrible.

Sometimes social surgery is possible on a more limited scale. Much of the immigration to our country from Europe was by the poor, and it was often encouraged by the foreign authorities, who wanted nothing more than to be rid of these people so that their land could be taken over and used for the new owners' profits.[24] More recently in the United States a similar motivation lay behind the willingness of some Southerners to see poor rural blacks leave the land for southern cities or the North.

The same principle operates in northern cities which are willing to raze or convert vast areas of low-income housing so that middle-income people can live there, or so highways for them can be built. Relocation of the poor is attempted, but only half-heartedly, since the purpose of these maneuvers is not really to make conditions better for the poor, but to substitute more affluent citizens in their place.

Specific treatment of the problem can, of course, take many other forms, but let us briefly consider the alternative: treatment of the whole system. This solution, though it needn't in principle be violent, does amount to a revolution. Since I am of the opinion that poverty is not just a chance byproduct of history but is built into our system, I think that poverty can only be eliminated by revolutionary change. Small-scale tinkering does seem to help some people—for a time, at least—but apparently it does nothing to alter the general situation. One evidence of this is the fact which Miller and Rein have very recently pointed out (as have others before them), that the unequal distribution of income in our country has followed almost exactly the same pattern for the past thirty years.[25]

There has never been a revolution that didn't involve lots of unhappiness and at least some violence. It would be foolish to think that revolution is a pleasant or an easy affair. But it would be equally foolish to think that all revolutions are steeped in violence, or that they result in new regimes that are just as oppressive as the old. In the Cuban revolution most of the violence was used by the old Batista regime against the revolutionaries, who in turn were relatively mild once they came to power. It is true, however, that after the Cuban revolution the Cuban middle class had to reorient itself to a new lifestyle or leave the country. The American Revolution was not particularly violent in comparison with other wars, and it did not result in a more oppressive regime.

Successful revolutions occur only under conditions of extraordinary disruption and tension in a society. Therefore, we cannot expect revolution at this juncture in the United States, even if we want it. The exact form a revolution takes and its outcome both depend on factors which are largely out of the control of the revolutionaries themselves. Still, it is of the utmost importance that anyone who favors revolution have in mind some general goals to guide his actions. My own goal is a system where important decisions are made in the interest of those most severely affected by them. That boils down to a system where profit is not the first order of business, but rather production of useful things, on the one hand, and good working and living conditions for the workers, on the other. It also means having a system where there is honorable work available for any who can do it, and adequate support for any who cannot work. This system would eliminate poverty and many other problems, although of course there would remain other difficulties. Revolutions do not produce perfect systems, but they can produce better ones.

Since I do not expect imminent revolution in the United States, I think the best we can do for now is to keep that goal in the back of our minds and try to create the conditions that will best lead to the change we want. This means fighting governmental attempts to become more secretive, less respectful of our civil rights, and more removed from public scrutiny and control. It also means keeping the government and the corporations from destroying society altogether through nuclear war or environmental catastrophe. These are goals on which I think most of us can agree, whether or not we consider ourselves revolutionary.

Now let's return to a consideration of what I've called "tinkering," that is, less-than-revolutionary change. Tinkering is usually called social policy by those who do it, or else it is called social planning. We might begin with the fact that a considerable portion of government spending goes for domestic programs that are normally considered social policy. So we do not start from scratch. Even the conservatives have to be concerned about social policy, because it already exists (although they would like to eliminate most of it).

Liberals, on the other hand, generally favor the expansion of government services. Their policy of "more is better" does not always work out, but at least it has the virtue of recognizing that the problems will not go away by themselves and that some help is required. A glance at a typical United States budget since World War II might make you think that the liberals could get a lot more money into domestic programs by whittling down the defense budget.[26] In fact, most liberals do not favor drastic cuts in arms spending. Before World War II, liberals were fond of the idea that "guns" could for the most part be eliminated in favor of "butter." But history seemed to demonstrate that the Great Depression, when poverty reached its most dramatic peak in this century, was not solved with the "butter" of domestic programs, but with the "guns" of World War II. Ever since, although they try to moderate war spending, liberals have favored a good-sized arms budget as an important prop for the economy.

Given our social and economic system, in which large corporations make the important economic decisions that affect us (basing their decisions not on what is useful but what is profitable), the liberals are probably correct about the need for arms spending. The system breeds many such absurdities, and this is why I believe that without full-scale change we are severely limited in solving our social problems.

However, it would be a terrible error to think that small changes are not worthwhile. It may well be, as Miller and Rein point out, that although the distribution of income has remained highly unequal in the United States, it would have probably been even more unequal if not for those social policies which give minimal benefits to the poor.[27] Our systems of social security and medical aid for older citizens are basically steps in the right direction. Our welfare system, although assuredly a "mess" that needs drastic alteration, is better than no welfare system.

But the most important steps in alleviating poverty would be a guarantee of full employment combined with a living wage for every job. These steps would require both increased labor-union activity and more large-scale government programs.

When it comes to the details of reform, you must go to other sources. The intricacies of social policy cannot be unravelled in this article.[28] Let me leave you with this thought. We drew a distinction earlier between poorness and poverty. Now suppose that you could eliminate poorness; that would be a profound accomplishment. Yet in doing so, you might not have eliminated some of the most fundamental aspects of poverty. People can be supported so that they are not destitute, yet remain without any real control over their lives or their communities. If we want to create a society which offers not only the basic material needs to its members but dignity and the opportunity for meaningful participation as well, then it is not the benevolent dictatorship we seek, but the participatory democracy.

SOLUTIONS

The most important fact to bear in mind when dealing with "solutions" to poverty is that its dimensions and its very nature are defined by the society in which it occurs. American poverty is in some ways peculiar to America because America is somewhat different from every other place. The very existence of poverty is part of the American social order: poverty will no sooner disappear than will the House of Representatives, the automobile industry, or any other of the major institutions which make it possible for some people to gain a great deal of wealth while others acquire very little.

Therefore, short of a change in the entire system—in our unrealistic belief in economic self-reliance for all, in our political system, and in our ideas about what constitutes a good life—poverty will stay with us. Yet this drastic change, desirable though it is, is unlikely in the near future.

Meanwhile, it is wrong to think that in the absence of a complete solution it is pointless to try to alleviate what poverty we can. Several possibilities are mentioned: labor organizing, government job programs, changes in the welfare system. But it is left to the reader to explore these possibilities independently.

SUMMARY

This chapter first describes three ways of looking at poverty: conservative, liberal, and radical. Each of these views has roots in the history of social policy. Both England and the United States, since the end of the Middle Ages, have seen a variety of social policies adopted to deal with poverty, none with great success. Poverty has continued to be the condition of large portions of the population, although it is periodically forgotten by the more affluent, and then rediscovered. Some solutions take as their basic premise that society provides appropriate economic rewards for all. This is the conservative premise. It does not always mean that everyone who works hard can live well. Some conservatives believe that no society in which there is a scarcity of goods should allow all its members to live well. In this chapter we have taken the first variant of the conservative position and looked at its implications.

Another set of solutions suggests that our society does not automatically provide a just or adequate way of distributing rewards, but that it is our obligation as social beings to be sure that everyone is guaranteed some minimal level of necessities and comforts. This is the liberal position. Finally, a third set of ideas forms the radical position. The radicals, as they are defined here, believe (like the liberals) that the social system does not distribute wealth adequately (or even create it adequately); but radicals (unlike liberals) believe the problem cannot be well dealt with except by profound changes at the roots of the system.

The chapter continues by examining the difficulty of defining "poverty" and "poorness." While poverty is first of all the lack of money and other property, it also involves one's access to various opportunities for advancement. Since such opportunities are not evenly distributed—take such obvious examples as two children of the same age from the same city, one of whose parents sends him to private school where he makes friends with wealthy children from around the country, while the other has to go through the city school system, which provides inferior education and allows him to know only children from his own neighborhood— the simple redistribution of money is not sufficient to cure poverty, except perhaps temporarily. However, since "poverty" is so hard to define, we grudgingly adopt the definition of the Bureau of the Census, which is made in cash terms.

According to this definition, and using a study of 1973 data, the poor lie largely among the nonwhite, the aged, Southerners, and people with limited educations. It is not true (contrary to common belief) that most of the poor live either in the central cities or in rural locations; Poverty is geographically widespread.

The second section of the chapter ends with a more detailed study of the urban poor. We find that most of the urban poor are children, elderly, or otherwise unable to work at all, or can only work part time or for low wages. We conclude that in the absence of any better system of alleviating poverty, a system of welfare (not necessarily the present one) is necesary.

The third section of this essay explores the "meaning" of poverty for our society. Of course, poverty has many "meanings" depending on who is thinking about it. In this chapter we dwell on the relation between being poor and not being poor: we look at the fear of poverty which motivates many people to look away from the poor (lest they see themselves there), or to dislike the poor (as they would dislike themselves if they felt they had "failed"), and to scramble for "success," which in our society means first and foremost having a good buffer against poverty. This section is illuminated by a long quotation from a novel by Edward Bellamy.

The chapter ends with a discussion of solutions to poverty. No solution is likely to be of great or lasting value unless it goes to the roots of the system—what is produced, how these things are distributed, and how men and women are recruited into the work force. Although the author favors a radical approach, he contends that such revolutionary changes are not feasible in the near future. Therefore he favors a combination of more liberal measures to alleviate and ameliorate poverty. The chapter ends with an invitation to the student to draw his or her own conclusions about poverty and its possible remedies.

NOTES

1. John 12:8.

2. *New York Times,* 23 November 1975.

3. The most influential statement of the problem was *The Other America* by Michael Harrington (New York: Macmillan, 1962).

4. See, for example, Freidrich Heer, *The Medieval World* (New York: Mentor, 1962), pp. 52–53.

5. William L. Langer, "The Black Death," in *Cities, Their Origin, Growth, and Impact,* ed. Kingsley David (San Francisco: W. H. Freeman, 1973), pp. 106–111.

6. William Lozonick, "Karl Marx and Enclosures in England," *Review of Radical Political Economics* 6, no. 2 (1974): 1–59.

7. Karl Marx, *Capital* (New York: International, 1967), 1:735.

8. G. R. Elton, *England Under the Tudors* (London: Methuen, 1955), p. 260.

9. Karl Polanyi, *The Great Transformation* (Boston: Beacon Press, 1957): pp. 77–85.

10. A good discussion of this and other aspects of poverty and its measurement can be found in David M. Gordon, ed., *Problems in Political Economy: An Urban Perspective* (Lexington, Mass.: D. C. Heath, 1971), pp. 223–276.

11. United States Bureau of the Census, *Characteristics of the Low-Income Population: 1973,* Current Population Reports, series P-60, no. 98 (Washington, D.C.: U.S. Government Printing Office, January, 1975).

12. Karl E. Tauber and Alma F. Tauber, *Negroes in Cities* (Chicago: Aldine, 1965).

13. Some of the major works in this controversy are James S. Coleman et al., *Equality of Educational Opportunity* (Washington, D.C.: U.S. Government Printing Office, 1966); Peter Blau and Otis Dudley Duncan, *The American Occupational Structure* (New York: John Wiley and Sons, 1967); Christopher Jencks et al., *Inequality: A Reassessment of the Effect of Family and Schooling in America* (New York: Basic Books, 1972); Samuel Bowles and Herbert Gintis, "I.Q. in the U.S. Class Structure," *Social Policy* 3, nos. 4 and 5 (1972–73): 65–96; and Samuel Bowles and Herbert Gintis; *Schooling in Capitalist America* (New York: Basic Books, 1976).

14. This figure is not part of table 6-3. The exact number is 3,355,000 women with children under eighteen years of age (page 110 of the census report).

15. Anthony Downs, *Who Are the Urban Poor?* (New York: Committee for Economic Development, 1970).

16. I put "social problems" in quotation marks because it seems strange to suddenly become a "social problem" when one reaches the age of sixty-five, or if one happens to be born with black skin. Are *you* a social problem?

17. For a novelistic treatment try Harriet Arnow's *The Dollmaker* (New York: Macmillan, 1954) or Joyce Carol Oates's *Them* (New York: Vanguard, 1969). An excellent study by an anthropologist is Carol Stack's *All Our Kin* (New York: Harper & Row, 1974), as well as the fine books by Oscar Lewis. A standard and still excellent study by a sociologist is *Tally's Corner* by Elliot Liebow (Boston: Little, Brown, 1967). One excellent collection, easily available, is David and Sheila Rothman's *On Their Own: The Poor in Modern America* (Reading, Mass.: Addison-Wesley, 1972).

18. Edward Bellamy, *Looking Backward 2000–1887* (Cambridge, Mass.: Harvard University Press, 1967), pp. 96–99.

19. A standard account is Matthew Josephson, *The Robber Barons* (New York: Harcourt Brace Jovanovich, 1962).

20. See Stewart Ewen, "Advertising" Selling the System," in Milton Mankoff ed., *The Poverty of Progress* (New York: Holt, Rhinehart & Winston, 1973).

21. A classic fictional account of such a case is Budd Schulberg's *What Makes Sammy Run?*

22. See the fascinating account of some important labor struggles in Jeremy Brecher, *Strike* (Greewich, Conn.: Fawcett Books, 1974).

23. Francis Piven and Richard Cloward, *Regulating the Poor* (New York: Random House, 1971).

24. See, for example, John Prebble's masterful account of Scottish expropriation and immigration, *The Highland Clearances* (London: Penguin Books, 1969). Or see Oscar Handlin's *Boston's Immigrants* (New York: Atheneum, 1968), for a similar story of the Irish.

25. S. M. Miller and Martin Rein, "Can Income Redistribution Work?" *Social Policy* 6, no. 1 (1975): 5.

26. Of the entire projected U.S. federal budget (including social security payments, which have special sources of funds and account for 20 percent of expenditures), direct defense appropriations take up 26.9 percent and interest (mostly on past defense debts) another 9.9 percent—something in the area of 120 billion dollars.

27. Miller and Rein, "Can Income Redistribution Work?" p. 3.

28. You might begin by consulting Martin Rein, *Social Policy: Issues of Choice and Change* (New York: Random House, 1970), and proceed to look through recent issues of *Social Policy* magazine.

QUESTIONS

1 Imagine that every person or family were given enough money each year to raise it above a generous "poverty line." What would be some possible consequences of this action?

2 Find the most recent report on poverty in your area of the country, probably published by the Bureau of the Census. What is the distribution of poverty among the cities and towns near you, and among racial and ethnic groups (as presented in table 6-3)? Does this correspond with your impressions? Does it correspond with efforts being made to alleviate poverty in your area?

3 Think of several different kinds of jobs. How would you go about finding each job if you wanted it? What methods would most likely get you the job? Finally, how does this relate to poverty?

4 What does poverty mean to you? What image do you have of the poor? Try to write down in detail what you think the poor are like: how they dress, their family life, their attitudes toward work and crime, and so forth. *After* you have done this try to find information that will tell you whether your ideas are correct.

5 It is commonly believed that some ethnic groups have advanced (economically) much more quickly than others. Is this true? And if so, why?

6 What does "poverty" mean for specific groups? For example, what does it mean for migrant farm workers, if there are any in your state? What does it mean for Indians on a nearby reservation? Choose a specific group and investigate what poverty means for it by reading and by investigating firsthand.

7 Look through the newspaper and find some major current effort to deal with poverty. Then, for two or three months, follow various publications, of different political viewpoints, to see what their opinions are. What is your own opinion?

8 Do you think poverty will ever be eliminated?

READINGS

Gordon, David M., ed. *Problems in Political Economy: An Urban Perspective.* Lexington, Mass.: D. C. Heath, 1971.

Rowbotham, David and Rowbotham, Sheila, eds. *On Their Own: The Poor in Modern America.* Reading, Mass: Addison-Wesley, 1972.

Stack, Carol. *All Our Kin.* New York: Harper & Row, 1974.

Piven, Francis Fox and Cloward, Richard. *Regulating the Poor.* New York: Random House, 1971.

7 | THE PROBLEM OF PRISONS*

DAVID F. GREENBERG

> Imprisonment as it exists today is a worse crime than any of those committed by its victims; for no single criminal can be as powerful for evil, or as unrestrained in its exercise, as an organized nation. Therefore, if any person is addressing himself to the perusal of this dreadful subject in the spirit of a philanthropist bent on reforming a necessary and beneficent public institution, I beg him to put it down and go about some other business. It is just such reformers who have in the past made the neglect, oppression, corruption, and physical torture of the old common gaol the pretext for transforming it into that diabolical den of torment, mischief and damnation, the modern model prison.
>
> If, on the contrary, the reader comes as a repentant sinner, let him read on.
>
> George Bernard Shaw[1]

One of the most difficult and one of the most ignored of our social problems is the problem of prisons—a problem which might be ameliorated through drastic prison reform, but which can be solved only through the abolition of prisons.

The elimination of imprisonment may at first seem like a radical step, but alternatives to imprisonment are already widespread—fines and probation are often used, and traffic law violators are sometimes sentenced to attend classes in driver education. The advocacy of prison abolition implies simply that other courses of action, including, sometimes, doing nothing at all, are preferable to imprisonment. This conclusion is far from obvious—it might follow from a distaste for the use of violence—prisons resting fundamentally on the use of violence or the threat of its use—or from a careful consideration of prisons, their effects on inmates, and the

---

*This article was originally published as an educational service by the National Peace Literature Service of the American Friends Service Committee in June, 1970.

relationship they have to the society at large. Here we take this latter viewpoint. The problem of prisons differs from other important social problems in at least one respect; most of the situations which present themselves as problematic, whether race relations, militarism, or air pollution, are widely recognized as problems, and receive much discussion and public attention. This is not true of prisons, and it is this that makes prisons one of the most difficult of public problems. With rare exceptions, only present or former prison inmates and their friends and family perceive prisons, per se, as presenting problems, and they are rarely in a position to do much about them, Neither periodic scandals and horror stories nor occasional prison riots have succeeded in awakening lasting public interest, though almost everyone recognizes that imprisonment is to be avoided if at all possible.

This lack of interest is to be explained only in part by the fact that most people never expect to be imprisoned. Yet the number of those involved is not so small either: at any one time, roughly 400,000 persons are imprisoned in federal, state, or local penal institutions, while another 800,000 are on probation or parole, many of them former prisoners. During the course of a year, institutions receive 2.5 million persons as inmates, probationers, or parolees; an additional 5.8 million family members are affected.[2] Besides, expectation of possible future incarceration cannot be the only relevant consideration, since conditions in public zoos are often superior to those in many jails, even though no one expects to be locked up in a zoo. And political groups whose members have often been imprisoned have shown comparatively little interest in prisons. Rarely do they go beyond the familiar complaints about lack of rehabilitation programs to a more fundamental analysis.

To understand this absence of concern about prisons it is necessary to examine the several roles that prisons play in our society, and to explore popular beliefs about the functions prisons serve.

Most people believe that prisons exist to protect the public from those who commit antisocial acts, such as murder, rape, assault and theft. Another commonly accepted rationale for prisons is that they deter potential criminals. Historically, the common use of a fixed prison sentence is in fact roughly contemporary with the acceptance of the idea that crime could be deterred by imprisonment for a period sufficiently long that the rewards of crime would be outweighed by the inconvenience of long imprisonment. Prior to this time, corporal punishment and deportation were commonly used as punishment, and imprisonment was reserved primarily for those awaiting trial. The notion that imprisonment deters potential criminals rests on the belief that the decision to violate a law is a rational one, decided by weighing the rewards of the criminal act against the sanction of imprisonment, which is presumed to increase in severity with the length of the sentence. On this basis, longer sentences are considered more appropriate for crimes in which the rewards are especially high or the dangers to society particularly great.

A third role, the most ancient in origin, is that of punishment. In biblical times, transgression of divinely inspired rules for human behavior fell into the category of "sin," to be punished according to divine command. In modern times, the state has, for most people, replaced religion as the ultimate source of authority, and most people believe that the state has both the right and the obligation to punish violations of its laws. Most people believe that such punishment insures the survival of an orderly society because they believe that anarchy would follow the elimination of punishment; some also believe that punishment improves the offender, just as it presumably improves small children who are punished by their parents.

By contrast, modern day penologists and prison administrators, at least at the level of rhetoric, consider the most important function of a prison to be rehabilitation, the improvement of a defective individual so that he can return to society as an acceptably functioning member.

In addition to the roles prisons play—or supposedly play—in the eyes of the public, prisons perform functions of which the public is often unaware, even though these unrecognized roles are the ones that involve the public the most intimately. Crime, police, courts, and jails serve, for many, a psychological function by providing the occasion for fulfillment of vicarious thrills and punishment, mental acting out of suppressed desires to participate in antisocial behavior, and transference of guilt feelings to others, differentiated as sharply as possible from themselves through the label "criminal." Prisons are important in helping to make that distinction. Obviously, the importance of this role cannot be measured quantitatively, but the wide consumption of detective novels and crime films leads one to feel intuitively that this factor is an important one.

Although little use now has been made of prisons as a laboratory for social experiments, prisons have considerable potential for experiments in social control of human behavior, in directions that may be far from desirable. The growing interest on the part of the government in developing sophisticated techniques of managing populations without provoking rebellions, coming at a time when penologists are attempting to find new ways to control prison populations without the methods of physical coercion used in the past, provides some grounds for concern.

An important function of prisons is helping the public to avoid facing certain unpleasant problems. Neither individuals nor groups wish to be reminded of difficult problems, and in such circumstances they often prefer to avoid the problems by physically removing them, or at least their most visible manifestations. To choose a nonpenal example, many people in our highly youth-oriented society are afraid of aging and of death. To avoid being confronted with these phenomena, we frequently place elderly people in special homes for the aged so that we don't have to see them; a variety of rationalizations whose factual basis is nonexistent may be used to justify doing so.[3]

Prisons sometimes serve a similar function. Society has so far not developed methods for dealing with problems that arise from certain kinds of deviant social behavior through noncoercive means; such problems are more easily avoided than faced, and so society develops elaborate ways to remove problems from its midst. Among the principal means of doing this in our society are commitment to mental institutions or prisons, the choice being made on somewhat of an *ad hoc* basis. One reason prisons present a difficult problem is that their elimination requires the finding of other ways to deal with problems prisons are intended to solve; as with many social problems, solutions may not be easy to find, and the motivation to find them may be lacking as long as prisons, however inadequate they are, are still available.

Such considerations, however crucial for an understanding of popular support for imprisonment, are in fact relevant only for an extremely limited number of prisoners, since the great majority of prisoners do not in fact represent particularly serious problems. The most important factor in determining who goes to prison and how long he stays there is not the antisocial character of an act someone commits, but the social and economic class of the person committing the act, a fact which has far-reaching consequences for the presumed necessity of imprisonment.

A few examples will illustrate the point. Although the most frequently violated federal law is without doubt the income tax law, hardly any of the 20,000 federal prisoners are tax law violators—delinquent taxpayers are not usually imprisoned or even arrested; they are simply made to pay back taxes, with interest and a fine. By contrast, a very substantial fraction of federal prisoners are young men who have been convicted of taking a stolen car across state lines. Those who steal cars are not allowed simply to return the car and pay interest on its value for the time it was "borrowed," with a small fine. The tax evader, who in the conventional view has stolen from the public, is not punished severely, and is usually not considered to need rehabilitation. The tax evader is pitied for having been caught, and is admired when he succeeds. Typically he comes from a middle- or upper-income group. By contrast, the car thief, usually from a low-income, working-class background, is branded a "criminal" and imprisoned. The one represents no more of a threat to society than the other, and imprisonment is a priori no more appropriate to one than to the other.[4]

Petty burglars may be imprisoned for years. The officials of General Electric, convicted of stealing millions from the public through price fixing, got thirty days; they returned to business careers, and were not widely thought to present a problem to society. Hundreds of fellow business executives who do the same thing are ignored. If we can survive without locking up the latter, we can surely get along without imprisoning the small-time thieves, whose take is so much less.

Sex distinctions are also important. In New York, thousands of men are arrested each year, and many imprisoned, for homosexuality, but women are hardly ever arrested for that reason, perhaps because male judges feel more threatened by male homosexuals than by lesbians. The number of female prisoners in the United States is extremely small when compared to the number of male prisoners, though no one seems to know whether this reflects a smaller real crime rate or a reluctance to arrest women and sentence them to prison.

On the face of it, incarceration is not necessarily closely correlated to behavior which is objectively harmful to society. Those who seek to stop a disastrous war, or to eliminate racial discrimination are imprisoned—not those who lead the country into war, or practice racial discrimination. Frequently the big-time criminals go free, while small-time crooks are locked up for years. The distinction between "political prisoners" and "ordinary criminals" therefore loses a good deal of its meaning, for the mere designation of certain acts as "criminal" and others as acceptable is already "political" and in our society strongly reflects class, racial, and sexual biases.

The above argument, taken by itself, is incomplete, since it shows only that imprisonment is selective: lower-income offenders and members of certain other minority groups, such as hippies or radicals, are treated differently from wealthy criminals. It is nevertheless widely believed that prisons at least protect us from lower-class criminals, thereby performing a useful and even necessary function; the economic bias could presumably be eliminated by imprisoning wealthy criminals, though this will never happen to any extent in a society based on economic privilege. To carry the argument to completion, it remains to examine the relevance of prisons to the various functions listed earlier: protection, deterrence, punishment, and rehabilitation.

Even modern-day prison administrators nominally committed to rehabilitation regard protection as the principal function of a prison. All other functions are relegated to a secondary role. This concern leads to an almost unbelievable fanaticism with regard to security inside the prison. Obsession with security might be amusing, were it not so annoying to the men inside, who have to put up with frequent counts, searches, a host of unnecessary regulations,[5] and continual surveillance. The extremely low escape rate (over a thirty-year period, roughly 8 prisoners out of 700,000 have escaped from the federal prison system[6]), the large number of unapprehended criminals not in prison and the growing successful use of minimum security prison camps without walls show how silly this obsession is, as does the fact that almost all prisoners will sooner or later be released from prison, usually within a few years of incarceration, and regardless of any changes in the personality of the prisoner. Many prisoners are in fact released despite virtual certainty that they will soon return to prison. On a long-term basis, then, prisons provide no protection; escapes are presumably feared because of the bureaucratic problems they create, and because of possible negative reactions among the public.

On a short-term basis, prisons may protect those outside their walls, but under anything like present conditions, they are unable to protect inmates from the crimes that flourish within their walls. Chicago experienced 1,397 forcible rapes[7] *outside* the walls of Cook County Jail in 1967, a figure probably smaller than the number of rapes committed within its walls. Similar figures have been reported in the Philadelphia prison system.[8] County jails in large cities are notorious for frequent rapes and beatings, and occasional murders. Most of those confined in this atmosphere are not even convicted criminals: only about 25 percent of the inmates at Cook County Jail are doing time on a sentence[9]—the remainder are there awaiting trial because they cannot afford bail. The crimes committed against the inmate population by other inmates or guards are almost always neglected when considering the "protective" aspects of imprisonment. This is a vivid example of how the label "criminal" is used to dehumanize a human being.

Prisons are also supposed to deter crime.[10] To what extent deterrence inhibits crime is mostly unknown, though one statistical study[11] indicates that increased length of sentence has little or no effect on crime rates. Psychologists generally believe that rewarding desired behavior is more effective than punishing undesired behavior. It is known that capital punishment does not deter murder more effectively than long-term imprisonment for the same crime.[12] It seems likely that most crimes are not deterrable by imprisonment or any other form of punishment because the decision to commit them is not a rational one in which consequences are weighed in advance; probably few criminals are able to estimate accurately their chances for success, for example. In those cases where the decision to commit a crime is made rationally, certainty of punishment is likely to be a more important factor than the severity of punishment. Since most crimes are not cleared through arrest, most of those arrested are not convicted, and most of those convicted initially are not imprisoned,[13] certainty of punishment does not exist in our judicial system, nor is it possible to conceive of a judicial system consistent with civil liberties that could ensure such certainty.

We *do* know that imprisonment is remarkably ineffective in deterring prison inmates from returning to crime after their release. Recidivism rates depend somewhat on the type of institution and the type of offender, and figures quoted are not always reliable,[14] but figures of 60 to 85 percent are commonly accepted.[15]

These figures, while obviously not encouraging, are open to interpretation: it can be argued[16] that since "hardened criminals" are more likely than others to be sent to prison, the low "cure rates" are perhaps not so surprising. This, however, amounts to an admission that imprisonment is not an effective way of preventing those convicted of crime from returning to it. Also, the assumption that only hardened criminals are sent to prison is unreliable. While multiple offenders are less likely to be granted probation, many other factors enter. For example, the frequency with which probation is granted varies widely from one state to another.

Furthermore, the economic status of the defendant is crucially important in determining the disposition of his case. The amount of money he has available will determine whether he is able to make bail or must remain in jail until the trial. The factor is highly correlated to the rate of conviction and to the rate of incarceration following conviction.[17]

Given the conditions in almost all jails, what is perhaps remarkable about recidivism rates, as many have commented, is not that they are so high but that they are so low. A man held in prison for a crime tends to classify himself as "a criminal," rather than as someone who has for one reason or another violated the law. This self-conception, linked as it often is to a lack of self-esteem, could be an important factor in determining behavior after release, especially when a released inmate has difficulty in finding a job because of his criminal record or lack of job skills, or when he encounters personal difficulties.[18] Furthermore, the stray pieces of information about crime techniques that every prisoner picks up casually in conversation with other prisoners make his return to crime all the more tempting when he encounters difficulty.

Other factors that enhance rather than deter crime after release are the sexual tension and undercurrent of violence found in almost all prisons. The sexual tension arises from the close confinement[19] and sexual isolation of prison society. This gives rise to a need to reassert masculine patterns of domination[20] as a psychological defense against forced submission to the authority of prison guards and administration. The repressed hatred of guards may erupt after release from prison, if not in prison riots or attacks on guards or other inmates before release. The feeling that a sentence is too long[21] and prison conditions unduly oppressive may lead to additional resentment[22] and a desire to "get even" with society after release. Furthermore, the denial of conjugal visiting rights tends to disrupt families and other relationships, making it more difficult for the inmates to do time and to resume stable relationships on the outside after his release. This enhances the recidivism rate[23]—as can only be expected from one's intuitive feelings that personal and sexual maladjustment must be a factor in at least some instances of law violation.

The notion that punishment by itself might *improve* the prisoner is even more curious than the notion that it might deter him from breaking laws in the future. George Bernard Shaw observed that no zookeeper would expect to turn a tiger into a Quaker by locking him in a cage,[24] yet most jailers believe this of their prisoners, as evidenced by the almost universal practice of using solitary confinement, sometimes disguised as "administrative segregation" but just as solitary and just as confining, for unmanageable prisoners, including those who are emotionally disturbed or mentally ill.

While it may be true that children's behavior can be improved by punishment, the analogy with socially deviant adults is misleading. For punishment seems to succeed in improving children's behavior only when administered by a loving adult or respected authority in the context of a generally supportive emotional environment, which, needless to say, is not present in prison. In addition, *punishment* of a child's misbehavior can succeed in modifying that behavior only when the child is *able* to act differently. In those instances when undesirable social behavior arises from addiction to alcohol or drugs, lack of those educational or vocational skills needed to survive by legal means in our society, or, in rare cases, mental disorders, punishment is at best irrelevant and in some cases may be quite harmful.

Going beyond the question of whether punishment does any good, to the question of whether punishment should be administered anyway, even when it is known to serve no useful purpose, as Kant believed,[25] one immediately becomes entangled in a web of essentially unanswered questions such as the relative degree of individual versus societal responsibility for law violations, and our inability to formulate self-evident criteria for determining standards of justice in meting out punishment.[26]

Quite apart from these questions, punishment by the state often appears as it did to Thoreau—childish and vindictive—a mere emotional outburst in which the state expresses anger at its inability to control its subjects. It is much like a temper tantrum, disguised by the ritual formality and cold impersonality of courtroom procedure.

In a moral sense, the propriety of punishment at the hands of the state seems especially questionable. A government responsible for the murder of thousands or millions in war is not in a very good position to pass judgment on domestic killers, whose body count has no hope, in a lifetime, of matching what the state frequently accomplishes in a day or week. The overwhelming majority of murders committed in this century have been committed legally, by governments in wartime. The largest thefts in our country have been thefts of land guaranteed by treaty to Indian tribes and Chicanos in the Southwest—thefts sponsored by our government. The largest number of kidnappings—those of Japanese-Americans during World War II—were carried out by the government with approval of the courts. Government kidnappings for ransom take place every time a person is arrested and held in jail before trial because of his inability to pay bail. Suppression of civil rights and civil liberties for minority groups and unpopular political organizations by governments at all levels is a familiar and sad story. The assumption of moral superiority implied when a government punishes a lawbreaker is incongruous and unjustified by reality. A black robe is no more a proof of purity than a white wedding gown.

We come now to the topic of rehabilitation—a word that can cover a multitude of sins and serves as the source of a good deal of bitterness to prisoners: despite much talk and slick government brochures (often printed in prison print shops) about rehabilitative programs, very few such programs can be found inside most prisons. Rehabilitation is still regarded as a luxury, something to think about after security and maintenance are ensured. As a result, neither adequate funds nor staff is available for rehabilitation or treatment programs in most prisons.

Rose Giallombardo's study of the Women's Federal Reformatory at Alderson, West Virginia,[27] illustrates this point. Officers are instructed to do what they can to "treat the inmates," after other duties are finished. However, there seem to be so many other duties that not much time for this is available. Officers who do have free time prefer to spend it alone in their offices. Only 3.3 percent of the officers are college graduates. Most come from rural areas, work in the prison system primarily for the money, and are considered by inmates to be ignorant of the urban conditions in which the inmates are accustomed to living. Most have no training in counseling or any type of rehabilitation work. The remote location of the prison (a typical feature of many federal and state institutions) makes the recruitment of officers difficult, since few are anxious to accept the social isolation. Indeed, the captain, before interviewing applicants for jobs as officers, is quoted as remarking, "I'll be happy just to have a warm body."[28]

The scarcity of trained, competent staff is a problem everywhere. Alfred Schnur,[29] quoting figures from the Federal Bureau of Prisons, points out that for the 161,587 inmates in state and federal prisons in 1954, there were 23 full-time psychiatrists employed; on the basis of a forty-hour week, each inmate was able to receive 82 seconds per month of psychiatric care. The 67 psychologists and psychometrists were able to supplement this with an additional four minutes per month for each inmate. On the same basis, the 96 institutional parole officers were able to spend six minutes each month with an inmate, the 155 chaplains, ten minutes a month and the 257 employees responsible for individual casework, less than sixteen minutes a month. These figures are based on the ridiculously over-optimistic assumption that the relevant staff member spends *all* of his working hours with inmates. This is of course not the case. Much of his time will be spent in administrative tasks, handling records, working with the custodial staff, and sometimes leading group therapy sessions. It seems clear that an inmate who needs psychiatric or psychological therapy of some kind is not too likely to get it in prison. Even the Bureau of Prisons admits the inadequacy of therapeutic programs in the federal prison system, where standards are generally higher than those in state or local institutions.

It should not be assumed, however, that all, or even most inmates are mentally ill and in need of psychiatric treatment, although this view is a popular one among members of the "enlightened" public. The fact that adult crime rates increase directly with the unemployment rate, especially for property offenses,[30] which constitute about 90 percent of all crimes committed, or that rates of delinquency among nationality groups whose children at one time figured prominently in juvenile court statistics declined as these groups improved their economic and social status and moved out of neighborhoods with high delinquency rates,[31] indicates that much crime is socially produced.

A substantial number of prison inmates simply lack the educational and vocational skills to function successfully within the law on the outside. Vocational rehabilitation programs are intended to help these inmates. Too often these involve unskilled labor whose main purposes are to help maintain the institution at the lowest possible cost, and to keep the inmates occupied during the day, not to help inmates prepare for a good job outside. Such programs help to keep inmates at the bottom of the economic ladder and increase the likelihood that the inmate will return to crime after his release: crimes committed for financial gain are usually not very lucrative, and hold little appeal to someone with a good job, but even crimes with small financial returns may appear worthwhile to a person who is unemployed or employable only at bare subsistence wages.

Some programs, such as those in Prison Industries, Inc., may prepare inmates for decent jobs outside, though the prison record is still a significant handicap in getting them. The number of prisoners allowed to participate in such programs is usually quite small. Furthermore, the programs are often closely involved with the military. Like much of what passes for higher education in the colleges and universities, prison industry programs serve primarily to train workers and technicians for the military-industrial complex at public expense.

Rehabilitation programs also include education. The low level of educational attainment of most inmates suggests that educational programs might be one of the most valuable services a prison could offer to its inmates. But the quality of educational programs is often poor, and the results have not been outstanding. In fact, for most prisoners, the usual duration and type of involvement in prison education programs is associated with higher-than-average postrelease failure rates.[32] In many institutions, inmates attend courses in the hope of impressing the parole board with a good institutional record, which may explain this surprising result. Technical innovations such as teaching machines are being introduced in some institutions, and could conceivably help to compensate for the lack of qualified teaching staff, but often at considerable cost: the introduction of teaching machines in a number of federal prisons was accompanied by the abolition of the prison libraries.[33]

A certain number of prisoners may in fact be unrehabilitatable, in the sense that their ability to acquire a stable life pattern and marketable skills may be quite limited. At best, they may be able to eke out a subsistence living at the most tedious and unpleasant jobs our society makes available, while others may be totally unemployable. In a productive economy based on sharing, this would present no difficulties at all. In a society based on competition, difficulties arise when such individuals acquire the values of the society where status is determined primarily on the basis of success in material acquisition, but lack the ability or motivation to compete successfully within the legal framework. The unsuccessful individual may respond to his situation in a number of ways, including law violations. Unfortunately for the individual involved, his incompetence may limit his success in this area also.

Such an individual is not a good candidate for rehabilitation, both because he is less likely to refrain from law violation after release, and because he is more likely to get caught. These two factors presumably help to explain why thieves have a high rate of recidivism compared to other criminals.[34] Another obstacle in the successful rehabilitation of this category of law violator is that unlike some prisoners (such as conscientious objectors) whose values differ in some way from those of society, his values coincide with those of society; a rehabilitation program revolving around a change in attitudes runs up against some of the most basic attitudes of our society. The inmate pictures himself, not unrealistically, as no different from the hustlers and con men on the outside, who didn't get caught or bribed the judge or whose actions happen not to be illegal even though they had the same character and motivation as those committed by the inmate.

As with many categories of criminal activity, we have the choice of tolerating this category of crime as one of the costs of living in an acquisitive society, or of modifying our values and social structure. For example, much theft might be eliminated if we had a guaranteed annual income or a socialized economy. Likewise, insurance, because it socializes the costs of theft, makes theft more tolerable because it is then less costly to any one individual victim. Other examples of institutional arrangements that would minimize crime and/or its cost to individuals can easily be multiplied. Frequently such arrangements would result in other benefits as well. A drastic reduction in private car ownership in favor of publicly owned transportation would have ecological benefits in addition to reducing the rate of car theft and traffic accidents. Similarly, a guaranteed annual income would have benefits reaching far beyond the reduction of theft.

The room for improvements in rehabilitation programs is clearly great, though the precise direction in which improvements and innovations should be made is not always completely clear due to our astonishing lack of knowledge concerning the relative effectiveness of various programs now in existence. The design of such improvements, however, is not our present aim. Here we want to emphasize that any rehabilitative program, to the extent that it aims to change only the inmate, is inadequate. Rehabilitation is no substitute for changes in the larger society that will make rehabilitation, whether psychiatric or vocational, unnecessary.

We also want to stress that within the prison framework, severe limitations exist in the extent to which improvements in rehabilitation programs are *possible*.

A person incarcerated after conviction for a crime experiences what have come to be known as the "pains of imprisonment."[35] These psychological "pains" arise from his being deprived of the liberty to which he was accustomed before his incarceration, from his being deprived of all material belongings, which in our society play a major role in helping an individual to form and maintain a sense of his own identity, from the denial of heterosexual relationships, the lack of autonomy, and the forced association with others, resulting, as it does, in a feeling of anxiety over lack of security when these others are also criminals. To this list we may also add the monotony of the prison routine and the almost total lack of privacy. These deprivations are significant for us both in themselves and because of the compensating mechanisms inmates develop to cope with them.

The denial of liberty and autonomy is an obstacle in preparing an inmate for life outside prison, where he will have to make decisions on his own affecting both himself and others. An individual's ability to act responsibly can be acquired or strengthened only through his being given the opportunity to exercise responsibility. Prisons subvert the development of an inmate's autonomy by reducing him to a wholly dependent status in which every aspect of his life is governed by rules, whose reasons the inmate is not entitled to know and in many cases may not exist, and in whose formulation the inmate was allowed to take no part. The reasons for this are obvious: it is much easier to manage a herd of docile, obedient creatures than a group of responsible, thoughtful human beings. In a prison setting, the goals of responsibility and autonomy will always be sacrificed in the interests of trouble-free maintenance of the institution.

The denial of heterosexual relationships is likely to compound difficulties an inmate may have in relating to those of the opposite sex, particularly when the denial takes place in the context of a prison, which in other ways challenges an inmate's sense of his own masculinity.[36] And the endless monotony of prison days and nights following one another in unchanging succession tends to dull the mind, destroying alertness and initiative, again subverting rehabilitation goals for the long-term prisoner.

The prisoner responds to his unpleasant position in such a way as to minimize his discomfort and to maximize the small benefits he may receive while in prison, by assuming one or another of the fixed social roles that differentiate prisoner society and by adopting social values of the inmate society, values whose adoption helps to neutralize the pains of imprisonment. (We are oversimplifying here, since not every prisoner accepts these values to the same degree, and since, to a certain extent, inmate society values are not created only by the prison society but may also be brought into the prison from the outside, and may reflect values and attitudes of the larger society, though perhaps in distorted or intensified form.) The inmate social system promotes group solidarity and provides emotional support to an inmate in dealing with the degradations and humiliations of prison life.

One of the most pronounced features of this counter culture is its hostility toward the guards and members of the prison administration.[37] This seems to arise partly from the need to inhibit informers, partly from the natural resentment of those who forcibly impose submission, humiliation, and obedience to senseless and annoying regulations, and partly as a psychologically protective device that deflects the self-hatred that might in many cases accompany imprisonment, from oneself to members of another group.

Hostility of inmates for guards is often so great as to prevent ordinary conversations between guards and inmates; communication between members of these two groups must ordinarily be limited to an absolute minimum to prevent an inmate from being suspected as an informer. Ernest Ostro, recently released from a federal prison, tells of one prisoner at Lewisburg Federal Penitentiary who claims never to have spoken to his cellblock guard in thirteen years of imprisonment, with the exception of once on the day of his incarceration, and once when he was released.[38] An unusually humane guard may in some instances be able to overcome this barrier, but this is rare. The jobs a guard has to do ordinarily prevent him from showing much humanity. Needless to say, this hostility precludes the possibility of guards' playing an effective role in "treating" prisoners, even if they were competent to do so.

Furthermore, the conflict between organizational needs and the needs of individual treatment, whether vocational or psychological, make these two incompatible: to a considerable extent, the existence of a prison and the regimentation imposed by its organizational needs make rehabilitation programs impossible to carry on.[39]

The guards at Alderson[40] who spent their free time alone in their offices instead of following the meaninglessly vague instructions to "treat the inmates" when they had time, were merely recognizing the mutual incompatibility of incarceration on an involuntary basis, and the needs of treatment. Treatment by nonsupervisory staff may be less subject to this limitation, but trained, competent staff are ordinarily not available for this purpose, and when they are available, they may be looked upon with suspicion by the custodial staff, which may sense a threat to its authority. Furthermore, the success of any program of psychological or psychiatric therapy is ordinarily thought to depend on the voluntary character of participation. A recent book describing the counseling programs in the California state prison system, which has gone farther than any other state in implementing widespread treatment programs by noncustodial personnel, concludes, "Until the present time there have been no satisfactory studies offering the essential data regarding the effects upon the inmates exposed to the correctional community."[41] The authors express their personal beliefs that the results will be no worse than the traditional prison routine, which is not saying very much.

One important experiment, at Highfields, New Jersey,[42] strongly suggests that counseling programs, at least for delinquent juveniles, tend to be much more successful than traditional reformatory programs, at least in terms of reducing recidivism, when conducted in a noncoercive atmosphere. This program was established for delinquent sixteen- and seventeen-year-old boys without previous prison experience, who would live together in a building housing about twenty people, for a period of about four months, instead of being sent to the penitentiary at Annandale for at least a year. The group meets daily for group counseling with a counselor, who is also director of the center; other staff include a husband and wife who serve as houseparents and do maintenance work, and a handyman, to help boys with their hobbies. There are no guards, nor is there any other visible sign of coercion—no walls or fences. Boys are able to go to nearby towns with an adult, may go to church in nearby communities, or home on furloughs. A comparison study was done to determine changes of attitude and comparative recidivism rates with boys who had been sentenced to Annandale, and who had similar backgrounds and criminal records. In neither case were the changes in attitude very striking between the time of imprisonment and release, but the recidivism rates were impressively smaller for boys sentenced to Highfields, especially for blacks.

Vocational training and educational programs, if upgraded, could be valuable to those whose primary motivation for crime was economic; but this training need not take place in prison, as is recognized by those few institutions making use, on a very limited basis, of work release programs. There is no need to put a person in jail before training him for a job. In fact, it seems somewhat irrational to provide job training only to those who have first committed a crime. The time for education and vocational training is *before* a crime has been committed. Other factors that diminish the value of in-prison job training are the small numbers such programs can accommodate, the low standards of workmanship, and the deliberately slow work rates maintained by prisoners who resent being forced to work, especially at the extremely low pay scale of prison industries. It would be much more sensible to free the prisoners and provide vocational and educational programs on the outside.

These aspects of prison life which subvert the goals of "rehabilitation" are reinforced by the moral corruption of prison life, in which small-scale embezzling, bribery, and favoritism abound. These factors seem to appear in the functioning of any large, total institution, not just prisons.[43] The role of officers in these activities is frequently not small, and may lead to a good deal of cynicism on the part of inmates; it is likely to be admired by the other inmates as a successful violation of administration-imposed rules, particularly when the fruits of corruption are shared. Clearly the prison environment is not one that is likely to encourage the development of respect for law.

If we rule out purely retributive punishment as pointless, our survey of the functions that prisons are supposed to serve leads to the conclusion that prisons are not known to serve any useful purposes. The vocational, educational, and psychological treatment programs are largely under-mined by the precedence given to security and maintenance of the institution, and could be operated much more successfully for those who want them outside of prison, and on a voluntary basis. Since such programs would also be open to those who have not yet committed any crimes, this could also become a major contribution toward crime preven-tion. At the same time it will be necessary to eliminate the economic factors that lead to crime. In the long run, reorganization of society could eliminate much of the crime we see today. Probably no social reorganiza-tion will ever succeed in wiping out all manifestations of antisocial behavior, but this need not be a serious problem, even if alternatives to imprisonment are not found. A society that is prepared to tolerate 56,000 traffic fatalities a year has no reason to be worried about occasional murders; a society that squanders many billions a year on armaments is not really worried about petty theft; it only thinks it is.

Imprisonment is not very effective in deterring those who commit crime, and there is not much reason to believe that it deters those who have not yet done so. In particular, there is no reason to believe that different kinds of penalties, whether monetary or other, are less effective than imprisonment in obtaining adherence to laws. The use of rewards, such as cash incentives to prevent recidivism, remains wholly un-explored. We are not likely to know more about this as long as we can rely on prisons. The abolition of prisons, on the other hand, will clearly stimulate experimentation in other methods of preventing crime.

Yet, while the degree of fear generated by occasional murders may be irrational, people nevertheless are afraid, and will have to be shown alternatives, if they are to support a step like prison abolition. One simple possibility is to follow those who have committed crimes of violence, and physically restrain them from repeating their acts. Another possibility is to make guns inaccessible. A third possibility is suggested by penal institutions in other countries. Mexico, for example, maintains Tres Marias,[44] an island penal colony for prisoners with long records of previous offenses, with sentences of twenty years or more for murder, assault, and other crimes of violence. Prisoners have complete freedom on the island's 34,000 acres. After an orientation period, the prisoner's family may join him, and he selects a house in which they live. Prisoners can farm, start a business, or work for one of the businesses on the island; male and female prisoners may marry one another, and they may marry someone from the nonprison population on the island. Prisoners are counted only once a month, the only day on which they must wear the prison uniform. There seems to be no difficulty in maintaining a normal, healthy environment, so that Tres Marias is not plagued by the homosex-uality and constant violence of American prisoners—there are only occasional fights between two men over a woman—and prisoners are not plagued by problems of psychological readjustment after their release.

Need such a program operate only on remote Atlantic islands? The experience of the van der Hoeven Kliniek in Holland[45] indicates not. Holland has a very low rate of criminality compared to the United States—the per capita crime rate is only one-fifth of ours, so that the total prison population is only about 2,600. These are divided among forty-three prisons, on the basis of sex, age, character and length of sentence, mental problems, type of crime, and the prisoner's preference for solitary confinement as compared with dormitory living. This results in a highly homogeneous prison population of small size, making individual treatment much more feasible than in this country. The criminally insane are sent to the clinic in Utrecht, where they undergo intense psychotherapy. There are no guards and only a low wall. Inmates may go outside to visit families in the vicinity, and may participate in a work-release program. Despite the lack of security restrictions, only one serious incident occurred in ten years of the clinic's operation. The success of this clinic allows one to imagine small centers located in a community, where those who have committed very serious crimes of violence might undergo highly individualized voluntary treatment, not isolated from their families and friends and looking toward reintegration in the community. It goes without saying that cooperation and support of community groups would be essential to the success of a program of this kind.

Just as prison abolition would force us to find new ways of dealing with the problems prisons were invented to solve, the success of new experiments, along the lines just indicated, or perhaps along quite different lines, would do much to stimulate a movement for prison abolition. Another approach to prison abolition involves the efforts of those inside at making prisons unworkable. Prisons . . . function primarily through the cooperation of those whom they oppress. Both systems are highly vulnerable to systematic organized opposition from within.[46] The task of those outside is public education and support for the efforts of those inside. This will obviously be no light task given the present climate of public opinion.

In the meantime, a number of reforms could be instituted to improve the situation of those in prison, and bring closer the day when prisons can be eliminated. It should be understood, however, that all reforms are not equally desirable. Prison reforms that serve to increase control over inmates while presenting the image of a liberalization are clearly undesirable. Reforms involving special privileges to certain classes of inmates, especially the overtly political prisoners, fall into this category. Their effect is to divide those who must be solidly united if their opposition to the prison system is to have any chance of success. Especially desirable are reforms that help a prisoner to keep his head together and thereby resist the efforts of the prison system to break his spirit, and those which will give the prisoner weapons that he can use to fight the prison system.

My own suggestions for reforms, consistent with these criteria, follow.

1. Prisoners should be entitled to all civil liberties guaranteed by the Constitution, including the right to unlimited, uncensored correspondence with anyone, the right to receive any books, magazines, or newspapers, to receive visits from anyone, the right to publish articles, and to hold political meetings in prison. These rights would help reduce a prisoner's isolation, will reduce the power an administration has over inmates, and above all, will allow him to publicize conditions in the prison.

Prisoners should be entitled to all rights of due process for infraction of prison regulations. The present disciplinary committees do not meet this requirement. The inmates should be able to appeal any decision to an appeal committee of nonprison personnel. Solitary confinement, when involuntary, should be eliminated as cruel and unusual punishment. To a certain extent, it may be possible to win some of these rights in the courts, but the efforts of prisoners will be crucial.

2. Indefinite sentencing should be eliminated. Although the Federal Bureau of Prisons hails this procedure as "a milestone in Federal Sentencing,"[47] inmates find that it has more the character of a *millstone* about the neck. Inmates find it difficult to adjust to a sentence of indeterminate length. Prison officials like the practice because it increases their control over the inmates. Unfortunately for the inmates, those sentenced on this basis frequently find themselves doing much more time than those given a fixed sentence for the same offense.[48] The argument in favor of this type of sentence, that it allows for "individual treatment" of the prisoner, is vitiated by the absence of such treatment in prison, and indeed the virtual impossibility of providing it in an institutional setting. It also poses a serious threat to civil liberties.

3. No prisoner should be forced to work. Most work in prison is tedious labor necessary for the maintenance of the institution, or for the purpose of presenting a favorable image to the public. While many inmates are willing to work to help pass the time, no one should be forced to do so. Pay and working conditions should both meet union standards. Pay comparable to that earned for equivalent work done on the outside is given in Finland, in the Netherlands, and in the U.S.S.R.[49] Much of the additional cost would be absorbed by the removal of inmates' families from welfare roles, and the reduced probability that a prisoner with substantial cash savings will recidivate if he is unable to find a job immediately after his release.

4. Each prisoner should be entitled to a monthly cash allowance to pay travel expenses for friends and relatives who wish to visit. At

Alderson,[50] only 12 percent of the inmates received visits in 1962, presumably because the distance and expense involved in travelling to a remote spot were prohibitive to friends and relatives of many of the other inmates. The value of frequent visits to the emotional well-being of prisoners is considerable, and the expense involved need not be prohibitive.

5. Widespread use of recognizance bonds would drastically decrease the population of county jails. This alone would make county jails much more livable for those doing time in them. The money saved could be used in a variety of ways to improve living conditions for prisoners. The fact that imprisonment rates for those arrested could be expected to drop dramatically[51] as the use of recognizance bonds increased would result in further savings. Experiments with recognizance bonds in several cities have indicated that forfeiture rates can be kept quite low. The need felt by some for "preventive detention" might be obviated by the speedy scheduling of trials.

6. Many "crimes" could be eliminated from the lawbooks as unnecessary or harmful. Laws against crimes without victims, such as narcotics laws, abortion laws, and laws against a variety of voluntary sex acts—such as homosexuality or prostitution—between consenting adults . . . fall into this category.

7. The use of probation as an alternative to imprisonment should be extended widely. Judges are frequently reluctant to overburden an already greatly overextended probation service. (More than two-thirds of those under felony probation and more than three-fourths of those under misdemeanant probation are in caseloads of more than 100, and hardly any are in caseloads under 50.) In such circumstances a judge is likely to substitute incarceration for probation. Prison administrators estimated[52] that from 25 to 40 percent of their inmates could have been sentenced to probation, and the number is very likely larger, even using a prison administrator's standards, since a prison administrator may be biased in applying his own standards to an inmate population.

Clearly the situation could be alleviated by significantly increasing the size of the probation staff and the facilities available to it. Since the financial cost of keeping a man in probation is small compared to the cost of imprisoning him, the money saved could be used for financing the expansion of parole and probation programs.[53] The Swedish and Japanese practice of obtaining small caseloads by using volunteers should be tried.

8. A prisoner should be able to see and to insert material in the records kept on him by the prison administration. This is important because negative reports inserted by the administration in his records may jeopardize his chances at parole.

9. Prisoners should have the right of conjugal visits or furloughs at frequent intervals, from spouse or other men or women. No laws are needed to allow this. So far as I am aware, any warden could institute such a program any time he wanted to do so. In the United States, only the Mississippi State Penitentiary at Parchman[54] permits conjugal visits. The program there, begun in 1956, is limited to wives of prisoners. In the opinion of the warden, homosexuality has been reduced, and the program has worked out well. This seems to be the case in Sweden and in Soviet penal labor colonies[55] where visits are allowed twenty-eight times a year. The value of conjugal visits to the prisoner and his family is obvious.

10. Prisoners are entitled to educational and vocational training programs consistent with their interests. When these are not available inside the prisons, the inmate must be allowed to participate in such programs either through correspondence courses or through study and work training programs outside the prison at government expense.

Caveat Captor!

SUMMARY   In order to find solutions to the problem of prisons in this country one must first ask several important questions: what are the basic beliefs people have concerning why prisons exist; what functions do prisons really perform; and what alternatives are there to the prison system as it exists today?

An examination of the public's certainty that prisons are necessary reveals that it is based on a variety of beliefs. Primary among them, however, is the conviction that such institutions protect the public from antisocial acts by incarcerating those prone to commit such acts. In fact, prisons do no such thing, as is evidenced by the continuing existence of crime itself. Furthermore, the very fact that large numbers of people who commit "white collar" crimes do not go to prison indicates that the most important factor in determining who goes to prison and how long he stays there is not the antisocial act but rather the individual's social and economic class.

Deterrence is yet another frequent justification for the existence of prisons. It seems likely, though, that the deterrent effect does not occur except in those instances when the would-be perpetrator of a crime thinks rationally about what he is planning. In any case, for prisons to work as an effective deterrent to crime there must be certainty of punishment. This does not exist. More importantly, the ineffectiveness of prisons as a deterrent is demonstrated in the behavior of those who have already done time: they have a 60 to 85 percent recidivism rate. It is apparent that prison living, with its sexual tensions, undercurrents of violence, and absence of liberty and autonomy, customarily leads inmates to reassert patterns of domination once they leave prison. The prison experience breeds no respect for the law.

The punishment and rehabilitation of the offender are also common functions cited by those who uphold the conception of imprisonment. When one investigates these goals, however, one cannot help but see that they are contradictory. The only way an individual can increase his ability to act responsibly is to be given responsibility. Indeed, few useful rehabilitation programs exist within prison walls, due to the lack of adequate funding and trained staff and to the obsession with security on the part of those in charge of the system.

A strong case can also be made against the notion of punishment, since the violence of the State far exceeds that of any individual. Yet no one is convicted and imprisoned for the murders of citizens of other nations or of antiwar protesters, for the theft of millions of acres of land from Native Americans and Mexicans, or for the kidnapping of those of Japanese heritage during World War II.

Many people are unwilling to accept the idea that lawbreakers may not be solely responsible for their actions. Much crime results from social conditions, as can be seen in the striking increase of adult crime as unemployment rises. In this intensely competitive society, where one's status is determined by the acquisition of material goods and where prisons demonstrate such a dismal record in obtaining jobs for released prisoners, it is not surprising that many inmates perceive themselves as hustlers just like those outside the walls. A reorientation of social values, coupled with a reorganization of society along cooperative rather than competitive lines, would go far toward eliminating the need for much of the crime that exists today.

Since none of the objectives people give as the goals of imprisonment can be proven effective, it seems reasonable to conclude that the solution to the problem of prisons is to abolish them and substitute in their place more humane, rational, and effective methods of dealing with socially irresponsible behavior.

NOTES

1. George Bernard Shaw, *The Crime of Imprisonment* (New York: Philosophical Library, 1946), p. 13.

2. "The National Profile of Correction," Correction in the United States, Crime and Delinquency (National Council on Crime and Delinquency, January 1967), pp. 229–60.

3. Dorothy Rabinowitz, "Among the Aged," *Commentary*, March 1969, p. 61.

4. This paragraph should not be interpreted as meaning that the author believes people should pay federal income taxes. He believes it would be better if they did not.

5. For a sample set of penitentiary rules, see "Rule Book for Iowa State Penitentiary" in Norman Johnston, Leonard Savitz and Marvin E. Wolfgang, *The Sociology of Punishment and Correction* (New York: John Wiley & Sons, 1967), p. 87.

6. *Thirty Years of Progress* (Washington, D.C.: Federal Bureau of Prisons, 1967), p. 14.

7. Virgil W. Peterson, *A Report on Chicago Crime for 1967* (Chicago: Chicago Crime Commission, 1968).

8. Alan J. Davis, "Sexual Assaults in the Philadelphia Prison System and Sheriff's Vans," *Transaction*, December 1968.

9. On November 30, 1967, Cook County Jail held 1913 inmates. Of these, 88 were awaiting trial in federal court, 1449 were awaiting trial or court action in local courts. Only 464 inmates were serving sentences (see note 7). Of the 1654 women held in Cook County in 1964, only 99 were sentenced to do time there.

10. The deterrent effect of prisons is familiar to anyone involved in draft resistance: the number of draft resisters would no doubt increase were there no prison sentence given for resistance, though by how much no one knows. This illustrates that imprisonment may deter socially desirable as well as socially undesirable acts.

11. George Rusche and Otto Kirchheimer, *Punishment and Social Structure* (New York: Russell and Russell, 1968), pp. 193–205.

12. Thorsten Sellin, "The Death Penalty Relative to Deterrence and Police Safety," in Johnston, Savitz and Wolfgang, *Sociology of Punishment*, p. 74.

13. Paul W. Tappan, *Crime, Justice and Correction* (New York: McGraw-Hill, 1960), p. 363.

14. Due to cases of arrests not being reported, quoted figures may underestimate the true rate of recidivism, especially for older data. Another factor that leads to underestimation of the true recidivism rate is that data report only arrests, that is, cases where the criminal was caught. If the crime was committed successfully the information will not be reflected in recidivism rates. This factor is never mentioned in sociological studies of recidivism, showing how even impartial and "objective" observers tend unconsciously to accept official values of the prison administration, which mostly concern themselves with the narrow functioning of the prison system, rather than with the society at large.

15. S. Glueck and E. T. Glueck, *Unravelling Juvenile Delinquency* (New York: The Commonwealth Fund, 1950); *After-Conduct of Discharged Offenders* (Oxford: Oxford University Press, 1949), p. 20; *500 Criminal Careers* (New York: A. A. Knopf, 1930), pp. 191–2; *Criminal Careers in Retrospect* (New York: The Commonwealth Fund, 1943), pp. 121–2; Stanley B. Zuckerman, Alfred J. Barron and Horace B. Whittier, "A Follow-up Study of Minnesota State Reformatory Inmates," *Journal of Criminal Law, Criminology and Police Science* (January–February 1953), p. 622; John C. Ball, "The Extent of Recidivism among Juvenile Delinquents in a Metropolitan Area," *Journal of Research in Crime and Delinquency* (July 1965), p. 77; Daniel Glaser, *The Effectiveness of a Prison and Parole System* (New York: Bobbs-Merrill, 1964).

16. George Vold, "Does the Prison Reform?" *Annals of the American Academy of Political and Social Science*, May 1954, p. 42.

17. Caleb Foote, "The Bail System and Equal Justice," *Federal Probation*, September 1955, p. 43.

18. Glaser, *Effectiveness of Prison and Parole System*, pp. 504–13.

19. When the population density of caged rats exceeds a critical level, the rate of violence and sexual deviation increases dramatically. Although the extrapolation to human behavior is of course an uncertain one, the rat experiments are at least suggestive in their implications for prison society.

20. John H. Gagnon and William Simon, "The Social Meaning of Prison Homosexuality," *Federal Probation*, March 1968, p. 23.

21. According to James V. Bennett, former Director of the Federal Bureau of Prisons, in "A Cool Look at the Crime Crisis," *Harpers*, April 1964, p. 125, "Our criminal laws are the most severe in the world, and our legislative bodies are still at work making them more severe. . . . Only in America do we find, occasionally, sentences of 199 years and 100 years, and regularly sentences of 30, 40 and 50 years. In England in the course of a year no more than 150 men are likely to be given sentences of 5 years or more. In the United States the number is about 15,000."

22. Alfred Hassler, *Diary of a Self-Made Convict* (Chicago: Regnery, 1954), p. 97.

23. Glaser, *The Effectiveness of Prison and Parole System*, pp. 504–13.

24. Shaw, *Crime of Imprisonment*, p. 18. Quakers have long been concerned about prison conditions. Solitary confinement, in fact, is a reform urged by Quakers, who thought it would help wrongdoers repent. Such has not proved to be the case. Today solitary confinement is one of the forms of punishment most feared by prisoners.

25. I. Kant, *Rechtslehre*, trans. E. Hastie (Edinburgh: 1887), pp. 195–8.

26. For a thorough exploration of such questions, see A. C. Ewing, *The Morality of Punishment* (London: Kagan, Paul, Trench, Trubner and Co,. Ltd., 1929); Edmund L. Pincoffs, *The Rationale of Legal Punishment* (New York: Humanities Press, 1966); Brand Blanshard, "Retribution Revisited" in *Philosophical Perspectives on Punishment*, ed. Edward H. Madden, Rollo Handy and Marvin Farber (Springfield, Ill.: Charles C. Thomas Publishers, 1968) pp. 59–93; and Sir Walter Moberly, *The Ethics of Punishment* (Hamden, Conn.: Hamden, 1968).

27. Rose Giallombardo, *Society of Women: A Study of a Women's Prison* (New York: John Wiley & Sons, 1966).

28. Ibid., p. 29.

29. Alfred C. Schnur, "The New Penology: Fact or Fiction?" *Journal of Criminal Law, Criminology and Police Science*, November–December 1958, p. 331.

30. Daniel Glaser and Kent Rice, "Crime, Age, and Employment," *American Sociological Review*, October 1959, p. 680.

31. Clifford R. Shaw and Henry D. McKay, *Juvenile Delinquency and Urban Areas* (Chicago: University of Chicago Press, 1942), pp. 151–57.

32. See note 30.

33. The Federal Bureau of Prisons issued a memorandum in 1967 ordering prison libraries closed. At present, some libraries are closed while others are still operating, according to current inmates of federal prisons.

34. See note 30.

35. Gresham M. Sykes, *The Society of Captives* (Princeton: Princeton University Press, 1958), pp. 68–83.

36. Gresham M. Sykes and Sheldon O. Messinger, "Inmate Social System," in *Theoretical Studies in Social Organization of the Prison* (Social Science Research Council pamphlet #15, New York, 1960), p. 93.

37. N. Hayner and E. Ash, "The Prison as Community," *American Sociological Review* 5 (1940): 527.

38. Ernest Ostro, *National Catholic Reporter*, 27 August 1969, p. 1.

39. Donald Cressey, "Limitations of Organization of Treatment in a Modern Prison," *Theoretical Studies in Social Organization of the Prison*, (Social Science Research pamphlet #15, New York, 1960).

40. See note 27.

41. Norman Fenton, Ernest G. Reimer, and Harry A. Wilmer, *The Correctional Community: An Introduction and Guide* (Berkeley: University of California Press, 1967), pp. 114–16.

42. H. Ashley Weeks, *Youthful Offenders at Highfields* (Ann Arbor: University of Michigan Press, 1958); Lloyd W. McCorkle, Albert Elias, and F. Lovell Bixby, *The Highfields Story* (New York: Henry Holt and Co., 1958).

43. Erving Goffman, *Asylums* (Garden City, N.Y.: Doubleday, 1961), pp. 321–86.

44. Donald P. Jewell, "Mexico's Trés Marias Penal Colony," *Journal of Criminal Law, Criminology and Police Science* 48 (1957): 410.

45. N. S. Trimasheff, *Journal of Criminal Law, Criminology and Police Science* 48 (1957): 608; Giles Playfair, "Without Bars: Some Bold (and Some Timorous) Experiments," *Harpers*, April 1964, pp. 174–75. I am grateful to Gene Keyes for this reference as well as for other helpful suggestions and comments.

46. Lowell Naeve, with David Wieck, *A Field of Broken Stones* (Glen Gardner, N.J.: Libertarian Press, 1950); Holley Cantine and Dachine Rainer, *Prison Etiquette* (Bearsville, New York: Retort Press, 1950).

47. *Thirty Years of Progress* (published by the Bureau of Prisons), pp. 22–24.

48. Sol Rubin, *Crime and Juvenile Delinquency* (New York: Oceana Publications, 1961), pp, 121–44.

49. John P. Conrad, *Crime and Its Correction: An International Survey of Attitudes and Practices* (Berkeley: University of California Press, 1967).

50. See note 27.

51. See note 17.

52. Will C. Turnbladh, "Substitutes for Imprisonment," *The Annals of the American Academy of Political and Social Science*, March 1954, p. 293.

53. According to "The National Profile of Correction," state institutional cost for adults is about 14 times that of probation (see note 2).

54. Columbus B. Hopper, "The Conjugal Visit at Mississippi State Penitentiary," *Journal of Criminal Law, Criminology and Police Science*, September 1962, p. 340.

55. See note 49.

1   Have you ever thought of committing a crime? What prevents you from committing crimes?

2   Do you personally know anyone who practices crime and is *not* arrested? What do you think of them and what they do?

3   Do you know any people who have served time in prison? What have they told you about what institutionalization is like?

4   Why do you think that almost all inmates in prisons are from the lower social and economic classes? Why are so few middle- and upper-class people in prison?

5   Who decides what is a crime? Have you ever been in a courtroom where a criminal offense was being tried? Describe what you saw there.

6   What kinds of words do you use to describe a person who is incarcerated? What perceptions do you have of prisoners? Would you associate or become friends with anyone who had been in prison?

7   Is an individual completely responsible for a crime he commits? Where else might responsibility lie? Do you agree with the author's view that society's values may lead some people to commit crimes?

8   Do you think that the abolition of prisons is a responsible and realistic goal?

READINGS

Jackson, Bruce. *Outside the Law: A Thief Primer.* New Brunswick, N.J.: Transaction Books, 1972.

Klockars, Carl. *The Professional Fence.* New York: The Free Press, 1974.

Quinney, Richard. *The Social Reality of Crime.* Boston: Little, Brown, 1970.

Rossett, Arthur, and Cresey, Donald. *Justice By Consent.* Philadelphia: J. B. Lippincott, 1976.

Schur, Edwin. *Radical Nonintervention.* Englewood Cliffs, N.J.: Prentice-Hall, 1973.

Sommer, Robert. *The End of Imprisonment.* New York: Oxford University Press, 1976.

Sykes, Gresham. *The Society of Captives.* Princeton: Princeton University Press, 1958.

HIGH COURT BACKS ARRESTS IN PUBLIC WITH NO WARRANT

(Washington, D.C.) Over the harsh dissent of its two most liberal justices, the Supreme Court ruled today that the Constitution does not require law officials to get warrants before they make arrests in public places, even when there is adequate opportunity to obtain a warrant.

All the Constitution requires, the Court said by a vote of six to two, is that the official have "probable cause," or good reason, to believe that the person being arrested committed a felony.

[*Lesley Oelsner,* New York Times, *27 January 1976.*]

WIDELY USED FOOD COLORING BANNED FOR SAFETY REASON

(Washington, D.C.) Capping a fifteen-year controversy, the Food and Drug Administration yesterday banned the country's most widely used food coloring because of questions about its safety.

However, millions of food, drug, and cosmetic products containing Red Dye No. 2 which are still on store shelves or in warehouses will not be recalled and will be sold to consumers.

[*Michael J. Coulon,* Boston Globe, *16 May 1976.*]

STAGGERING EXPENSES OF HAVING A BABY

Forget, for a moment, the buzzing confusion that greets infants at birth, and consider instead the rude awakening some parents experience —when they learn what childbirth costs.

Joan Weiss, who recently gave birth at New York-Cornell Hospital, had in her mind that the charges would run, oh, maybe $1,000 from start to finish, and when her doctor told her the fee would be $850, she thought that was the total. But that was his bill. Then came the hospital's which was in the vicinity of $1,200.

"I just didn't realize it would be up in the $2,000 range," she said, "and that my insurance would only cover about $300 of it."

[*Richard Flaste,* New York Times, *23 January 1976.*]

FBI MAN ADMITS ROLE IN BREAK-INS

(Washington, D.C.) An agent of the Federal Bureau of Investigation has testified under oath that he participated in "between fifty and ninety" burglaries of the Socialist Workers Party headquarters in New York, according to a deposition made public today.

[*Nicholas M. Horrock,* New York Times, *28 July 1976.*]

W HAT *shall we do with our great cities?" intoned the Reverend Lyman Abbott. "What will our great cities do with us? These are two problems which confront every thoughtful American." The year was 1819. The census of 1820 listed 100,000 persons living in New York City, the largest city in the country. It was a prophetic and sad comment on the city in American society.*

The American attitude toward the city has been at best one of ambivalence—at worst, one of outright rejection. Novels, short stories, plays, movies, television, and songs have sung the praise of rural, small-town, and farm America and have essentially scorned the urban areas. The veneration of pastoral life with its alleged contact with the Deity and all virtue is to be contrasted with the image of the city, filled with conflict, violence, human corruption, and environmental pollution.

Simply put, the complex problems confronting the cities in contemporary America are not merely the consequence of age or size, racial tension, density, or economic malaise, but to a large extent the result of our refusal to accept the city as a viable place in which to live and bring up our children—in short, to call home. Moreover, as Robert Ross has deftly noted, the special problems of the city go beyond antiurban bias; they are "the results of industrial capitalism, which sorts out the rewards and burdens of its way of life according to one's class."

One of the promised places of escape from the city has traditionally been the region adjacent to but removed from the city proper, the suburb. A frontier for the middle class, the suburb has provided the best of both worlds. The suburban dweller has had the benefits of a semipastoral existence in the form of land (backyard and front lawn), nature (flowers, trees, grass), cleanliness (refuse-free streets), low density and limited structures, and many single-family houses; at the same time he has reaped the economic and cultural benefits of the city. Jay Ostrower maintains, however, that this scene is turning sour. In "The Future Suburbs: The Closing of the Frontier," he predicts that future suburban agglomerations will confront problems similar to those now plaguing the cities. As the distinction between the two areas narrows, the housing problems of this country demand a comprehensive policy.

TROUBLED DWELLINGS

8 | THE STATE OF URBAN SOCIETY

ROBERT J. ROSS

Most Americans do not live in big cities. They fear and avoid them, but need them. Of the big-city dwellers—one of every three Americans (31 percent)—a majority would rather live elsewhere. They complain of fear, poor public services—especially schools—and the burden of numerous petty hassles in everyday life. Inadequate public transportation, rising housing costs, a surly climate of ill-will—the list can be extended indefinitely. Though the fires of racial insurrection no longer glow in the cities' summertime skies as they did between 1964 and 1971, the city itself remains an issue in American society. By the mid-seventies the form that issue assumed was the vituperative debate over the fiscal crisis of New York City in 1975, epitomizing the financial woes of other big cities. Yet our contemporary experience is no different from our past: the big cities have always been a focus of controversy in America—and usually despised because of it.

For Thomas Jefferson cities were sources of corruption, the enemies of democratic small landowners. Before the Civil War, such enlightened figures of American letters as Emerson, Thoreau, and Melville distrusted the new life emerging in the East Coast ports. Later, between 1880 and World War I the massive immigration of Catholics and Jews from eastern and southern Europe caused many to renew their view of urban degeneracy, adding the bitterness of ethnic hatred. This culminated in the bigoted Quota Act of 1924, which virtually curtailed immigration from these areas.

The first important signs of suburbanization occurred in the twenties, as automobile registration zoomed. In 1910 there were fewer than 500,000 motor vehicles registered in the United States; by 1930 just under 27 million were registered.[1] The Depression and World War II saw attention

United Press International

shift first to the problems of a failed industrial capitalism and then to the war against fascism. By the fifties, the suburban exodus was in full swing. Metropolitan areas outside the central cities grew by 46 percent between 1950 and 1960, and then again by 27 percent between 1960 and 1970. In the meantime large numbers of blacks were moving to the cities both within the South and from the South to northern and western cities. Their numbers in central cities increased 51 percent in the fifties, and then 32 percent in the sixties.

The rapid expansion of black areas of residence in big cities—ghettos—since the fifties is still creating controversy about the city. Some of the words have changed, but the melody is the same.

From the founding of the republic, many of the privileged and articulate members of American society have seen the city as the place of strangers—and the city's diversity of cultural backgrounds has made many Americans feel unwelcome in what they chose to define as their own land. The strangeness is sometimes activity: "we" are farmers; "they" are laborers. Sometimes it has been nationality: "we" are American—that is, from northern and western Europe; "they" are foreigners—from south and east of where our forebears lived. Now it is "we" who are fair skinned, earning our way; "they" are dark and poor.

Racism is not the whole of the "city" issue, not even the largest part. But it holds our attention because it is so familiar—and so intractable. Having lost the battle to control their own neighborhood schools, blacks now uneasily acquiesce to busing—and are faced by angry white residents who do not. When we think of the cities, the issue of race relations is never far from our minds.

II

When people talk about the social problems of cities they usually mean problems which afflict the people who live there. To be sure, big cities have collective problems which can be distinguished from those afflicting specific groups. The eroding tax base of most cities is one of these collective issues. It affects city dwellers powerfully (for example, in the form of rising property tax rates and rents), but is a step or two removed from the direct experience of the high cost of living. More typically, when people talk about social problems in the city they mean that long list of fears and conditions that are associated with lives less than whole, hopes frustrated, possibilities ignored. Drug addiction, alcoholism, crime, poverty, racial oppression, slum housing—these are the conventional social problems of the city. There ought to be some way to link the larger structural or collective issues to those which are experienced by the different urban groups. This chapter tries to establish that link by focusing on specific groups of people and placing their problems in a historical and structural context. The groups we shall discuss are the white working class; the white middle class; the poor; and minority groups. Though it is possible and necessary to discuss them separately, the fact is that these groups share a place and a time in history; whether they like it or not (and they don't), their fates are interdependent. This was never clearer than during the period from 1965 to 1975. A quick look at this decade will set the stage for our discussion.

By 1965 two great movements of people across the country had culminated in riot and insurrection. The migration of southern blacks to northern, western—and southern—cities had finally transformed black Americans from a southern agrarian to an urban people.

A Decade Which Opened in Turmoil Ends in Squalor

The simultaneous suburbanization of white city dwellers resulted in what amounted to an exchange of populations. A rough estimate indicates that over ten million whites left the central cities between 1950 and 1970, while over three million blacks entered.[2] By 1970 this meant that over 58 percent of all blacks were living in the central cities of metropolitan areas; this contrasts to the situation in 1950, when 44 percent of all blacks lived in the central cities.[3] The opposing trend is the suburbanization of whites. In 1950 28 percent of all white persons lived in suburbs, and 35 percent in central cities; by 1970, about 28 percent lived in the central cities, and 40 percent lived in suburbs.

The black migration began during World War I, when labor contractors promised jobs and freedom to blacks who had known the poverty of cotton cropping and the terror of the lynch mob. Responding to the need for labor during the war, this wave ended in the bloody race riots of 1917 and 1919 in east St Louis, Chicago, Washington, and Houston. Once again, during World War II (but even more rapidly) blacks went north for work. Again, in Detroit in 1943, blacks and whites found the auto industry and the city too small for both of them. But this time the flow did not stop—and through the fifties, blacks continued north for jobs and for relief from violent racism.

They found some measure of both: but there were not enough jobs and there were more subtle forms of racism. By the time the fires of insurrection flared in Harlem in 1964 and in Watts (the black section of Los Angeles) in 1965, black rage and political militancy had become a significant factor in urban life. For six years every summer brought civil strife in hundreds of cities. The climax was in 1968. There were eighty riots, the largest of which were in Newark, Chicago, and Detroit. The damage was counted in hundreds of casualties and billions of dollars. Over fifty persons were killed between April and June alone.[4]

These were the years when poverty gained national attention and the administration of President Lyndon Johnson attempted various reforms.

But the underlying poverty was more than racial. The fact was that the decent jobs in manufacturing and industry were leaving the cities—following the white labor force and cheaper land and transportation costs to the suburbs. Black people had arrived as a force in urban life in time to inherit a drastically changing urban economy.

In manufacturing employment grew more than three times as fast in the suburbs as in the central cities during the mid-sixties. In retail trades, jobs were being created ten times faster in the suburbs during this period, while in wholesale trades suburban employment grew eight times as fast as city employment.[5]

This pattern of job creation was a symptom of the generally weak economic position of the central cities in relation to the metropolitan areas in general. Eighty-five of every hundred new jobs in manufacturing, retail and wholesale trades, and selected services were found in the suburbs between 1948 and 1967.[6] Thus, the entry-level jobs that might have given the poor and minority group members footholds in the changing economy were moving out of the cities, just as the proportions of such people were growing within the cities.

This pattern was fairly evident to social observers from the end of the 1940s on. One of the chief strategies used to deal with the problem was to design incentives to keep middle-class white residents in the city. By so doing, mayors and city planners hoped to keep within the central cities and their central business districts the shopping dollars of the more affluent (and the jobs these create), and also the kind of well-kept residential properties which produce more in taxes than they cost to service. To public officials and business people the matter of taxes is important because city services—especially health, police, and fire protection—are more costly in poor neighborhoods than in well-to-do ones. As the cities became poorer, their ability to pay for needed services fell behind their ability to raise revenue.

The most visible program used to effect this strategy was urban renewal. Briefly, this program was enacted at the federal level to subsidize investment in housing and commerce in the older neighborhoods and business areas of the cities. It allowed cities to use federal funds to pay for land taken by the city by the right of eminent domain, and to sell it back to real estate developers at less than the purchase price. Although originally intended to clear slums and improve housing for the poor, the program changed emphasis during the fifties. It had become evident that even with large subsidies developers could not or would not provide low-rent housing and make a profit. Moreover, in many places city officials and business people decided that providing housing for the well-to-do (and the shopping and civic improvements which would attract them) was more important.

Depending on one's point of view, the result was merely an unsuccessful attempt to solve a virtually insoluble problem, or a vast injustice to working people and poor citizens. Although the suburban exodus went on, the program tore down more housing than it built, and replaced low-rent with high-rent housing. Thus, the government subsidized the already affluent at the expense of the rest of the citizenry. In the process of doing so, two kinds of victims were specifically affected. As vividly described by Herbert Gans (in *The Urban Villagers*), one kind of victim was the ethnic working-class resident of a stable but low-income ethnic community. Gans's study, for example, was of Italians in the west end of Boston. These residents prized the stable, family-oriented life of a community in which they felt at home. When forced to leave because urban renewal was slated to bring in luxury high-rises and commercial facilities, many of these families experienced genuine grief and loneliness in new and strange surroundings.[7]

The other victims of these changes were black (or Spanish-speaking) and poor. Forced out of housing or areas to which they did not necessarily have strong attachments, these residents had to find their new housing in the segregated ghetto. An already overcrowded ghetto housing market was forced to expand to accommodate these new residents. In the black communities of the big cities urban renewal was known as "Negro removal," and was held responsible for making bad housing conditions worse.

United Press International

The resentment created by the urban renewal program was but one of many similar grievances that were shared by minority and poor white communities. As a small part of the War on Poverty (the rather dramatic title President Johnson gave his program to aid the poor during the period from 1964 to 1969), some funds were made available to support community organizations in poor areas within the big cities. The general idea (which was supported by some influential social scientists) was that poor people suffer from not having the opportunity to master their environments—compounding their lack of purchasing power, and making them even more helpless.

Thus, although expanded job training was seen as the major component of the antipoverty campaign, another small part was devoted to creating community organizations which would represent the interests of the poor. It was hoped, for example, that in a black community leadership would develop in such organizations, and that this leadership would then be better able to represent the community and resist the destructive uses of urban renewal.

One reason the Democratic Party leadership tolerated or supported this potentially contentious strategy was that the change in the cities' composition was having an impact on politics. The Democratic Party needed to ensure its ability to command very high percentages of the black vote in the cities. Poverty program money did go to almost every black neighborhood in the big cities. But party leaders did not anticipate one of the results of the program.

As the poverty program (and later the model cities program) was learning that its problem was in part based in the structure of society and of black communities, and was not just due to the failings of poor black individuals, the civil rights and black liberation movements were becoming influential in the northern cities. Black liberals, black militants, black revolutionaries, white liberals, white radicals, white professionals, city officials, and business people all fought to control the available federal funds. The shifting coalitions were complex, but in general black, Hispanic, and some poor white community leaders would unite around the position that they should control poverty and other federal-program spending in their areas. They argued that only they knew the reality of the problems of the poor. Moreover, only by creating self-governing institutions could such communities enter the mainstream of political life and create an atmosphere encouraging enough to counter the despair of life at the edge of indignity .

These demands were most frequently resisted by the cities' elected officials, who were reluctant to allow programs of such size to escape their control—especially when they knew they would be held responsible by the voters for demonstrations or other political embarrassments which might stem from such programs.

The professionals, as always, were divided. However, a very visible and sizable minority tended to support the claims of the black and the poor. When the residents of poor neighborhoods did frequently generate "militant" leadership, these professionals supported what became known as "community control."

The sense of crisis created by the riots of the sixties made the conflicts over these programs a dramatic symbol both of the questions raised by black militants and of the radicals' demands for the decentralization of power. Gradually, the storm passed as community organizing funds were cut due to the costs of the Vietnam War, the anger of the big-city mayors, and (most significantly) the election of a conservative administration under Richard Nixon in 1968.

The years of the conservative Nixon and Ford presidencies created a temporary lull in the storm. The potential conflict over the relative importance of integration versus self-government for the urban minority poor was barely joined before it became irrelevant. The change in Washington brought hard times and the retreat of the federal government from active involvement in the social problems of the cities. Americans of all classes and races turned their attention to the cost of living and to unemployment, for by 1973 a depression had begun.

We can now examine the condition of the classes and races in urban society in the mid-seventies.

For those who can afford it, the city still offers a variety of work and leisure opportunities that simply can't be found elsewhere. And if we focus on the very big cities which are also the centers of national life—Los Angeles, New York, Chicago, and Boston—we find the glamor of fame and the possibility of high style. However, except for a very few places, one senses an intense demoralization of the urban middle and upper classes. They are afraid, at least one-third of them, to walk outside their homes at night.[8] This is part of a larger fear of the night-time city: a fear of violence and theft, of using what public transportation exists, a fear of the mugger and the junkie. The affluent share this fear, of course, with working-class city dwellers, whose anxiety is even greater. Indeed, the neighborhoods of the well-to-do are safer than those of the less affluent, while their financial ability to use private transportation renders fear of public transport less relevant. For the more affluent classes, however, the promise extended to them by city life is frustrated by environmental conditions which seem to have accumulated into ugliness and despair.

Density itself is not a problem. There is little empirical support for the popular notion that high-density living creates social pathology. But density and over-centralization do slow down traffic; they may create a concentration of pollutants that irritates the eyes and lungs; they may put open space at a premium. For those who want to stroll on boulevards, take the kids to a playground, or dash downtown to pick up some gifts in

The Urban Middle Classes: Problems of Comfort and Convenience

a specialty store, the city becomes a hassle. Nothing comes easy. These are problems of convenience which cities are not solving. So the attractions of urban life for the middle classes are decreasing. The trend is quite clear: for those who can afford it, the move to the suburbs continues to be the chosen path.

The affluent classes have more serious grievances, but these are frequently things which they can do something about on a personal basis. Education is an important example. The public schools of the city are not working, in the view of many of the educated and affluent urbanites. They want effective college preparation for their youngsters, and their preferences in educational styles are more oriented towards high culture and individual initiative than are those of other parts of the population. However, school financing continues to be mired in crisis, and the rather inflexible educational bureaucracies find keeping order in the classroom barely within their power. One solution for those who can afford it is to remove their children from public schools and put them in private schools. This is very costly, so the free public schools of the suburbs become more attractive still. The removal to the suburbs of many middle-class white youngsters who are apt to be academically successful further depresses the attraction of the city schools for the middle-class families who remain.

Another problem for the middle class is the spreading effect of the concentration of poor, minority, and deviant types within the city itself. As the middle classes cluster in suburban rings, they bring their shopping dollars with them. The suburban shopping plaza increasingly includes the kind of specialty store and smart shops which the well-to-do cherish as part of city life. In consequence, as the downtown shopping areas lose their distinctive charm, they lose their share of the retail trade. The shops age, profit margins decrease, and they carry smaller selections. Some shops go out of business or move to suburban areas. Finally, the porno shops and cheap dry goods stores move in. Daytime purse snatching and robbery become a problem, panhandlers embarrass passers-by. For these reasons, too, the middle-class urban family with school-age children is likely to succumb to suburban flight.

In the city, the singles bar and the "smart scene" are highly visible because much of the urban middle class is young, unmarried, or childless, and at the beginning stage of their careers. For some of these people, the city can be a lonely and confusing place. Away from their families and the homes and neighborhoods in which they were raised, frequently migrants from other cities, they are also away from childhood friends. Despite its superficial conviviality, the singles scene is a rather dreary mating game—and as most young men and women settle into the city and pass into their mid-twenties, it fades into a slightly embarrassing memory. Without ties of family, though, the single or childless young member of the middle class is not likely to develop strong neighborhood roots. A kind of cordial anonymity with apartment-house neighbors is maintained, but this is very different from the support and warmth of the extended family or of old neighborhood friends.

The high cost of housing in areas near entertainment and white-collar downtown jobs leads many young adults to share apartments. These residences, in turn, have a high turnover as yesterday's stewardess living on New York's East Side or in Chicago's Old Town becomes tomorrow's married suburbanite.

During the sixties, many members of the middle class saw urban problems as an expression of black poverty. But as the economy weakened in the seventies and the black movement waned, the economic pressures on middle-class life itself increased. These pressures are likely to continue and to grow. The move to the suburbs is becoming more expensive, as mortgage and construction costs put new housing out of the reach of all but the wealthiest families. Automobile commuting is also cutting into the family budget, as gasoline and automobile prices increase. Thus, the coming generation of middle-class urban families are apt to be discontent. They will want to move, but many will not be able to; the compensations of urban life will pale beside the anxiety and cost it entails. These frustrations may take different political directions—some of which are already taking form.

One response to these economic pressures is the end of the liberal-black coalitions which defined many cities' politics from the mid-sixties to the seventies. If middle-class people define taxes and street crime as the villains, then austere budgets and aggressive policing—a swing to the right in city politics—can triumph. This happened in the victory of Mayor Frank Rizzo in Philadelphia, in Ralph Perk's election in Cleveland, and was characteristic of the late Mayor Richard J. Daley's dominance in Chicago. Contrary to expectations, this political thrust has not recaptured the glamor of city life for the middle class.

The prospects for a middle-class reformist movement are not bright. After the War on Poverty and the Great Society programs of the sixties, many people became disillusioned. They did not quite understand the turmoil of the early seventies, but they knew that nothing worked very well and that prices were high. New Yorkers, once proud of their city's extensive social services, found themselves confronted with just as much misery and addiction and poverty as before—and with municipal bank-ruptcy as well.

These trends add up to a kind of political passivity—a loss of will and nerve. The urban middle class is hunkering down. They feel they are in a state of siege. The weak economy of the seventies appears more person-ally and immediately threatening than the environment of the city itself. So the accountant hangs on: he hopes he keeps his job, that his taxes (which rose 200 percent from the early sixties to the seventies) stay level, and that his kids will not be beaten up in school or beaten out of competition for a place in law school. He goes to concerts or plays less frequently and does less fancy eating. The trip downtown is more hurried, and the 11 P.M. return more anxious. Yesterday's brave rhetoric about new directions in city life has become today's grim resignation to keeping one's own family above water—and the noble intention to help the less fortunate now seems like quixotic idealism. For the urban middle classes the mid-seventies were not a time to dare, but to protect. In this attitude the once affluent are forced willy-nilly towards accepting a position the white working class have held for a long time. If the sixties were "go-go" for the affluent and the stock market, they were clearly not so for those whose jobs, neighborhoods, and schools were the victims of the period.

The White Working Class: Once More, Scarcity

High unemployment, rising consumer prices, and depression in such key industries as construction and automobile manufacturing have pushed working-class purchasing power back to the levels of the early sixties. In the meantime, the processes which created working-class discontent during the sixties continue. Chief among these are the changes disrupting the neighborhoods and schools central to working-class life.

For the second, third, and fourth generations of immigrant Catholics, success has meant attaining a steady job and a small house in a quiet neighborhood. Expanding productivity and unionization appeared to provide steady increments in real income, this making possible credit payments for many of the possessions which came to symbolize security. But in the postwar the neighborhoods settled by Lithuanian, Italian, Polish, Czech, and Irish workers have repeatedly come under sustained attack through shifts in the shape and context of urban life.

Federal highway and urban renewal projects have bulldozed many such neighborhoods, forcing their residents to move—many times to anonymous places where the comfort and support of extended family and familiar parish churches were not present. The expansion of black communities, caused frequently by the same programs, has meant that working-class neighborhoods were changed racially. As poorer black neighbors settled in higher densities, the resultant overcrowding outpaced city services such as garbage removal, and landlords followed reduced-maintenance programs even though the population rose. Thus, policy and population changes have disrupted the stable neighborhoods so greatly prized by ethnic workers.

No less disturbing has been racial change in schools—including busing. Paying taxes for public schools (and, in shrinking numbers, tuition for parochial schools), many working-class families look out on a city which seems dominated by affluent whites and poor blacks, denying them even the solace of secure and safe neighborhoods.

To many such families, programs of aid to the poor were programs for blacks. This was not completely true, but it was especially galling to workers whose families had known want and attained stability through great hardship. The bitterest pill now is competition for jobs and for places in schools and in colleges for their children. "We made it," they believe, "why can't the blacks!" Such families built their livelihoods and neighborhoods in periods when unskilled labor was still in demand within the cities' boundaries . The next groups in the waves of city-bound immigrants, the blacks and the Spanish-speaking, find no such demand for their labor. Consequently, high unemployment rates among the poor minorities are seen by white workers as laziness, and they thereby mistake a new period in economic history for cultural character.

Whatever the source of racial and cultural antagonism, the ethnic working class feels pressured: in their neighborhoods, at work, and now in their moral values. Since many are Catholic, the changes in social values which became so visible during the sixties are especially threatening. Abortion and liberalized divorce are on the surface of this sense of injured values. Below the surface lie the traditional values and lifestyles that present the patriarchal family as the ideal, offering a sense of satisfaction from family life which cannot be gained through wealth or fame as a city worker or in the construction trades. The image of the "liberated" woman has connotations which appear to demean what these working-class families have achieved. If an Italian woman married to a plumber works as a clerk, it is not because she has liberated herself and can now fulfill herself by using her talents in meaningful employment, but because she must do so to make ends meet. She is all the more bitter when her ideal of domesticity is attacked by young women campaigning for admission to law school or for free abortions.

The standard of living which many Americans now call "middle class" had been attained by many such working-class families by the late sixties. Two incomes insufficient in themselves were combined to produce a family income which purchased, with credit, the possessions and homes which have come to define comfort. When unemployment is at the relatively high levels of the mid-seventies, such families are apt to lose that all-important second income, for unemployment is high among women but below the national average for white men who head families. The effect of unemployment plus inflation has been to drive working-class purchasing power back to the levels of the early sixties. This is the first time since World War II that so much material progress has been wiped out. The insecurity and anxiety it produced are understandable.

Even as the economy began to improve in late 1976 and early 1977, the outlook was for continuing high levels of unemployment through the rest of the decade. And inflation, while lower in 1976 than it had been for the four years preceding, was still high enough to hold back working class purchasing power. The expansionist economic horizons of the sixties are not likely to be repeated for working people, even though the recession of the mid-seventies is technically over.

Added to the pressures of an economy gone sour is the soaring crime rate which appears to have been (in part at least) caused by that economic retreat. In the big cities, when people are asked about the problems of their communities, they name crime more than any other problem—and workers are no exception. One-third of the respondents to a Gallup poll conducted in the biggest cities in 1975 reported that they had been victimized in the last year. Over 50 percent of that sample reported that they were afraid to walk in their neighborhoods at night. The poorer one was, the more apt one was to report such fears—reflecting the greater dangers of working-class and poor neighborhoods.[9]

In cities today, white workers are the victims of an economic insecurity unknown since the Great Depression of the thirties. They are victims of neighborhood changes which threaten the small social worlds which protected them from a larger society that does not value their achievements. They feel victimized by racial and social changes which challenge their values of thrift and hard work, their way of life, and their cultural ideals. They share with others anxiety about crime. As a result they sometimes support a defensive politics given to right-wing populism.

In this environment of pressure and change, there is a constant temptation to blame blacks and "middle-class liberals" for a quasi-conspiratorial attack on what the workers call the "American way of life." Governor George Wallace of Alabama successfully appealed to this during most of his career. On the other hand, the jobs, credit, and homes that workers want, and the dignified stability they want in their neighborhoods, could provide the basis for a political program benefiting both blacks and whites. A politician who could formulate a credible populist program for the left could perhaps defuse the racist populism of the right.

In the meantime, defense of the working-class neighborhoods has become the most characteristic working-class response to the seventies. There is no other place to go: new homes in the suburbs are out of reach, and there are no new tracts of land for development in the cities themselves. Fear of crime, blacks, and cultural change, resistance to taxes which take from one-quarter to one-third of their incomes, and fear for their children's future have added an angry tone to the community life of the working class. The direction of that anger is the great question for the remainder of the seventies.

The Poor and Minority Group: Survival

While the economy was booming and the Great Society programs growing, a feeling of anger pervaded the black ghettos and Hispanic barrios of the big cities. The riots of the sixties announced the arrival of a "new ghetto man," no longer content to be a last-hired, first-fired, second-class citizen.

But hard times, the conservative Nixon and Ford administrations in

Washington, and the breakup of the black movement have come together to shift the national focus of attention away from the problems of poverty and racial inequality. Despite substantial gains made by new black and Latin entrants to the stable working class and lower middle class, for the bulk of the poor minorities life is a grim search for enough money to keep families together and adequately nourished. Housing for these groups continues to be disproportionately dilapidated, income from welfare and laboring jobs trail behind rising prices, and neighborhood life is filled with fear, crime, and violence. While many courageously cope as best they can, other families fail to keep together. Youngsters drop out of hostile schools only to find no work, and fall prey to the pathologies of street life: heroin, hustling, and petty crime. Fathers and husbands despair of finding and wander off in search of jobs elsewhere, or avail themselves of the ever-present solace of drink and drugs. Left with welfare, mothers adapt as best they can, leaning on sisters, aunts, and parents to help raise children who *do* have hope—in fact, high hopes—but poor prospects. The honky-tonk verve of life in the streets masks the despair of lives fated never to be fulfilled. During hard times life back in the southern countryside or on Puerto Rico becomes, perhaps, a fond memory. But few return. There are fewer jobs and worse pay back home and, however inadequate and despised, northern welfare programs can keep people alive.

Despite the comparative advantages of city life, the infants of the poor die before they reach their first birthday about twice as often as the children of affluent whites. Their parents' poor diet and poor living conditions produce much more physical and mental illness. The care they receive in overburdened public health institutions is impeded by red tape, and is frequently a long journey away.

Transportation—or the lack of it—prevents many workers from following manufacturing jobs to the suburbs; and restrictive zoning in the suburbs makes it impossible to build low-rent housing near these jobs. Since the economics of the big cities are not growing even in good times, the prospects for the post–Vietnam War poor are not good. They suffer more than any other group from inflation and unemployment, and their poverty is all the more bitter because our standards for material decency have increased so much.

At the turn of the century working class immigrants were poor, but they had work and they had the solace of sharing the condition of their class. For the new poor, without work or in service jobs at the bottom of the occupational structure, the images of affluence surrounding them are a constant reminder of their lowly condition. The psychological distance between them and their material ideals presented in "television normality" makes them feel further from attainment than ever the immigrants did.

In this context the recourse to crime by teenage and young adult men (and increasingly by women) is a double burden. For residents of poor neighborhoods, the danger of a life of poverty and ill health is doubled by the danger of the mugger or thief. Indeed, the poor fear crime about twice as much as the affluent. Mothers fear for their children's safety, but fear too that their older children will become a threat to others. For those who become entangled with the law, a dreary series of probation and ineffective social programs finally becomes jail and ultimate brutalization. A cynical matter-of-factness grows up in the neighborhoods. The law neither protects effectively nor proceeds justly. People want police protection, but they do not trust the police, who, they feel, despise them. The poor and minority community is a sea of violence in which islands of residents try to shut out a threatening world.

From time to time an event or an issue mobilizes anger, and militant demands for jobs, income, schools, or protection from police brutality are heard. In some places this anger has been capitalized upon by a new generation of black and Latin politicians. However, even where there is a black and Latin city majority, the necessary change in the urban economy is not within the power of city government to generate.

The emphasis on community participation and control which characterized the late sixties has faded now. As a black planner cynically titled his skeptical article about neighborhood participation in social planning, "Model Cities, Model Airplanes, Model Trains." The banks and the Washington decision makers decide the direction of the economy, not the neighborhood. The demand for citizen participation did significantly affect the ways in which social programs are administered. But it did not greatly affect the content of the programs. Now even these have dried up.

It is difficult to see much improvement for the urban poor, for the American economy is sluggish and it is jobs, not services, which reduce poverty. In this the poor and the white working class share a common need—jobs for all who can and want to work. Whether this community of interest will overcome the racial tensions in schools and neighborhoods remains to be seen. In the meantime, in the center of the great cities, American civilization is being tested and found wanting. That failure, and its underlying economic structure, is making the dream of city life a nightmare for city residents.

An Epilogue on Issues and Problems   Between lack of money and race hostility our big cities are being ground into deeper squalor. We should realize, of course, that our standards change, and our expectations always increase. Eldridge Cleaver, the black American who was once a revolutionary, wrote that being oppressed in America is like being crushed between two pieces of silk. American cities house most of America's black people, and that fact lurks behind every issue, every attitude, and every program concerned with urban policy.

But racism and social oppression are only starting points for understanding the city as an issue and as a problem. To go further one must clarify the difference between a social issue and a social problem. A social issue is matter of public concern around which organized groups contend for advantage or survival, and about which large numbers of people believe some public decision is necessary. A social problem is or may be more diffuse: it is publicly recognized as distressing by significant numbers of people, some of whom have public influence, but has not stimulated the organization of interested classes and parties. Thus, for example, the *problem* of energy consumption and conservation had been recognized for a long time before it became an *issue*. A problem is what someone claims is causing distress or will cause distress in the future; it becomes social when numbers of others besides the claimant agree, or when they experience that distress and communicate with each other about it.

Given these concepts, the cities have a few key problems. These are primarily problems of finance, investment, and the creation of work. Of course there are scores of groups which focus on such symptoms as child abuse and drug addiction. They thereby perceive and define social problems. Only a few of these socially-perceived problems become broad matters of contention—social issues.

The social problems of the cities are only rarely specifically urban. They are usually the results of industrial capitalism, which sorts out the rewards and burdens of life according to one's class position. When lack of opportunity produces despair, or competition creates intense stress, the personal problems produced appear to be individual problems: alcoholism, drug addiction, school failure. But the issues about which people become angry and active rarely focus on the causes of the problems. New York City, for example, was attacked for having too many employees and too extravagant a pension program. But it was a lack of jobs in business which created the poverty resulting in a need for the public payrolls and the city workers' demand for security through pensions.

The "solution" to the issue of New York's fiscal crisis—firing people and cutting back services—will merely reproduce and intensify the cycle. New York's problem is that sources of investment capital (to produce jobs) and public revenue (to support services and income for those unable to work) are at the mercy of banks, and not made available to a city the size of many countries.

Taking urban power from fast talking politicians and giving it to slick bankers will not solve the problems behind the racism, poverty, and insecurity which plague so many urban dwellers. During the mid-seventies, long after America had become a corporate society, the very rich maintained national power and local influence by cloaking their ambition in the mythic garments of free enterprise. More than any other advance, solutions to our cities' problems now depend on discarding these myths and confronting the nature of our economy. This will entail widespread understanding of the nature of advanced capitalism and opening once again the historic discussion of the meaning of socialist democracy and its possibility in America. The crisis of the late seventies for urban America is forecast in New York. When we are done with shadowboxing against phony issues perhaps the economic solutions will be found, solutions which will produce work and income to ease the cities' problems.

SOLUTIONS THAT DIDN'T WORK

A handful of federal programs which during the post–World War ll period composed the major national response to the changes in the central cities. Since America has never had a coherent urban policy, these programs worked at cross-purposes. The federal highway system and the urban renewal program were contradictory in effect, though some of their negative consequences were similar. Public housing and the War on Poverty—programs which by contrast have been oriented to the less privileged—have had mixed outcomes. When their achievements were compared with the inflated expectations their supporters aroused, these programs were publicly perceived as disappointments.

The federal highway system has provided a multibillion-dollar subsidy to the complex of interests centered on the automobile and trucking industries. It has made suburban real-estate speculation and suburban population growth possible. It has therefore been a major force in attracting both jobs and affluent residents from the city. In all these ways, the interstate highway system redistributed income from those people and uses most in need to those less in need. Mass transportation, an alternative form of public investment, has been so neglected that it may be too late, given the decentralized population of the metropolitan areas, for it to reverse the trend.

Even as the highways were built to take suburban residents to office jobs downtown, the urban renewal program was vainly trying to keep the middle class in town by subsidizing the costs of high-cost real-estate development for them. As this failed or became insufficient, the program attempted to resuscitate the waning attractions of central business districts (CBDs). But the blight of the cities, combined with highways offering a way out, spurred a white migration to the suburbs, and the CBDs continued to deteriorate.

Though the highway and urban renewal programs spent billions negating each other, they had the common effect of appropriating large amounts of land occupied by lower-income and working-class residents, thus disrupting neighborhoods and putting available housing at a premium for those in the lower third of the housing market.

public housing was thought to be a remedy for the
in our aging inner-city slums. A number of aspects of
ve weakened its positive potential. White Anglo
and politicians resisted the incursion of blacks and
g people from the ghetto and the barrio. The limited
program and the punitive ideology which dictates austere
e poor have made most low-income housing projects very
ated, and barren. Without simultaneous development of
child care, and other services, the concentration of hun-
sperately poor families in barrackslike structures has fre-
ulted in demoralized and even terrorized housing projects. As
ncreased maintenance costs beyond the ability of residents to
ased rents during the seventies, standards of security and
ss declined terribly. And new apartments were still not substi-
new job and educational opportunities. Public housing propo-
re now more modest in their claims for the social effects of
g than they once were, and they advocate low-rise, scattered site
ts.

The War on Poverty was a potpourri of programs which never
unted to much more than a large skirmish. Nevertheless, community
vices and organization were begun which had a major impact on the
pectations of residents of poor and minority communities, and on their
ility to represent themselves on the urban scene. From 1969 on these
programs were dismantled. In part, their emphasis on social services
seemed out of step with the renewed interest in employment and income
redistribution as the chief routes out of poverty. But the major reason for
their demise was a conservative mood which had become impatient with
racial conflict and was hostile to aiding the poor.

It is important to note that poor and black persons made great strides
during the sixties. However defective the programs of counseling, job
training, education, and community development for the poor were, their
virtue was that they were oriented to those most in need. In turn,
progress for these groups is the essential element in progress for our
cities. What we have learned is that subsidies to the affluent cannot deal
with poverty and that gross inequality—poverty—concentrated in the
cities creates a social climate injurious to all. Moreover, we now perceive
that the social programs of the sixties needed much greater backing in the
form of tax and income redistribution and economic policies of employment which would result in public investment. Without these essential
national policies, community-level services are built on hills of sand.

SUMMARY   This chapter reviews the deteriorating conditon of our big during the fifties and sixties. The great population shifts of these saw the exit from the cities of more affluent white residents leavin the suburbs, and the entrance of lower-income black and minority dents. Long-term changes in the structure of American industry sh employment opportunities in the cities during this period, creating a l demand for supportive services and income support; at the same time, tax base of the cities did not grow proportionately. Out of these pressu came the fiscal crises of cities like New York.

The state of urban society is examined by analyzing the problems three large groups of residents: the affluent whites, the working-cla whites, and the poor and minority-group residents. For the affluent whit middle class, the urban crisis is one of convenience—crime, poor schools poor services, and a weak economy all add up to a continuing pressure to flee to the suburbs. For those who can no longer afford the escalating price of new housing, resentment and a withdrawal from social innovations is predicted.

For the white working class in the cities, many of whom are members of Catholic ethnic groups, the weak economy has made the struggle for jobs and a decent standard of living much harder. Added to this economic insecurity, social and culture changes in society have challenged the religious, racial, and family ideologies of many working-class residents. Their resentments are expressed sometimes in rightist, sometimes in populist ways. The future of the city's political life depends to a great extent on the response its white workers make to the economic situation.

For poor and minority persons, the hope, militance, and modest gains of the sixties appear to have halted. For blacks, the attacks by Presidents Nixon and Ford on the Great Society poverty programs also resulted in a lull in militant activity. For the poor generally, the economic situation—and prospects through the 1980s—appear grim. More afraid of and victimized by crime than the other groups, the poor and the minorities often find themselves entangled with the law, the harsh life of the streets, and dependence on welfare. Coalitions with white workers could forge a program to aid both groups, but present racial tensions and the myths surrounding the fiscal crisis must be overcome for this to occur.

In the recent past the major federal investments in urban affairs have added to the problems of the central cities at least as much as they have alleviated them. The federal highway program made the suburbanization of people, industry, jobs, and services easier and probably more rapid than it otherwise would have been. The urban renewal program disrupted working-class and minority neighborhoods and actually reduced rather than increased the housing supply.

At the heart of the crisis of urban life is the long-term decline of job opportunities in the central cities as opposed to in the suburbs. Thus, the fiscal crisis of cities like New York (or to a lesser degree, Boston) is but one part of a general condition: the inability of city governments to pay for services out of current tax revenues. The other part of the crisis, more structural and more powerful in its impact on the lives of city dwellers, is the inability of urban economies to keep up with other sectors of the economy.

This analysis leads one to ask: What is the real problem which lurks beneath the surface of the ostensible public issues of the cities? The author concludes that it is the lack of capital investments in the central cities—which must be overcome to create jobs and improve the quality of life. Since the private sector will not, by current evidence, provide this solution, public or publicly regulated investment and job programs are the only alternative. Thus, the crisis of city life requires once again in the history of American politics the evaluation of capitalism, socialism, and other economic systems as effective ways to provide decent lives for all of our people.

NOTES

1. Department of Commerce, Bureau of the Census, *The Statistical Abstract of the United States: 1974* (Washington, D.C.: U.S. Government Printing Office, 1975), p. 547.

2. This figure corrects for natural increase due to the excess of births over deaths in both groups, but it does not correct for immigration from abroad for either group.

3. Ibid., p. 17.

4. *Statistical Abstract*, p. 148.

5. Noel Gist and Sylvia Fava, *Urban Society* (New York: Thomas C. Crowell, 1974), p. 267.

6. Ibid., p. 273.

7. Marc Fried, "Grieving for a Lost Home," in *The Urban Condition*, ed. Leonard Duhl (New York: Basic Books, 1963).

8. *The Gallup Opinion Index: Report Number 124* (Princeton: American Institute of Public Opinion, October 1975), p. 16.

9. Ibid.

1 How has the population mix of central cities changed in terms of race and income over the last generation?

2 How do suburbs and cities compare in terms of the growth of job opportunities?

3 Why were the urban renewal and highway programs adopted? What problems did they solve? to which did they add?

4 What were some features of the Great Society programs? Why did they come to an end?

5 What were some of the problems of middle-class urban dwellers?

6 What pressures are there on white working-class families in the cities?

7 What is different about the situation of minority and poor persons today contrasted to that of ethnic immigrants seventy years ago?

8 How would you define the "problems" of the cities? What would you do about them?

READINGS Drake, St. Clair and Cayton, Horace. *Black Metropolis*. New York: Harcourt Brace Jovanovich, 1945. The classic discussion of black communities.

Gans, Herbert. *Urban Villagers*. New York: Free Press, 1965. One of the best discussions of (Italian) ethnic working-class life, this book also treats urban renewal.

———. *People and Plans*. New York: Basic Books, 1968. Includes essays on suburban life, and many discussions of social problems.

———. *Levittowners*. New York: Pantheon, 1968. A superb case study of the move to the suburbs.

Gist, Noel, and Fova, Sylvia. *Urban Society*. 6th ed. New York: Thomas C. Crowell, 1974. A useful survey of urban sociology, this book has an extensive bibliography.

Liebow, Elliot. *Tally's Corner*. Boston: Little, Brown, 1967. An excellent study of a black community.

Moynihan, Daniel P. *Maximum Feasible Misunderstanding*. New York: Free Press, 1969. A critical conservative discussion of the War on Poverty.

O'Connor, James. *The Fiscal Crisis of the State*. New York: St. Martin's, 1973. A socialist discussion of the contemporary economic crisis in American cities.

Palen, John J. *The Urban World*. New York: McGraw-Hill, 1975. Another useful survey of urban sociology.

Pettengell, Robert, and Uppal, Jogindan S. *Can Cities Survive: The Fiscal Plight of American Cities*. New York: St. Martin's, 1974. A discussion of the finances of cities, this volume includes references to many more technical sources.

Piven, Frances Fox, and Cloward, Richard A. *The Politics of Turmoil*. New York: Pantheon, 1974. A series of discussions of recent social policy.

Report of the National Advisory Commission on Civil Disorders (the Kerner Commission). Washington, D.C.: 1968. A discussion of the racial change in cities and of the condition of black people.

Rothstein, Richard. "The Urban Ethnic Working Class." An influence on this chapter, this essay was published in *The Green Mountain Quarterly* and is available from the publisher (462 N. Main Street, Oshkosh, Wisconsin 54901).

Suttles, Gerald. *The Social Order of the Slum*. Chicago: University of Chicago Press, 1968. A discussion of an ethnic working-class neighborhood.

Tauber, Karl, and Tauber, Alma. *Negroes in Cities*. Chicago: Aldine, 1965.

Warner, Sam B., Jr. *The Urban Wilderness*. New York: Harper & Row, 1973. A good history of American cities which emphasizes economic forces.

Wilson, James Q., ed. *Urban Renewal: The Record and the Controversy*. Cambridge, Mass.: MIT Press, 1966. An extensive examination of urban renewal.

9 | THE FUTURE SUBURBS:

The Closing Frontier

JAY OSTROWER

The suburbs have been America's twentieth-century frontier. Urban dwellers in search of green, a house, the image of prosperity, and a better life for the children have been moving to the fringes of the cities. Potato farms, apple orchards, and swamps were bought by real estate speculators; over time land was subdivided; trolley lines, subways, and highways provided access to the hinterland; and the new pioneers moved from the city.

However, the suburb and the move to the fringe of the city is not new, nor exclusively American. In the Middle Ages the cities kept growing beyond their original walls. In the nineteenth-century the street-car companies brought residents to the suburbs in mid-Manhattan and Roxbury. In the twenties, the wilds of Brooklyn and the Bronx, small villages that are now the urban neighborhoods of New York, developed on the land opened to mass development by the expansion of the subway.

Because of the availability of large tracts of inexpensive land at the fringe of the developing cities, it has always been cheaper to continue to build outward on this land at lower densities than to redevelop land closer to the existing population. With the continued availability of relatively inexpensive new housing at the fringe, the movement out from the center traditionally became associated with the "expected" upward mobility of the American dream. The immigrants of the Lower East Side would move to an apartment in Brooklyn and their children subsequently would buy a house on Long Island. For most, the movement to the suburbs has signified a change in lifestyle: the suburban move of a young family meant buying their first house, rather than renting an urban apartment. The initial suburban move was accompanied by new experiences: having to drive a car to go shopping, having a backyard and grass to mow, and having upwardly mobile neighbors like oneself. The patio, the barbecue, and the carport all represent new terms related to this new lifestyle.

The suburban movement signified an antiurban bias, rooted deep in American tradition and values: the country was good, honest, and pure; the city was bad, evil, and corrupt. In *Levittowners: Ways of Life and Politics in a New Suburban Community,* Herbert Gans investigated the motivation of residents moving into this community at the fringe of the Philadelphia metropolitan area:

> People's reasons for moving to Levittown were primarily the need for more spacious housing and the desire to own a free-standing house—"to own our own home" as many put it . . . . those who came from aging apartments and row houses (in the city) placed special emphasis on getting a brand-new house and having a yard for children.[1]

The desire for more space and a pleasant environment also reflected a concern about position. A higher-paying job meant that one would have to demonstrate this increase in status: the more successful one became, the larger the house, the more green, and the richer the neighbors.

Although the suburban movement had been occurring for many years, after the second World War the full support of federal policy was placed behind the suburban lifestyle. Veterans were guaranteed no-down-payment, low-interest mortgages. Homeowners could deduct their mortgage interest payments from their taxes. Highways were built with federal and state funds. With the support and encouragement of the federal government, suburban expansion during the years after the war was massive. From 1950 the suburbs received about two-thirds of all the country's population growth: 64.3 percent between 1950 and 1960, and 70.5 percent from 1960 to 1970.[2]

Since World War II, the percentage of Americans living in cities and rural areas has declined. By 1970 76.3 million Americans or 37.6 percent of the nation lived in the suburbs of metropolitan areas of the nation. This is contrasted to 63.8 million or 31.4 percent in the cities, and 63.0 million or 31.0 percent outside the metropolitan areas. The number living in the suburbs has been projected to increase, and the increase in suburban political domination is already reflected in the membership of state legislatures and the Congress. People now are more likely to move from one suburb to another than from the city to the suburbs or from the rural areas to the suburbs. The residential population shift has been paralleled by a growth in suburban jobs. Between 1960 and 1970, in the fifteen largest metropolitan areas of the nation the number of persons employed in the suburbs increased by 43.6 percent, a gain of 3,086,000 jobs, while the number employed in those central cities declined by 6.9 percent, a loss of 836,000 jobs. With the increased suburban employment, fewer suburbanites are now commuting to central-city jobs. In 1960, 68 percent of all suburbanites worked in the suburbs. By 1970, this had increased to 72 percent.[3]

In the 1960s, Jean Gottman developed the term "megalopolis" to identify the growing together of the major metropolitan areas.[4] Major urban concentrations have developed along the East coast from Boston to Richmond, Virginia; on the West coast from San Francisco to San Diego; and in the Midwest from Chicago to Pittsburgh. New concentrations have been developing in Florida and along the Gulf Coast. These concentrations are basically suburban agglomerations that now dominate our national life.

The suburban nation is often viewed in contrast to the central cities of the metropolitan areas. The suburbs are largely white and the cities are increasingly occupied by blacks, Puerto Ricans, and other minorities. The suburbs are viewed as having fewer poor people and more rich people. The perception has been that the suburbs are free of crime and have good schools, while the city is unsafe and has bad schools.

The Suburban-Central City Conflict

This distinction between city and suburb is becoming one of the most divisive forces in American life, with consequences for our entire society. The growth of the suburban nation and the contrasting increased concentration of the poor and the black in the central city have not been independent phenomena.

In the fifties and sixties, the migration to the fringes was paralleled by a movement into the center. The central neighborhoods, occupied by older immigrant groups, had aging populations. The children of these older families moved to more "suburban" neighborhoods within or near the city, or bought the new single-family homes at the fringe. At the same time, black families migrating from the South, white families migrating from the Appalachian region, and rural families migrating from Puerto Rico moved into these neighborhoods to seek available and relatively inexpensive housing. The movement of the new families into the urban neighborhoods prompted those older residents still remaining to move. Some real estate brokers devised "panic selling" techniques; they encouraged black migration into new neighborhoods by playing to the racial fears of the residents. They "block busted" areas on the fringes of minority settlement, opening new neighborhoods to the continued movement from the South. In the early seventies, the continued movement of middle-class families out of the urban neighborhoods and the increasing spread of black and other new residents across the city was accompanied by the tapering off of migration from the South. Without a continued large-scale migration into the older and deteriorating sections of the city that were losing population, the inner-city neighborhoods began to experience wholesale abandonment. These deteriorating sections and the areas that lower-income populations live in comprise a major portion of America's cities.

The white movement from the city in the fifties and sixties was the result of continued prosperity and only incidentally a flight from new neighbors. Without the financial ability to move and to obtain credit as well as the continued desire for a suburban lifestyle, those families who moved would never have been able to leave the older neighborhoods. As black families began to benefit from Vietnam-era prosperity in the late sixties, they too began to move from their initial areas of settlement and to buy homes in less densely populated residential neighborhoods. Class differences began to become increasingly evident in the black community, and areas of slightly more prosperous black families began to exist distinct from the original areas of black settlement, which were now occupied by the poorest members of the black community.

As the city grew outward one would have expected the municipal boundary to change to follow this development. But as development continued the new suburban communities became parts of existing small towns with already formalized municipal structures. In only a very few cases, such as the growing Texas cities, could the corporate boundaries expand to include the fringe developments. In other states new residents could incorporate themselves as a municipality, and then it was impossible for the city to annex its newly developed neighbors. The result of this process has been described for the New York region, a

> governmental arrangement perhaps more complicated than any other that mankind has yet contrived or allowed to happen. A vigorous metropolitan area, the economic capital of the nation, governs itself by means of 1,467 distinct political entities (at latest count), each having its own power to raise and spend the public treasure, and each operating in a jurisdiction more by chance than design.[5]

Basically, each municipality is given the power by the state to regulate its own development, tax its citizens, and finance its services independent of regional considerations. The separate communities in the metropolitan areas have generally used these powers to strengthen their own position in relation to the central city. Most local services are financed from property taxes that are levied on the value of the homes, businesses, and industries within the municipality. In order to increase tax yield, communities have regulated or attempted to attract new development to produce increased revenues. This is called "fiscal zoning." Industry and large commercial developments provide good tax yields with minimal service requirements. In the past, local governments felt that low-density single-family housing would generate fewer school costs than dense single-family or multi-family housing; although this belief is not correct, they have zoned to attract such uses and discourage others.

Those suburbs with new highway access, large available low-cost land areas, and lower taxes have been able to continually attract the new large-scale developments. Those towns and cities with wealthier citizens, who pay high property taxes, have been able to finance the "good"

schools and services that have continually attracted young families with children. Because of higher property values and a low-density population, they have been able to provide better services at lower property-tax rates.

The consequences of the political division of the metropolitan area is that the social divisions between suburb and city are continually reinforced by the ability of suburban communities to attract new industry and middle-income housing, with the parallel exclusion of low-income housing. This has resulted in the continued concentration of the lower-income population in the central cities. As industrial and residential wealth has moved to the suburbs, the ability to finance city services has moved with it. The central cities require increased revenue to finance services for a growing lower-income population at a time when the wealthier populations are continuing to concentrate at the fringe. The financial plight of the City of New York has roots in this situation. At a time of increasing need, suburban municipalities are now even more anxious to maintain their tax base for their own citizens, rather than to contribute broadly to regional needs.

The suburbs have also regulated their development simply to preserve their "distinctive character." They have used zoning as a tool to maintain the class uniformity of the community. Many communities have allowed only single-family home construction, on large lots, with specific design requirements that increase home prices. Some communities have not allowed sewer construction that would accommodate multi-unit housing. While now allowing higher-density housing, they have restricted these apartments to units with few bedrooms and therefore few children. When suburban communities have allowed low-income housing, it has been solely for occupancy by the elderly.

The Suburban World: A Precarious Alliance

Even though the suburban-central city conflict is becoming one of the major elements in American political life, the contrasts and distinctions among suburban communities are becoming increasingly significant. Most people tend to maintain a uniform image of the suburban lifestyle, an image reinforced by films, television, and books. This image has been the picture of the middle-class suburb: Protestant family with two or three children, ranch house, station wagon, little theater groups, and husband who commutes to his corporate job in the city. However, in spite of the lower density, greenery, and several perceptions they share, the suburban white population is extremely varied. They reflect significant differences in income, social class, age, family status, politics, ideas, ethnicity, and religion.

These differences tend to correspond to whole suburban municipalities, with each community attempting to maintain its unique character. Not only are blacks isolated from large portions of the white population, but whites are separated from each other by community differences that are strongly maintained.

Most suburbs developed during a short time, with similar houses sold at comparable prices. Because of this, individuals who moved into a town were generally similar in age, income, occupation, and lifestyle. Despite America's high mobility, most families have maintained a stable home while the children were in school. Communities have therefore tended to change and "age" collectively.

As these individual communities change, the suburban coalition of interest erodes, with some municipalities beginning to develop a closer identity with the central cities. However, other suburban communities, in spite of a growing similarity to the cities in population and problems, are attempting to maintain the distinction between themselves and the cities even more vociferously than before. At the same time, the newer and wealthier communities maintain their aloofness and attempt to protect their own character and environment, avoiding the concerns of the other communities.

The older suburban communities closest to the cities generally contain the older population. These communities were built at a higher density, often with multi-family dwellings combined with the traditional suburban single-family homes. Some suburban communities are similar in character to the city neighborhoods to which they are adjacent. In some metropolitan areas these inner suburbs are served by mass transit lines radiating out from the city, and often they serve as the terminus of these lines. The newer, more distant communities are generally lower-density, and almost solely single-family-home communities dependent upon the automobile. Because they were built more recently, they generally have a younger population than the inner ring of communities.

THE INNER-RING COMMUNITIES

The inner-ring communities can be classified to highlight key issues of the current policy questions metropolitan areas must face. Some of the important community types are:

- the suburban community with an increasing older population,
- the community undergoing a major population transformation, and
- the more stable and generally working-class suburb.

The people in many of the inner-ring communities moved in during a limited time span of ten to twenty years, and in some of the towns the children have grown up and left home, leaving their parents alone in large houses. Communities with large elderly populations present problems that most suburban governments are not accustomed to dealing with. Greater health and social services are required, rather than the traditional school construction. Local transit systems are needed when automobile transportation is no longer appropriate. Little money and effort is invested in home maintenance and improvement because of the lack of financial resources and a physical inability to do home maintenance. Tax increases present an excessive burden to older residents living on Social Security and fixed incomes increasingly affected by inflation. Houses may increase in value, but older homeowners have less and less ability to pay the higher levies required to finance the new services necessary for their survival.

In one such community, Brookline, Massachusetts, approximately 10 percent of the population was over the age of 65 in 1940, 13 percent in 1950, 17 percent in 1960, and 20 percent in 1970. Over 25 percent of the population is now over 65.

Given the life expectancy of about seventy, it is obvious that the population of the community will be changing rapidly in the next few years. The presence of large elderly populations in suburbia is a trend that will be increasingly common. Communities that have excluded multifamily housing will either have to build it or force its elderly citizens to move. Most suburbs in the past have been single-age environments, designed for young adults and children. This has changed significantly, but suburban communities have yet to see this change as desirable and to provide housing and services for all age groups, thus encouraging community responsibility toward older citizens and their integration into community life. Overcoming the traditional age segregation common in American life must be a conscious objective for community development.

Many of the inner-ring communities have already experienced a shift in population. Some have attracted new waves of young white working-class or professional families buying large, inexpensive older homes. Some of these communities, because of their proximity to public transit, the central city, and inexpensive land, have attracted large-scale high-rise construction. Those with no obvious housing advantages have begun to deteriorate. One of the most interesting phenomena is the development of the black suburban community, generally adjacent to the older areas of black settlement in the city.

Black families seeking better schools, a safer community, and a home to own moved to these communities at the height of mid-sixties prosperity. With the increasing inflation and rising unemployment of the seventies, many of these communities, born in optimism, became the centers of problems, with many citizens unemployed and on welfare. At a time when increasing revenues are needed, these communities, like the central city, have a declining tax base. Given no change in state and federal policy, black suburban growth will continue to be concentrated in a few inner-suburban municipalities, rather than spreading throughout the entire metropolitan region.

As the populations of many of the inner communities changed in the fifties and sixties, the children of white working-class neighborhoods also moved in search of the suburban lifestyle. Many of these families left as their neighborhoods changed from white to black. Both the black and working-class suburbs were severely affected by the shaky economy of the seventies.

Many of these communities have ethnically homogeneous populations: Irish, Italian, Greek, or Eastern European. In several important ways they duplicate the old ethnic neighborhoods of the central cities, but with the newer look of the suburbs. Because the citizens of these suburbs recently lived in the central city themselves, they are anxious to demonstrate their separateness from their former, changing neighborhoods. Many residents of these suburban communities initially moved in response to black incursion, and they are fearful of having their lives disrupted again. They share the attitudes toward school desegregation and "forced busing" of their counterparts in the ethnic city neighborhoods, from which many have moved. In some of these communities, citizens are already organizing in anticipation of metropolitan school plans.

Both the black and working-class suburbs are particularly vulnerable to changes in the economy. The move to suburbia and particularly the purchase of a home has placed a financial strain on the working-class family. The social, psychological, and economic dislocations caused by these changes will continue to have a major impact on these communities.

THE OUTER-RING COMMUNITIES

The outer-ring communities have been growing and are strong. They still have significant tracts of undeveloped land and have been experiencing continued increases in density. Three of the most significant types of these communities are:

- the community experiencing growth in high-density housing, employment, and commercial activity, becoming a new suburban core community;
- the middle-income community whose development has stabilized; and
- the community on the fringe of development, only now undergoing the pains of urbanization.

Some communities, because of a location at the junction of two highways or railroads, have become points of concentrated development. These developments, which include major shopping centers, industry, offices, and more recently high-density apartments, have resulted in suburban communities with growing and increasingly diverse populations. They are the new prosperous urban concentrations of the latter part of the century. They were the sites of major shopping mall construction during the sixties, followed by the construction of multifamily housing units for childless couples and singles. With increased residential density, new restaurants and other places of entertainment have begun to develop. The old single-family residential base in these communities is generally strong. The residents do not go into the central city; increasingly they commute to suburban jobs.

Access to the growing number of suburban jobs for lower-income residents of the city has been a focus of debate since 1965. After the riots in Watts (an area of Los Angeles), it was realized that residents could not get public transportation to areas with newly developing jobs. A variety of transportation experiments were conducted in many cities, but with little impact on the employment of low-income central-city residents. Since the failure of these experiments, continued questions have been raised about how to link lower-income central-city residents with suburban jobs. Policy recommendations suggesting the need for better ways to get lower-income residents to suburban jobs stress regular and effective mass transit and extensive suburban low-income housing construction. Probably the most fundamental policy recommendation, springing from the realization that discrimination still exists, is that major inroads in suburban employment will not be made without large-scale affirmative action. But affirmative action cannot be effective until the means to get to suburban jobs exists. Affirmative action and improved transportation must also be accompanied by improvements in education and a growth in the number of jobs.

Many of the outer-suburban communities (and even some of the inner-ring communities) have homogeneous and relatively wealthy populations. In most of these communities there are few single individuals. Houses are mostly single-family units of high value. Residents have high educational achievement and high incomes. There are no poor people, few elderly people, and relatively few blacks. These communities, because of their wealth, generally have sufficient resources for excellent public services and have established local development controls that are effective in limiting or slowing growth.

Unlike the new central suburbs, which are experiencing an increase in density, many of the outer fringe communities are undergoing development for the first time. Communities of this type still have open options, and currently many of these small towns or agricultural settlements are afraid of the consequences of urbanization: population growth, the destruction of the land, and increased taxes. For many longtime residents who wish to stay in these developing suburbs, staying may mean a change in lifestyle and a loss of political power. For those anxious for the change, it may mean business opportunities or opportunities for profitable land sales. The process of development is fraught with conflict in these communities. An increasing number of residents are finding urbanization undesirable, and are attempting to develop ways to restrict growth. Many of those moving into developing communities are anxious to be the last in, hoping to then "close the gates behind them." Environmental objectives, land-use control, and good community design are receiving increased attention.

Fringe development is increasingly the province of the large developer. The home builder of the mid-fifties who built ten homes a year is fading. Developments are larger and developers are therefore interested in constructing commercial enterprises as well as residential units. Most developers are inherently conservative and are anxious to follow the tastes of the consumer. Innovations are incremental and reflect market and cost considerations. Low-income housing cannot be built at a profit without subsidy, and at present little governmental funding is available. Suburban communities not anxious to encourage low-income housing are matched by developers who cannot build it. Without substantial government intervention, there is little chance that the population composition of newer suburban communities will be any different than that of the presently stable wealthy communities.

Moreover, the desire to increase job and housing opportunities has begun to conflict with the desire for environmental protection. The term "green bigot" has been used to describe individuals who present the desire to protect the environment as an excuse for restricting growth that might benefit the poor. Equal financial opportunity and a protected environment are not necessarily mutually exclusive. But it takes conscious planning to accommodate both objectives and reach a consensus through objective compromise. Although these conflicts over development will continue in the fringe and the wealthier communities, many factors are operating that may significantly change them.

The Arab oil boycott and the Yom Kippur War of 1973 signalled the end of the post-World War II era of suburban development. All the suburban communities are being forced to question their traditional assumptions. The increased price of gasoline, home heating fuel, and electricity after the boycott was only one problem. The mid-seventies inflation combined with high unemployment and low economic growth also had a variety of consequences, which when combined with basic social changes in population distribution and families have affected the major components of the contemporary suburban lifestyle. These components are:

Suburbanism: A Precarious Lifestyle

- the dependence on the automobile
- the large single-family house
- the child-centered community
- the cohesive nuclear family
- continued prosperity, employment, and expectation of growth
- continued increase in community services
- the perception of safety and isolation

All these factors have been crucial to the development of suburban communities as they now exist. Each of these factors is changing, with the consequence that major disruptions can be expected in existing suburban communities and a new metropolitan structure will begin to evolve.

THE DEPENDENCE ON THE AUTOMOBILE

More than any other element, the easy, inexpensive use of the automobile is the cause of the development of a low-density suburbia. Any major change in the ability to use an automobile will significantly impair suburban functioning. A number of factors are rapidly increasing the cost of maintaining an automobile at a time when few people can afford the increase. The higher price of fuel when combined with an increased purchase price, maintenance, insurance, tolls, and taxes makes it difficult for some families to afford the two or three cars necessary for mobility in a low-density environment, where the independence of each adult and teenager requires an individual automobile. Smaller, more gas-efficient cars and car pooling may improve the situation slightly, but an energy conservation policy will require families to decrease automobile dependence significantly. In addition, subsidized highway construction will diminish. State and federal governments, faced with increased costs and the pressure to provide mass transit, will have to divert resources from highway building, preventing any major spread of suburban development to areas now without highway access. The increased cost of driving, a national policy of energy conservation, the lack of new highway access, and the rising cost of the extension of such necessary utilities as sewerage and water will generally confine new fringe development to areas already experiencing urbanization.

THE LARGE SINGLE-FAMILY HOUSE

With the confinement of suburban development to already accessible areas, the price of land will continue to rise. Combined with the increasing cost of borrowing money, the increasing cost of labor and materials, the increasing cost of local property taxes, the increasing cost of home heating and furnishing, and the decreasing ability of a family to afford these added costs, this means that houses and home lots will be getting much smaller and sparser. Houses are already being built without extra bedrooms, dens, playrooms, or garages. When single-family homes are built they are generally a repeat version of the post–World War II tract home.

With the increased cost of single-family home construction, there is an added incentive to build higher-density housing. The townhouse, garden apartment, cluster development, and high-rise building will become more and more common on the suburban scene.

With decreased dollar value being received for new housing, older homes will become increasingly attractive. Areas not previously considered for family occupancy, such as the older inner-suburb and urban neighborhoods with large well-built homes, will increasingly experience the incursion of young families.

THE CHILD-CENTERED COMMUNITY

National changes in the birth rate have resulted in smaller families. Therefore, in addition to the difficulties of affording a large suburban home and automobile mobility, there is in fact less need for the large amount of space that precipitated many of the past moves to newer and larger homes in the more expensive outer suburbs. Many of these communities occupied in the early and mid-sixties are now experiencing major reductions in their elementary-school populations. These reductions will soon be felt on the junior-high and high-school levels as well.

With the decline in the number of younger children, the era of suburban school construction will be over. The politics and social lives of these communities have centered around school activities and issues for many years, and a major adaptation will be required. Proposed school closings will become a major source of community conflict.

THE COHESIVE NUCLEAR FAMILY

The continued movements to the fringe were family growth decisions. Decisions were made for "the benefit of the children." With an increasing rate of divorce and family separation, the suburban communities so dependent upon interfamily relations are finding increasing disruptions in the traditional social patterns. Since most social functions in the suburbs involve husbands, wives, and children, women or men living alone are isolated from the community social life. The single parent forced to combine work and child rearing has difficulty locating work in or near home, delivering the children to schools and piano lessons, shopping, and still finding time to maintain a viable life as a productive and creative individual.

CONTINUED PROSPERITY, EMPLOYMENT, AND EXPECTATION OF GROWTH

More than any other factor, prosperity has determined the suburban lifestyle. The suburbs have been the frontier of upward mobility. As with the western frontier in the nineteenth century, the ability to move to the suburbs has in some ways been an outlet for expectations in the twentieth century. But with the increased costs of the suburban move, the declining ability to sell houses in some urban neighborhoods, and continued unemployment, the hope for a suburban move has almost died. The consequences of this loss of expectation are still to be felt among the urban, working-class, black and white populations. The increased costs of suburban life at a time of economic hardship have made many of these outer communities unavailable even to many relatively wealthy families. Changing jobs and thereby moving has become more difficult. Family difficulties with roots in increasing economic hardship make marriages less stable. Myriad businesses based on suburban growth and located in the suburbs have faced increasing difficulties: building contractors, furniture suppliers, and landscape gardeners, to name a few. Economic hardship in the suburbs is more and more common. It is also probably less bearable than unemployment faced in the city or in a rural area. Suburban families have such fixed costs as several cars, expensive home heating, and high mortgage payments. These are basic requirements of suburban survival. Adjustments downward and shifts in lifestyle are

therefore more difficult to make without major family dislocations. The dependence on the nuclear family rather than extended families and communal environments has also made it extremely difficult to share these burdens.

THE CONTINUED INCREASE IN COMMUNITY SERVICES

The continuing inflation has severely increased the costs of municipal services at a time when citizens can least afford major tax increases. Even in the wealthy suburbs, local governments are trying to control the increasing municipal budget. Reductions in school populations will allow some cost savings, but forced budget cuts and layoffs will begin to create splits in communities that had expected a consensus on the continued need for an improvement in services. Even with cost savings, local taxes will continue to increase, raising home prices and the cost of construction and making home sales and new development even more difficult. It is necessary to note, however, that the rise in tax rates in the central city and lower-income communities can be expected to be much greater, and the differential between the high taxes and lessened services of the city will become even more blatant.

THE PERCEPTION OF SAFETY AND ISOLATION

The major reason cited for many suburban moves has been the desire for a "safe and secure" environment. However, crime rates in recent years have been increasing faster in the suburbs than in the cities. In the city, crime is not a novelty and the "eyes" of the street often protect individuals and homes. In the wealthier suburbs, privacy and isolation behind shrubs and fences have made homes particularly vulnerable. With the safety of the suburb no longer assured, the comparative advantage of the outer suburbs in relation to the older areas and particularly the inner suburbs will increasingly diminish.

Suburban communities adjusting to these factors will experience increasing social disruption, with consequences as yet unclear. Because of these factors inner-suburban communities of higher density with mass transit access, varied populations, good schools, a broad range of services (easily accessible employment, shopping, day care), and less-expensive older housing will become increasingly attractive to young families traditionally attracted to the outer areas of new suburban development. Given these circumstances, one might also expect a middle-class influx into urban neighborhoods, to occupy housing units now available to lower-income and working-class families. Although some particularly attractive urban neighborhoods will draw young professional couples without children or with young families, the cities will probably not experience any major growth in family population. Further increases in taxes, a decline in services, perceived continued high crime rates, and the continued poor quality of the urban public schools will increase hardships for those already living in the older urban neighborhoods. If any of these factors change, city neighborhoods with good housing might experience a middle-class influx. With more pressure on housing markets in existing communities of the inner ring and relatively less development at the fringe, the price of existing housing units will increase substantially, and in a situation of increased competition for land and housing, the poor will have less access to the older suburbs traditionally open to working-class migration. Existing suburban communities will have to come to terms with the need to develop mixed housing opportunities for a variety of lifestyles, the need for public transit, and the need for local services to lessen dependence on the suburban shopping center. In short, their survival depends upon their becoming increasingly urban.

THE FUTURE OF SUBURBAN POLICY

The problems of suburban communities are increasing and the assumptions behind the suburban lifestyle are changing, paralleled by continuing problems in the central cities. The central city and the suburbs are inexorably linked. Changes and actions in each have major effects on the other. The limitation of suburban growth at the fringe raises land prices at the center. The migration of lower-income residents out of the center causes movements in the metropolitan area that reverberate to the outer, rural communities. But the conflicts are confined to urban neighborhoods and the inner-ring communities, with little overt impact on the fringe. Little improvement can be made in the central-city conditions without the resources of the wealthier suburbs and the opening of suburban jobs and housing to lower-income residents of the cities.

With constant changes in the suburbs and central cities affecting the entire metropolitan area, ideas once only mentioned in the classroom have begun to surface in political discussion: abandon the property tax, equalize tax revenue, establish metropolitan government, construct mass transit, build suburban low-income housing, design new communities, organize metropolitan school systems, freeze development in undeveloped communities. Whether or not these policies will help provide an equitable social and racial structure in the 1980s, there is currently no framework within which the development of our metropolitan areas can be discussed, evaluated, planned, and resolved. Existing metropolitan planning agencies shun issues of potential political conflict and work only on areas of possible consensus. They have no power and represent only the collective will of their member communities. All the important questions raise conflict and are therefore avoided. The state is the only level of government on which the issues for each metropolitan area can generally be fought out. However, the legislatures include significant rural representation as well as the growing suburban forces, and therefore the resolution of issues of suburban-central city conflict is generally skewed towards the suburban and rural interests.

These issues affect the entire metropolitan area. It is impossible for any of the poorer and changing communities to affect their own destinies—to increase their tax yields, serve the growing concentrations of poor people, or develop jobs for their residents. These communities are at the mercy of factors beyond their individual control. Only the wealthier communities can truly meet their citizens' needs.

The Congress and the executive branch would seem to have the greatest potential to consider the issues out of the context of local parochial interests. However, each member of Congress is affected by the opinions of the constituents; special interests and local issues do play a part in national decisions. However, national decisions and programs, no matter how grand their intentions, have to be implemented locally. Without cooperation and commitment on the local level (particularly from the wealthier suburbs), the objectives of any program can be shifted and have different effects than those intended by the legislative draftsmen.

The issues to be resolved in a metropolitan development policy involve the fundamental values of this society: the taxation and distribution of income; the nature of our neighbors and communities; the education of our children; the availability of jobs; the freedom and cost of mobility; restrictions on the use of private property; and limitations on profit. Questions such as these are rarely discussed as parts of a comprehensive policy, but are resolved by small incremental decisions or are generally resolved through avoidance. Given the inherent conflicts of interest—between rich and poor, black and white, urban and low-density suburbs, old and young, the childless and the child-rearing, owners and renters, investors and consumers—unless interest predominates and can force a resolution on an issue, market forces will generally be allowed to operate, with the attendant benefits to wealthier suburban interests.

This incremental method of implementing decisions also means that victories that may appear significant may turn out to have little real impact in resolving fundamental questions. Legislatures may only be able to pass laws that will have little impact. The Massachusetts legislature passed a law requiring all communities to construct a "fair share" of low-income housing. In 1976 approximately 100 units were constructed under the provisions of this legislation. The Urban Development Corporation in New York State had powers to override suburban zoning and build suburban low-income housing. When it tried to do so, its powers were taken away. If the courts eliminated exclusionary zoning barriers tomorrow, little or no low-income housing would be built in most suburban communities. If communities are hostile and if the federal government does not subsidize and encourage low-income housing, it will never be built.

An increasing number of economic and political factors will limit expansion at the suburban fringe. The legal restrictions imposed by communities have been supported by recent Supreme Court decisions. In addition, the slow growth of the economy and the lack of financial resources increasingly restrict the mobility of nonwealthy families and their ability to buy homes. These constraints on traditional suburban movement are probably not temporary but reflect permanent changes in the ability of American families to meet their goals through moving. The suburban frontier may be closing. The loss of this outlet will require that metropolitan areas deal with issues of the distribution of land, development of tax resources, and access to jobs and services within existing communities, with particular emphasis on providing resources, jobs, and housing in the central cities. Without a deliberate process of distribution, internal metropolitan social and racial inequities and conflicts can only increase.

The problems discussed in this chapter are not the simple consequences of governmental inefficiency, easily rectified by new programs or new tables of organization. But governmental structures such as community land-use decision making and enduring programs such as home-interest tax deduction are reflections of politics: basic assumptions about

SOLUTIONS

personal goals backed by the power and influence to see that they prevail. Current conflicts over school busing are a perfect example of this. The issues of tax redistribution, nonlocal control of development planning, affirmative action in hiring, large-scale suburban low-income housing construction, and metropolitan schools might raise an even more angry debate. The fact that politicians have not picked these issues up as part of their platforms is not accidental.

However, it *is* important to think in terms of policy. The policies and program areas that follow probably require economic growth, a reduction of military spending, or increased taxes to finance them.

A Program of National Planning and Investment. Both private and public resources are increasingly being invested away from the older metropolitan centers. A conscious policy of national planning and investment is required that would emphasize the older, declining regions. This would have the effect of channeling growth and resources where they are needed most. The investment should be focused on the metropolitan regions. Regional development banks should be established as part of a national development banking system. A program to rebuild the railroad network and other urban-oriented public works would be a major part of this development plan. Energy investments and alternate energy development should be planned and encouraged to lower energy costs for developed regions, and organized so as not to cause the development of some regions at the expense of others.

A Program of Investment in Developed Areas. Regional investment should be focused on the centers and growth should be encouraged in these areas. A publicly supported jobs program focused on housing construction, rehabilitation, and municipal facilities and services would both provide jobs and improve the competitive position of the centers.

A Program to Restructure Metropolitan Decision Making. A variety of models are available, but the policy should control those areas which larger-scale metropolitan decision making involves, including transportation, utilities, and taxation. The new metropolitan unit would also have jurisdiction over the proposed new development zones. A careful and slow metropolitanization of decision making is necessary, because otherwise the suburban areas will dominate the process, to the detriment of the cities and the poor.

A Program to Restructure the Development of Metropolitan Areas. This would include public transit development (not necessarily fixed rail) to and around the suburban and fringe areas, but with a major improvement of service to already developed communities. Publicly owned development zones should be created in and around these lines, with a program of incentives for firm location, housing, publicly supported mixed-income housing construction, and concentrated public-service investment. Profit earned in land sales would be used to pay for the program. This development program would be accompanied by a program of development controls in other communities and a program of disincentives for automobile use.

A Program to Redistribute Public Revenue. The property tax must be eliminated as the major tax supporting local services. A graduated income tax would be ideal, with redistribution based on need rather than wealth. The federal revenue-sharing program or some other means (federal assumption of welfare payments or school costs) should be used as a supplement for those units of government that might have difficulty even under the new redistribution system.

A Program of Housing Subsidies. With a major increase in the construction and rehabilitation of center-city and new suburban housing, families should be given a subsidy based on income to purchase or rent, depending upon their tastes and preferred location.

A Program of Metropolitan Services. The new development zones might provide the basis for organizing schools and other public services on a metropolitan basis. A major program to provide the best schools and services in the cities and new suburban zones might provide the basis for increased metropolitan integration.

SUMMARY

More Americans now reside in suburbs than in cities or the rural areas of the nation, and the urban culture and politics of the United States is increasingly dominated by that of the growing fringes of the metropolitan areas. This suburban growth has been spurred by a federal policy, in operation since the post–World War II period, that has paid for massive highway construction, insured single-family home mortgages, and allowed home buyers to deduct home-mortgage interest from their income taxes. One consequence of this massive development (from 1960 to 1970, 70.5 percent of all the country's population growth was in the suburbs) has been to increasingly isolate and diminish the influence of the older central cities that have become increasingly poor and black, without sufficient revenue to cope with growing costs.

The growth of the wealthier population at the fringe has been paralleled by massive suburban job growth. The shift in population and employment has not been followed by any change in governmental or municipal boundaries or any major redistribution of public revenue. The newer communities, isolated from the older cities, manage their own development so as to exclude large families and the poor, and attract industry and commercial development. The poor do not have access to suburban jobs and housing and have minimal resources with which to obtain them, even if they were available.

The growth of the suburbs in the older metropolitan areas has proceeded for so long and has been so massive that there are few generalizations that one could make about the population, politics, and physical condition of the multitude of suburban communities, even given the recognized reality of the suburban-central city conflict.

Some of the older suburban communities closer to the cities are facing aging populations, deterioration, rapid population transformations, and fiscal dilemmas. At the same time others are experiencing new development pressures and growth. Some suburban communities are becoming centers in their own right—centers of transportation, employment, shopping, entertainment, and new high-density housing—serving the population of surrounding suburbs. As many of the other communities have grown rapidly, with the attendant problems of traffic, pollution, destruction of natural amenities, and the inevitable tax increases, fringe communities watching these changes have become increasingly cautious and exclusive. Better planning, although desirable, has resulted in increased and more rigid control of new construction in the fringe and outer communities, with rapidly increasing costs for the lower number of housing units available. The outcome of this will be intensive development pressures in some of the inner suburbs and also possibly those city neighborhoods with desirable older housing.

Lower-income families still possess the suburban dream, but they will find it increasingly difficult to realize. Families now living in the suburbs are finding the suburban lifestyle increasingly difficult to sustain. The costs of important elements of the suburban lifestyle have increased rapidly: the single-family home, home heating, the required automobile, and local taxes. With continued unemployment and a slow-growth economy, family incomes have not kept pace with costs, and the construction and expansion that the suburbs have grown to expect and depend on have diminished. Slowed growth has been accompanied by social changes such as the declining birth rate, increasing family instability and growing female employment, changing the nature and expectations of suburban life.

The bloom is off the suburban dream; the suburban migration has ended, and there is a perception that less money is available for public needs. Conflicts between central cities and suburbs, as well as within suburban communities, will therefore undoubtedly increase, with the issue being who has the power to determine the character and population mix of communities; the availability and location of jobs, housing, and education; and the nature and character of a transportation system that might alter those market forces that in the past have determined the distribution of wealth to the benefit of the presently dominant suburbs. Without a deliberate process of allocation and redistribution (which is exceedingly unlikely), internal metropolitan social and racial conflicts can only increase.

1 Postwar federal policy has been implemented to the benefit of the suburban areas. How can this be so considering the emphasis on urban renewal, the antipoverty program, the model cities program, and revenue sharing? What do you know about each program and how it operated?

2 Why do people move? How do they select where to live? What are the reasons for either renting or buying a house?

3 Analyze the presidential election issues and results in 1976 from the perspective of the conflicting interests of suburban, rural, and urban areas. How might these conflicts and the changes in population distribution affect future elections?

4 Identify the issues in your community and state. Do they reflect the issues discussed in this chapter? Given your local community, how do you think it should respond to the issues?

5 No community fits exactly into a given category, although certain traits might predominate. Can you match communities that you know with the examples given of different types of communities? What do the locations of these communities and their differences reveal about the development of metropolitan areas—about their history, geography, transportation, governmental policy, and economic history?

6 The protection of the environment and the construction of low-income housing are both desirable objectives. Can you provide instances in which these objectives are in conflict and situations in which they are not? How can these objectives be reconciled? Are there cases where one objective should predominate?

7 Identify several different communities in your area. What do you think the impact of each of the following changes would be on each community: tripling the price of gasoline; a major increase in unemployment; an increase in the rate of inflation; an increase in the birth rate; a metropolitan school plan; and a freeze on development?

8 The authors use the analogy of the American frontier to describe the growth of metropolitan areas. Do you think the analogy is valid?

NOTES
1. Herbert J. Gans, *Levittowners: Ways of Life and Politics in the New Suburban Community* (New York: Random House, 1967), pp. 32, 36.

2. Anthony Downs, *Opening Up the Suburbs: An Urban Strategy for America* (New Haven: Yale University Press, 1973), p. 17.

3. Ibid.

4. Jean Gottman, *Megalopolis—The Urbanized Northern Seaboard of the United States* (New York: The Twentieth Century Fund, 1961).

5. Robert C. Wood, *1400 Governments: The Political Economy of the New York Metropolitan Region* (Cambridge, Mass.: Harvard University Press, 1961), p. 1.

READINGS
Downie, Leonard, Jr. *Mortgage on America: The Real Cost of Real Estate Speculation.* New York: Praeger, 1974. A journalistic account of the development process.

Downs, Anthony. *Opening Up the Suburbs: The Urban Strategy for America.* New Haven: Yale University Press, 1973. A plan and program for urban America, focusing on the suburbs.

Gans, Herbert J. *The Levittowners: Ways of Life and Politics in a New Suburban Community.* New York: Vintage Books, 1969. Probably the best suburban community study.

Glazer, Nathan. *Affirmative Discrimination: Ethnic Inequality and Public Policy.* New York: Basic Books, 1975. A discussion of some of the political problems associated with suburban integration and other affirmative policies.

Warner, Sam Bass, Jr. *Streetcar Suburbs: The Process of Growth in Boston, 1870–1900.* New York: Atheneum, 1962. A history of suburban development in Boston. The dynamics have not changed considerably.

Wirt, Fredrick M., et al. *On the City's Rim: Politics and Policy in Suburbia.* Lexington, Mass.: D. C. Heath, 1972. Recent studies of suburban politics and the implications for suburban policy.

Wood, Robert C. *1400 Governments: The Political Economy of the New York Metropolitan Region.* Garden City, N.Y.: Anchor Books, 1961. An older book now, but nothing has changed.

COST CUTS IN BURIALS PROPOSED

(Washington, D.C.) Funeral homes should be forced to give consumers accurate information to dispel myths concerning caskets, vaults, embalming, and other burial practices, presidential consumer Virginia Knauer said yesterday.

On embalming alone, she said, consumers might save as much as $1,000 per funeral if they realized it has no long-term effect. Additional savings would also result, she said, if more people knew they had the option of renting rather than buying a casket to display the body.

[*Michael J. Coulon, UPI,* Boston Globe, *15 January 1976.*]

IN THIS CASE, EQUALITY STOPS AT THE HAIRLINE

(Hartford) It's all right for an employer to tell a male worker to get a haircut while allowing a woman employee to wear long hair, the Connecticut Supreme Court has ruled.

In a unanimous opinion, the court held that while men and women have an equal right to jobs, employers may distinguish between the sexes in matters of hair grooming. The court said hair length was related to the company's method of doing business and was not a question of equal opportunity.

[*AP,* New York Times, *4 May 1976.*]

G.I.S "TOO HEAVY" ON THE BOOZE

Enlist Now.

But beware the boozy bonhomie of the military happy hour.

In a blockbuster report that has shaken the military establishment, *Stars and Stripes,* the newspaper for overseas service and government personnel, paints a picture of hard drinking and widespread alcoholism among United States servicemen.

[*Bill Fripp,* Boston Globe, *20 December 1975.*]

TAX NOTES

Over 50 percent of the taxpayers who go to the IRS for help in completing their tax returns receive bad advice, according to the Tax Reform Research Group. What's worse is that the IRS isn't bound by its own bad advice—says a recent tax court decision.

[Equal Times, *19 December 1976.*]

THE *traditional institutions of society reflect the intense changes, conflicts, and currents so familiar in contemporary America. The fact that the most powerful of these institutions—the family, education, and work—are groping toward new and different definitions clearly indicates the need for rethinking the socioeconomic basis upon which society rests. Roslyn L. Feldberg and Janet A. Kohen's article, "The Custom-Made Blues," notes that although the problems of society are associated with family life, the type of social change required to alter these basic problems threatens the priorities and privileges available to those in power. They point out that people should not resign themselves to this situation but should analyze their own lives and organize with others to change the conditions in which they live.*

One of the popular tunes in Walt Disney's film Snow White and the Seven Dwarfs *was sung by the dwarfs as they went to work. With tools in their hands and music in their voices they regaled Depression audiences of the thirties with "Whistle While We Work." But it is clear that humming is not often heard in factories, offices, and schools today. The sounds of protest have been heard for some time and are growing louder. Unless the basic values and institutions of the working place are reoriented toward the autonomy of the individual and the elevation of the creative impulse, the concept of work will be further eroded.*

The educational system, a most sensitive social institution made more so by the busing controversy of the sixties and seventies, is dealt with by Paul Nash in "Education for Justice and Freedom: The Economic Dimension." The thrust of the piece is that education is interwoven with the values of freedom and justice and that regardless of the place of education, in schools or in other settings, it should have as its primary objective the autonomy of the individual.

Increasing attention is being focused on the elderly in our society. Advances in medicine have increased the life span. More and more people are living to old age. But what does America offer the aged? Robert N. Butler explores the ways in which people "grow old and poor in an affluent society."

Without the implicit understanding that one's words and actions carry meaning and have import—that they are vital to the maintenance of open communication— democratic society will simply cease to exist. The article by David Kunzle, "Scratching Our Revolutionary Itch—How Advertising Absorbs the Imagery and Slogans of Radicalism," explores the complicity of advertising in its attempt to defuse radical ideas and expressions, not only by controlling all avenues of expression but also by using these very ideas and slogans in advertisements, thereby distorting and diluting their original meanings.

INSTITUTIONAL DIMENSIONS

10 | THE CUSTOM-MADE FAMILY BLUES[*]

ROSLYN L. FELDBERG/JANET A. KOHEN

Every family has difficulties, from the everyday hassles of family life to the occasional but serious problems which threaten the well-being of all concerned. The children may fight all day; the vacuum cleaner breaks; one child doesn't get into college; another disrupts the classroom; a father loses his job and is unable to find another; a mother finds a job but can't get child care. Families experience the immediate and direct consequences of personal difficulties and, regardless of the conditions which produced them, they, rather than other organizations, are expected to solve them. The wife of the unemployed father may extend her work hours or the children may take after-school jobs. Families may move to subsidized housing, eat cheaper foods, and eliminate nonessentials from their budgets. The unemployed father may return to school to get formal training for a different type of work or spend his days at the unemployment office or the nearby bar. Whatever the family members' responses, they will deal with the difficulty only as it affects them. Whether the family handles the difficulty successfully or not, the social conditions which produced it remain, creating the same difficulties for other families.

In contemporary America, personal troubles—delinquency, alcoholism, unemployment, marital breakup, violence of all varieties, mental illness, variations in sexual response—are associated with family life. Academicians, the press, and other public commentators often look to the family for clues to explain these troubles. Although people with these personal troubles spend most of their time outside the family in schools, at work, in the streets, or at businesses, their experiences in these other places are not given equal attention as a source of their problems. For

[*] © Roslyn L. Feldberg and Janet A. Kohen, January 1976.

example, most delinquents have been or are students, but the schools are not given primary attention as the source of delinquency.

Both the source of the troubles and the troubles themselves are defined in a simple way. Social policy makers, professionals, and others with power define the troubles as individual, personal problems. They tie the problems to the individual people who display them and they find the source of these problems in their personal lives. Since the family is the one place where people expect to have a personal haven and act on the basis of their individual needs and choices, it is seen as the source of and cure for individual variation. But relating personal troubles to family life ignores the social patterns which are the conditions for both the troubles and their solution.

In the following pages, we will examine personal life in the family and the personal troubles which families are expected to solve, but analyze them within a societal context. We will examine the cultural belief that the family is to blame for personal difficulties and show how that belief developed historically, as the family changed from a multipurpose to a specialized living unit. We will analyze the consequences for the family of the development of industrialization, as bureaucratic organizations replaced the home-centered production of goods and services and dominated personal life beyond the realm of organizational responsibilities. We will show how a conflict emerged from the opposing natures of the family as personal haven and other organizations as rational, impersonal units, and how this conflict created difficulties for members of contemporary American families, limiting their ability to respond to one another's personal troubles. As a result, the family came to be blamed for these troubles, and was left to suffer the consequences of them.

Personal Life Is Equated with Family Life

People have not always felt that the home was the only place where they could express their personal interests and desires. Nor did they feel that it was the only place where they could get personal support and care. That has been a relatively recent idea, and the elimination of personal life from the nonfamilial areas of people's lives has also been a recent phenomenon. There were no books prescribing child rearing as an emotional and nurturant relationship in America until about 1830.[1] Child rearing had been more disciplined and formal; the home was a work-oriented, productive place organized around family relations. The acceptance of family relationships outside of the home was evident in one of the early forms of factory hiring. At the turn of the eighteenth century in Rhode Island and Connecticut factories, the whole family rather than an individual laborer was employed by the factory.[2] Furthermore, poorhouses and asylums were built to resemble common homes in the community rather than large warehouses as they later did.[3]

With the flowering of industrialization in the early nineteenth century, several important changes took place within the home. Responsibility for the production of essential household items moved progressively from the home to the factory at the same time that responsibility for personal behavior and interpersonal relationships moved from the community and the workroom to the exclusive domain of the family and the home. By the end of the nineteenth century the family was almost completely responsible for the personal behavior of its members. This change can be seen in the response of various public agencies to children's needs.

Early in the nineteenth century, day-care centers were initiated as a service to women (often widows) who had to work outside their homes.[4] By the mid-nineteenth century, many day-care centers had sprung up in neighborhoods with poor and immigrant populations. These day-care centers often had service components attached to them which provided education in housewifery and motherhood as requirements for their use. This service component was introduced because the centers' founders and benefactors believed that if the poor, immigrant mothers who used the centers were schooled in the proper ways of managing their homes and training their children, then their children would not exhibit the problems of unemployment, delinquency, drinking, and other "social evils" that were often publicly linked to the immigrant family. Platt aptly refers to these and similar welfare efforts as "child saving."[5]

By the turn of the nineteenth century, the family's responsibility for personal life was made clear in the courts. Judges were regularly interpreting the "best interests of the child" to be with the mother in the home rather than in orphanages or "houses of refuge" which had previously been seen as appropriate for problem children. In fact, some officials claimed that a bad home was better than a good institution. Thus the family, not the public, was to be responsible for personal behavior, and various regulatory measures were instituted to ensure that the family accepted this responsibility. The ideology which developed to justify these policies emphasized the home as the cure for social evils. The practical effect was to make families accept the consequences for the personal problems of their members.

The epitome of this ideological change can be seen in the application of scientific management to the home, justified by the idea that a well-run home would keep husbands and children from "evil ways." Evil ways were associated with the street life of the cities and were believed to result from the lax moral standards of immigrant and poor families. Middle-class families began to move to "suburban" settings to avoid the influence of these people. Even the use of immigrant women as domestics in middle-class homes came to be seen as a "bad influence" on family life. Scientific management was the means by which the mother became the manager who kept the home both physically and morally clean for her family. Thus, the home came to be seen as the place where moral problems were prevented or cured, much as illnesses could be prevented or cured. It was the shield from bad influences, providing the armor against corruption. The family in which moral problems persisted was pathological and a failure. Poorer families were doomed to fail. Not only was their public behavior defined as problematic by the powerful in the community, but also their ability to maintain clean, hygienic homes was limited by their not having the money to secure gas stoves or carpets, or to maintain an adult out of the paid labor force full time.

The Traditional Family within a "Rational" Society

Changes in the family followed patriarchal and capitalist patterns. The family was traditionally patriarchal, and relationships within the family were defined by tradition and custom. Family members related to each other in personal ways, and most of the family's goods were produced within the home. With industrialization much of domestic production was taken over by factories. Clothes, linens, soaps, and foods no longer were produced within the home. They came to be produced, as they are today, by wage labor according to technological methods. Production of domestic goods was not the only part of traditional family life to be taken over by nonfamilial organizations. General and technical education, medical care, religious training, and social services have also been relocated from the home to formal organizations. They are now organized according to rational/bureaucratic principles rather than according to the personal/traditional principles which are the bases of family life.

But the rise of the rational, bureaucratic structure did not merely relieve the family of certain tasks. It had two important by-products which changed the nature of family life to what it is today. First, a major function was added to family life. Goods and services which people had produced within their homes and communities and which they could expect to find there were taken over one by one, each by a separate organization. Family members now had to devote time and energy to coordinating the consumption of goods and services provided outside of the home by a multitude of organizations. Second, the rational organization produced goods and services for family members according to technical principles which stripped the production process of the personal component it had had within the family and community. This had the effect of pushing onto the family most of the responsibility for taking care of personal needs, personal differences, moral training, and encouragement and support, and for creating the special environment where the personal choices of daily life could be made.

This change can be seen in the history of unions and political organizations. Originally, these organizations related to the community and to individual problems and needs. Entertainment, job placement, and the provision of food in time of family crisis were considered services integral to these organizations. Now, neither of these organizations considers these services within their domain. They are rational and impersonal, like all the other organizations family members must use in their daily lives. People participate in them only as "parts" that are essential to the organization's delimited operations. On the other hand, they expect to participate in the family as "whole persons." The family has become an island of traditional and personalistic relationships within a society which is primarily rational and impersonal. In commenting on the importance of the family in taking care of the personal needs and troubles of individuals, Bernard points out:

> Marriage is a cheap way for society at large to take care of a lot of difficult people. We force individuals—a wife or a husband—to take care of them on a one-to-one basis. If or when these caretakers refuse, we are left in the lurch. Marriage is a nice way to parcel individuals out for individualized care and support, but if we did not have such care and support available, what alternatives would there be?[6]

The division between rational organizations and traditional family relations provided the social conditions for maintaining a sexual division of labor. Historically, the family has been both traditional and patriarchal. To the extent that the family remained traditional, it remained patriarchal. The woman remained subservient to her husband, supporting his interests, and the man remained responsible for the material condition of his wife and children. Industrialization did not change the basic responsibilities of husband and wife. Man's breadwinner role was translated from productive work in or near the home to wage labor in the factory. Although he was physically divorced from the domestic scene of wife and children, his spiritual presence remained as a contribution to most family tasks. His responsibility was fulfilled within the rational-technical organizations outside of the home; her responsibility, even when she was employed, remained within the home. Woman's situation, however, became worse than before. Her husband no longer contributed physical effort to domestic tasks but his authoritative role in defining and supervising the standards of housework and child care remained. Although women were under less and less pressure to produce domestic items (depending on their social class), they were allocated more and more responsibility to do the emotional and nurturant work of reducing stress or motivating family members to participate in organizations outside the family.

It is exactly these latter tasks for which the rational/bureaucratic organizations do not accept responsibility. The isolation of the personal from the productive creates a dichotomy between external institutions and the family which parallels the sexual division of labor within the modern family. Just as the family is responsible for personal life vis-a-vis the rational organizations, so is the wife/mother responsible for personal difficulties within the family. The family must respond to the "whole person"; the wife/mother is the chief contractor in seeing that these needs are met. Lillian Robinson's poem, "Political Economy," captures this situation.

> *. . . Monday through Friday*
> *nine hours*
> *(don't forget to record*
> *your down-*
> *time).*
> *He peels the check*
> *out of his oil-stained*
> *pocket*
> *and gives it*
> *to his wife:*
> *one hundred fifty-*
> *six dollars*
> *and forty-three cents*
> *I'm making a living. He says,*
> *I'm making a living.*
> *In the morning*
> *she gets up*
> *to make his lunch:*
> *two sandwiches*
> *(baloney and cheese)*
> *an apple, a piece*
> *of cake.*
> *I'm making life.*[7]

Invasion of the Personal Haven   We have shown how the contemporary family has come to be responsible for the "whole person," and the home has come to be considered a private place where individual and idiosyncratic choices should be expressed rather than in other places. Family members are supposed to resolve one another's personal troubles. At the same time they also implicitly accept the notion that if they live "right" and can create the proper home life, they will be happy. Most parents, for example, maintain that they should choose how to raise their children and should be able to do so according to their own values and ideas. Opposition to day-care centers is often based on the belief that children may learn the wrong ideas or values in such centers, creating problems within the family. A one-to-one individualized parent-child relationship in the privacy of the home is the valued approach to child care and training for many families.

Nevertheless, families exist in a social world created in the interests of rationalized organizations and capitalist control. Families must adjust to the conditions of this social world in order to survive, but the adjustments are often difficult, creating both routine and extraordinary problems within families and limiting the choices of family members. It is not always possible for family members to achieve what family life is supposed to be.

REGULATING PERSONAL LIFE

A variety of constraints that the state and other organizations have imposed on family life prevents family members from finding a personal refuge from the competitive, impersonal world and from making personal choices. The state regulates marriage, school attendance, and the selection of medicines and drugs. The juvenile justice system includes a wide array of laws which regulate children's behavior, from curfew to leaving home. The state even regulates the conditions of birth. Midwifery, once a system of exchange of services among neighbor women, has largely been eliminated through regulatory policies.

The state is not the only institution that channels or intrudes upon family privacy and personal choice. Professional practices and ideologies prescribe appropriate behavior within the family. Professionals promote child-training philosophies, define appropriate nutrition, condemn certain sexual practices while perpetuating others, and encourage people to accept stereotyped sex-role behaviors. Professional invasion is especially common among the poor (particularly among welfare families), who may be proffered menus, budgets, homemaking training, and moral lectures as a routine part of welfare services.

Formal regulation of the family has increased as the responsibility for personal behavior has been relegated to the home. Early efforts at regulation were privately organized, primarily directed at the poor and at immigrants. Mid-nineteenth-century day-care services, schools, and welfare programs attempted to control the personal decisions of the families who used them. However, public regulation through the state expanded at the end of the nineteenth century and the beginning of the twentieth. Between 1890 and 1920, compulsory school attendance, enforcement of child-labor laws, prohibition of alcohol consumption, enactment of sanitary codes, judicial determination of child brutality, criminalization of heroin use, establishment of juvenile courts and separate juvenile laws, licensing of midwives, prohibition of pornography, and other state controls restricted self-determination by family members. With personal life largely relegated to the family, control of personal choices ultimately restricted family life. Many of them required that family members adapt their lives to the rules and conditions of organizations specified by the state—schools, hospitals, welfare, and work places. What was on the one hand protective legislation was on the other hand restrictive legislation.

CONFINING FAMILY PATTERNS TO MARKET INTERESTS

State and professional regulatory measures are not the only constraints which determine the patterns of contemporary family life. Two other important factors define the options for family members' day-to-day lives: the consumer choices available to family members, and the consumer schedules and practices of economic, political, educational, religious, and welfare institutions. Both of these factors restrict the possibilities for family members to meet one another's individual needs and introduce additional problems into the daily life of the family. State and professional regulatory policies define the limits of personal life and affirm family members' responsibility for one another's inappropriate behavior. The limits created by consumer choices and organizational rules and practices have a different impact. They make it difficult for family members to secure resources for their personal needs, or to resolve the personal troubles which people bring to the family setting. At times, they create conditions which intensify personal troubles.

The ideology of the family includes the idea that the family is an arena of personal choice. The ideology of capitalism also includes the idea of choice, choice in the marketplace. In neither case does the ideology correspond to the reality. With most production of needed domestic goods located outside the home, families must rely on the marketplace to secure individual needs. But consumer choices are limited by the options presented by corporate decisions—the types of products and their quality. Which products are developed and marketed depends on corporate decisions, not individuals' interests. Mothers can choose between cloth and paper diapers but usually have no choice of infant day-care services. Nor can families choose to buy a steam-powered, alcohol-burning, or electric-powered car. Children's toys are largely plastic and breakable rather than wood or metal and repairable.

Choices are further limited by the family's income—the lower the income, the fewer the choices and the lower the quality. As Gans points out, one function of poverty is to provide a market for otherwise useless goods—the secondhand, the irregulars.[8] We might add that the poor also have few choices of consumer services. They are likely to be "guinea pigs" for clinics attached to medical schools; they cannot buy private education.

Consumer choices available to any class are consistent with the values of profit-oriented corporate structures. Household products embody values created by the marketplace and condition family members to use that set of values in determining the direction of family life. They affect the standard of life, the energy requirements, and the budget expenditures of American families. Household products carry with them the image of what a home *should* look like and determine the time and energy which housewives feel they must put into it. Soap is presented as making clothes sparkling and white, not just cleaning them. Wax does not just protect floors, it makes them shine. It is up to the housekeeper to make the product do what the advertisements say it should. The time necessary to do so (usually longer than claimed in the advertisements) must be subtracted from family members' needs. The "fine print" describes the additional effort that is required when the housekeeping task differs slightly from the picture in the glossy ad. It is a difficulty of the home or the user when the product can't be used as simply as the publicity portrays. In addition, products are made to be replaced, not repaired. Business is organized to produce new models to sell, not parts necessary to repair older models. The very design of products frustrates repair even by specialized service agents, let alone by the average consumer. As a result, household budgets must cover the costs of replacing furnishings, toys, and appliances which are produced to have a short life span.

Family members' time and energy, the organization of household work, and the family budget are largely determined by the type of products available. People can choose only what is available on the market and what they are offered in the market is not necessarily what they need. Products represent what corporate managers can produce for the largest profit. Managers, more than anyone else, know that many products are not needed. They pay to create a market for unneeded items. Added to the frustration of not being able to get what family members need or want are the problems created by the products themselves. Injuries and health hazards are among the worst problems, but even the time and energy used to replace, restyle, or adjust products to family life create problems.

Related to limited market choice are attitudinal values which accompany products. Breakage, malfunction, or poor quality are generally blamed on the purchaser or user of products rather than on their producer. A bad meal is blamed on a bad wife; injuries from toys are explained as the result of poorly socialized or unsupervised children; malfunction of appliances may be attributed to the homemaker who does not use them according to the "directions" or fails to do the necessary preparatory work such as rinsing dishes before putting them in the dishwasher. Difficulties in using products may be attributed to idiosyncratic tastes, the nonstandard quality of the home, or even the neglect of family members to buy the additional devices necessary for the product to run or be used. The blame that accompanies product difficulties affects low-income families to a greater extent than other families. They must rely on poorly made or low-quality goods. When their home looks a shambles, when shoes wear out or clothes tear, they are presented as irresponsible, uncaring, undisciplined, or hedonistic. They must suffer the consequences built into the product and be blamed for them as well.

The tendency of family members to accept blame can be related to marketing practices. The most common form of marketing is self-service. Department stores, drug stores, supermarkets, and appliance stores have eliminated sales personnel, leaving the customer to select a product. Under these circumstances, customers no longer have an informed salesperson who can counsel as to quality, warn about use, or advise in terms of the needs of the individual family. They have only themselves to blame for a "wrong choice" should the item be defective, unusable or inadequate.

Services present some of the same problems, but these are more subtle. People are expected to choose services. The American Medical Association (AMA) or the American Bar Association will not recommend a good doctor or lawyer. Personal references are the only source of recommendation for professional as well as any other services. If the services of an electrician or a psychiatrist do not eliminate the problem brought to their attention, or if they make the problem worse, it is the consumer who made the wrong choice. With professionals, the consumer is often held responsible for choosing the doctor or lawyer, yet disqualified from judging their performance. Thus, when a problem recurs or worsens they have little recourse. Services have an additional component which limits family members' ability to take care of their problems in their own way. Access to services is often restricted to those who have the appropriate appearance or lifestyle. Securing a mortgage, getting credit, or obtaining the services of a doctor or dentist requires a show of assets or at least a middle-class lifestyle. Often services are class defined, with better-quality services extended to the middle and upper classes. Poorer families may have to use legal aid, paraprofessionals, loan companies, and unlicensed repair people.

Restriction of choices by those who provide them rather than by those who use them means that family life is what the producers allow it to be rather than what the users need it to be. Although the family has responsibility for managing personal life, family members don't usually have the opportunity to choose the goods and services which they may want for their own satisfaction or which they may need to resolve personal troubles. What they can get may make it difficult to resolve individual family members' problems. Even worse, what they can get may produce personal problems.

MANIPULATING FAMILY LIFE TO CONFORM TO ORGANIZATIONAL ROUTINES

Making a life within the family requires money, usually a paycheck. But the paycheck has contingencies. To have money available for goods and services, family life must be adapted to the schedule and work requirements of the organization that pays the wage or salary. Family members must accept the absence of the wage earner (almost always the father and much of the time the mother as well) during most of the day. Nonpresence means nonresponse to needs that arise for family members. But it means more than that. The work day is defined according to the convenience of the employer, not the convenience of the employee. It is usually inflexible. Consequently, the wage earner's needs must be met after hours, and response to the needs and problems of family members

can take place only outside of the routine work day. Personal problems of the worker or the worker's family are not legitimate reasons to come to work late, leave early, or miss the job altogether. Just to be able to go to a job means making arrangements. When the mother is at home, she is expected to coordinate child care, meals, medical care, and routine services. When she is employed, she usually has to do the same tasks as well as arrange services to replace some of her efforts.

Coordination of routine family needs or services for special problems is hardly easy. Since most rational-formal organizations serve only one need or service for their clients and their schedules are set up for their benefit and convenience, families who must use them have to arrange their lives to adapt to these organizations. Yet, families do not use only one organization at a time. They rely on many outside organizations: businesses, schools, repair services, medical services, and so forth. Managing family needs and resolving family problems becomes a matter of coordinating these services and fitting them around the work day.

Family life can hardly be seen as an arena of personal choice. What looks like individual variation and idiosyncratic behavior merely represents the structuring of individual behavior by a combination of organizational schedules and procedures. Coordination of schedules and procedures is in itself problematic for family members. When special problems or needs arise, family members are pressed to find the time to take care of these problems immediately. To obtain the services of one organization may mean jeopardizing access to the services of another or to the paycheck which secures the services. Nonroutine but nonserious problems may be postponed or neglected in such situations until they become serious. Dental care may wait until a toothache occurs; treatment of a child's hearing difficulty may be postponed until the child fails in school. If a serious problem results, it becomes the fault of the family members, not of the conditions which led to the neglect.

Family Work: Women's Work

The constraints on family life disproportionately affect women. The division of labor within the family along sex lines results in women's being responsible for the domestic work and the internal organization of the family. Most people would agree with Brenton that women are the central figures in the family, that "every day is Mother's Day."[9] But the flowers and special appreciation associated with Mother's Day hardly reflect the reality of women's minute-to-minute family responsibilities and problems.

As the domestic workers, women put meals on the table, provide clean clothes, and push back the daily accumulation of "dirt" that results from the activities of the family. As wives and mothers, they are the child-care workers, consumers, and service workers for their husbands and children. This means that they not only work for their families in the home but also go outside the home to make purchases and arrangements for family needs.

If services were available on a flexible basis that meshed easily with the schedules of family members and if quality goods were available at prices families could readily afford, women's family work would still be difficult (labor intensive, menial, repetitive), but it would be "do-able." However, in the social organization of the United States neither of these conditions exists. Services are scheduled according to the priorities of the managers of service organizations. Prices are set according to profit margins, consumer demand, and production costs, not family incomes. The result is that the social and material conditions in which women do their family work interfere with the doing of it. When the work does not get done, the routine basis for family living is upset and the woman, as the adult responsible for doing it, is to blame. This allocation of responsibility is not merely customary, it is institutionalized. Students of child brutality view evidence of malnutrition or neglect as the basis for charges against the mother.[10] Because she is supposed to provide nutritious meals and supervise the care of the children, she is "liable" when this work is not properly done.

THE LOVE/DUTY TRAP

It is not, however, being "liable" that structures women's family work. Their labor is shaped by the constraints under which they work and their love for and sense of obligation to the members of their families. When the goods and services women need for their families are unavailable or too expensive, they do not shrug their shoulders and stop trying. With limited household budgets, women may shop around for cheaper foods and put extra time into preparing casseroles so that their families continue to have satisfying meals. They devise substitutes or find alternatives because they are working for people they care about. If they fail in their efforts, the consequences may be sick children, lost educational opportunities, or disappointed loved ones, as well as their own awareness of their inability to meet what they see as the needs of their families.

Because of the way women mediate between the available resources and their families they work against themselves. If they worked for pay by contract, they could evaluate the resources and say, "I can only do this much work with these materials." Since they work without pay to make a life for their families, they attempt to stretch their resources so that all the work gets done. In so doing, they obscure the material basis of family problems, while reinforcing the view that the quality of family life is determined by the efforts and capabilities of the wife/mother.

THE COSTS OF THE TRAP

The wife and mother's unintended support of the status quo is costly for her. It maintains her in the position of continually trying to solve, on an individual basis, insoluble problems. Using her own time and energy to stretch resources, she faces continual frustration and possible failure. If she manages to stretch the household budget by preparing nutritious or at least appetizing meals with inexpensive ingredients, she cannot simultaneously be teaching a child to ice skate or be repairing clothes. Her situation is comparable to that of the early aerospace engineers, who worked for months on insoluble problems. Those who felt responsible not only for working on the problems but also for solving them suffered severe mental strain and eventually had to leave their jobs. Because the family, and within the family the woman, is defined as responsible for dealing with recurring insoluble problems, it is not surprising that married women show high rates of mental illness.[11] Bernard has argued that the condition of being married includes two marriages—his and hers—and that hers takes a considerably greater toll than his.[12] Motherhood, as it is currently organized in the United States, also contributes to the strain on women.[13] The love/duty trap is clearly an expensive one.

Although organizations and individuals benefit from this arrangement, the costs are concentrated in the family and borne most heavily by the women themselves. The mental and emotional consequences women suffer are regarded as trivial and treated symptomatically through chemical or psycholanalytic therapies aimed at adjusting women to their circumstances. The source of the problems remains untouched and the woman continues to do her work for the family with the added burden of what are now seen as *her* personal problems.

MATERNAL EMPLOYMENT

Until quite recently maternal employment itself was considered the source of social problems. Students of family life and social commentators argued that the family required woman's full-time attention. Anything less was expected to have negative consequences. Researchers studying delinquency and other problems which were at least partly attributed to family life routinely scrutinized rates of maternal employment as a potential cause of such problems.[14]

Today, with 43 percent of married women employed, public opinion has shifted.[15] Employment for mothers of school-age children, especially those over twelve, is encouraged. Additional income is an important factor in alleviating family burdens. Many women have accepted employment as one aspect of their familial responsibilities. In addition, women are being urged to "work" as a way of overcoming the isolation of individual households.

The woman's acceptance of new responsibilities does not reduce her old ones. Within the family, the division of labor along sex lines remains relatively unchanged. Women continue to be responsible for both domestic work and internal organization of the family. Societal recognition of maternal employment does not eliminate maternal responsibilities; it merely permits a new manifestation of them. Working wives are expected to provide quality goods and services to substitute for their own labor in the family. The difficulties of finding or inventing such substitutes remain the woman's problem and she remains accountable for failure.

In the context of the Women's Liberation movement, women analyzed the problems of family life. They did so by comparing their experiences and identifying common features. The discussions were concrete, dealing with daily routines, difficulties that arose, and the ways these were handled. Striking similarities were observed—common patterns of problems too widespread to be explained as the consequences of individual failure. Seeking an explanation for common problems, women began to look at what was common in their circumstances. The structure of family work was identified as an underlying problem. **A New View of an Old Problem**

Analyzing family work revealed the contradiction involved in doing domestic labor, coordinating the purchase and use of goods and services with limited resources, and meeting the emotional needs of family members. The next two questions came easily. Why is family work structured in this way? And why is it so difficult to change the structure of family work? Answering these questions focused attention on the institutional arrangements which constrain family life. For example, housework and child care are tied together because women are responsible for both of them, but these activities are often incompatible. Small children typically "undo" housework as it is being done—dirtying a half-washed floor or scattering food over the vacuumed portion of a rug.[16] Inexpensive, high-quality child care would allow women to separate these activities so that one would not be done at the expense of the other. Such family patterns are maintained because alternative arrangements are not readily available. Thus, the incompatibility of domestic work and child care is a feature of women's family work, with the attendant problem of harried mothers and their children isolated together for the major portion of the day.

The difficulties in changing the structure of family work are evident in the rigidity of the sexual division of labor within the family. Men resist induction into housework in many ways.[17] Their resistance is supported both by custom and by the fact that men's employment has been organized on the assumption that men live in families in which women do the household work. Their hours and their pay reflect that assumption. Furthermore, women's employment, organized on the complementary assumption that women are supported by men, pays less than a family wage, and therefore increases the pressure on women to continue to do the family work as the remainder of their "equal" contribution.

<table>
<tr><td>

**Personal
Problems Are
Social Products**

</td><td>

By locating the problems of family life in the structure of family work and in the institutional arrangements which support that structure, feminist analysis challenges the tradition of individualizing problems and finds their source in the social aspects of life. In contrast, those who adopt the traditional approach to family problems (or to the family's failure to deal with individual personal problems) seek the source of problems in personal character structure, family history, or, more recently, in genetic disposition. Violence within the family provides one example. Researchers studying this problem analyze the personal backgrounds of family members, family histories, socialization patterns, and related information about the individuals in order to explain such violence. Undoubtedly, all of these factors contribute to one's behavior. However, the approach remains simplistic because it ignores the social conditions which promote such behavior.

</td></tr>
</table>

The limitations of this explanation can be shown by an analogous problem from the health sciences. Heart attacks can be explained partly by heredity (genetic disposition) and partly by medical history, but that does not mean that diet, exercise, stress, and smoking do not affect the likelihood of heart attacks. In fact, some health scientists argue that the incidence of many diseases, including cancer, is greatly influenced by such social conditions as chemical additives in foods, pollution levels, and diet. These researchers are not, of course, ignoring the finding that such diseases also appear to have a genetic base. Instead, they are arguing that social conditions influence which biological potentials are realized. Thus, medical researchers have at least established that various socially produced phenomena create conditions favorable to disease even though medical treatment is still individualized. We have been arguing in parallel fashion that a wide variety of difficulties may produce problems affecting family life. Which problems do develop and their actual effects on families depend, to an as yet unknown extent, on the social conditions in which we lead our personal lives.

<table>
<tr><td>

**More of the
Same or
Social Change?**

</td><td>

Social policy makers are continually pointing to the social problems surrounding families and announcing that these must be dealt with. The services available to families symbolize policy makers' analysis of and concern for eliminating personal troubles and difficulties. Services are generally available only when families have used all of their personal

</td></tr>
</table>

resources and the family as a unit is likely to "fall apart," or when family members' lives are seriously threatened. They are individualized services, based on an after-the-fact corrective model rather than on a preventive model. Such services attempt to adjust people to the social conditions underlying trouble rather than eliminating the source of problems for all who are "at risk." Because policy makers act on the premise that the family is the setting in which problems must be resolved, they fail to consider the ways in which social institutions and conditions produce problems. As a result, their policies and the services created by these policies deal only with families.

This approach does provide patchwork servicing, but its long-term effects are not known. Forcing individuals to adjust to what may be harmful social conditions may create additional problems or exacerbate existing ones. Couples having marital difficulties are viewed as personally troubled and counselled to adjust to their marital roles or to divorce. They are not helped to change the conditions of their married life—to find better jobs, locate acceptable child care, or otherwise reduce socially produced stress which impacts on their marriage.

It is unlikely that current policy makers will attempt to change the conditions which we have associated with problems in family life. The kind of social change which is needed would reorder priorities and threaten the privileges of those in top positions. We do not think people should resign themselves to this situation, accepting patchwork services or being satisfied with the few liberal policies that from time to time are legislated and then often "revoked" through lack of funding. People can analyze their own lives and, together with others, organize to change the conditions in which they live. And they must do so. Only through their own efforts at organized change will people create the conditions and institutions for a satisfying family life.

SOLUTIONS

The most common method of change in the past has been regulation of personal behavior. Starting with a cultural ideology of individual responsibility, policy makers have treated social problems as character flaws or disorders which could be eliminated by more and more complex rules and laws. Regulation has not solved the problems. Rather it has created new ones which constrain and interfere with family life and personal happiness.

Such an approach has resulted in the continual containment of personal efforts to create a satisfying life. From our analysis we would argue that we need to organize for change on two fronts. We must provide new services and support to help families cope in the existing social conditions. An example here would be organizing extended child-care facilities so that care is available for infants or sick children. On the other hand, we must change the social conditions of our lives so that family members can do what they need to do. A parallel example is the location of facilities for children in or near work places, with hours for parent-child contact during the day.

New services have become necessary as the conditions of our lives have changed. For instance, the move from rural to urban settings has made rural methods of child care inappropriate at the same time that new child-care needs have arisen from the urban environment. Changes in the organization of work and community life have created the need for new services for the elderly. Changes in the products we use in our homes have mandated the need for more flexible service.

Most importantly, the contemporary conditions of life often make it impossible for people to do what they need to do for their families. The boundaries we have created between interpersonal relationships and rational institutions interfere with family life. For example, health care has moved from the home to the hospital and clinic. In the process the care itself has become fragmented and the patient has been separated from the supportive environment which personal attachments supply. Some people have countered this trend of extreme rationalization by moving some aspects of their families' personal health care back to the home, such as the delivery of babies or the care of dying patients. However, this approach is limited. Rationalized institutions do provide needed specialized services, some of which cannot be provided on a house-to-house basis. In most cases, we need to change the hospital into a home rather than the home into a hospital. This means incorporating interpersonal relationships by making room for friends and family and their belongings, especially for long-term patients and children. But hospitals are not the only places that need to become more like home. We need to bring personal concern and emotional support into all of the organizations in which we spend so much of our lives.

In the long run, we need two kinds of change. First, we need to move away from the simplistic notion of personal responsibility and recognize the contribution of social policies and organizational schedules and procedures to personal problems. Second, we need to reassess priorities. We have concentrated on the material environment—products, efficiency, and profit—and let it structure our personal concerns. It is time to make our personal and interpersonal needs paramount in determining the organization or our material environment.

SUMMARY Every day families face difficulties: children behave "badly" at school, mothers or fathers lose jobs, someone becomes ill. These difficulties create problems which family members try to solve within the family. These problems are defined as "personal" problems: problems whose source and solution are located in individual families. This definition is imposed by social-policy makers and organizations and accepted by most families. In this chapter we examine two major historical changes in the family which have contributed to defining families' problems as "personal" ones: changes in cultural ideology and changes in the organization of economic activity and social services.

In American society "personal life" is equated with "family life." Only in the family is a person expected to have a "personal life," a life in which people relate to him or her as a person. In other settings people are expected to relate impersonally, according to their positions in organizations or social groupings. This has not always been the case. At one time, people were expected to relate fully to each other in all settings and family relationships were integrated into activities that we now distinguish as "work," "school," or "religion." Changes in the organization of economic and social activities have produced a separation of personal life and social life. These activities came to be organized rationally, in a manner which specifically excluded any concern for personal relationships. The family became the repository of personal relationships. This transformation changed the functions of the family. The basic production of goods and services no longer took place in the home. Instead "home" became the place where not only personal life but also personal problems were located. The family became solely responsible for emotional and nurturant work.

These are important responsibilities, important not only to family members but also to the existing social order. To ensure that families carried out their responsibilities properly, regulations were introduced by the state on such matters as school attendance and the use and practice of medicine. Professionals offered expert pronouncements on proper techniques of child care and home management. Additional pressures for conformity in family life were introduced through the marketplace of goods and services. Using available products and services shapes families' styles of living, their organization of time and energy for household maintenance, and their budgets. While the market is celebrated as the "arena of choice," the choices are limited. Refusal to conform to the market choices is expensive, making nonconformity a luxury. At the same time, participating in the market is also expensive, ensuring that poor families will rarely be able to provide what looks like a "good home." Finally, the organization of goods and services that structures the families' choices also structures their daily routines. Family life must be organized around the schedules of other organizations because families rely on these organizations for the paychecks that support them, the products they use, and the services they require.

The division of functions and the interdependence of the family and other organizations means that the family faces contradictory demands. Meeting children's emotional needs may not be compatible with maintaining the home or meshing with the schedules of stores and service agencies. The work involved in all these areas is assigned, according to the traditional division of labor by sex, to women. As wives and mothers, they undertake this work and they, most directly, pay the costs of attempting to solve insoluble problems. The women's movement has analyzed the difficulties women experience in doing family work and has pointed out the contradictory demands on families in general and on women in particular. This analysis has located the source of personal problems outside the family, in the social conditions in which families live. While the analysis has been powerful in affecting women's consciousness and their approaches to family work, it has not yet affected the organization of social services. Social services are still based on the assumption that families are the sources of problems and the places where problems must be solved. Therefore services continue to be attempts to "patch up" families—by adjusting them to the situation and encouraging them to function as well as possible within it. The chapter closes by arguing that people can and must organize to provide new ways to deal with the socially produced difficulties that we all experience as "personal problems" in our families.

NOTES

1. Sister Monica Keifer, O.P., *American Children through Their Books, 1700–1835* (Philadelphia: University of Pennsylvania Press, 1948), pp. 82–85.

2. Robert H. Bremner, ed., *Children and Youth in America*, vol. 1 (Cambridge, Mass.: Harvard University Press, 1970), p. 146.

3. David J. Rothman, *The Discovery of the Asylum: Social Order and Disorder in the New Republic* (Boston: Little, Brown, 1971), p. 42.

4. M. O. Steinfels, *Who's Minding the Children: The History and Politics of Child Care* (New York: Simon & Schuster, 1973), p. 36.

5. Anthony Platt, *The Child Savers* (Chicago: University of Chicago Press, 1969), pp. 3–4.

6. Jessie Bernard, *The Future of Marriage* (New York: Bantam Books, 1973), p. 181.

7. Lillian Robinson, "Political Economy," *Radical America* 7 (1973): 129–130.

8. Herbert J. Gans, "The Positive Functions of Poverty," *American Journal of Sociology* 78 (1972): 275–289.

9. Myron Brenton, *The American Male* (Greenwich, Conn.: Fawcett, 1966), p. 119.

10. Richard J. Light, "Abused and Neglected Children: A Study of Alternative Policies," *Harvard Educational Review* 43 (1973): 589.

11. Walter R. Gove and Jeanette F. Tudor, "Adult Sex Roles and Mental Illness," in Joan Huber, ed., *Changing Women in a Changing Society* (Chicago: University of Chicago Press, 1973), pp. 65–66.

12. Bernard, *The Future of Marriage*, pp. 16–58.

13. Jessie Bernard, *The Future of Motherhood* (New York: Penguin Books, 1975), pp. 69–89.

14. Compare Ruth Brandwein, Carol A. Brown, and Elizabeth M. Fox, "Women and Children Last: The Social Situation of Divided Mothers and Their Families," *Journal of Marriage and the Family* 36 (1974): 498–514; Mary C. Howell, "Employed Mothers and Their Families," *Pediatrics* 52 (1973): 252–263; F. I. Nye and L. W. Hoffman, eds., *The Employed Mother in America* (Chicago: Rand McNally, 1963), and L. W. Hoffman and F. I. Nye, *Working Mothers: An Evaluative Review of the Consequences for Wife, Husband, and Child* (San Francisco: Jossey-Bass Publishers, 1974).

15. United States Department of Labor, *Manpower Report of the President* (Washington, D.C.: U.S. Government Printing Office, 1975), p. 58.

16. Ann Oakley, *Woman's Work: The Housewife, Past and Present* (New York: Pantheon, 1974), p. 94.

17. Pat Mainardi, "The Politics of Housework," in Robin Morgan, ed., *Sisterhood is Powerful* (New York: Vintage Books, 1970), pp. 447–454.

QUESTIONS

1 What do the authors see as an important but neglected source of difficulties which become "problems" for people as members of families? How do they explain this oversight?

2 How did the development of "rational bureaucratic" organizations change the functions of the family?

3 Several historical trends are discussed as examples of changes in social life which affect family relations. How are these trends related to the development of social problems in other areas?

4 What are three of the most pressing problems in your family? What social and economic arrangements contribute to these problems? How do they contribute?

5 The authors argue that women, as wives and mothers, are particularly burdened by the difficulties that existing social and economic institutions create for their families. Explain the main reasons why the wife/mother comes to accept the responsibility for personal problems of family members.

6 What assumptions about the nature of family life are reflected in the kinds of services American society provides for families when they have difficulties?

7 Give some examples of ways family members either individually or collectively have overcome or gotten around the difficulties created by political and economic organizations.

8 The authors have given historical examples of political and social policies which attempted to control the personal life of family members. Give some contemporary examples of political and social policies which are also attempts to control the personal lives of people in families.

READINGS   Bernard, Jessie. *The Future of Marriage*. New York: Bantam Books, 1973.

———. *The Future of Motherhood*. New York: Penguin Books, 1974.

Brandwein, Ruth; Brown, Carol A.; and Fox, Elizabeth M. "Women and Children Last: The Social Situation of Divorced Mothers and Their Families." *Journal of Marriage and the Family* 36 (1974): 498–514.

Bremner, Robert H. ed. *Children and Youth in America*. Vol. 1. Cambridge, Mass.: Harvard University Press, 1970.

Brenton, Myron. *The American Male*. Greenwich, Conn.: Fawcett Books, 1966.

Feldberg, Roslyn, and Kohen, Janet. "Family Life in an Anti-family Setting: A Critique of Marriage and Divorce." *Family Coordinator*, April 1976, pp. 151–159.

Gans, Herbert J. "The Positive Functions of Poverty." *American Journal of Sociology* 78 (1972): 275–89.

Gordon, Linda. *Families*. Boston: New England Free Press Pamphlet, 1970.

Gove, Walter R., and Tudor, Jeannette F. "Adult Sex Roles and Mental Illness." In *Changing Women in a Changing Society*, edited by Joan Huber, pp. 50–73. Chicago: University of Chicago Press, 1973.

Hoffman, L. W., and Nye, F. I. *Working Mothers: An Evaluative Review of the Consequences for Wife, Husband, and Child*. San Francisco: Jossey-Bass, 1974.

Howell, Mary C. "Employed Mothers and Their Families." *Pediatrics* 52 (1973): 252–63.

Keifer, Sister Monica, O.P. *American Children through Their Books, 1700–1835*. Philadelphia: University of Pennsylvania Press, 1948.

Komarovsky, Mirra. *Blue Collar Marriage*. New York: Random House, 1964.

Light, Richard J. "Abused and Neglected Children: A Study of Alternative Policies." *Harvard Educational Review* 43 (1973): 556–98.

Lynd, Robert S., and Lynd, Helen M. *Middletown*. New York: Harcourt Brace Jovanovich, 1956.

Mainardi, Pat. "The Politics of Housework." *Sisterhood Is Powerful*, edited by Robin Morgan, pp. 447–54. New York: Vintage Books, 1970.

Manpower Report of the President. United States Department of Labor, Washington, D.C.: U.S. Government Printing Office, 1975.

Nye, F. I., and Hoffman, L. W., eds. *The Employed Mother in America.* Chicago: Rand McNally, 1963.

Oakley, Ann. *The Sociology of Housework.* New York: Pantheon, 1974.

————. Woman's Work: *The Housewife, Past and Present.* New York: Pantheon, 1974.

Platt, Anthony. *The Child Savers.* Chicago: University of Chicago Press, 1969.

Robinson, Lillian. "Political Economy." *Radical America* 7 (1973): 129–30.

Rothman, David J. *The Discovery of the Asylum: Social Order and Disorder in the New Republic.* Boston: Little, Brown, 1971.

Sidel, Ruth. *Women and Child Care in China.* Baltimore: Penguin Books, 1973.

Steinfels, M. O. *Who's Minding the Children: The History and Politics of Day Care.* New York: Simon & Schuster, 1973.

Vogel, Lisa. "The Earthly Family." *Radical America* 7 (1973): 9–50.

11 | LABORING IN CONTEMPORARY AMERICA:

CAN WE WHISTLE WHILE WE WORK?

JOSEPH BOSKIN

> A Christian should follow his *Occupation* with INDUSTRY . . . . It seems a man *Slothful in Business*, is not a man *Serving the Lord*. By Slothfulness men bring upon themselves, What? but Poverty, but Misery, but all sorts of Confusion . . . . On the other Side, a man by Diligence in his Business, What may he not come to? A *Diligent* man is very rarely an *Indigent* man. Would a man *Rise* by his Business? I say, then let him Rise by his Business . . . . I tell you, With Diligence a man may do marvellous things. *Young* man, *Work hard* while you are *Young:* You'll Reap the Effects of it, when you are Old. Yea, How can you ordinarily Enjoy and Rest at *Night*, if you have not been well at work, in the Day? Let Business engross the *most* of your Time . . . . Come, come For shame, Away to your *Business:* Lay out your *Strength* in it, Put forth your Skill for it; Avoid all impertinent *Avocations*.

So did Cotton Mather exhort his fellow colonists in the early part of the eighteenth century to their dual calling: to serve the Lord and to pursue their own "particular employment." To ignore this counsel was not only an affront to the Deity but also the opening wedge for a secular existence of poverty and misery, and certainly an afterlife of soulless drudgery administered by Satan. The notion of the work ethic was thus all-encompassing. It combined the secular with the supernatural; it affected the young and old of both sexes; and it provided rewards and punishments. The work ethic provided strong extrinsic motivations: an angry God who would punish work failure, and later, failure in the eyes of one's fellows in a system of competition based on work accomplishments.

The early Puritan aspects of the ethic were further buttressed by environmental factors. The survival of a new community in a hostile environment was dependent upon the cooperative work of its people. Indeed, the settlement of and movement across the North American continent resulted from communal rather than individual effort. Success was counted individually but the community demanded loyalty and a sense of identification. But it was clear that an inherent contradiction existed between the values of individualism and community, a contradiction which would continue to wrench American society. The clash between the individual and the majority was often resolved in favor of the former, who was relatively free to pursue his own ends at the expense of the community.

From these roots there developed a uniquely American creed, the gospel of individual striving and success. Until recently, this gospel was one of the most powerful of societal goals. Moses Rischin, in his imaginative anthology, *The American Gospel of Success,* noted early in his introduction that "the magnetism of individual success" has been more potent than any other inspiration in the United States. "Indeed," he argued, "perhaps nowhere else in the world has a seemingly materialistic cult been so uninhibitedly transformed into a transcendent ideal, indeed into a veritable gospel that has been called a dream."[1]

Paeans hang like fruit from the tree of the work ethic. Poets, novelists, politicians, workers, minorities, and many others have honored its profitability. Work became acquisition and acquisition became the great quest, the test of worthiness, the cry of the powerful, and the anger of the powerless. Compounding the ideology of work was a real or imagined scarcity of goods. Only those who could control a large share of the available resources were regarded as important and knowledgeable. Into their hands went the instruments of change, the determination of the future, and the continuation of the primacy of the ethic. Eventually, as the religious origin of the work ethic became less meaningful, the secular manifestations of the creed became the sole measure of the individual.

In the beginning, the work ethic was seemingly egalitarian. Everyone (especially white males) could apply it. It was unrestricted: physical size, religion, and background were secondary. Immigrants joined native Americans in seizing upon its simple pronouncements to achieve a place in the American sun, passing on its tenets to succeeding generations. The work ethic, then, was a primary value system for the majority of Americans. Work was at once a powerfully mediating, separating, and yet cohesive force in society.

Work has often been perceived as a beneficial experience for the individual—work for the sake of work. President Richard Nixon in his 1973 inaugural address counselled holding fast to the ethic:

> The work ethic holds that labor is good in itself; that a man or woman at work not only makes a contribution to his fellow man but becomes a better person by virtue of the act of working.

However, there were other reasons why people worked. Some worked to ensure a better life for their children, a motivation which characterized many immigrant and minority-group parents. Others worked because of the lack of alternatives. Institutionally and attitudinally, American society was geared to labor. This becomes evident in the stereotypes of the nonproducers: the hobo has been portrayed as a romantic figure, the tramp as a scorned individual, and the welfare recipient has been barely tolerated. Regardless of their external plight, they have all been regarded as unworthy persons by the middle and upper classes.

There has always been implicit in the ethic that someone, somewhere and somehow, is shirking, not doing the job. This ever-present notion was communicated in one of the many travelling graffiti that cross the land in sub-rosa fashion. This one was in the form of a news release:

> Washington—The 1960 census stated that the population of the United States is 160 million. 62 million people are over 60 years of age.
>
> This leaves 98 million people to do the work
> 54 million are under 21.
> This leaves 44 million to do the work.
> 21 million are government employees.
> This leaves 23 million to do the work
> 6 million are in the armed forces.
> This leaves 17 million to do the work.
> 14 million are in state, county, and city offices.
> This leaves 3 million to do the work.
> 2,500,000 are in hospitals, asylums, etc.
> This leaves 500,000 workers.
> 450,000 are bums or others who will not work.
> This leaves 50,000 to do the work.
>
> It may interest you to know that there are 49,998 people in jails and prisons. That leaves just two people to do all the work, brother—that's *you* and *me* and I'm getting sick and tired of doing all the work by myself, so let's get with it.

In the late nineteenth and early twentieth centuries, the work ethic was severely challenged. Cotton Mather's argument was undermined by the very success of the ethic, the success of American industrialism, organization, and technology. Though the individualistic core of the ethic continued to be lauded, it was obvious that a considerable amount of the talk was rhetoric. To the economic and financial decision makers, individualism was no longer a prime determinant. Clearly, the organization had assumed control. John D. Rockefeller, who played a primary role in the development of the corporation, said bluntly of the consolidation process:

> This movement was the origin of the whole system of modern economic administration. It has revolutionized the way of doing business all over the world. The time was ripe for it . . . . The day of combination is here to stay. Individualism has gone, never to return.

By the turn of the century, those influencing the work process came to identical conclusions and furthered the development of the new system. One of the most important innovators was Frederick Winslow

Taylor. Though practically unknown—there is not a line about him in most American history texts—Taylor contributed to the mechanization of daily work by applying the stopwatch to the minutest of details. Out of his endeavors came the time-and-motion and efficiency experts. In his significant work, *The Principles of Scientific Management* (published in 1911), Taylor, who remodeled the work process at Bethlehem Steel and other corporations, wrote that "in the past the man has been first; in the future the system must be first."[2]

At the middle and lower levels of society the ethic continued to operate, but in a narrower context. As white- and blue-collar workers came to realize, their coglike existence in a huge machine system meant limited mobility. They applauded others who made it into the entrepreneurial class and fantasized about the few who made it big, but were dubious about the viability of the ethic.

Major erosion of the work ethic was caused by the failure to reconcile the basic conflict of individualism and the organization. (The inability or refusal to cope with this contradiction led to the failure of the major reform movements of the twentieth century). Moreover, in the work arena the conflict between individual and organizational values led to a deepening hostility on the part of the worker toward his environment and circumscribed his expectations. Large-scale business enterprises tried to solve the problem, but their conclusions only made the situation bleaker. The Du Pont Corporation is a case in point. In 1964 Du Pont issued Number 26 in its publication series, appropriately called *The Organization and the Individual*. In a large, slick pamphlet over thirty-two pages in length, replete with illustrations, woodcuts, and pictures, Du Pont began its message with an encompassing theory of nature and human life:

> Organization is a fundamental impulse of nature. Ants march as armies; fish weave through ocean currents in millions of schools; bees not only live and move in swarms but maintain a highly structured group existence. Man has applied human intelligence to the exercise of this impulse in order to create infinitely more useful groupings of effort. Skills of organization are in truth one index of the advance of any civilization. For society discovered long ago that the effective organization accomplishes work far in excess of the sum of its parts. Individual effort is multiplied when carefully planned and skilfully directed.

Du Pont's adulation of the organization identified human skills and talents, but only after the successes of the firm had been detailed and its importance to society eulogized.

How was the worker to respond to Du Pont's statements about organizational power, goodness, fealty, and importance? How was the work ethic, with its individualistic component, to be fully expressed? The enormous gap between the reality of the structure of American society and the values perpetuated by its institutions has wreaked havoc with the ethic. A sophisticated populace on all levels has noted the hypocrisy behind vaunted expectations when they are compared with actual exis-

tence. Witness, for example, the actions of the University of California at Berkeley students in 1964 in the first major student uprising in recent American history. Taught in elementary and high school, in college, in countless speeches and novels, in church sermons and in parental education that the individual was the capstone of American society, the students were more than chagrined when they read Chancellor Clark Kerr's work on the functions of the "multiversity," expounding the secondary role of the university in supporting a technological society. In short, Berkeley was not to gear its curriculum to solving problems, expanding knowledge, or honing curiosity and thinking, but was rather in the business of turning out students for the organization. Kerr's words were buttressed by the university itself, which presented students with a monolithic, impersonal labyrinth. Taught that the individual was important, students from high schools of several thousand suddenly found themselves in monstrously large classes. A *single* course—for example, the survey of American history—numbered several thousand students. Students watched the instructor on closed-circuit television and then asked questions of teaching assistants. For these reasons, students in the first several days of the Free Speech movement first held aloft a large IBM card (symbol of the organization) showing the dark letters at the bottom, DO NOT FOLD, MUTILATE OR BEND, and then, with utter disdain, marched through the campus folding, mutilating, and bending IBM cards and tossing them onto the ground. The contradiction between the values of the organization and the individual proved too great to be overlooked, repressed, or denied.

Workers, too, have protested and rebelled against this contradiction. Du Pont's publication is only one of many in the corporate world which attempt to create a fealty that clearly does not exist. That many workers do not identify with their organizations is illustrated by widespread sabotage, equipment theft, embezzlement, and protest. Moreover, workers are cognizant of the disparity between their condition and the power of the organization, between the decision-making process and their own inability to effect change.

The vaunting of the system as primary and essential to the individual led to the acceptance of the assembly line, the conveyor belt, and other mass-production techniques. If production was to be the main goal, then the health and welfare of the worker could be, at very best, only a secondary consideration. The assembly line had been developed before Henry Ford applied it to the automobile industry, and the industrial patterns developed in Great Britain a century before already comprised a system in which the worker was demeaned; but the refinement of such production techniques made the work process a secular horror.

The result was a factory system in which the word "creative" became a blasphemy. Work became stultifyingly dull and harsh, excruciatingly monotonous and repetitious, and extraordinarily hazardous. Pay scales in no way ameliorated the situation; they were kept slightly above survival level for half a century. The vagaries of capitalism kept the worker in a state of constant flux, from full-time employment at twelve hours a day to layoffs for months. Although the Progressive movement produced some reforms in the system before the first World War, it was not until the New Deal period that some degree of protection was given the worker and some aspects of the factory were altered. But even these efforts were meagre.

The harshest parody of the scene was Charlie Chaplin's brilliant film, "Modern Times," in which a worker had to turn two knobs in opposite directions as the conveyor belt carried parts, its speed increasing as the management announced additional requirements. The rotating hands did not cease when the belt came to a partial halt for a lunchtime break. When the belt picked up again, this time carrying Charlie's lunch, the soup spilled in his lap. Eventually he was caught up in the machine's huge rollers and travelled through the plant until the machine coughed him out. The symbolism was apt enough. Workers have been coughed out by the system for over a century. In the quest for efficiency they have been made the "human sacrifices" of our society.

Time is a crucial factor in the American work process. Although workers no longer spend fourteen to sixteen hours a day on the job as they did in the nineteenth and early twentieth centuries, they nevertheless spend a substantial proportion of each day, week, and year in the work process. It is not until the minutes are totaled up that one gets a clear picture of the actual amount of time that working consumes. Consider the following chart.

The inordinate amount of time spent on the job results in an environment which produces feeling of anomie, boredom, frustration, and anger, and a desire to somehow strike back. In July, 1970, for example, a thirty-five-year-old factory worker, James Johnson, shot and killed his foreman and two other workers at the Eldon axle plant in Detroit. At the trial his attorneys argued that working conditions at the factory were so pitiful that Johnson went temporarily insane. Both the judge and jury toured the plant and acquitted him.

Johnson's hostile actions were limited to the plant. But it is certain that such anger is carried into the community, where it is expressed with great hostility and violence. Alfred J. Marrow, President of the American Board of Professional Psychology, in a seminar on "Man and Work in Society" conducted by the Western Electric Company in 1974, explained this relationship between work and the community: "There is a great danger to America in the pent-up feelings of restlessness, anger, and hatred that silently fulminate in our country's factories, shops, and office buildings and spill over after work into our streets and homes."[3]

Workers' actions clearly indicate a pattern of fury. Automobile-factory absenteeism increases 100 percent between 1960 and 1970; drug intake in many factories rose precipitously and corresponded to occupation—sales workers were shown to have the highest rate of hard (and illegal) drug use, including heroin, LSD, and methedrine. Alcoholism and alcoholic abuse rates rose in staggering proportions. The figures indicate that the cost of alcoholic addiction alone was as high as fifteen billion dollars in 1973, and much of this cost was in lost worker time for business and industry. Strikes increased from 3,614 in 1962 with a total loss of 18,600,000 work hours to 5,010 in 1972 with a total loss of

27,066,000 work hours. Many persons chose to collect unemployment compensation rather than remain at a position that paid better but was boring.[4]

It is clear that the issue is not merely higher wages or benefits. *New York Times* labor writer Agis Salpukas related the story about a Detroit auto worker who was always absent on Fridays and worked only four days a week. "How come you show up every day except Friday?" the union steward asked. "Because," retorted the worker, "I can't make enough money by working only three days."[5]

Disenchantment with the work process and its environment was not limited to factory workers. Miners, executives, teachers, doctors, store clerks, managers, and millions of others openly and bitterly complained about their work. Over the decades, government, university, and business groups have conducted surveys and studies in an attempt to uncover the intense antiwork attitudes which have become prevalent in American society. Although their conclusions vary, they all note that the issue is not work itself; work seems to be essential to the human psyche. Rather, the issues are the prevailing settings and structures of the work. Plainly, at every level of society, too many people feel that their work is unfulfilling, unexciting, bureaucratic, and dangerous. Too much energy is given for too few psychological rewards.

Ironically, the strength of the system has produced its most serious weakness. As psychologist Daniel Yankelovich has noted, "The cult of efficiency may well be breeding inefficiency. It is quite possible that the gains in productivity achieved annually by technology, by the infusion of capital, and by foment and organization are more than offset by the tendency to create conditions that make it impossible for people to feel that they are doing a good job or that what they do on the job counts."[6]

Moreover, the concept that competition is the motivation of human development and the measure of individual worth has only added to the intense resentment of work. The American version of competition pits each individual against everyone else in a never-ending series of experiences, at first subtly and then quite directly as the individual becomes aware of society's demands. Although cooperation is often ballyhooed, it is quite clear that its value is mainly rhetorical. Most persons recognize that their livelihoods and their children's future depend much less on cooperation than on economic standing. The chasm between the values of competition and cooperation has led many to regard the vaunting of cooperation as the ultimate societal hypocrisy.

One of the most far-reaching consequences of the nearly universal dismay towards work in this century is that as the rewards of work diminished, the leisure life became increasingly attractive. The coining of "workaholic," a derisive term for a person who held to the ethic in an addictive manner, revealed these changing values.

And so a second factor undermining the work ethic was the substitution of the bourgeois ethic of the good life for the traditional values which viewed work as leading to religious reward and as being a good in itself. In sixties advertising jargon this became the "Pepsi Generation," the "You-Only-Go-Around-Once-Go-For-Gusto" syndrome. In the twenties, the middle-class ideology of the good life assumed command, and has since directed American values toward leisure, pleasure, and excitement—in essence, toward the avoidance of pain, of which work is but one example. How is it possible to maintain the traditional work ethic in the face of mass media which unceasingly entice, cajole, and exhort the populace to take advantage of a consumer lifestyle?

From the twenties to the early sixties, this leisure-life goal went virtually unchallenged. Its success was due not only to the expansion of industry and purchasing power, but also to the ingenious solution of another conflict, the age-old clash between saving and spending. The work ethic had counselled saving for old age, as Mather advised. But a consumer society called for a reconciliation of the conflict between saving and spending. Madison Avenue came to the rescue with a dictum that has become so much a part of our purchasing as to go unnoticed. It is the concept of the savings achieved when one buys in bulk or at certain times or to replace more costly forms of spending: buy ten cans and save twelve cents; shop now at the sale; buy a washing machine and save on the laundromat. In the early sixties a soft-water company which advertised that one could save enough on laundry soap to pay for the softener received an unexpected reply from a housewife:

> We are already paying for our food freezer on the money we are saving on our food bills, we are paying for our storm windows on the fuel we save, we are paying for our car on the carfare we save, and we are paying for our washing machine on the laundry bills we save—frankly, we just can't afford to save any more money at this time.[7]

Recognizing organizational dominance and responding to consumer-oriented directives, lower- and middle-class groups have altered the work ethic in another way. In the original Puritan schema, there was a nobility of *all* labor; now workers distinguish between status and nonstatus occupations. Assembly-line, clerical, menial, and unskilled occupations have been rejected as not producing work satisfaction. Professional executive, managerial, and white-collar jobs, though perhaps not overly satisfying, make possible pleasure-laden activities at the conclusion of the work day. Work for joy rather than the joy of work was the result of these changes.

But there has occurred a third major challenge to the work ethic, a more serious jolt than the others because it attacks the basic philosophical and psychological assumptions of the ethic itself. The Mather work ethic was based upon two interrelated, external notions, the concepts of scarcity and competition. The former, as Philip Slater acutely observed in his provocative book, *The Pursuit of Loneliness*, was the core of the "old culture":

Everything in it rests upon the assumption that the world does not contain the wherewithal to satisfy the needs of its human inhabitants. From this it follows that people must compete with one another for these scarce resources—lie, swindle, steal, and kill, if necessary. These basic assumptions create the danger of a "war of all against all" and must be buttressed by a series of counternorms which attempts to qualify and restrain the intensity of this struggle. Those who can take the largest share of the scarce resources are said to be "successful," and if they can do it without violating the counternorms they are said to have character and moral fiber.[8]

The other notion was that competition would help direct men and women toward the goal of hard and constant work. In the sixties, many noncommitted members of an older generation joined with what came to be known as the counter culture in calling for a different set of values. The creation of an abundant society, or rather a society technologically *capable* of providing the essential needs of the entire population, made the old values of scarcity and competition appear obsolete. With a vast economic and mechanical apparatus fully installed, it is now possible to significantly reduce hours of work, rearrange work priorities, alter work patterns, and produce working conditions which are more pleasurable and creative. More importantly, the counter culture criticized the notion of competition as the mainstay of American values and has attempted to create an atmosphere and a lifestyle based on cooperation. The "war of all against all" is to be replaced with the "good of all for all and with all," with no one denied or rejected, and with feeling and perhaps even love between people.

Secondly, the counter culture has questioned the extrinsic approach to values, arguing for a different consciousness. Although various groups in the eighteenth and nineteenth centuries also rejected the external view of man and woman, they had little impact on society. The counter culture, in arguing for an inner awareness and consciousness, has influenced many persons of the older generation. What the counter culture has specifically suggested is a set of satisfactions and joys which emanate from within. In this sense they have joined David Riesman in rejecting the other-directed self and, while not arguing for a return to the nineteenth-century inner-directed concept, have sought to establish the means whereby individual values, attitudes, and perceptions can have greater expression.

The ideas of the counter culture—equality of distribution based on a technology of abundance, social welfare based on cooperation, inner rewards based on spirituality—present the most powerful assault on the Puritan concept of work as the basis of social organization. *Time* magazine assessed these changes with some insight:

> What is happening is that the work ethic is undergoing a radical transformation. Workers, particularly younger ones, are taking work *more* seriously, not less. Many have abandoned the success ethic of their elders, but they still believe in work. Young and old are willing to invest more of their efforts in their work, but are demanding a bigger payoff in satisfaction.[9]

A vice president of the United Automobile Workers, Douglass Fraser, viewed the situation in larger terms when he exclaimed that "people look at life in different ways than they used to. Maybe we ought to stop talking about the work ethic and start talking about the life ethic."[10]

The growing acceptance of the notion of a "life ethic" has produced many suggestions and some changes to make work more satisfying. Two areas have received attention: work operations and decision making. In the first instance, techniques have been devised to further individual creativity and to allow for idiosyncratic work habits. To counter the monotony and hazards of the assembly line—on which a single worker must keep pace with a moving conveyor belt, repetitiously performing the same movement with no sense of the finished product—the team approach of decades ago has been revived. Some factories have instituted small assembly teams which are completely responsible for a finished product. Manufacturers of the Saab automobile, for example, ran an ad in *Newsweek* and other magazines in 1976 heralding this approach:

SOLUTIONS

Working on an assembly line is monotonous. And boring. And after a while, some people begin not to care about their job anymore. So the quality of the product often suffers.

That's why, at Saab, we're replacing the assembly line with assembly teams. Groups of just three or four people who are responsible for a particular assembly process from start to finish.

Each team makes its own decisions about who does what and when. And each team member can even do the entire assembly singlehandedly. The result: people are more involved. They care more. So there's less absenteeism, less turnover. And we have more experienced people on the job.

Adapting to individual differences, various business and governmental offices have established a system called "flexible time." Initiated in West Germany in the sixties and used extensively in Switzerland and other countries, the stretchable time system was introduced in the United States in 1973 and has slowly made headway. Approximately five hundred companies, organizations, and governmental agencies have adopted this method, whereby employees can vary their starting and stopping times provided they work the required total number of hours.

Minor changes include refurbished environments, with green plants adorning floors and hanging from ceilings, multicolored walls, and movable interiors; four-day work weeks to create more available time for nonwork activities; and special spaces for workers' suggestions, which are answered by the management.

Most important, however, are discussions of the larger issue of powerlessness. Simply stated, neither blue- nor white-collar workers participate in the decisions of the agencies, businesses, or corporations in which they spend the bulk of their adult lives. Although the term is rarely applied to their situation, they can be properly labelled "victims." They have virtually no input into management and are forced to accept decisions made "upstairs." Talk about workers' having representation on a board of corporations, whether industrial, educational, or governmental, has occasionally been heard but little serious action has been taken in this area. There are *some* establishments in which workers now play a primary role in assisting management to make the basic decisions of company policy; indeed, there are instances in which workers have successfully taken over factories after management either declared bankruptcy or permitted the workers to enter the decision-making process during a financial crisis. But there are powerful institutional and psychological forces acting against this sort of participation.

The risks of worker exclusion, however, are profound. Andrew Levison placed the situation into perspective in a provocative article, "The Working-Class Majority":

It is precisely the extension of democracy to the main social and economic areas of American life—the creation of a society without injustices toward blue-collar workers—that is the real issue. It is the fulfillment of the democratic ideal that goes all the way back to the French and American

Revolutions—the ideal of equality and general popular rule which has lain dormant throughout our history.[10]

Without these substantial modifications, it is clear that few people will whistle while they work in contemporary America. Whistling reflects inner harmony. Work cannot be perceived as separate from the totality of being—rather it is expressive of the self. When the concept of work and its physical manifestations are altered to reflect a culture in which creative impulses have first priority, then and only then will work make emotional sense. The restoration of the individual as an integral part of production, as worker *and* as policy maker, is the crucial goal—not in competition with fellow beings, but in cooperation.

In the United States definitions of work were once intimately related **SUMMARY** to religious values. To work hard and rightly in one's particular place was to please God, honor the community, and avoid the ways of the devil. Moreover, hard work was regarded as essential to create new communities and a larger society. In time the definition was expanded to apply to the nation as well. Thus, not only were personal pride and salvation at stake, but national pride as well.

Eventually work came to be regarded as a measure of worth. As the concepts of competition and acquisition became institutionally fixed in American culture—competition not with one's prior achievements but *against* other people—it became necessary for all to adhere to the system. Those who chose neither to compete nor to acquire property or goods were regarded as "bums," "losers," "tramps," or "no-goods," epithets which reflected their status as outcasts. The rewards of society went to those who worked without question or protest and especially to those who went as far as possible beyond the normal desire to make ends meet. In short, the riches of applause went to those richest in material wealth.

There was another aspect to work values. It was argued that the economic system would *automatically* provide rewards to those who worked hard and diligently and followed the rules of the game. Remarkably, despite countless recessions and major depressions, this idea held fast.

Consequently, those who failed to achieve a certain economic position were blamed for their failure. Their own limitations and not those of the economic system were to blame. Those who were forced onto the welfare rolls as a result of a depressed national or regional economy (it was maintained) had either not worked hard enough or had not saved enough for a "rainy day."

But that is the past. Two major depressions in the twentieth century, an overpowering and stultifying factory system, countless recessions, and an economic system which enables only a minority to acquire bounty and comfort have led to a vast protest against the present concept and processes of work. Hence, this article notes that there exists a serious malaise surrounding work in this country. In the thirties, the Walt Disney animated cartoon "Snow White" contained a song the dwarfs sang as they cheerfully skipped off to work: "Whistle While You Work." But while virtually everyone today rightfully talks about the *scarcity* of jobs, the issue of the *quality* of work goes begging. Work is no longer regarded as the path to righteousness or as the way to the good life in a secular society. Millions of white- and blue-collar workers find work tedious, unfulfilling, and demeaning—in short, endurable only because of its absolute necessity for survival. Personal satisfaction is frequently derived from activities outside work.

It is clear that work can no longer be separated from the other facets of life. Moreover, the competitive mode of existence in American society must give way to cooperation. To accomplish this, the entire work environment must be seriously altered and workers, regardless of their positions, must participate in making the decisions governing all our institutions. Democracy does not apply only to the political sphere, but must encompass the economic world as well.

NOTES

1. Moses Rischin, *The American Gospel of Success* (New York: Quadrangle, 1965), p. 3.

2. Frederick W. Taylor, *The Principles of Scientific Management* (New York: Harper & Bros., 1911), p. 7.

3. Susan Trausch, "Work: Labor of Love—or Lifetime of Drudgery," *Boston Globe*, 1 December 1974.

4. Ibid.

5. David Hess, "Money Alone Not Enough to Keep Workers, Especially the Young, on the Job," *Boston Globe*, 15 September 1974.

6. Ibid.

7. Newsletter of the Michigan Department of Health, reprinted in *Consumer Reports*, May 1961, p. 240.

8. Philip Slater, *The Pursuit of Loneliness* (Boston: Beacon Press, 1970), p. 103.

9. Donald A. Morrison, "Is the Work Ethic Going Out of Style?" *Time*, 30 October 1972, p. 12.

10. Andrew Levison, "The Working-Class Majority," *The New Yorker*, 2 September 1974, p. 61.

1 What is your personal attitude toward "work"? What were the influences upon your life that produced this attitude?

2 What have been your work experiences? Regardless of whether they were part-time or full-time, were they satisfying? did they permit expression of your talents and ideas?

3 Do you think work is an integral part of human personality? Have people always worked? Is it possible to live a creative existence without work?

4 Work has not always been what it is today. Describe the work process in the preindustrial period. How does it differ from work in industrial societies?

5 Is education a type of work? Would you describe education as rewarding work, as work which stimulates creativity and personal growth?

6 Is all work equal? What are the different types of work in American society?

7 What kind of work would you prefer to do? Why?

8 If you had the opportunity, how would you structure society to make work more creative, satisfying, and responsive to human needs and desires?

READINGS

Berger, Bennett M. *Working-Class Suburb*. Berkeley: University of California Press, 1960.

Blauner, Robert. *Alienation and Freedom*. Chicago: University of Chicago Press, 1964.

Hunnis, Gerry; Garson, G. David; and Case, John. *Worker's Control: A Reader on Labor and Social Change*. New York: Vintage Books, 1973.

Mills, C. Wright. *White Collar*. New York: Oxford University Press, 1956.

Special Task Force to the Secretary of the Department of Health, Education, and Welfare. *Work in America*. Cambridge, Mass.: MIT Press, 1971.

Turkel, Studs. *Working*. New York: Pantheon, 1974.

Vroom, V. H. *Work and Motivation*. New York: John Wiley & Sons, 1964.

Whyte, William H. *The Organization Man*. New York: Simon & Schuster, 1956.

12 | EDUCATION FOR JUSTICE AND FREEDOM:

THE ECONOMIC DIMENSION

PAUL NASH

Justice demands that the state intervene in the lives of individuals to reduce harmful and unfair inequalities. Freedom demands that individuals be permitted to discover and pursue their own notions of human excellence. These conflicting demands produce one of the most persistent and irreducible tensions in society. It is possible to see much of history in terms of a series of battles between opposed views about how best to deal with this tension. Let me look back briefly at a number of ways in which people have tried to resolve it.

In the Middle Ages, the feudal system weakened the power of the state to control men's lives. Effective power was in the hands of small, independent rulers and private landowners, who profited economically by exacting punitive levies on trade and industry, especially through tolls on canals, rivers, and roads. What was good for the landowner turned out to be disastrous for traders and travelers. It was private enterprise at its most unrestrained. It is instructive to note that an absence of governmental control did not lead to individual freedom. It merely meant that those with minor power were freer to exploit those farther down the scale.

The system of mercantilism attempted to deal with this problem. Mercantilism has been variously seen as a system of economic protection, a method of achieving economic unity within the state, and an attempt to use economic power for political purposes. It consisted of a collection of state regulations and controls that were imposed at a national level, thus bringing some order out of the chaos of local variations and reducing interference with trade and commerce. For example, in England the

Justice and Freedom: from Mercantilism to Keynes

Statute of Artificers (passed in 1562 under Elizabeth I) created a national system regulating trade and industry that lasted on paper until the early nineteenth century. Mercantilism was at its height in the seventeenth and eighteenth centuries. Not only did it protect national industry and trade against foreign competition, but it determined that individuals should be subordinated to the state in their economic affairs.

By the second half of the eighteenth century the regulations of mercantilism had become anachronistic and were experienced as increasingly irksome by the aggressive, energetic entrepreneurs of the nascent industrial age. These men found their spokesman in the Scottish economist Adam Smith, who in 1776 published *The Wealth of Nations*,[1] which became the classical critique of mercantilism and the standard justification of individualism and laissez faire. Smith argued that a country's economic life would prosper best when the government intervened minimally, confining its activities to the preservation of law and order and the enforcement of business contracts through the courts. There should be a large measure of freedom for the individual producer to pursue his own self-interest, for the nation's interest would be best served when each individual actively sought his own good without regard for the good of his fellows. This philosophy arrived at a most opportune moment for the industrialists and merchants of the developing industrial revolution. It released considerable aggressive energy that could be channelled into increased production and it provided a justification for an active pursuit of self-interest by those who were not inclined to waste time on an overscrupulous concern for the social consequences of their business operations.

Although stemming from economic life, the doctrine of laissez faire came to be applied to many aspects of human activity in the nineteenth century. It was argued that the State had no right to attempt to remove or reduce "natural" inequalities among men by interfering in their private lives. The writings of Charles Darwin were distorted to lend a specious credence to this view, by writers who suggested that since "the cream always rises to the top" anything that interferes with the process of natural selection will harm the quality of leadership. The doctrine of Social Darwinism, in the hands of men like Herbert Spencer (whose books were read by millions in both Europe and America), became a justification for economic exploitation under the guise of obeying the eugenic law of the survival of the fittest. Men best serve their society, it was argued, when they concentrate on their own economic gain. The role of government should be to give such hard-driving leaders the greatest scope for their activities. It was, in fact, government of the people, by the minority, for the minority.

In arguments that have a strangely contemporary ring, nineteenth-century laissez-faire writers maintained that if the state provided free education and welfare services for the lower orders, it would destroy the development of their powers of self-help. It was also claimed that for the state to impose taxes on an individual in order to provide schools for his and others' children was an unwarranted infringement of his freedom. If the state fails to provide a child with an education, it was argued, it takes away no freedom that he already holds.

Like mercantilism before it, laissez faire remained the orthodox way of viewing the economic world until it became clear that its principles were in conflict with the facts of life. This moment of truth came for laissez faire with the massive unemployment and economic breakdown of the 1920s and 1930s. Once again the time found a man to make the diagnosis and write the prescription. John Maynard Keynes brought about the most profound revolution in economic thinking in this century. He argued that with the development of large-scale industrialization and huge corporations the individual is now subject to economic forces beyond his influence. There is a need for large-scale intervention by the central government to prevent economic disaster and individual suffering. The period from 1921 to 1939 in Britain was marked by economic depression and persistent unemployment. This was the main period of Keynes's theoretical writing, in which he repeatedly advocated governmental intervention to provide employment, especially through public works. He also showed how the central bank could help by controlling interest rates. His most influential work was *The General Theory of Employment, Interest, and Money*.[2]

Although during the last three decades Keynesianism in the United States has progressed from being viewed as radical socialism to becoming the prevailing orthodoxy,[3] the doctrine of laissez-faire individualism, bolstered by the myths of "private enterprise," lingers on nostalgically in a few places. One such myth is the belief that a laissez-faire governmental posture is justified because, under such a policy, private enterprise built the United States and made it the most economically powerful country in the world. The truth is that from the earliest beginnings of American history governmental intervention and support were the essential foundations of private enterprise. It was government (local or national) that made the economic activities of the private entrepreneur possible and profitable by driving out competing groups (Indians, Dutch, French, Spanish); by making huge land grants to railway builders; by protecting American industries against foreign competition through high tariffs; by constructing huge dams, water systems, and irrigation works; by building an enormous road system for the transport of goods; by providing cheap power through agencies like the Tennessee Valley Authority; by instituting soil conservation and other agricultural services; by supplying a public health service to provide better health for workers; by building schools and employing teachers to make the working population more skillful and productive; and in countless other ways. These things, if left to the agency of private enterprise, could not be done or would not be done adequately. And yet they constitute the very basis of a prosperous economy. The services of federal, state, and local governments now account for about one-quarter of all economic activity in the United States. This proportion is much greater than that in such purportedly socialist countries as India, Norway, or Sweden.

Another myth is that under the American private enterprise system the consumer's freedom and sovereignty are protected, for it is the consumer who calls the economic tune. J. K. Galbraith has most effectively disposed of this myth in his analysis of *The New Industrial State*.[4] He points out that the giant industrial corporation is the typical economic institution of the modern industrial state and he shows how this fact alters the pattern of consumer sovereignty. Outside the industrial system, Galbraith acknowledges, what he calls the accepted sequence still largely prevails, a sequence of instruction and control that flows from the consumer to the market to the producer. But within the industrial system the accepted sequence is of diminished importance in relation to what Galbraith calls the revised sequence. That is, the producer, instead of waiting for the consumer to decide what he wants to buy, reaches forward to control market behavior, shaping the social attitudes and economic demands of the consumer through advertising and the media of mass communication. Because of its gigantic scale of operations, the modern corporation cannot afford to allow its fortunes to be determined by as capricious an agency as the desires of the consumer. Instead, the technostructure (that is, the leadership of the modern industrial enterprise) decides what it needs to produce, produces it, and then proceeds to ensure that people will discover that they want to buy it.

> The Pentagon pursues wars and builds weapons systems in accordance with its own dynamic. Similarly NASA. So the Department of Transportation in relation to the SST. So General Motors as a producer of automobiles that threaten to smother cities and as a sponsor of highways that have already gone far to devour them. So other industry as it subsumes countryside, water and air. This and the resulting discontent could not occur in a society in which the consumer or the citizen is sovereign. It is predictable in a society in which producing organizations are sovereign—in which they have the power to pursue purposes of their own that are different from those of the consumer or citizen.[5]

In reality, then, in the United States neither the consumer nor enterprise is "free." Nevertheless, much energy and ingenuity are spent trying to deny this reality. There remains a widespread suspicion of governmental intervention that renders it difficult to bring about the economic and social control needed to ensure social justice for those consumers and citizens unable to protect themselves adequately from producers, sellers, and advertisers.

A nation like the United States that has not yet altogether thrown off its old laissez-faire myths finds it hard to take the steps necessary to strengthen social justice. We are widely aware that most people need economic security before they can begin to strive for individual excellence. But it has proven difficult to persuade the American government to implement the measures that ought to flow from that fact. Thus, the debate about the stingy provisions of Medicare drags on, at a time when every other advanced industrial country has long ago taken care of the medical needs of all its citizens. One of the problems is that the people who pass legislation are themselves economically secure and hence lack the ability to make that leap of imagination that can take them inside the intellectual and emotional prison constricting those debilitated by poverty.

There is much facile talk about freedom in America. But we know, from the examples of Italy, Germany, Spain, and Greece, that if people suffer enough economic and political insecurity they will reject freedom in favor of security and order. It is not enough for a government to provide a political environment in which all people have maximum access to opportunities: it must also provide an economic and social environment that enables people to grasp and use those opportunities.[6]

Besides the myth of free enterprise, another handicap that keeps America from instituting economic justice is the ethic of Puritanism. One aspect of this ethic is the view that man must work and that it is sinful to reward those who do not. However, in the United States, it is becoming ever more difficult to justify this position in the light of the endemic underemployment of the poor and the poorly trained. So the cruel, Puritan dogma that individual consumption must be linked to individual production becomes a tyrannical anachronism. It is time to break this link through guaranteed minimum wage provisions, so that those who are unable to produce can still consume and live decently.

Another disability is the religious belief that man's lot on earth is lonely and tragic, that the real task is to save men's souls and not their bodies, and that social amelioration is therefore trivial at best and at worst pernicious.[7] Another debilitating argument is that greater social justice and equality will lead to individual and social stagnation by removing the frustration that is a necessary stimulus to effort and achievement. But frustration, in order to be creative, must be accompanied by *hope* (of overcoming the frustration): frustration without hope is destructive. Rather than providing unnecessary frustration for its citizens in order to strengthen their moral fiber, a society ought to help them to adapt. The ability to adapt continually to constantly changing environments saves energy that can be released for creative purposes. We need not fear that such a process would lead to stagnation. A society that removes everyday frustrations by providing basic economic and social security strengthens its members to overcome the frustrations that accompany the creative

Economic Security and Individual Excellence

endeavors that they will then feel able to tackle. Without economic and social security, we lack either the hope or the energy to achieve personal excellence.

Two Nations Under Mammon   In the past, it has been customary to argue that we do not possess the economic resources to build this floor of security under every man, woman, and child, even if that bounty were desirable. This argument has always been vulnerable, but today it is totally untenable in the United States, as well as in some of the other industrialized countries of the West. For in this country we are incredibly and unprecedentedly rich. Our economic resources and power are so great that we can do, in an economic sense, virtually anything we, as a nation, decide to do. It has become more important to ask *what* to produce than *how* to produce. And it is more crucial to ask how to distribute our wealth more equitably than how to produce always more wealth. And these, of course, are inescapably questions of values.

When we examine the values underlying our present national decisions regarding the economics of production and distribution, some disturbing conclusions emerge. The United States contains what Galbraith has called "the affluent society."[8] The number of millionaires in the country increases at the rate of about 6,000 every year, and now totals over 100,000. We were able to fight a major war in Asia, costing $30 billion a year, without apparently reducing private domestic consumption. We were able to siphon enough resources from our economy to pay for the enormously costly moon explorations.

But we can also find in this country what Michael Harrington has called "the other America."[9] Many investigations have corroborated Harrington's claim that a large minority of the American population live in poverty amidst the galling and provocative spectacle of the richest society the world has ever known. Estimates of the number of poor people vary slightly according to the criterion employed, but there is wide acceptance of the figures calculated by the authoritative Keyserling study, that about one-fifth of the nation are living in poverty and another fifth living in deprivation.[10]

Moreover, there are ominous indications that the gap between the rich and the poor is increasing. Robert Lampman's studies of the distribution of wealth in America have shown that the richest people in the country have steadily increased their share of the country's assets. While they held 21 percent of all personally held assets in 1949, their share rose to 25 percent in 1953, and to 28 percent in 1961.[11]

Similarly, Gabriel Kolko's extensive investigations revealed not only that America has suffered from a drastically unequal distribution of income since at least 1910, but that this inequality has not lessened over the years. Indeed, the real situation has worsened for the poor, since those at the higher income levels have benefited from a series of tax exclusions and special rates, while obtaining increasing proportions of their income in nontaxable and nonreported fringe benefits.[12] Kolko's findings also demonstrated that stock ownership in the United States is concentrated in the hands of a small percentage of the population and that, among those who do own stock, an even smaller percentage control the great bulk of it, despite popular myths to the contrary.[13] At the other end of the scale, he showed that 24 percent of the spending units in the country had no liquid assets at all, 27 percent had between $1 and $500, and 63 percent had less than $1000.[14] An earlier study by Lampman showed that 1.6 percent of the adult population owned 80 percent of the personally held corporate stock, almost all the state and local bonds, nearly 90 percent of all corporate bonds, and between 10 and 35 percent of all other types of property.[15]

This gap between rich and poor is constantly exacerbated by other changes in society, such as developments in technology. Technological changes in the cotton industry in the South have removed work opportunities for countless lower-class workers, leading to a mass exodus from the rural areas and an enormous migration to the cities of the North. Developments in automation and cybernation are similarly changing the occupational structure of the country, rendering highly trained labor more valued and rewarded, and diminishing even further the demand for unskilled and semiskilled labor. We face a real danger of producing a large, permanent minority excluded from the affluent society who are liable to continue to be left out because of their inability to do anything for themselves. They lack political power, as is repeatedly demonstrated by their failure to bring about desperately needed improvements in their children's schools, resulting in an educational loss to the entire nation. And they lack effective economic power, for their real needs cannot be expressed in terms of purchasing ability. Their endemic poverty constitutes a brake on the entire economy. The satisfaction of their basic needs could provide a stimulus to healthy economic growth, which would contrast sharply with much of the trivial or pernicious products of affluence. It has been estimated that to raise the American families living in poverty to an adequate standard of living would require a transfer of payments of about $10 billion to $15 billion—an increase smaller than half of the annual cost of the Vietnam war at its height.[16]

Tax reform in the United States as a means of redistributing income and wealth has usually been unsuccessful. The tax system is supposed to be progressive—that is, the proportion of income paid in taxes rises steeply as income rises. But massive loopholes render the taxation pattern not very progressive and permit the rich to keep most of their wealth. It has been calculated that in the last two decades, the *effective* federal tax rate on the richest 1 percent of the population has declined from 33 to 26 percent.[17] This failure of taxation to effect significant redistribution of income is even more marked in the case of local and state taxes. Since property and sales taxes ignore income, they bear most heavily on the poor. This is significant, because state and local taxes are becoming increasingly important sources of revenue. Federal tax revenues rose only from 18 percent to 19 percent of the gross national product between 1955 and 1975, while state and local taxes rose from 8 percent to 13 percent of gross national product during the same period.[18]

At the same time, the poorer classes are kept in line by continuous inflation. As prices continue to rise, workers must always earn more in order to keep up. This need renders them more docile and accepting of the economic and social structure. When inflation gets out of hand, instead of controlling it through a redistribution of income—which would alter the social structure—a recession is decreed, with an increased "acceptable level of unemployment." This constitutes another whip over the poor. In a recession the lower levels of workers are thrown out of work first. The upper levels have a better chance to maintain their jobs and their incomes. The social structure remains intact.

The wealthy are less vulnerable to inflation and recession. Their affluence is less closely tied to salaries and wages: significant proportions of their wealth come from dividends, rent, interest, and capital gains, which have many protective devices to shelter them from economic vicissitudes. The group representing the top 1.5 percent of the country's wealthholders receive only 10.8 percent of all salaries and wages, but they receive 74.8 percent of all dividends received, 71.4 percent of all capital gains, 52.5 percent of all rent, and 27.9 percent of all interest.[19]

The greatest danger in the present situation is the possible development in one country of two nations, growing increasingly farther apart in wealth, education, lifestyle, and understanding. The first nation, already clearly visible, adopts a lifestyle that stems from a long and secure immersion in affluence. Its cultural values reflect this security: at best they transcend gross materialism and represent a sensitive tolerance for diversity and individuality; at worst they betray a selfish complacency or a willful obtuseness. The second nation has until recently been largely invisible, but has become increasingly difficult to ignore. Its cultural values stem from scarcity or poverty; they are not refined or softened by abundance or security and hence are usually viewed with abhorrence by members of the first nation.

It requires little social analysis to become aware that such a dichotomized situation is inherently explosive. As the gap between the two nations grows larger, it becomes a formula for violence.

The Cost of Inequality

The nation that permits gross economic disparities to persist among its citizens must be prepared to face certain consequences and incur certain costs. The heaviest cost is the loss of human excellence. Societies that fail to compensate for natural inequalities among people or

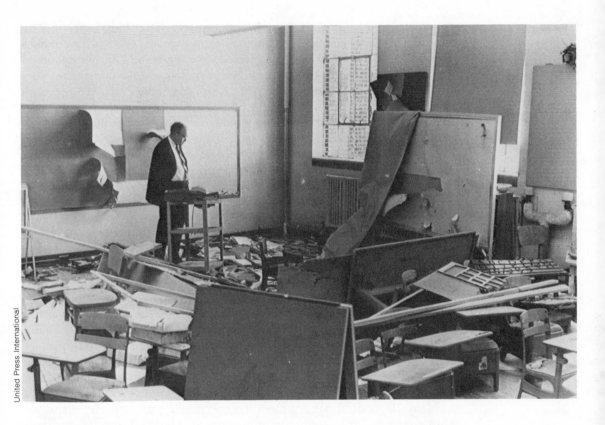

to mitigate the harsh effects of deprivation find that those in positions of superiority often display arrogance and complacency, while those in inferior positions are often debilitated by feelings of impotence and resentment. Such feelings serve to destroy the motivation of people to work cooperatively to bring out the best in one another.[20] The principal casualty is the quality of human relationships that prevails in such a society. In his classic defense of equality, R. H. Tawney placed cardinal value on the kind of human relations that violent disparities of income and opportunity are apt to impair.[21]

In the United States, despite all the fine egalitarian words in commencement speeches, we are suffering from costly inequalities and injustices. These injustices are most obvious in the treatment of blacks, Puerto Ricans, Chicanos, migrants, and Indians at home; and of Asians, Latin Americans, and others abroad. This treatment is bound up with the distorted values of the economic system, which make it profitable to produce napalm to deepen human suffering and unprofitable to produce works of art to enhance human joy. The injustices are maintained through official support for superficial but conscience-calming gestures of "charity" (such as income tax allowances for "gifts"), which encourage us to postpone the fundamental changes that justice requires.

Postponing these changes becomes ever more inexcusable in an increasingly affluent society. "The soil grows castes; the machine makes classes," Michael Young has suggested. We might add to his aphorism the thought that electronics creates lifestyles. We now have the technological knowledge and resources in this country to enable everyone to choose his own style of decent living and intelligent work. But we have not yet created the economic reforms that would enable these conditions to exist. Our failure has a cost. "It is impossible for a highly industrialized society to attain a widespread high excellence of mind," wrote John Dewey, "when multitudes are excluded from occasion for the use of thought and emotion in their daily occupations."[22]

It can be—and has been[23]—argued that the real enemy is capitalism, which encourages competition and selfishness, sets man against man, and engenders hierarchy and inequality; and that the solution is socialism, which encourages cooperation and altruism, unites man with man, and engenders fraternity and equality. There is much validity in this theoretical argument, and I can well understand why Russians feel that their "schools for altruism" are superior to American "schools for selfishness," as I have been told by visitors from the Soviet Union. Nevertheless, an examination of practice in the United States and the Soviet Union leads to the impression that the similarities between the two countries are more significant than their differences.[24] And this is strengthened by the conviction that these nineteenth-century terms, "capitalism" and "socialism," bear ever less relevance to contemporary conditions and problems. If modern nations meet their economic problems successfully it will be because they define them in terms of twentieth-century technology, not nineteenth-century ideology.

However, if technology gives us the *possibility* of decent living conditions, meaningful work, diversified lifestyles, and widespread human excellence, it *guarantees* none of these things. For these things to happen, there must be deliberate intervention in the processes of economic life to bring about a more equitable distribution of the fruits of technology and more humane decisions about what to produce. And this requires planning.

Planning and Responsibility

The concept of the responsible state arose originally out of moral considerations, including concern for those people who suffer misfortunes through illness, unemployment, old age, or bad luck in choosing their parents. But it has often been discovered that the establishment of the responsible state also has an important economic consequence: it strengthens the nation's prosperity by spreading effective economic demand widely through the population by means of social security and welfare payments. This building of large-scale consumer demand helps the economy to avoid depression and reduces business risks.

The creation of the responsible state has been the appropriate political response to the economic conditions brought about by industrialization. In taking this step the state recognizes its responsibility to intervene actively in order to establish the conditions for greater equality of opportunity, for national prosperity, and for individual creativity and excellence. Andrew Schonfield has shown that those industrialized countries that have been less inhibited in adopting central planning and public control in their economic affairs have had much higher rates of economic growth since 1945 than those industrialized countries whose "free enterprise" traditions have caused them to hang back from the exigencies of planning.[25]

The concept of the responsible state is the logical extension, in economic terms, of the political concept of the equality of all men before the law. If this latter concept is to have any operational meaning, it must be supported by the equalization of economic opportunity that the responsible state is designed to provide. This is what justifies the state's imposition of restrictions on the opportunity of one individual to exploit others or to degrade the quality of their lives.

It is sometimes argued that the supportive climate of the responsible state harms economic progress by removing or reducing the incentive provided by the prospect of economic hardship and the subsequent effort to avoid it. It is true that suffering, poverty, and hardship *can* be stimulants to effort and even to creativity; but more often they act as depressants, notwithstanding romantic stories of starving artists and writers. In terms of unused, unexplored talents, the social cost of permitting avoidable hardships to continue is grossly out of proportion to the possible learning that might be gained from such misfortunes. The responsible state is a way of reducing valueless inequalities of material circumstance, without determining the ways in which the subsequently released energies will be used.

It is an American tragedy that the concept of "welfare" has become associated with *passivity*— with a passive person accepting handouts that serve to reduce his self-respect and remove his incentive to work— instead of with *activity*—with a person being lifted up so that he can exercise more initiative and gain a stronger hold on his own life. This unfortunate development has come about because of an unintelligent approach to the problem of welfare. The basic welfare right that a person needs is the right to work, for a person who cannot find work is, in effect, being told that society can get along quite well without him. Hence, it would really make no difference if he were to die or disappear. Many lower-class fathers have indeed disappeared or even died because they could in this way better "provide" for their families, under our archaic welfare rules, than if they stayed around. If a person cannot find work on his own, then the responsible state must find work for him. To argue that work cannot be found for all who want it is absurd. One need only look at our decaying cities, with their unswept streets, dangerous parks, rotting bandstands, unpainted buildings, unplanted flower beds, broken playgrounds, and absent amenities, to see one outlet for available workers.

The chief enemies of the responsible state are war and poverty. War is an abuse of our resources, diverting them from creative, welfare-producing activities.[26] Poverty drags down the whole economy, for the poor lack the money to make their demands effective and hence they hinder general economic growth. An appropriate alteration in our national values would shift the power of effective demand from the military to the poor. The budget of the Department of Defense dwarfs that of the Department of Health, Education, and Welfare: the situation should be reversed. As the expenditure on military activities and preparation is reduced, it becomes necessary for the state to increase expenditure on health, education, welfare, and culture, for otherwise the inability of private consumption and investment to compensate for massive reductions in military expenditure brings a grave risk of economic depression.

Of course, the Department of Defense would argue that its enormous budget is necessary in order to protect the welfare of the country. Apparently, however, it does not regard this argument as self-evident, for it reportedly employs more than 6,000 public relations personnel to present its case to the public. When an agency is clearly necessary for the public welfare it does not need a regiment of public relations men.

Another notion that threatens the responsible state is a narrow concept of "efficiency," which would measure everything in terms only of financial profit and loss. When the British government announced in 1967 its program for the reform of the financing and administration of the British Railways, it stated that it would spend 55 million per year on subsidizing unecomonic passenger services. As long as we in this country persist with the archaic idea that public transportation must "pay for itself," it is hard to be optimistic about its future. To be moved safely, quickly, pleasantly, and with a minimum of noise, dirt, and atmospheric pollution from one place to another is a basic good. In the United States, we have allowed the automobile lobby to cheat us of this good. Transportation is an aspect of human welfare. Like education, it cannot be expected to show an immediate "profit." It must be provided, even at a loss. Conventional accounting methods of evaluating such services must give way to methods based on human values.

It is now clear to most people that one of the most crucial aspects of human welfare is the nurture and improvement of the natural environment. It is futile to expect to raise the quality of life in a country if individuals and corporations are permitted to profit by destroying the environment. In the United States we have allowed military, industrial, and agricultural interests to take incredible risks with the lives of present and future citizens by polluting the earth, air, and water with destructive agents. The evidence concerning the harmful nature of radioactive fallout, industrial waste, and pesticides is too well documented and too widely known to need repeating. The hazards of stockpiling atomic, bacteriological, and chemical weapons are similarly recognized. At long last people are beginning to realize that something is wrong when the same oil interests whose "private enterprise" despoils the natural beauty of Santa Barbara and destroys fish and seabirds by the million are protected by enormous tax benefits and protective tariffs, so that the consumer may pay inflated prices for oil and gasoline, which could be purchased much more cheaply if admitted freely from abroad. The inequality between the protection of the oil industry's interests and those of the consumer is thus linked to a reduction in the quality of the human environment. In a genuinely responsible state, the quality of life as it is shaped by the environment would be given precedence over private profit.

It is worth noting that there is a clear connection between inequality and environmental destruction. The rich do most of the polluting. This is true both within a single country and in the world as a whole. It has been estimated that the United States, with 6 percent of the world's population, uses between one-third and one-half of the world's raw materials and about one-third of the world's energy. One person in the United States has the same impact on energy consumption as twenty-four persons in the developing continents. Affluent people and nations use a disproportionate and increasing amount of the world's natural resources, including clean air and water. The movement towards ecological balance needs to be accompanied by a movement towards more equitable income balance. One way to restore both balances is to tax private industries (such as those producing oil and automobiles) that are major polluters and to invest this tax revenue in subsidized housing, public transportation, schools, hospitals, urban restoration, and the preservation of natural resources.

A government that takes its responsibility for the total welfare of its people seriously can make significant contributions to the quality of cultural life. For example, the vitality and creativity of the British theatre since 1945, in contrast to the relative torpidity and derivativeness of the American theatre, has been due in large part to the fact that British playwrights, directors, and actors are freed for daring innovation because the theatre is government-subsidized, while the American theatre is rendered timid and cautious by its dependence on the box office.[27]

In 1966 a group of concerned people, under the leadership of A. Phillip Randolph, developed a plan to attack the social problems of the United States. This plan was called "A Freedom Budget for All Americans" and it suggested six objectives to be attained in the seventies. These objectives were: to provide full employment for all who are willing and able to work, plus education or training for those who need it in order to become employable; to assure a decent living standard to those who cannot or should not work; to wipe out slums and provide decent housing for all Americans; to provide adequate medical care and educational opportunities for all, at a cost they can afford; to purify our air and water and develop our public transportation and natural resources on a scale suitable to our growing needs; and to unite sustained full employment with sustained full production and high economic growth.[28] This program, modest as it is, provides a basic minimum for the creation of a responsible state in this country.

Inevitably, the responsible state involves some loss of immediate gratification in the cause of long-term gains. It is a form of discipline that we undergo so that we and our successors can have greater enjoyment in the near and distant future. Essential to the responsible state is long-range planning of social and economic priorities. If the individual citizen shows a tendency to sacrifice the future of others for his own immediate satisfaction, the state must step in and act responsibly towards the future, through planning, conservation, environmental control, welfare legislation, income redistribution, and the use of taxation to improve the cultural level. The most important of the responsible state's activities is education, for it is through this means that people can be helped to see for themselves the need to be responsible to the future—to their children and to those who will come after them. When this happens, the people themselves become the designers of excellence, and inequalities between those who plan and those who are planned for disappear.

Education and Justice   Given the present harsh gradient of inequities in the world, the achievement of greater justice requires a redistribution of economic and educational resources in favor of the poor, both within countries and among countries. This necessitates some reconceptualization of the nature of education, interdependence, planning, and productivity. Let me examine some of these concepts in an attempt to gauge what changes will be demanded of us in the coming decades.

In classical economics, the three factors of production are land, capital, and labor. The relative importance placed upon each of these three factors has varied throughout the last two hundred years, the period of industrialization. In the late eighteenth and early nineteenth centuries, the era of economic theorists like Smith, Malthus, and Ricardo, land was seen as the vital productive element. From the mid-nineteenth century to the mid-twentieth century, capital came to assume greater relative importance. In the second half of the twentieth century, it is becoming clear that labor—especially the *quality* of workers, industrial managers, technicians, and technological innovators—is the crucial factor determining productivity. And the most important element in determining the productive capacity of labor in a technologically advanced society is education. Hence, education must now be viewed not as economic *expense*, but as economic *investment*. Expenses are those economic costs that are regarded as necessary but from which we do not expect any return. Investments are outlays that are made in the expectation that they will more than pay for themselves in the future.

A basic dilemma in the process of using education as an agent of greater justice concerns the kind and amount of central government action that is necessary to bring about whatever educational and cultural changes are appropriate. It is unlikely that major cultural changes can be achieved without planning and intervention by the central government to a degree that is sure to elicit protest and opposition. In the United States it is clear that the federal government must be an active educational agent on a massive scale if equality of opportunity is to be anything more than a slogan. No other agency has access to the necessary economic resources. The federal government has already intervened massively in education (through support of land-grant institutions, the GI Bill, the National Defense Education Act, and the Elementary and Secondary Education Acts) without surrendering to the temptation to control day-to-day educational processes and results.

Nor is there any ineluctable reason why increased national planning and intervention in education need result in increased uniformity and conformity. We can plan for diversity as well as for uniformity. Indeed, there is evidence to support the belief that a central government is more likely than a local school committee to leave important educational decisions to teachers and students. However, unless there is a consistent national commitment to the achievement of a just society, the educational system is always liable to be thrown into disarray and despondency by the capricious withdrawal of central government support. One of the worst recent examples of this was Richard Nixon's decision, in his second term of presidential office, to make a massive shift in federal support away from the public educational sector of the economy and towards the private business sector.

It is not enough, moreover, that the central government be strongly active in the educational life of the country. For it makes a fundamental difference *how* the planning and intervention are done. There are several criteria by which good central intervention can be distinguished from bad. In most circumstances, it should be complementary rather than complete; stimulating rather than satisfying; and transitional rather than permanent. Even more important, the planning should be participatory rather than autocratic. Those who will be affected by educational decisions must be able to participate in making those decisions. Several other requirements follow from this demand. Planning must be sufficiently loose and flexible to permit important dimensions to be worked out as the implications of a decision made at the center are followed through and translated into action at the periphery. This means that those who are to be involved in the planning and implementing at *all* levels must be provided with the necessary data and raised to the cultural level that will enable them to make good decisions. Hence, planning becomes an educational enterprise, not only in its promise but in its actual operations.

Education and Freedom

Just as the economic dimension of life does not exhaust the definition of life, so schooling does not exhaust the definition of education. Man neither lives by bread alone nor grows by schooling alone. Education is a larger concept than schooling because persons are larger than institutions. We tend to forget this in a period of bureaucratic dominance, but it remains true that institutions are merely man-made abstractions, while persons are the mysterious, tangible expressions of the life force of the universe and therefore of ultimate importance.

There is no greater cause in the world than the liberation and enhancement of human life. I have argued in this chapter that this cause can be served by large-scale intervention to bring about a more equal distribution of economic resources and educational opportunities. The problem is that this redistribution tends to focus on schools (meaning all formal institutions of education, including higher education) as the vehicles of change. This presents no problem when schools actually perform redistributive and liberating functions. The question is whether they in fact do this or whether they make things worse.

Schools are central institutions in society. It would therefore be naive to expect them to represent values antithetical to the predominant societal values. If a society is marked by inequality, hierarchy, competition, and acquisitiveness, it is not surprising that its schools manifest the same qualities. If a school is large it can also be expected to bear the characteristics of most large institutions of any kind, and be bureaucratic, impersonal, quantity-conscious, and rigid. However, schools have a special function, in that they are supposed to be concerned with fostering the growth, liberation, competence, creativity, and joy of human beings. This complicates the picture and makes the task of evaluating the productive contribution of schools very diffcult.

If we look at the history of the public schools in the United States during the last hundred years, it becomes clear that their development has occurred principally as a response to changing economic conditions. The second half of the nineteenth century saw the creation of the common school in response to the economic need to create from a predominantly agricultural population a labor force able to man the rapidly growing factory system. In the late nineteenth and early twentieth centuries the comprehensive high school arose as the institution geared to the economic demand of welding into a working force the European peasant immigrants whose social relations and lifestyles were incompatible with the demands made of the American labor force. In the mid-twentieth century the urban ghetto schools became the custodians of the inadequately socialized children of black, southern, agricultural laboring families that had been driven to the northern urban factories as a result of technological unemployment. The result of these changes was the development of a hierarchical, centralized school system with prevailing values similar to those of an efficient factory: docility, subordination, external motivation, and passivity, with an absence or scarcity of initiative, creativity, flexibility, nonconformity, collaboration, and autonomous judgment.

Henry Perkinson has shown convincingly that the American public school has not been an effective instrument in achieving its purpose of equalizing opportunity and solving the major social problems of the country, despite the claims of its supporters that it is a panacea. Perpetuating the divisions and inequalities in society, the schools have served as selectors to separate winners from losers on the basis of socioeconomic class and to polarize society into self-satisfied whites and victimized blacks, despondent city dwellers and indifferent suburbanites, conformists and rebels. Perkinson saw little hope of the American people's being able to recognize the inefficacy of the schools as agents of democracy.[29]

Paulo Freire, in speaking of aid to developing countries, has made a distinction between *modernization* and *development* that might provide an analogy for the distinction between schooling and education. Modernization, in Freire's view, is a mechanical, nonreciprocal process in which the local recipients of aid are controlled and manipulated by outside experts. The locus of initiative and decision making lies outside the community undergoing change, which is thus prevented from becoming the agent of its own transformation. Development, on the other hand, is a genuine transformation through which new structures and practices emerge. This transformation grows out of a critical dialogue between the outside educators and the local peasants. The peasants' own common sense and wisdom become vital aspects of that dialogue. In order to be effective in facilitating this kind of change, the educators must enter into the cultural universe of the peasants and make themselves vulnerable to reciprocal transformation.[30] Much schooling throughout the world has resembled modernization. In order for education to be a liberating force in the lives of individuals it must become more like development.

What prevents schooling from being educational in this sense? One problem is that much of the impact of schooling on the development of students' values, attitudes, and beliefs comes not from the formal curriculum but from the "hidden curriculum," that is, the social relationships that arise in the schooling process. Factors like competition or collaboration among students, authoritarian or egalitarian attitudes among teachers, and creative or alienated attitudes on the part of teachers and students towards their work become crucial.[31] These factors in the school are usually reflections of the dominant values of society. In American society, with its emphasis on material productivity in response to external motivation by those higher in the hierarchy, it is not surprising that in schools students are not customarily in control of the educational process but are motivated by those above them to work for external, material rewards (grades) rather than finding their own work fulfillment in the product of education (knowledge) or in the process (learning).[32]

This alienation of the student from his work through external motivation and hierarchical authority has become the central problem in education. It reflects the problem of work alienation that has become the central problem in economics. Keynesian economists focused on finding a solution to the problem of unemployment. Monetary theorists tried to find a solution to the problem of inflation. Neither has found a solution to a more basic problem: even with employment and controlled inflation, workers in industrialized societies still feel alienated and oppressed. Freedom comes from gaining a sense of unity about ourselves. We risk losing this when we put our faith in things external to ourselves. The danger is that we lose our identity to them, whether they are positions (such as professor of education) or possessions (such as antiques). Then the role or thing comes between us and our sense of self. To the degree that schools foster this process of identification with things, positions or successes external to the student's self, they fail to serve the purposes of liberation and education.

Are education and schooling incompatible? Many thoughtful critics think so. The most eloquent and celebrated of these critics is Ivan Illich. There is something in the very nature of schooling, argues Illich, that thwarts the development of a personal capacity for autonomous and initiating social activity and reduces its victims' resistance to the blight of commodity fetishism. "People who have been schooled down to size let unmeasured experience slip out of their hands . . . . They do not have to be robbed of their creativity. Under instruction, they have unlearned to do their thing or 'be' themselves, and value only what has been made or could be made."[33]

Illich and his followers are bringing to our attention something of basic importance: it is foolish to assume that by putting someone in a school for a number of years something educationally beneficial will inevitably happen to him. The experience may be educationally meaningless or even harmful, if we define education as a process of learning to liberate oneself from oppressive and alienating forces. Illich's prescription of deschooling society sounds radical, but it is not radical enough. It may benefit many people, especially those who are apparently prospering in the affluent society but who at present pay a heavy price for their success by surrendering much autonomy in the process of learning to please the boss. But I suspect that under Illich's "cure" those who are at present doing badly in our society will fare even worse. The more open educational structure that Illich recommends will reward those who can gain access to information about educational resources (that is, mainly middle- and upper-class people) and penalize those (mainly lower-class people) who lack the money, mobility, contacts, and information to take advantage of the educational opportunities available.

Schools are not likely to disappear just because they are educationally disappointing. Too many vested interests support their retention. Moreover, I cannot entirely share Illich's condemnatory picture of the effects of schooling. If we look only at the structural pattern of relationships in the school, Illich's gloomy view is warranted. But I am impressed by the ability of human beings to relate humanely, sensitively, and lovingly to each other even within dehumanizing institutions. Much of the growing and learning that occur in schools take place in the nooks and crannies of the formal structure. I am encouraged by the number of young people who define school as the place they go to meet their friends. It is impossible to control or manipulate the vast majority of human events that happen in school. They constitute the stuff of spontaneous interactions among people, especially peers, and out of this stuff growth, learning, and liberation can come.

However, this is not enough. We need to break down the rigid, formal authority patterns that make it so difficult for good educational things to happen in school. One way to do this is to weaken the monopolistic position the school holds over the process of education. There is a need for a multiplicity of educational alternatives, both outside and inside schools. This is already occurring, though not yet on an adequate scale. More and more people are recognizing that the school is not the only route to self-realization or vocational competence. The United States Census Bureau indicated that the percentage of eighteen- and nineteen-year-old men enrolled in college dropped from 54.4 percent in 1970 to 49.9 percent in 1975. The percentage of twenty- to twenty-four-year-old men in college dropped from 29.3 percent to 26.4 percent during the same period.[34]

We also need to develop a principle of client sovereignty in education to match the principles of consumer sovereignty in economics and of citizen sovereignty in politics. It is absurd that those who are paid to be the servants of the educational process (such as university administrators) should wield autocratic power over those who are the clients and raison d'être of that process (the tuition-paying students). This absurdity is destined to disappear. I see more and more students learning to use schools (as they use other resources) for educational purposes, rather than permitting themselves to be *used* by schools for bureaucratic or institution-building purposes.

Schools provide not only education but also accreditation. People are often willing to tolerate educational abuses from their school in return for the promise of being licensed to practice a profession. But here, too, there is a prospect for change. While performance-based or competence-based schooling has some serious dangers and pitfalls, it also holds the possibility of breaking the monopolistic grip of the school on the process of accreditation. If licensing becomes a matter of demonstrating professional competence rather than enduring a term of years in an institution, the school will become only one of a number of routes to the attainment of that competence.[35]

An education that transcends the dialectic of justice and freedom will enable the student to enjoy productive, self-fulfilling, nonalienated work. Whether this education takes place in schools or in other settings, it will have to respect the autonomy of the individual to decide for himself the nature of that productivity. If schools are capable only of training people to be obedient producers in response to others' orders, they will increasingly be bypassed in favor of educational settings where people can learn to fulfill themselves through self-chosen work.

SOLUTIONS   The following proposals are offered as promising ways of meeting the problems and dilemmas outlined in the preceding chapter.

1. There is a need to strengthen the powers of those federal and state agencies whose responsibility it is to protect citizens and consumers from manipulation, exploitation, poisoning, injury, and premature death. The Federal Trade Commission, the Federal Communications Commission, and similar agencies are pitifully impotent in their ability to protect us from being cheated, misled, and harmed by business and political interests.

2. The federal and state governments need to recognize their responsibility to enter the lists on behalf of the individual citizen in order to balance the scales that are at present heavily tilted in favor of the large corporations.

3. Schools and colleges should assume the responsibility of killing the myths of consumer freedom and sovereignty that hinder understanding and good decision making.

4. One of the best reforms this country could carry out would be to transfer 50 percent of the budget of the Department of Defense to the Department of Health, Education, and Welfare. This single act could transform and renew our society.

5. We need a negative income tax or minimum income guarantee that will ensure that every person in the country will be able to eat adequately, live decently, and be cared for when sick, whether he or she works or not.

6. The concept of the responsible state includes the demand that the state find work for everyone who wants to work and cannot find employment in the private sector.

7. Our major polluters, such as the oil and automobile industries, should be assessed a special ecological tax, the proceeds of which should be invested in subsidized housing, public transportation, schools, hospitals, urban restoration, and the preservation of natural resources.

8. There should be a massive redirection of federal support away from the private business sector and towards the public educational sector of the economy.

9. Educational and economic planning must be done in such a way

that those who will be affected by decisions are able to participate in making them.

10. It is necessary for us to understand the distinctions between schooling and education, between modernization and development, and between the formal curriculum and the hidden curriculum.

11. We need to break down the rigid, formal, authority patterns in schools and colleges that hamper educational efforts.

12. We need to develop a multiplicity of educational alternatives, both inside and outside the schools.

13. We need to develop the principle of client sovereignty in education to match the principles of consumer sovereignty in economics and citizen sovereignty in politics.

14. We need to help students to see themselves at the center of the educational process rather than on the periphery, and to learn how to use schools for educational purposes rather than permitting themselves to be used by schools for bureaucratic or institution-building purposes.

15. Competence-based education should be explored as one way to break the monopolistic hold of schools and colleges on the process of accreditation and licensing.

16. The major task is to help each individual to define productivity for himself, rather than merely accepting an externally determined definition.

SUMMARY

This examination of the economic dimension of education takes us into the center of the tension between the demands of justice and the demands of freedom. Can we reconcile the claim of justice—that the state intervene in individuals' lives in order to reduce unfair inequalities—with the claim of freedom—that individuals be permitted to discover their own forms of self-determination? The author tries to grapple with that problem by exploring the dialectic between the distribution of economic wealth and the opportunity to learn to enjoy productive, fulfilling, nonalienating work.

Focusing primarily on the United States, he suggests that there have developed in this country two nations—the affluent society and the "other America"—which are growing dangerously farther apart in wealth and mutual understanding. This split is reflected in the world at large, where the industrialized nations constitute an economic upper class and the underdeveloped nations an economic lower class, also growing farther apart. He goes on to argue the merits of the concept of the responsible state as a manifestation in economic terms of the political concept of the equality of all people before the law.

He next examines the distinction between education and schooling and assesses the possibilities of schools being the agents of greater economic justice and personal freedom. After discussing the problem of student alienation as a consequence of external motivation and hierarchical authority relations in schools, he considers the arguments of Illich and others in favor of deschooling as the solution. He concludes that schools are seriously defective, but not hopeless, vehicles for the reconciliation of the justice/freedom dilemma.

NOTES

1. Adam Smith, *An Inquiry into the Nature and Causes of the Wealth of Nations,* ed. Edwin Cannan (London: Methuen, 1950).

2. John Maynard Keynes, *The General Theory of Employment, Interest and Money* (London: Macmillan, 1936).

3. For an amusing and incisive analysis of this metamorphosis, see John Kenneth Galbraith, "How Keynes Came to America," in *Economics, Peace and Laughter* (Boston: Houghton Mifflin, 1971), pp. 43–59. See also Harry G. Johnson, "Revolution and Counter-Revolution in Economics," *Encounter* 36, no. 4 (April 1971): 23–33.

4. John Kenneth Galbraith, *The New Industrial State* (Boston: Houghton Mifflin Co., 1967), especially chapters 6 and 19.

5. John Kenneth Galbraith, "Economics as a System of Belief," in *Economics, Peace and Laughter*, pp. 76–77.

6. See Dorothy Lee, "Equality of Opportunity as a Cultural Value," in *Freedom and Culture* (Englewood Cliffs, N.J.: Prentice-Hall, 1959), p. 44, for an illustration of this position.

7. C. P. Snow has pointed out that "there is a moral trap which comes through the insight into man's loneliness: it tempts one to sit back, complacent in one's unique tragedy, and let the others go without a meal." C. P. Snow, *The Two Cultures and the Scientific Revolution* (New York: Cambridge University Press, 1959), pp. 6–7.

8. John Kenneth Galbraith, *The Affluent Society* (Boston: Houghton Mifflin, 1958).

9. Michael Harrington, *The Other America: Poverty in the United States* (New York: Macmillan, 1963).

10. In 1962, "poverty" was defined as the condition of a family with an annual income under $3000 or of an unattached individual with an annual income under $1500. "Deprivation" was the term applied to the condition of families with annual incomes between $3000 and $5000 or individuals with annual incomes between $1500 and $2500. Leon H. Keyerling, *Progress or Poverty: The U.S. at the Crossroads* (Washington, D.C.: Conference on Economic Progress, 1964), pp. 16–25. (See also note 15.)

11. Robert J. Lampman, *The Share of Top Wealthholders in National Wealth: Paper No. 74* (Princeton: Princeton University Press, 1962), p. 6.

12. Gabriel Kolko, *Wealth and Power in America* (New York: Praeger, 1966), pp. 13–23.

13. Ibid., pp. 50–54.

14. Ibid., pp. 47–49.

15. Robert J. Lampman, *Changes in the Share of Wealth Held by Top Wealthholders, 1922–1956: Paper No. 71* (New York: National Bureau of Economic Research, 1960), pp. 29–33. Subsequent studies have confirmed that, despite the liberal policies of recent decades, national income remains as inequitably distributed today as a half century ago. The percentage of national personal income received by each income-tenth of the population has been largely unchanged since 1910. See Gus Tyler, *Scarcity: A Critique of the American Economy* (New York: Quadrangle, 1976), chapter 4. It has also been confirmed that wealth holdings among different sections of the population have not changed significantly since 1947, a period in which so much has allegedly been done for the poor of the United States. See Charles Sackrey, *The Political Economy of Urban Poverty* (New York: W. W. Norton, 1973), chapter 1. See also Mihajlo Mesarovic and Eduard Pestel, *Mankind at the Turning Point: The Second Report of the Club of Rome* (New York: E. P. Dutton, 1974).

16. Robert L. Heilbroner, "Priorities for the Seventies," *Saturday Review*, 3 January 1970, pp. 17–19.

17. Richard Parker, "The Myth of Middle America," *The Center Magazine* 3, no. 2 (March 1970): 61–70. See also Tyler, *Scarcity*, chapter 4, and Sackrey, *Political Economy*, chapter 1.

18. U.S. Bureau of the Census, *Statistical Abstract of the United States: 1976*, 97th edition. (Washington, D.C.: U.S. Government Printing Office, 1976), pp. 256, 393.

19. Parker, "Myth of Middle America," p. 65.

20. For an argument supporting this position, see Daniel Jenkins, *Equality and Excellence: A Christian Comment on Britain's Life* (London: SCM Press, 1961), p. 30.

21. R. H. Tawney, *Equality* (London: Allen and Unwin, 1931), p. 239.

22. John Dewey, *Individualism Old and New* (New York: Minton, Balch, 1930), p. 133.

23. "Capitalism, which consecrates the profit motive, tends to make a man think, in the context of his livelihood, first and mainly of himself, and so produces an atmosphere unfriendly to goodness—to the going out of his self into a union that realizes selfhood. The capitalist way of living encourages greed: discourages altruism: makes gentleness, tolerance, mercy, fellow-feeling very much harder than they might have been. . . . The machinery of socialism—nationalism and the rest—can make it easier for men to be good, if certain conditions are fulfilled: and can do so positively as well as negatively, because the right kind of socialism (a) has abolished the climate of pushfulness in workaday life (this is its negative contribution) and (b) has replaced it by a climate of altruism (this is its positive one): and altruism, cooperation—in an activity so ubiquitous as earning our livelihood—must encourage our other-regarding impulses over our whole way of thinking and feeling." Victor Gollancz, *More for Timothy* (London: Gollancz, 1953), p. 25.

24. Writing of the United States and the Soviet Union, Galbraith has said, "Both systems [of economic management] are subject to the imperatives of industrialization. This for both means planning. And while each uses different techniques for dealing with the individual who contracts out of the planning, planning in all cases means setting aside the market mechanism in favor of the control of prices and individual economic behavior. Both countries, quite clearly, solicit belief for what serves the goals of the industrial mechanism. Instead of contrast leading to implacable conflict, a more evident economic

tendency is convergence." Galbraith, *The New Industrial State*, p. 332.

25. Andrew Schonfield, *Modern Capitalism: The Changing Balance of Public and Private Power* (New York: Oxford University Press, 1966).

26. Speaking of the 1970 United States military budget of $80 billion, Robert L. Heilbroner wrote that it "has sucked into the service of fear and death the energies and resources desperately needed for hope and life." "Priorities for the Seventies," *Saturday Review*, 3 January 1970, p. 17.

27. "If you don't have to worry whether a show can pay for itself, then the sky is the limit and the cow can jump over the moon." Peter Hall (English director of the Royal Shakespeare Company), *Boston Globe*, 6 June 1967.

28. See Jervis Anderson, *A. Philip Randolph: A Biographical Portrait* (New York: Harcourt Brace Jovanovich, 1972), p. 344.

29. Henry J. Perkinson, *The Imperfect Panacea: American Faith in Education, 1865–1965* (New York: Random House, 1968).

30. Paulo Freire, *Pedagogy of the Oppressed*, trans. Myra Bergman Ramos (New York: Herder & Herder, 1970); Denis Goulet, "On Critical Consciousness in the United States: The Relevance of Paulo Freire," *Perspectives on Development and Social Change* (Cambridge, Mass.: Center for the Study of Development and Social Change, 1973).

31. See Samuel Bowles, "Cuban Education and the Revolutionary Ideology," *Harvard Educational Review* 41, no. 4 (November 1971): 472–500.

32. Ibid.

33. Ivan D. Illich, *Deschooling Society* (New York: Harper & Row, 1971), p. 40. See also his *Celebration of Awareness: A Call for Institutional Revolution* (Garden City, N.Y.: Doubleday, 1970), and *The Metamorphosis of the School* (Cuernavaca, Mexico: Cidoc, 1969).

34. U.S. Bureau of the Census, *Statistical Abstract*, pp. 119–20.

35. For an attempt to explore the tension between performance-based teacher education and humanistic values, see Paul Nash, *A Humanistic Approach to Performance Based Teacher Education* (Washington, D.C.: American Association of Colleges for Teacher Education, 1973).

QUESTIONS

1 Are the claims of justice and of freedom necessarily antithetical or can one reasonably hope to reconcile them in a society like that of the United States?

2 What are the major advantages and dangers of strengthening the powers of federal and state agencies to protect citizens and consumers from exploitation and manipulation?

3 Should everyone in our society be able to eat adequately, live decently, and be cared for when sick, even if he does not work? Or should those who will not work be abandoned by the state?

4 What is the difference between education and schooling? between modernization and development? between the formal curriculum and the hidden curriculum? Are such distinctions worth making? Why?

5 What is your own experience of authority patterns in school and college? What changes would you advocate in such patterns? What are the consequences of the patterns you experienced and what consequences do you expect to flow from your recommendations?

6 What does it mean to help students to learn how to use schools for "educational" purposes? Does not education automatically occur in schools and colleges? If not, what hinders it?

7 Who defines "productivity" for you? What does it mean to you to be "productive"? What difference would it make if you insisted on defining "productivity" for yourself?

8 What do you think of the notion of "deschooling" as a solution to the problems of student alienation? What advantages and disadvantages could flow from it?

READINGS

Freire, Paulo. *Pedagogy of the Oppressed*. Translated by Myra Bergman Ramos. New York: Herder and Herder, 1970.

Galbraith, John Kenneth. *The New Industrial State*. Boston: Houghton Mifflin, 1967.

Harrington, Michael. *The Other America: Poverty in the United States*. New York: Macmillan, 1963.

Illich, Ivan D. *Celebration of Awareness: A Call for Institutional Revolution*. Garden City, N.Y.: Doubleday, 1970.

Keynes, John Maynard. *The General Theory of Employment, Interest and Money*. London: Macmillan & Co., 1936.

Marx, Karl. *Capital: A Critique of Political Economy*. Chicago: Kerr, 1925–26.

Myrdal, Gunnar. *An International Economy: Problems and Prospects*. New York: Harper & Row, 1956.

Nash, Paul. *A Humanistic Approach to Performance-Based Teacher Education*. Washington, D.C.: American Association of Colleges for Teacher Education, 1973.

Smith, Adam. *An Inquiry into the Nature and Causes of the Wealth of Nations*. Edited by Edwin Cannan. London: Methuen, 1950.

Tawney, R. H. *Equality*. London: Allen and Unwin, 1931.

Ward, Barbara. *The Rich Nations and Poor Nations*. New York: W. W. Norton, 1962.

13 | HOW TO GROW OLD AND POOR IN AN AFFLUENT SOCIETY*

ROBERT N. BUTLER

In our image of affluent America we tend to think of poverty as isolated in self-contained "pockets," rather than in terms of the dry statistics that tell us that up to one-fifth of our nation are poor, and that one-fifth of the poor are citizens over 65 years of age. In our mind's eye the poor are black ghetto children playing in the streets, or "welfare mothers," or a formal front-stoop portrait of a white family in Appalachia. We are less likely to see the old as poor because they are literally less visible. They rarely make newsworthy scandals in the daily papers or models for the posters of the United Givers' Funds. They escape notice by staying in their homes, locked in by timidity, illness and disability, lack of money, poor transportation and fear of crime. Some have been left behind in rural backwaters after the young reached out for work in the city or life in the suburb. Others are lost even to the Census Bureau, when they hole up in "hotels" or boardinghouses, or even wander, transiently, from town to town. A few are tucked away in institutions, their aloneness safely hidden from view.

Many we don't see because we don't care to look. One research group describes what can happen:

> If too many of them frequented a cafeteria where food was low in cost and where it was possible to sit for a long time over a cup of coffee and a roll, younger people began to go elsewhere to eat, repelled by the sight of arthritic hands carefully counting out coins, dragging feet, and clothes unkempt or clumsily restyled. All too often even a friendly proprietor was obliged to change the rule or close his restaurant. Then the customers disappeared, to hot dog stands or to the hot plate in a furnished room.[1]

A vast number of older people in America are poor by government definition.[2] Many more are economically deprived by anybody's definition. In 1970 one in every four older persons had *less* income than the

*Published as Chapter 2 of *Why Survive? Being Old in America* (New York: Harper & Row, 1975), pp. 22–36. Reprinted with permission.

Everett English

official, very conservative poverty estimate based on the government's own emergency food budget.[3] By 1972, with the passage of significantly increased Social Security benefits, there was a reduction in the number of the "officially" poor. Nonetheless, a minimum of 3 to 3.6 million older Americans remain poor by government standards. Millions more barely manage to survive.[4] Moreover, virulent inflation erodes new benefits.[5]

Over half of our elderly population live in deprivation. I am not speaking of lacking money enough to visit one's grandchildren, keep chilled drinks in the refrigerator or buy a subscription to the local newspaper. I mean lacking food, essential drugs, a telephone in the house to call for help in emergencies. Some take desperate measures to make ends meet:

> A 69-year-old widow was apprehended while trying to steal a 25-cent can of soup in a supermarket in Miami Beach with its opulent waterfront hotels. Shoplifting is seen as a necessity by some old people. This widow had $114 each month to live on in 1971.

The problem of *relative deprivation* cannot be ignored either. The daily ordeal that so many of the aged experience occurs in the context of an affluent society. Bare economic survival erodes the body and spirit even when it is the common condition. It is the more painful and humiliating in a country where the needed resources are not scarce but merely distributed unevenly; where the top fifth of the population has over 40 percent of the wealth and the bottom fifth less than 5 percent;[6] where the average aged family lives on half of what it had in earlier years. This country grosses almost a trillion dollars a year and spends only 4.2 percent of it toward aiding the old. With much smaller resources at their disposal, Britain and France spend 6.7 and 7 percent of their respective gross national products on their elderly. The denial of an active part in the social life of a nation or in a fair share of its benefits increases the feeling of isolation, fear and deprivation.

The Total Income Picture

To understand the poverty of older Americans in an affluent society we need to see how the old currently are supported and the difficulties they experience. Those 65 and older as a group receive their aggregate income as follows:

Table 13-1	PERCENT OF INCOME	INCOME SOURCE
	46	Retirement benefits (Social Security, 34%; public pensions, 7%; private pensions, 5%)
	29	Earnings from employment
	15	Income from assets
	4	Public assistance
	3	Veterans' benefits
	3	Other (contribution from family, etc.)[7]

Two crucial and distressing facts about poverty and old age are clear. **The Old Grow** First, although the numbers of those in poverty in other age groups are **Poor** said to be decreasing, there has been an increase in both the number and the proportion of aged poor. The U.S. Senate Special Committee on Aging, using the conservative government-established poverty threshold, reported that in 1969 there were approximately 4.8 million people aged 65 and older who were living in poverty, almost 200,000 more than in 1968. In this same period, said the committee, poverty declined by 1.2 million for all other age groups.

Second, the elderly are the fastest-growing poverty group. This is new poverty, not simply the poverty transmitted from generation to generation within the same family. Independently of previous means and previous socioeconomic status, one may be thrown into poverty for the first time in old age. Catastrophic diseases, or the sheer cutback of income in retirement, may create instant poverty where none previously existed.

In fact, *many—I think most—elderly poor have become poor after becoming old.* What does it mean in the lives of retired persons to receive a total pension income from both public and private sources of one-quarter to one-half or less of their average preretirement earnings?

> Mrs. Woods: an old lady with a lightly made, stately body, carried with pride and some pain. Her beautifully wrinkled skin was almost translucent, showing her high cheekbones.
>
> She would be pretty if not for the worried strain in the voice, face and hands, the shifting feet, distant eyes. A successful lawyer's wife, she had always been able to live in comfortable circumstances but was now under increasing financial pressure. She had outlived her savings.
>
> When her lawyer makes a visit she puts on the violet and blue print dress. She does not change her flat brown shoes. She pins her hair in a soft white knot in back. The lawyer was the family attorney for years. He comes to receive her endorsed checks and pay her bills. He makes out a check to the realty company for rent, and two other checks, one for the housekeeper who comes once a week, the other for food. He continues to help her now, when she is on public assistance of $92 per month.

Why should Mrs. Woods's last years have become mired in the struggle to survive? She is not the exceptional case—her situation is commonplace among the old.

The words "poor," "poverty" and "relative deprivation" have become **What Is** so commonplace that they have lost all reality. Anyone who reads **Poverty?** newspapers is apt to be familiar with the images of the outstretched hands of some of the six million starving, homeless refugees fleeing from East Pakistan, or of the distended stomachs and empty expressions of malnourished children in our own rural backwaters or city streets. If one keeps these painful images in mind, it becomes tempting to imagine that less dramatic poverty is "only relative," and therefore less worthy of concern.

How does one arrive at a realistic idea of what constitutes poverty in old age? The official government estimate of poverty,[8] that is, the amount of income necessary to meet essential needs, is based on the Department of Agriculture's Economy Food Plan for emergency use, designed to keep a healthy person alive and functioning reasonably for thirty days. Since the average family spends approximately one-third of its income on food, government economists multiplied this amount for food by three to obtain the total minimal budget that one could possibly live on; those with less are considered poor. In 1973, for an individual this was an income of $2,100 a year or less. The 1973 weighted average for a two-person older family was $2,640.

What if we take a less biological view of poverty and consider more than brute survival by examining the lot of the aged in terms of America's standard of living? The Retired Couple's Budgets of the Department of Labor estimate what a "modest but adequate" standard of living would cost, rather than an emergency budget. These budgets are detailed listings of items and quantities to meet the normal needs of an urban retired couple as judged adequate by the staff of the Bureau of Labor Statistics (BLS), which intermittently revises them.

The "experts"—economists, statisticians and social-science analysts—develop these hypothetical budgets for a hypothetical standard of living, assuming an existing inventory of clothes, furniture, appliances and so on. The retired couple is defined as a husband, age 60 or over, and his wife, who are self-supporting, living independently in their home, in reasonably good health and able to take care of themselves. More recently the Bureau of Labor Statistics has designed two additional Retired Couple Budgets, one at a somewhat lower standard of living and the other at a higher standard. "All three budgets provide for the maintenance of health and allow normal participation in community life, taking into account social and conventional as well as physiological needs." So say the government experts—but is this the case?

DO THE OLD NEED LESS?

The total Intermediate Budget for the Retired Couple, calculated in 1971,[9] was $4,776.[10] Let's look at what that detailed budget allows. The staff concluded that $24 per week was adequate for groceries. (An elderly couple was allotted a little over $3 per meal plus tip in a restaurant once every week.) Housing averaged $139 per month, including household repairs and furnishings. For example, 1 percent of a sofa could be purchased every year. In the way of clothes, every year 7 percent of a topcoat was allowed for a man, one and one-fourth of a street dress for a woman, one house dress, two-thirds of a bra, etc. The husband was allowed 15.3 haircuts a year and his wife 1.7. For each person, one-fifth of an eye examination for glasses was allowed and one-half pair of glasses. Needless to say, it is not possible to live statistically.

America advertises and fantasizes old age as a period of leisure, travels and hobbies, but the recreation allotment in 1971 was $91 a year for both the husband and wife. No allowance was made for visits with children, travel away from home or vacation costs. The retired couple was allotted $5.30 a year to provide for a pet animal, which is for many people their major solace in loneliness, and often an aid to safety as well. Traditional American virtues have emphasized providence, but no money was allotted for savings.

The Retired Couple's Budgets in themselves tell us something about popular conceptions about the old "needing less." The Bureau of Labor Statistics has developed a whole set of budgets to describe a modest but adequate income for different family compositions. To compare the itemized accounts of these budgets for retired and younger couples with those for the four-person family is informative. One might expect housing, transportation and certain other costs to be greater for the larger younger family and some personal-care costs to be higher for the older family, which is, indeed, reflected in the budgets. But the reasoning behind the appreciably smaller clothes allowances for the adults in the older family or for home furnishings or gifts and contributions is less understandable. In the intermediate budget,[11] for example, the retired man was allowed $94 for clothing, the younger man $204. The older woman was given $100 for all clothing, and the younger wife $211.[12] Should we automatically assume that retired men and women are going to be leading drab and inactive lives? The older family was allotted $231 for gifts and contributions, the younger family $270. Yet the older couple might well have children and grandchildren to make gifts to, as well as churches and special causes to which to contribute.

Retirement budgets are calculated on the assumption that the older couple have already accumulated much of what they will need for the rest of their lives. This is asking a lot of the healthy, potentially active older couple who may have twenty or more years ahead of them—if not the hundred years it would take to save the 1 percent a year allotment toward a new sofa! Are the elderly expected to keep their appliances and furniture in better shape than the rest of the population in our economy of planned obsolescence? Are they expected to care less for the satisfaction of wearing something new on those special occasions when they go out? What do we know about the spending patterns of older people?

In studies of consumer expenditures high-income families—whether younger or older—tend to show similar expenditure patterns.[13] In other words, if older couples have the money, they are as interested in recreation, clothes and a pleasant home environment as anyone of any age. *The reason old people spend less is that they have less to spend.*[14]

To put these two government estimates—the poverty line and the modest but adequate budgets—into perspective, let us note that economist Leon Keyserling considers those who are above the poverty line but below the Bureau of Labor Statistics budget to be living in "deprivation."[15] In terms of elderly couples and individuals the following are the poverty "definitions" and "guidelines" available at the time of the 1971 White House Conference on Aging:

Table 13-2	ORGANIZATIONS WHICH HAVE DEFINED POVERTY	POINT BELOW WHICH POVERTY OCCURS	
		COUPLE	INDIVIDUAL
	Official poverty level, 1970	$2,328	$1,852
	Retired Couple's Budget (Bureau of Labor Statistics, 1971) Intermediate		
	"Modest but Adequate"	4,776	2,627*
	Higher Budget	7,443	4,094
	National Welfare Rights Organization, 1971	**	2,250
	Chairman, National Caucus on Black Aged, 1971	9,000	6,000

*Estimated as 55 percent of couple.
**No "guideline" available.

Hobart Jackson, chairman of the National Caucus on the Black Aged, affirms that an adequate income is the chief need of the elderly. He sets a minimum floor of $6,000 for a single old person and $9,000 for an aging couple. Jackson's figures are much more realistic than the official guidelines. They begin to approximate the median income of Americans regardless of age. The National Council of Senior Citizens, however, only supports the recommendation of the 1971 White House Conference on Aging for approximately $4,500 a year per couple, which was less than the 1970 Retired Couple's Intermediate Budget. Official 1967 analyses of the Retired Couple's Budgets against actual income levels, completed by the Bureau of Labor Statistics, found that 56 percent of all older couples had less income than even this "modest but adequate" budget!

Estimates of government agencies and private organizations—other than the National Caucus—run low because of conceptions of "political realities." In other words, requests and estimates are determined by what politicians feel have a chance of being approved by Congress, or the President, or an appropriate state official, rather than by what is needed. Government agencies also feel pressures to minimize the estimate of need. Increasingly, mild reform proposals become no more than mere ritual, a tinkering with the lives of the old.

What would it cost to provide a better standard of living? The National Welfare Rights Organization estimated in 1971 that to bring all Americans up to their minimal budget estimates ($6,500 for a family of four, $2,500 for a single person) would cost between $30 and $50 billion. Other agencies and organizations have offered similar estimates. To support all age groups decently will cost a lot of money; it cannot be done cheaply. As a people we either want to direct our resources in this direction or we do not.

THE WIDOW'S MITE

Widows, single women and members of minority groups are particularly disadvantaged economically. As one leading economist, Dr. Juanita Kreps, views it, "The older woman is the poorest in society today."[16] In 1970, 51 percent of elderly women living alone fell below the poverty line. One reason for the poverty among older women is that more women than men become widowed because they tend to marry men older than themselves and outlive males by an average of seven years.

Since 1973, with the change in Social Security law, widows (and dependent widowers) now receive 100 percent of the spouse's Social Security benefits instead of the 82 1/2 percent that worsened the widow's economic plight before then. But other retirement programs remain prejudicial. Under the federal retirement system, for example, the survivor of a retiree gets only 55 percent of the retirement benefits received before the retiree's death. The wife who in a very real way helps in the support of her husband and family with the care of the home, food and children during working years is not supported in turn upon her husband's death.

The 1972 change in the Social Security law meant that nearly 3.8 million persons (widows and dependent widowers) would receive an additional $1.1 billion in benefits. An estimated 200,000 persons would be "removed" from official poverty. But note what this means in actual dollars—benefits for the average widow were increased $18 per month, from $138 in 1972 to $156 in 1973. That's not much!

Today's thirty million working wives will be in a better position when widowed than the present generation of widows. As Dr. Kreps points out, however, if women continue to earn less than men their retirement benefits will be proportionately smaller. Women's life opportunities have been restricted throughout the life cycle by sex-role conditioning, inequitable salary levels and prejudice, and this continues on into old age with pension benefits. Job discrimination early in life adversely affects an older woman's options. Department of Labor statistics show that a woman's median income is substantially lower in all major fields of employment.[17] In the labor force as a whole, 60 percent of women working full time the year round earn less than $5,000 annually, compared with 20 percent of the men. Only 3 percent of women earn more than $10,000, compared with 28 percent of men. On the average, women earn 58 percent of the income earned by their male counterparts.

These statistics, of course, refer to working women. The Department of Labor estimates that another 32.5 million women are not "working" because of home responsibilities. These women, mostly married, will be especially dependent on their spouses' retirement benefits. As they age, many will be forced increasingly to turn to the state for help.

MULTIPLE JEOPARDY

Minority-group elderly live in multiple jeopardy because of the effects of both racism and ageism. Blacks, Chicanos, Puerto Ricans and Chinese are among the minorities whose old age is often marked by grim poverty. It is frequently said that we have very little useful data about the relevancy of race to aging. But we know the overall truth: to be old is bad enough; to be old and not white is even more terrible. The likelihood of being poor, reports the Senate Special Committee on Aging, is twice as great for elderly minority groups as for the white population, and four times as great as for our total population at all ages.

America's one million elderly blacks continue to face discrimination and most live in poverty.

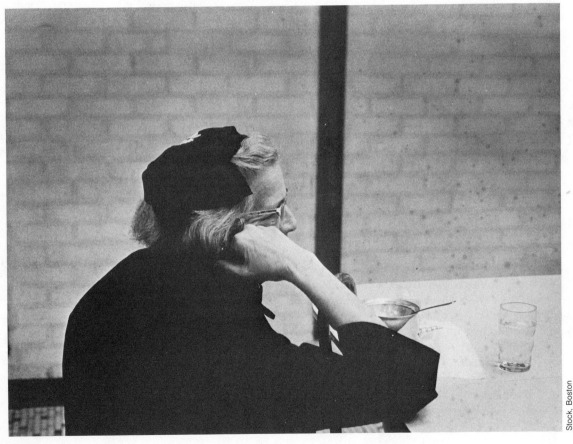

Stock, Boston

For them life has meant the slum, the public aid roll, the second-hand store and the empty table. They have lived through six decades of inadequate medical care and have survived the ravages of discrimination, poor education, slum conditions, and unemployment. . . .

Seven of ten elderly black Americans have incomes below $3,000 per year and half of them less than $2,000 per year.[18]

In absolute numbers more whites than blacks are elderly poor (85 percent of the total elderly poor are white, 15 percent black). Black poverty, however, is more profound than white poverty. The percentage of aged blacks living in poverty is twice that of aged whites. Forty-seven percent of all aged black females have incomes under $1,000. In rural areas two out of three aged blacks fall below the poverty line.[19] Furthermore, elderly blacks tend to have more people dependent on them than do the white elderly.

More elderly black people live with younger people than do white elderly: 28 percent of them live in families with a young head of household compared to 8.9 percent for all elderly regardless of race. There are many reasons why a larger percentage of black elderly live with their children: the importance of the role of grandmother because the mother works or is away; the need for the sharing of income within a family, including the older person's Social Security and public-assistance payments; and the respect and sense of responsibility, said to exist more strongly in black households, in caring for and protecting one's parents, particularly the aged mother.

Those older blacks who do not live with relatives are in a much more disadvantaged economic situation: 75 percent of all elderly blacks living alone fall below the poverty line, and Project FIND reported that of black widows an amazing 85 percent were living in poverty, with another 5 percent on the borderline. These are depressing facts indeed for an affluent society.

The impacts of racism upon aging are reflected in life expectancies at time of birth, which in turn affect retirement benefits. Robert Hill has emphasized that the average life expectancy of black males has actually declined by a year over the 1960–70 decade. Among males, nonwhite death rates were higher than those of whites through age 84, with a reversal occurring beyond that age. Nonwhite female death rates were higher than white through age 74.

Poverty is widespread among minority groups, and even the traditional kinship support of the family is broken down when the family as a whole is impoverished or the needs of the elderly outstrip the family's ability to help. Even East Asian–American elderly, usually thought of as much better off financially than other minority racial groups, experience the late-life consequences of lifetimes of discrimination.

The American Indian elderly suffer from a much lower life expectancy than blacks or whites; their average length of life is estimated at 44 years, so comparatively few survive to old age. Mexican-American elderly fare little better; for example, in Colorado their life span is 56.7 years compared to 67.5 for other Colorado residents.

In view of these differential life expectancies a number of people, including Dr. Jacqueline Johnson Jackson of Duke University and Dr. Inabel Lindsay, former dean of social work at Howard University, have called for the enactment of legislative changes in existing Social Security policies. There is a need to reflect differences in racial life expectancies by lowering the minimum age-eligibility requirements for beneficiary status for old age, survivors, disability and health insurance. This holds true for other pensions as well, since few elderly blacks live long enough to collect benefits.

THE RURAL ELDERLY POOR

Rural older people tend to be poor in part because self-employed farmers or agricultural workers were not covered by Social Security until recently. Few have private pension plans. Rural communities suffer from a shrinking tax base and an increasing scarcity of services when young people migrate to cities. The rural elderly are left with the task of maintaining their communities and services. A shortage of employment further hampers them in their attempts to supplement their income.

What about the War against Poverty?

One wonders what happened in the Office of Economic Opportunity (OEO), which was the one agency supposed to be concerned primarily with poverty. What did OEO ever do for older people? During 1965 and 1966 there were arguments as to whether the aged poor would be a prime target group or simply a minor concern of the agency. In the end, budgeting outlays for the aged in the OEO through 1966 ran 2 percent of the total. This was against the Congress's mandate in 1965 that directed OEO to consider special programs for the aged "wherever possible." In its early days, the only program to which OEO gave any priority was the Medicare Alert Program,[25] in which older people were given temporary jobs at $1.25 per hour in order to let other older people know of the benefits available under Medicare. One of the few other OEO programs for the aged poor was the Foster Grandparent Program,[26] which allowed older people to help neglected, institutionalized, or mentally retarded children. It was a very successful but very modest program.

In some measure the cost-benefit philosophy that was popular among many federal agencies contributed to a negative attitude toward the old; the elderly were felt to be a very poor investment. Indeed, this was the point of view that Sargent Shriver, then OEO director, seemed to take when he spoke before a Senate subcommittee. He felt that there was little that could be done for older people, that they had low educational levels and poor health, and could not compete for jobs.[27]

> . . . It seems to be extremely difficult to find efficient, economical ways of actually helping the very elderly poor to get out of poverty. Congress already has a magnificent record through the Social Security Administration, through the proposed Medicare bill, and through other programs, for bringing effective help to the aged, but when you get to the problem of how do you actually help the aged to help themselves to get out of poverty it is more difficult.

It was not clear from what Shriver said why, if Congress had such a "magnificent record," there was so much poverty.

Since those first years of OEO, the allocation for special programs for older people has increased somewhat, and several new service programs have begun. From the OEO's Office of Special Programs the following fund pattern was given for specific programs,[28] collectively called Senior Opportunities for Services (SOS):[29]

(Requested)	1968	1969	1970	1971	1972
(Millions)	$2.8	$6.4	$6.8	$8	$8

SOS is an appropriate acronym if one considers the enormity of the problems of old people and the short time available to them before death. But these yearly budget increases have been modest to the point of tokenism and light-years away from eradicating poverty among the elderly.

In addition to specific programs for the elderly, older persons have been served by Neighborhood Health and Legal Services, Emergency Food and Medical programs and others. One of the more creative programs was Operation FIND,[30] which employed 320 older persons as canvassers and reached more than 50,000 older persons. The objective was to find the friendless, isolated, needy and disabled to determine needs and to direct them to services.

THE IMPACT OF POOR SERVICES

We should be concerned not with income alone but with the *means* by which society provides for a decent old age. If we assured older people certain essential *public* and *social* services, such as transportation, adequate medical care, decent public housing, and rent subsidies, being "poor" would take on a different meaning; it would be less cruel and terrifying. But in fact, our country does not provide or provides inadequately such essential services. Government-backed medical insurance and public housing are still controversial and poorly implemented concepts in the United States, decades after they have become commonplace throughout Western Europe.

Neither money alone without services nor services provided under "means tests" without adequate income are desirable. Older people would prefer to be able to pay all their taxes, to pay full fare on transportation, to be able to afford an occasional movie. They don't really want to depend upon tax abatement, reduced transportation fares, food stamps, golden-age cards for the movies, Medicaid and Old Age Assistance. They should not be stigmatized by "special" cards and "benefits," nor be forced to hustle frantically to survive.

Myths about Poverty   We need to examine the myths about income that underlie the plight of the elderly.

THE MYTH OF IMPROVIDENCE

Many Americans tend to believe that poverty among the old is their own fault, attributable to their failure to prepare adequately for economic security. Consider, however, the hypothetical John McCabe,[20] born in 1900 and living his primary earning years during the Depression between 1929 and 1939—in which, at its height, 25 percent of the work force was unemployed. Between his twenty-ninth and thirty-ninth years his situation was greatly affected by the economic status of the nation. He, like the rest of today's elderly, bore the brunt of the Great Depression—as they have borne the brunt of the inflation of the 1960s and 1970s. Moreover, since retirement occurs much earlier now than formerly (the average man leaves the work force at 57[21]) and is increasingly compulsory, McCabe will have had to finance an extended retirement period. He has roughly 14 years in "retirement" if he dies at the average age of 71. (The longer one lives, of course, the more one has the chance of outliving private pension benefits and exhausting savings.)

McCabe entered the army or the work force in 1917. He would have been in the work force approximately 40 years. During those 40 years he would have had to earn enough not only for his immediate purposes but for his future needs in his old age. In addition, he would have had to provide for his wife, who probably will outlive him. He most likely helped support his own parents, who would not have been covered by Social Security. He started contributing to the Social Security fund at 35 in 1935.

It would have been difficult for McCabe to accumulate any savings during the Depression in his prime years, or in the inflation of his so-called golden years. Like other retirees, he is dependent on a fixed income from Social Security and possibly (but unlikely) a private pension now being radically eroded by the rising cost of living. Between 1948 and today the value of the dollar has fallen castastrophically. What was worth 100 cents then was only worth 57.6 cents by 1972.[22] Virtually half of the dollar's purchasing power was gone. Whatever McCabe had saved between 48 and 72 years of age, and whatever plans he had made, were profoundly affected by that erosion.

The pointing finger of "improvidence" becomes a cruel gesture to this man, who was told—when he was in his thirties—that only by spending every penny would he help remobilize the economy; unfair to a man with the burden of supporting both young and the old in his family during his peak middle years; misdirected onto a man living in a technology of planned obsolescence.

As a final indignity, the same people who claim old poor people have been improvident may accuse them of hiding their assets. But about 40 percent of single older citizens have total assets of less than $1,000.

THE MYTH OF AVAILABLE JOBS FOR THE ELDERLY

Against overwhelming odds almost one-third of the income of older people still comes from current earnings. This income is derived largely from part-time, unskilled and low-paid jobs such as janitor, night watchman and babysitter. Employment is often concealed "bootleg" work to avoid income taxes and Social Security penalties that could nullify any financial benefits of working.

Age discrimination, unemployment levels and arbitrary forced retirement drastically reduce the incomes of the elderly. (The problem of employment in America goes beyond the elderly, of course, with youth, women, minorities and workers over 45 particularly subject to underemployment and unemployment. We have also failed to develop successful techniques for the great transitions: from military to peacetime industries, from goods to services. Obviously, these problems have affected the old age of the elderly of today and will affect those of tomorrow.)

THE MYTH OF ADEQUATE SOCIAL SECURITY

Social Security keeps more than twelve million people of all ages out of poverty as officially defined. It is the source of 50 percent of the income of nearly 66 percent of retired single workers and 50 percent of elderly couples. It is essentially the sole source of support for some 30 percent of retired workers and 14 percent of elderly couples. In absolute numbers, for more than two million of the twenty million aged, Social Security is the *only* source of income.[23]

Nonetheless Social Security has not eliminated poverty in old age. Along with other forms of income maintenance, such as private pensions and the emergent "guaranteed annual income," it is under skeptical scrutiny. In January, 1973, the U.S. Senate Special Committee on Aging began a series of hearings on the "Future Directions of Social Security."[24] There are major problems with the concepts *and* the benefit levels of all kinds of income maintenance in old age, including Social Security. . . .

SUMMARY   The image of poverty in the United States has often focused on nonwhite ghetto residents or white rural communities in such areas as the Appalachian Mountains. Rarely are the elderly included in this picture. Because the elderly are invisible in the larger sense—because they are overlooked, shunted into nursing homes and housing projects for the aged, and denied visible forms of work—few people recognize their economic plight. The aged comprise one-fifth of the poor in this country, and one-half of them live in relative poverty and deprivation. Continuing inflation cuts into their fixed incomes, and meager Social Security checks makes it more and more difficult for the elderly to enjoy a minimum standard of life.

The image that the elderly need less to live on is equally distorted. Although they may no longer support children or require certain amenities they once did, they have many new needs. Funds for medical care, recreation, travel, gifts, and other expenditures are required by the elderly.

Widows, single women, and members of minorities are particularly disadvantaged. Retirement programs do not provide enough for the single aged person, and immediate families are often unable to help financially. Because of racist policies and attitudes, nonwhite elderly people fare even worse. They hover around the lower rungs of the socioeconomic ladder: the chance of being poor is twice as great for the aged minorities as for all aged, and four times as great as for the total of all ages.

What compounds the problem are the various myths about poverty. It is still a common belief that the poor have no one but themselves to blame, and that the aged are to blame for failing to save enough for a rainy day. In fact, the economic system has played havoc with those who attempted to provide for their retirement years. The Great Depression of the 1930s made it extremely difficult to save, and the inflation of the 1970s eroded savings of the previous decades.

Lastly, social welfare programs of the late sixties and early 70s failed to adequately aid the aged. Consequently, as the number of people over 65 increases in the 1970s and 1980s, the national problem will likewise grow into monumental proportions.

NOTES

1. *The Golden Years: A Tarnished Myth.* A report prepared for the Office of Economic Opportunity by the National Council on the Aging on the Results of Project FIND (1970), p. 4.

2. The facts and figures of poverty in America do change, although not remarkably. A few dollars may inch someone above the official poverty threshold, but is he—or more likely she—no longer really poor? This chapter was completed in July, 1973. It was possible to take the 1972 and 1973 Social Security legislation somewhat into account. I could not bring all the material in this chapter completely up to the *same* date since not all data necessary to complete analyses were available. The changing poverty statistics depend upon fluctuating prices, inflation, employment, property taxes, savings, the value of the dollar, and other factors as well as Social Security.

Lenore Epstein Bixby, Herman Brotman, Margaret Gordon, Michael Harrington, Juanita M. Kreps, James N. Morgan, Jack Ossofsky, Mollie Orshansky, James H. Schulz, Ben B. Seligman, Harold L. Sheppard are among those who have contributed much to an understanding of the economics and the poverty of the elderly in America.

3. The 30-day emergency food budget, or Economy Food Plan for emergency use, derives from Department of Agriculture data refined by Social Security Administration staff economists. See specifically Mollie Orshansky, "Consumption, Work and Poverty," in Ben B. Seligman (ed.), *Poverty as a Public Issue* (New York: The Free Press, 1965).

4. The 1970 poverty threshold for a single person was $1,852; for a couple, $2,328. The 1972 figures were $1,940 and $2,520 respectively; 1973: $2,100 and $2,650 respectively. Poverty-index increases are based on the Consumer Price Index (CPI) and do not reflect changes in the nation's standard of living.

   In the language of official government poverty indices the near poor are those whose income is below 125 percent of the poverty index.

5. The first six months of 1973, for example, saw further skyrocketing inflation in food, rents and other necessities. Food prices alone went up 12 percent.

6. Anthony Downs, "Who Are the Urban Poor?," Committee for Economic Development Supplementary Paper, November 26, 1969; revised edition, September, 1970.

7. Herman Brotman, "Income Resources of the Elderly, 1967," *Aging* (May, 1970), p. 25.

8. The Council of Economic Advisers provided the first "official" estimates of the numerical extent of poverty in its January, 1964, "Economic Report of the President." They chose $3,000-per-year income for a family of four as the dividing line.

9. Some of the figures given here for specific items such as a pet or haircut, rather than general categories such as food or recreation, are from 1967 calculations. Budgets updated since 1967 have been limited in detail and based on the Consumer Price Index rather than actually pricing the contents of the budgets in the marketplace. The intermediate was pegged at $4,776 (the lower at $3,319 and the higher at $7,443).

10. No budget has been developed for the single aged person, but unattached older people were much worse off economically than their married counterparts. The BLS estimates that the costs for one person are approximately 55 percent of the costs for a retired couple. Personal communication, Helen H. Lamale, Chief, Division of Living Conditions Studies, Bureau of Labor Statistics, U.S. Department of Labor, November 16, 1971.

11. Only 1967 figures are available for the specific comparisons that follow.

12. A case could be argued that younger active men and women wear their clothes out more quickly, but unfortunately inadequate money for clothing only reinforces the likelihood of forced inactivity by older people embarrassed by their appearance.

13. Herman Brotman, "The Older Population: Some Facts We Should Know," Administration on Aging, mimeographed, 1970.

14. See Sidney Goldstein, "Consumer Patterns of Older Spending Units," *Journal of Gerontology*, 332 (1959). See also Harold L. Sheppard, "The Poverty of Aging," in Seligman, op. cit., pp. 98–99.

15. Leon Keyserling, *Progress or Poverty* Washington, D.C.: Conference on Economic Progress, 1964).

16. Juanita Kreps, cited in *Developments in Aging*, Report (1970) U.S. Senate Special Committee on Aging, p. 5.

17. National Urban Coalition' *Counterbudget: A Blueprint for Changing National Priorities 1971–1976*, R. Benson and H. Wolman (eds.) (New York: Praeger, 1971), p. 289.

18. U.S. Senate Special Committee on Aging, *The Multiple Hazards of Age and Race: The Situation of Aged Blacks in the United States*, a working paper prepared by Dr. Inabel B. Lindsay, September 1971.

19. Ibid.

20. He is typical of older Americans; the median age of those over 65 is about 74.

21. Calculations producing this low average age of retirement include illness and unemployment as well as arbitrary or compulsory retirement rules.

22. Of the 42.4-cent loss, 19.4 cents occurred between 1965 and 1972, the period of escalation of the Vietnam war.

23. National Urban Coalition, op. cit., p. 294.

24. U.S. Senate Special Committee on Aging, *Future Directions in Social Security* (1973).

25. This model could be employed to register older people for the guaranteed federal income floor, SSI.

26. Now part of ACTION.

27. Sargent Shriver's testimony at hearings before the Senate Special Committee on Aging, June 16–17, 1965.

28. Personal communication, March 1, 1971, Cleonice Tavani.

29. Created in 1967 under amendments to the Economic Opportunity Act.

30. Conducted by the National Council on the Aging under Jack Ossofsky.

1 Describe and analyze the basic needs of elderly people. How do these needs differ from those of younger adults?

2 What are the motivations of the elderly? How do these motivations differ from those of younger adults?

3 How would you describe the particular world of widows and single women?

4 What is the relationship between poverty and aging? between the job market and the economic situation of the elderly?

5 How would you describe the particular situation of minority elderly people?

6 Is there a difference between the rural, small-town elderly people and those who live in large urban areas? If so, what?

7 What do you know about the Social Security system? What are its requirements and benefits? Are its payments to the elderly ample to meet their basic needs?

8 Does the image of the aged hurt their economic circumstances? If so, how?

READINGS   Altmeyer, Arthur J. *The Formative Years of Social Security*. Madison: The University of Wisconsin Press, 1966.

Burgess, Ernest W. *Retirement Villages: New Living Patterns for the Later Years*. Ann Arbor: University of Michigan Press, 1961.

Comfort, Alex. *The Process of Aging*. New York: New American Library, 1961.

Cumming, Elaine, and Henry, Willian E. *Growing Old: The Process of Disengagement*. New York: Basic Books, 1961.

Curtin, Sharon. *Nobody Ever Died of Old Age*. Boston: Little, Brown, 1973.

Harner, Ruth M. *The High Cost of Dying*. New York: Crowell-Collier Press, 1963.

Nader, Ralph. *Old Age: The Last Segregation*. New York: Grossman Publishing Co., 1971.

Stotsky, Bernard. *The Elderly Patient*. New York: Greene and Stratton, 1968.

14 | SCRATCHING OUR REVOLUTIONARY ITCH–

HOW ADVERTISING ABSORBS THE IMAGERY AND SLOGANS OF RADICALISM

DAVID KUNZLE

Who presumes to challenge the idea that politicians, in order to be elected, must find "the right image"; that institutions dependent in any way on public or corporate support must engage in "public relations"; that a book, in order to reach people, must be properly "marketed"; that a proposal of any kind, in order to be implemented, must be properly "packaged"—that any idea of value, in order to become effective, must be made to "sell"? We may "buy" the idea that this is *so*, but must we accept that it is *right?*

There will be a certain ideological sales resistance to the critique that follows. Some will find it an excessively harsh treatment of what is, after all, the "American way." It will be accused of falling into a "politically biased" rhetoric of its own, even as it tries to expose the rhetorical techniques of the media. My starting assumption is, however, not at all revolutionary, or even novel: it is that there is abundant evidence of a reality which the media seeks to distort and conceal, that the United States is structurally in pretty bad shape. The poor, the minorities, the unemployed, and many women have felt this for a long time; and a lot of people from the so-called middle-class majority are discovering how impoverished they really are, not so much economically as psychologically and morally, humanly.

Much of the rest of the world, that Third World which has been made dependent on the United States and has been taught that the United States is a friend, now sees this country as an enemy, and its own predicament as not just bad, but quite desperate. Small, weak countries such as Cuba, Vietnam, Angola, and (until crushed in 1973) Chile have risen in revolt against the system imposed by the United States. Within the United States itself "national minorities" and other oppressed sectors, including students, have protested, sometimes very loudly. The American governmental and corporate structures, through the media which serve their interests, have taken these revolutions, revolts, and protests seriously enough to consider it necessary to absorb them—in order to destroy them. I believe that their attempts to do so have not succeeded and that they have been frustrated by our scepticism, our critical consciousness, and our will to resist.

The extension of the hegemony of the United States over a large portion of the globe has been secured by psychological and cultural, as well as by economic and military, means. The increasing application of economic and military muscle has been facilitated by the growth of the communications media, which have proved a potent means of imposing American values upon alien cultures, reducing nationalist feeling, and paralyzing the desire to resist.

The methods applied abroad are also used to domesticate "alien opinion" at home, with effects potentially as deadly. As we have grown, since the sixties, increasingly restive, information production and processing have been unleashed to still our discontent. Let us look closely at the way in which a tiny portion of that arsenal, certain advertisements, has sought to turn our dissenting energies into new avenues of compliance. The system is geared to "scratch where it itches" and ignore—or pretend to ignore—the serious social disease of which the itch is a symptom. Our analysis, although confined to only a few advertisements, could be applied across the spectrum of the media—for while the technology may differ, the intention remains basically the same.[1]

The manner in which advertising has exploited and continues to exploit personal anxieties of an economic, emotional, and sexual nature is a dismally familiar phenomenon. Over the last decade, when even the most "apolitical" of Americans became aware, through the media, of loud demands for radical social change, a new—political—layer of public susceptibility was laid bare, offering fresh fields for media conquest. In the light of the new political consciousness, and the considerable incidence of revolutionary activity throughout the world, certain words, images, and concepts have acquired a new charge.

The terms "revolution" and "liberation" or "freedom" have long been used by Madison Avenue to promote anything, from a car to a potato peeler, of "improved" function or appearance. Such terms are now used with an additional, explicitly political reference, either playfully, as when the pitch is for some luxury object, or more seriously, when ideology is at stake. As an example of an entirely frivolous usage, we may take an advertisement (fig. 1) showing how Mr. Average Consumer "has joined the non-shrink revolution." The key (but through overuse, bland) word "revolution" is now accompanied, as it would not have been ten years ago, with the symbol and instrument of the authentic, armed revolutionary—the cartridge belt. It is assumed that the typical jovial sweater-wearer (who is also identified as a corporate executive) harbors a fantasy of rebellion, which the advertisement conjures up in order to neutralize it. Implicit is the existence of the real revolutionary, who may be rendered Red in sweater only, and moved off the street into a magazine, and absorbed into the corporate structure.

Here the advertisement works by disassociation, divorcing the symbol from the reality, and using incongruity to achieve a humorous effect. Fashion magazine illustration and advertising relies heavily on disassociation and incongruity in creating, for example, the exotic effect of the hyper-sophisticated model placed in a hyper-primitive environment. The real fears generated by the Third World "savage" are allayed by using him as a theatrical extra, as a backdrop, incorporating his magical (and

Fig. 1 (Horne Brothers, Ltd, London)

Gordon Young
has joined the
non-shrink
revolution...

He's sales director of a leading textile fashion merchants and knows good cloth; which is probably why he buys his clothes from Hornes. We've converted him to SUPERWASH, the latest development in Woolmark knitwear – machine washable pure new wool, treated with an exclusive process which *guarantees* against shrinking. He sports here two pullovers from our own classic collection. They each cost 5.95 and come in a range of well-chosen colours – with not a shrinking violet amongst them . . .

dangerous) primitivism into high fashion. Barbaric fashions are also symbols of revolutionary and repressive violence which the society absorbs, and suffers, and inflicts; locks, manacles, slave-collars, cartridge belts, commando boots, rough fatigue shirts, are donned casually by affluent Westerners, taught to slough off the anxieties of their personal lives by adopting exotic accouterments. The appearance affects casualness, but conceals the sadomasochistic tension between the desire and need to bind and be bound. These fears are not merely internal; fashion pays mocking homage to the sinister omnipresence of the military in American life, and tries to exorcise it by wearing military symbols as decoration (fig. 2).

Casualness is of the essence. The mask of the casual covers the fear of the real thing. And it is not only the clothing which nonchalantly bears the symbols of revolution, but also the language of fashion, the style of fashion reportage. Consider this typical editorial-cum-advertisement in a sophisticated newspaper announcing,

> the first major silhouette change . . . since 1970, right after the last peasant uprising. The first really full skirts since the petticoated '50s. If most of these new spring fashion insurgents didn't look so friendly and non-threatening, one might even be inclined to speak in terms of revolution. But they are so non-radical, so non-shocking that they may well turn out to be the first clothes to overthrow the existing fashion order without ever causing a ripple of protest.[2]

It may be that "ripples of protests" are discernible, if one looks hard enough, even among the ranks of those who produce the media. Several excellent, independently produced antiwar posters were honored by the advertising trade magazines. Co-optation? Another example of the establishment absorbing radical sentiment? Maybe. But how does one judge, otherwise than as deliberate, perhaps pained, self-parody, that feature from a French fashion magazine which concluded a series of full-page photographs of models posed sexily in the jungle wearing jungle combat outfits, war decorations, and machine guns, with an unposed, press photograph of American soldiers standing—in *their* jungle combat outfits and carrying *their* machine guns—over the mutilated corpses of Vietnamese (fig. 3)?[3] While one would hardly expect such self-exposure in an American fashion magazine, one cannot discount instances in which an individual conscience, under unbearable pressure, may force its way through some rigid institutional framework.

Women, traditionally targeted as the primary consumers in the United States, are considered particularly vulnerable to the blandishments of advertising. "Women's liberation" is offered to those buying labor-saving food or household equipment in advertisements which reinforce woman in her domestic role and ignore the fact that in order to earn enough money to pay for these goodies, she is likely to be stuck with a menial job. "Stand up for your dignity. No lady should stoop to this"—

"this" being cleaning an oven on her knees. Ironically, this exploitation of the women's movement in an advertisement for a self-cleaning oven was thought up by a woman featured in *Communication Arts* magazine as one of the subjects in a series on women designers, itself obviously a concession to Women's liberation.[4] Some advertisements have pushed hypocrisy so far as to suggest that the time saved by buying a labor-saving device can be used to attend a women's rights demonstration or protest march.

It has long been the practice of Madison Avenue to present the act of buying as a gesture of self-assertion and independence, when in fact it is the very oppostie. To buy attractive clothing is now one of women's rights. The association of consumption and liberation is particularly nefarious in advertisements for physically harmful products like cigarettes, where the trade has reacted to and absorbed the "cancer scare" by pitching directly against the desire to give up the habit, emphasizing that the pleasure is greater than the risk. The implied alternative is between

Fig. 2

Fig. 3

(Mode Internationale, Paris, Franc

private sensual gratification and grim governmental authority (the Surgeon General). By opting for the former, the smoker is supposedly engaging in an act of self-gratification and defiance.

One cigarette manufacturer links his product to the female liberationist slogan "You've Come a Long Way, Baby."[5] Feminists may take a grain of comfort from this process insofar as it testifies that their concept, at least, has impinged upon the public consciousness; but the predicament of socially progressive elements in a consumer society is epitomized by the fact that feminists are not only obliged to observe the process of co-optation and the dilution of their ideas, slogans, and images, but also to actively participate in it. Thus the major glossy feminist-oriented magazine *Ms.* is conspicuous for the quantity and quality (up to twenty color pages per issue) of its consumer advertising featuring the new "liberated" woman proclaiming her addictions as if they were convictions.

A more serious approach is called for in advertising which seeks to sell an idea, rather than a consumable object. A bank confronts and tries to undermine youthful resistance to the concept of personal financial investment. Under a photograph of a smiling, bushy-haired, denim-shirted (that is, moderately radical-looking) youth: "The X bank was one Society Pete Jenkins decided he'd opt into. Peter's not exactly what you'd call a dedicated capitalist. But he does a lot better than many who are. The X is one system you can't beat. The X gives it to you straight." The "straight" admission of the term "capitalist" (once a bogey), of the fact of youthful disaffection with it, and of the existence of "systems" to be beaten or opted out of is highly manipulative. Through a cunning appeal to self-interest, we are persuaded to cooperate with a system we do not necessarily believe in, and to identify ourselves with the true capitalists—who are not, of course, the Pete Jenkinses, the small investors, but the owners of the bank and the big corporations it serves.

A decade of active protest has put the ruling classes and the media they control on the defensive. In order to "win back" dissidents it is necessary to confront—or to appear to confront—their arguments and slogans. A series of recruitment advertisements for the Peace Corps, devised by the famous Rubicam and Young (the second largest agency in the United States), which has served that brainchild of liberal imperialism on a volunteer basis almost since its inception, ran the gamut of absorptive techniques. The rationale of the Peace Corps is that idealistic youths, armed with energy and American know-how, in conjunction with aggressive foreign investment policies, can show the underdeveloped world how to develop. The advertisements were accordingly designed to attract people with some vague sense of social responsibility and discontent, but without real political consciousness.

The Peace Corps played upon the youthful instinct for rebellion, as well as the maternal instinct, with a photograph of a pretty white girl hugging a native baby: "I didn't join the Peace Corps . . . for altruism

[but] because I had this idea of doing something I wasn't supposed to do." Disobedience is thus converted into patriotic compliance.

Another technique was the sleight-of-hand by which the idea of demonstration *against* American foreign policy was flipped into the idea of demonstration *on behalf of* American foreign policy—of which the Peace Corps is, of course, a part. Thus, in the style of a car bumper-sticker: "Peace Demonstration—every day you're in the Peace Corps." Another advertisement no less simply and deftly takes over a slogan coined by the peace movement to satirize the military ethos: "Kill for Peace." In the fine print, the killing turns out to be of Third World mosquitoes.

Yet another advertisement in this prize-winning series confronts—or appears to confront—the accusers of American foreign policy directly. The picture is of a Third World family posing in front of a hovel: "If you told these people the Peace Corps is the hypocritical extension of an imperialist establishment's military-industrial complex, they would think you were crazy. And you would be." The accusation is shrugged off, as if it were addressed to the victims, the ignorant and poverty-stricken people themselves, rather than against the managers of the "military-industrial complex." The advertisement ridicules an idea widely accepted by radical and liberal opinion alike by couching it in "typical" left-intellectual polysyllabic jargon obviously inappropriate to the unpoliticized and ignorant poor, and by playing this off against the plain-spoken word "crazy"—to criticize American policy in these circumstances is not just mistaken, it is plain "crazy."

The Peace Corps program presents itself as a kind of revolutionary reformism, but is in fact designed to prevent revolution and real change by "scratching the itch" of poverty. Government, business, and charity organizations all operate in this manner. Oxfam, the British charity which advertises prodigiously (and so successfully, it seems, that it always has funds for more advertising), calls itself "the quiet revolutionaries" rather loudly across full pages of consumer magazines. And it uses the classic revolutionary symbol, the hammer and sickle (fig. 4)—not, of course, as a symbol of violent revolution (which is its historic meaning), but as "the practical accompaniment to a very different kind of struggle. A radical yet peaceful attack on the unhappy statistics of the Third World—A Quiet Revolution." An attack on global poverty is conceived of as something "quiet" to reassure the reader-donors: just as their physical needs can be quietly assuaged by the simple act of buying the liquor or cigarettes advertised on the opposite page, so their social conscience (and global poverty) can be laid to rest by the even simpler act of writing out and quietly mailing a check to the Quiet Revolution.

The jading effect of so many pictures of starving children, served up amid luscious displays of food, drink, and other bodily comforts, is admitted by one American charity agency in copy accompanying a picture of yet another starving child who is feared to have lost his capacity to pluck our heart and purse strings: "It's getting easier to look at pictures of starving children. It's not getting any easier to starve." This, incidentally, is from a relief organization working with the United States Agency for International Development, funds from which were used to build the infamous tiger cages of Vietnam, where civilian men, women, and children were deliberately starved, crippled, and tortured.

The big international corporations like to pose as charity organizations who manage to combine philanthropy with profitability. Investors Overseas Services, a corporation concerned with the protection and expansion of American foreign interests (launched by a friend and associate of Richard Nixon's, Robert Vesco, who was eventually convicted of financial fraud through this company), adopted what appeared at first sight to be a surprisingly tolerant stance towards the idea of spontaneous popular violence that threatened those interests. The copy accompanying photographs of violent street confrontations, hands on Molotov cocktails, and burning cars seems to sympathize with angry people "who are only negotiating for a better way of life." But the solution offered is more of what originally caused the discontent—more American investment overseas, which will financially benefit the foreigner as well as the American investor: "There is more money to be made out of peace than out of war." This statement reflects, to a degree, a sincere belief: businesses not directly involved in arms production tend to disapprove of war (which does not prevent them from profiting from it when it happens), and to regard stability at the price of permanent repression as an acceptable form of peace.

If capitalism can sell ploughshares as profitably as swords it will do so, and even come out in favor of beating swords into ploughshares. It would rather see razor blades used for cutting beards than for slitting throats. *Ebony*, the glossy consumer magazine catering to the black bourgeoisie, says so in an advertisement designed to attract advertising revenues from white business (fig. 5). The slogan "What's the matter, don't you trust us?" in conjunction with the photograph of an aggressively outstretched black hand holding an instrument with lethal associations plays upon the white fear of black violence, and the vicious stereotype of the black youth as a kind of political Sweeney Todd (the English "Demon-Barber," who slit his clients' throats). It turns out, of course, that the *consciously* addressed white fear is only that blacks are not good consumers, and too poor to be worth advertising to.

Revolutionary activity is news copy and business opportunity. So is addiction to crime, drugs, and vice. Sensationalist media exploitation of these topics has been with us for a long time, almost as long as printing; a new development of the last decade is the bravado with which it is conducted. The advertising agencies not only know exactly what they are up to, but *boast* of what they and the media generally are up to. They boast of their deceitfulness, as if deceit, openly admitted, became a form of honesty. Macfadden-Bartell, the major publisher of "women's magazines," demonstrates to potential advertisers how the admittedly sensational and misleading headline to an advertisement can draw in advertisers and consumers, just as an admittedly sensational and misleading headline to a story can draw in a vast readership. The magazine boasts that some of their best salesmen were "bigots, hookers, pushers and fags" (actually, in smaller type, stories *about* these kinds of people); and, in another advertisement, about how an editor had "been through [stories of] a sexual assault, an abortion, a divorce, and an affair with a minister. Not bad for a day's work." Social problems are thus sold to a "special kind of reader. She's mainstream America [a market research formula, not a person], the wife of the blue-collar worker and the wageearner"—so illiterate that "if she reads at all, about the only thing she reads is *True Story*." All six million of her a month "keep coming back to *True Story* to learn about life through the experiences of others." Her own life, of course, is not an experience worth learning from. What is real (what is marketable) is the vicarious experience.

Fig. 4   (Oxfam, Oxford, England)   Fig. 5

"What's the matter, don't you trust me?" an ad for Ebony *Magazine asked.*

he Quiet Revolution.

In the world's political arena these apparently innocent tools can symbolise violent and often bloody upheaval.

To us, however, they act as a practical accompaniment to a very different kind of struggle. A radical yet peaceful attack on some of the unhappy statistics of the Third World – a Quiet Revolution.

In Asia, Africa and Latin America 80,000 people die each and every day through hunger. Oxfam's aim is to help the poorest in these countries overcome their agonising problems. To help them help themselves.

They're discovering how to grow more food, how to protect themselves against malnutrition and disease and how to acquire the basic skills their countries so urgently need.

For instance, in Africa the farmers of Upper Volta barely scratched a living from the land with hand hoes. It was heart and backbreaking work.

By buying 100 pairs of oxen we are helping them make revolutionary changes in their way of life.

In Guatemala we've helped poverty-stricken farmers increase yields of maize by up to six times

through the introduction of different agricultural methods.

These projects and many more were possible because of contributions of both time and money from people like yourself.

Anything will help.

For instance, 10 p has bought a chick for a poultry farm in Africa. £1 has purchased rice seed for an acre of land in India.

Such is the nature of this revolution, one which urgently needs your support.

OXFAM Quiet Revolutionaries

Please tick the box where appropriate and send to Room 17, Oxfam, Oxford.
☐ I would like to know how I can help Oxfam in my own area.
☐ I enclose the sum of £_____ as my contribution to the Quiet Revolution.
Name_____
Address_____

Communications claims to be a science. As "scientists," the communications managers do not merely interpret the world, they reshape it on the basis of their interpretations. They do so, moreover, in such a way that the interpretation is confused with the thing interpreted. The news of the event is substituted for the event; the media makes the event as well as the news, and before the news. "CBS gets the news *before* it happens." This is more than an instance of the self-fulfilling prophecy, for it confuses the nature of reality—the distinction between what is and what we think should be, or between the way we see ourselves and the way others see us. *Life* (before its demise) was based upon the equation of *Life* with life—or better yet, the precedence of the magazine over the real thing. The achievement of medical scientists who photographed an embryo in the womb was second to that of *Life* in reproducing the photograph (or thinking, daring to reproduce it), and was *announced as such* in advertisements. In the capitalist hierarchy, the media managers have become the entrepreneurs to whom scientists, artists, and even statesmen sell their ideas and labor. Duly processed by the media and effectively alienated from their true creators, events are offered up as consumable goods, as legitimate substitutes for real-life experience, purchasable for the price of a magazine. After reading *Life*, one had supposedly *felt* what it was like to be poor and black. Even scholarly publishers (who used to observe scholarly disdain for the hard sell of the mass media) have begun to resort to sensational headlines which play upon this substitution of a media product for reality: "Spend two decades under Fascist rule" invites

Fig. 6

Fig. 7

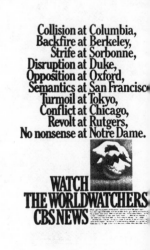

an advertisement for a learned history of Italian fascism in the august *New York Review of Books,* a publication which, ironically, has rendered signal services in criticizing the manipulations of the media.

Logically, if the account of the event is to be substituted for the event, he who reports it is the event's creator. The detective-reporter is the new hero, explorer, and activist of our time. Even a progressive political journal like *Ramparts* unwittingly reflects the perversion of values which places the agent of the media over the major historical figures of our age. A *Ramparts* cover used the Christ-like head of the dead Che Guevara (whose image, more than that of any revolutionary in history, has been exploited in the commercial media, especially for T-shirts and posters) as the monochrome background for a full-color portrait of a glamorous reporter. She had been sent (as she expressed it herself) to join the crowd of news vultures which descended on Bolivia in order to batten upon the martyr's corpse (fig. 6).

Media people, the purveyors of wisdom and benefactors of humanity of our age, are singularly lacking in that virtue which wisdom and benefaction once connoted: humility. A major news network like CBS presents itself as omniscient, omnipresent, omnipotent. A child asked to name the American president replied, "Walter Cronkite." And there he is indeed, his name up with Nixon's, Mao's, and De Gaulle's (fig. 7)—with the difference that he sees not just a part but (like God) encompasses all.

The "great" newscasters are the great reducers and packagers of knowledge, throwing out higgledy-piggledy tidbits of political information

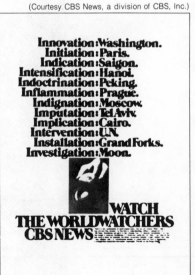

sandwiched between commercials. News and commercials operate in the same way, reducing ideas to slogans and inducing passive acceptance. Ideas, countries, problems, and statesmen are compressed into a pretty mosaic of sparkling chips. Racial confrontation is simplified and flattened into a pattern of complementary colors like an abstract painting which CBS alone can uncode, on the theory that only the artist can explain the mysteries of his art. Political differences between nations are reduced to a child's alphabet. Ideas, like words, are basically all the same; only their shapes are a little different here and there, and it is their very similarity that makes them manageable and palatable.

Rebellion in the universities is treated in the same way: the particular character of the revolt, that which made it real, is arbitrarily determined and effectively eliminated by chance differences in the initial letters of the place names. There are elements of an acrostic as well, reinforcing the news-as-game concept. And the significance of all the political games played at the universities around the world ultimately is reduced to the outcome of the game that *really* matters: the one at Notre Dame.

If ideas are merely counters in a game, one cannot ask if they are

Fig. 8 *"Radio works," this ad proclaimed.*

good or bad. All news is good that keeps you watching until the commercial. Or listening: a production company for radio commercials, in support of a medium which has become very conscious of its inferiority to television, reminds us that once upon a time, and not too long ago, radio *worked*—massively (fig. 8). Presumably, this company would make commercials for a Hitler if he paid them to.

We deal finally with advertisements where the co-optation of revolutionary imagery is left deliberately very much on the surface, where the process of fusion is left visibly manifest, and which, in certain circumstances, may be said to invite rather than to discourage thoughtful response.

No Londoner or visitor to London in the summer and fall of 1974 can have failed to notice an extraordinarily audacious and sophisticated campaign to sell classified advertising columns launched by the major conservative newspaper, the *Sunday Times* (figs. 9 and 10). With bold splashes of color and a "heretical" realist style, the posters effectively smashed out the edge-to-edge competition in the London Underground (where a captive audience waiting in crowded, confined spaces under artificial light

Fig. 9

Fig. 10

(Reprinted by permission of *The Sunday Times*, London, England)

is already peculiarly vulnerable). The style chosen was that of Chinese revolutionary art, which employs a kind of baroque academicism altogether alien to popular artistic sensibilities in the West, and which carries political and ethical associations altogether—and absurdly—alien to those of the *Sunday Times* and the spirit of private property that the posters proclaim. Figures in the attitudes and with the expressions of the most dedicated revolutionaries surge forward bearing aloft the banners of private property, linked in fraternal harmony, armed with the *Sunday Times* instead of the *Thoughts of Chairman Mao,* and the tools of the consumer revolution, umbrella and vacuum cleaner hose, in place of firearms. And, just in case you missed the point, the script of the lettering is adapted where possible to evoke the Russian Cyrillic alphabet.

This kind of advertisement, which seems to parody in pictorial style and verbal slogans the media tendencies we have been describing, has also appeared in the United States. The broad acceptability of the "Chinese style" presumably reflects the recent détente with China, whose Revolution is seen no longer as a direct threat to this country, and may be politically neutralized as an amusing and exotic commodity. A striking example (fig. 11) was conceived by the Warner Brothers art department, which calls itself "apolitical" and has put authentic Chinese posters on the walls. The advertisement plays upon the very absurdity of the idea that whoever purchases the promotional record (marketed below cost, as publicity for other records) is committing a revolutionary act and "outwit[ting] the running capitalist dogs at Warner Brothers." The pitch is to the young and "hip" who are assumed to be familiar with and in some sense attracted to the cruder kind of revolutionary rhetoric. Ironically, the running capitalist dogs at Warner Brothers have indeed been (indirectly) outwitted, and have had to run before the attack of angry feminists who objected to the blatantly sexist advertising for a Rolling Stones album which they distribute.

There was a comparable motivation behind the *Sunday Times* posters. In an interview, the art director of the campaign (which was managed by the well-known firm of Ogilvy, Benson and Mather) told me he had conceived it all in the spirit of détente and as a kind of "spontaneous joke." He admired revolutionary China and its art, and this was his way of paying homage. One should note in this connection that avant-garde taste admits Chinese social-realist art for its "camp" or "pop" quality, and the Chinese political posters which inspired the style of the *Sunday Times* posters, although originally intended for the Third World, have been successfully marketed in the West.

Using the Chinese revolution to sell Western capitalism may be considered a good joke by sophisticates in the advertising industry (as it was by the *Sunday Times* itself), but it offended certain members of the British public, who subjected the posters to the appropriate physical response: graffiti. These were of several kinds. One kind was solemn and didactic: "This ad exploits the revolutionary aspirations of the working class." Another was threatening: "Don't knock Chinese art—we'll put a bomb in the *Sunday Times*." A more considered and artistic response was that which altered and added to the signs and balloons in the spirit of the "original" Chinese art. Below the word Property borne by the right hand figure in the Bargaining Power poster, someone wrote in "is theft." The girl on the right with the upraised arm in the Property Power poster shouts, "Long Live Anarchy! Long live Libertarian Communism!" The central figure cries, "All power to the Workers' Councils"; and the whole was surmounted by the phrase "Forward to Revolution."

These graffitists understood a fundamental principle of people's war: seize arms from the enemy and turn them against him. Graffiti generally are a symptom of refusal to be co-opted, of resistance to the unilaterally imposed vision of the media. To deface a poster is to defy its power over us. In so doing we invite the sanction of the law, which would punish us for even the slightest attempt to talk back. But there is a limit to the capacity of the media to coerce and stun us into submission, and there are means, more potent than graffiti, of talking back and taking over.

Fig. 11

SOLUTIONS   We have discussed just one of many tactics employed by the media, which try to manipulate our minds and mold our behavior. It is not only this media monster's size which is frightening, but also its seeming intangibility—the miasma of what Herbert Schiller has called the "world's foremost message-producing and -transmitting society." We are or seem to be so completely engulfed by messages that there is nothing we can do about them, except to learn to live with them and perhaps ignore them. A paralysis of the will to think critically and act independently is the intended goal of the media, but there are increasing signs that people are refusing to be paralyzed.

Short of an anticapitalist revolution in this country (which is not likely to come quickly or suddenly), the problem of curbing and transforming the media and putting them if not under the actual control, then at least under the jurisdiction, of the people must be faced piecemeal and in a reformist spirit. Community-based action groups must be formed (they are already in the process of formation) to combat the worst manifestations of government and corporate advertising. Such groups would work at first on local levels and towards specific and concrete ends. Environmental and ecological protection, for which organizations already exist, might be the umbrella under which to mount campaigns to abolish billboards, the single major source of visual and mental blight.

The impetus of the feminist movement will facilitate the organization of resistance to the most blatant examples of sexist advertising. A particularly vile record cover and advertisement showing a bound and bruised female with the words "I'm black and blue from the Rolling Stones and I love it" has been attacked by an organization called Women Against Violence Against Women in Los Angeles[6] and by the Houston-based National Organization Against Sexism in the Media to such good effect that the record company involved was obliged to take down billboards and withdraw advertisements from magazines.

Demands for "equal time" to present opposing points of view, recognized in principle by the Federal Communications Commission, should be pressed to include the opportunity to rebut the claims and expose the tricks of advertisers. New educational, noncommercial television and radio channels and more publicity-free newspapers and magazines must be created. Advertising directed at children should be considered a primary target, and a vulnerable one. The possibilities are legion. Eventually it will be necessary—and possible—to attack the very *ideology* of consumerism, the very *idea* that corporations have the right to buy up our environment and invade our every level of consciousness for their personal profit.

The counter-ideology will be forged in our educational and intellectual centers, although it will be put into practice in work centers and homes everywhere. Our schools and colleges cannot continue as mere "knowledge factories" programmed by corporate interests. Over the last decade, intellectual workers throughout the United States have shown increasing scepticism towards the traditional structures of our society. Considering the efforts of government agencies to pressure universities and colleges into complicity in the war on Vietnam, the resistance exhibited—by many students and some faculty—is all the more impressive. The students developed their own media and their own attitudes, through massive demonstrations, occupations, teach-ins, protests, college newspapers, alternative ("underground") magazines, and posters of protest, all of which did much on the domestic front to force the government to abandon that savage enterprise.

A critical consciousness now exists on an unprecedented scale, one too great to be successfully co-opted. Due to the technological development of the media themselves, their controlling elements fall within the grasp of—or can be seized by—"ordinary citizens," a term which includes college students. College must become increasingly a place where we learn not just to think and to write, but also to act upon our society. I would like to close with a quotation from Herbert Schiller's *The Mind Managers*, a book which, shattering as it is in its exposition of the magnitude of the "(mis)information industry," ends upon this hopeful note:

> Already, a growing proportion of Americans no longer believe what they see and hear in the national media. Their cynicism, which now reinforces the *status quo*, could, with different stimuli, be transformed into clear-sighted opposition and political resistance.
>
> The mind managers have worked long and arduously at their task. Their resources, made available from corporate and governmental budgets, are substantial; their successes to date, many. Yet they have not been able to prevent, in at least one portion of the population, a growth in understanding, perhaps deeper than any achieved to this time, of what the system is really all about. This should be no small encouragement to the still weak forces of liberation.
>
> What is more, this understanding, derived from the realities of American existence, promises to be grasped by many others in the years immediately ahead. Thus, a gradually heightened consciousness, despite a more tightly controlled communications systems, may develop its own means to force the social changes so desperately needed in this country today.[7]

SUMMARY

American information networks have sought, both within and outside the United States to pacify restive populations which have become critical of the networks' economic and cultural hegemony. In moments of political crisis which also threaten a commercial crisis, the language of politics tends to infiltrate commercial advertising, and vice versa. This chapter analyzes certain advertisements devised by major commercial and political institutions to demonstrate how the system is geared to "scratch where it itches," ignoring the serious social disease of which the itch is a symptom.

Over the last decade advertising has increasingly exploited the new political consciousness and the currency of certain radical and revolutionary slogans and symbols to defuse the dangerous ideas they embody. The jovial man in a sweater advertisement sports a cartridge belt. High fashion models wear the symbols of war, oppression, and even torture. A new style of skirt represents a "peasant uprising." Women are told to "stand up for their dignity" by using a new oven cleaner. To buy attractive clothing is presented as one of women's rights, and to smoke a new and particularly dangerous cigarette is to "have come a long way, baby."

A bank advertisement suggests that it is "hip" to become a small investor, which is the same as being a big capitalist. The Peace Corp plays upon vague feelings of social discontent and the energies of the protest movement to channel them into patriotic compliance; reasoned antiimperialist argument is depicted as "crazy rhetoric." A major charity organization tells people to "join the quiet revolution" of private philanthropy, symbolized by the classic Communist symbol of the hammer and sickle. Another charity agency, while it collaborates in a program to build instruments of torture in Vietnam, tugs the heart and purse strings at home with pictures of starving children. A black bourgeois glossy magazine uses the white fear of blacks as natural throat cutters to stimulate advertising revenues from a white razor-blade company.

Magazines and advertising agencies boast openly of deceitfulness and sensation mongering. The news is nakedly presented as made not by events, but by TV stations and newscasters. A child asked to name the president replied, "Walter Cronkite." Reading a magazine or viewing a newscast is the proper *substitute* for real experience. A political atrocity is equated with a sporting event. Current history, political events and ideas, and rebellions at home and around the world are all so many commodities, so many sparkling chips in the pretty media mosaic.

An advertisement for a radio commercials production company justifies itself through the example of Hitler, for whom "radio worked." Is this meant to be funny?

Among the more sophisticated examples of advertising's absorbing revolutionary imagery are the large, gaudy posters designed to sell the property columns of a major newspaper, which precisely copied the style and slogans of Chinese revolutionary posters. This capitalist "rip off" of the Chinese revolution was heavily defaced by people who take that revolution seriously. The article concludes with the suggestion that the graffito is an appropriate response to advertisements and that it gives us a clue to more effective actions we can undertake to counter the media and eventually bring them under our control. A model action is that of the feminist group Women Against Violence Against Women, who forced a major record company to withdraw billboards and advertisements depicting the sadistic binding and beating of a young woman.

The major authority of the media, Herbert Schiller, gives us cause for hope:

> Already, a growing proportion of Americans no longer believe what they see and hear in the national media. Their cynicism, which now reinforces the status quo, could, with different stimuli, be transformed into clear-sighted opposition and resistance. . . .
>   . . . A gradually heightened consciousness may develop its own means to force the social changes so desperately needed in this country today.[8]

NOTES

1. In "the media" I would include avant-garde art as well. Two very recent examples are Tom Stoppard's *Travesties*, a play which absorbs the Russian revolution into a Wildean farce, and Andy Warhol's images of the Communist symbol, the hammer and sickle.

2. *Los Angeles Times*, 19 December 1976.

3. *Mode International*, Société d'Editions Alva, 1975.

4. I found most of the American advertisements cited here either in *Communication Arts* magazine or in the *Annual of Advertising, Editorial and Television Art and Design (The One Show)*, published by the Art Directors Guild in New York; these advertisements appear as award winners reflecting outstanding artistic merit. The volumes used are from 1967–1974.

5. Virginia Slims, the brand referred to, contain 16 milligrams tar and one milligram nicotine per cigarette. It is cited as the most dangerous of sixty-three brands compared in an article which indicates that women are smoking in greater numbers, at a younger age, and more heavily than ever before, and that because of their smaller lung capacity, they are more susceptible to lung cancer than men. (*The Better Way*, February 1977, pp. 217–18.)

6. The address of this organization is: c/o Feminist Women's Health Clinic, 1112 Crenshaw Blvd., Los Angeles, CA 90019. See also *Seven Days*, 14 February 1977, p. 37.

7. Herbert Schiller, *The Mind Managers* (Boston: Beacon Press, 1973), p. 191.

8. Ibid.

QUESTIONS

1 How does the phrase "scratch where it itches" relate to the way the media deals with social problems in general?

2 Why and how do the media try to "make" rather than merely relate the news?

3 Why did the media deal with the Vietnam war as a "spectacle"?

4 Why does the Peace Corps have to adopt an advertising technique different from that of the regular army, when their purposes are basically the same?

5 How do advertisements show charity organizations exerting a conservative political influence? What is the link between the concept of private philanthropy and capitalism?

6 "CBS *makes* the news." What are the implications of this claim?

7 How and why does advertising use calculated incongruities and absurdities? What is the point of using Chinese revolutionary images to sell capitalist commodities? Or of showing fashion models dressed up as guerrillas?

8 Take any familiar advertisement and "graffito" and adapt it in such a way that you expose and criticize (in a satirical or "straight" manner) its real function. Reconvert the image/ slogan to what you would consider a useful social purpose.

SOLUTIONS

Aronson, James. *Packaging the News.* New York: International Publishers, 1971.

Berger, John. *Ways of Seeing.* New York: Viking, 1973. Especially chapter 7.

Enzensberger, Hans Magnus. *The Consciousness Industry.* New York: Seabury Press, 1974.

Ewen, Stuart. *Captains of Consciousness: Advertising and the Social Roots of the Consumer Culture.* New York: McGraw-Hill, 1976.

Marcuse, Herbert. *One Dimensional Man.* Boston: Beacon Press, 1964.

Mills, C. Wright. *The Power Elite.* New York: Oxford University Press, 1957. Especially chapter 13.

———. *Power, Politics and People,* edited by Irving Horowitz. New York: Oxford University Press, 1963.

Packard, Vance. *The Hidden Persuaders.* New York: D. McKay, 1957.

Schiller, Herbert. *The Mind Managers.* Boston: Beacon Press, 1973.

Tuckman, Gaye. *The TV Establishment.* Englewood Cliffs, N.J.: Prentice Hall, 1974.

IS THERE LIFE BEFORE DEATH?

Graffito on subway station, Boston.

$40,000 DRUG FINES
HIT NFL CHARGERS

(New York) The San Diego Chargers, general manager Harland Svare, and eight players have been fined a total of $40,000 and the individuals involved placed on probation by the National Football League for violation of the NFL drug policies, Commissioner Peter Rozelle announced yesterday.

[*AP*, Boston Globe, *27 April 1974.*]

N.H. WOMEN'S PANEL
BACKS NAME FREEDOM

(Concord, N.H.) A married or divorced woman in New Hampshire has the right to use any name she chooses without resorting to legal procedures, the New Hampshire Commission on the Status of Women says.

[*AP*, Boston Globe, *21 April 1974.*]

5

ALTHOUGH *each chapter in this work posits solutions
to the problems posed, the concluding piece tempts
us with a powerful historical force in American
society, the movements which have produced rad-*
*ical cultural change. Despite the looseness of the term
made popular in the sixties, the "counter culture," as
Robert Rosenstone suggests in "The Mysterious Flavor of
Cultural Radicalism," offered us ideas that have long historical roots, ideas that have profoundly altered American
culture in the past and which still hold viable possibilities
for the future.*

AN
ALTERNATIVE

15 | THE MYSTERIOUS FLAVOR OF CULTURAL RADICALISM

ROBERT A. ROSENSTONE

Radicalism comes in many flavors. Most Americans are familiar with a variety of political and ethnic groups which loudly demand basic and far-reaching changes in the way society distributes political power and wealth. In fact, radicalism normally seems to imply organizations with programs for social reconstruction. But there is another kind that has little to do with political or economic change. The best term for it is "cultural radicalism." Shapeless and slippery as an amoeba, it is difficult to describe or analyze, but that in no way diminishes its importance. Indeed, cultural radicalism may be working greater changes in the U.S.—and other advanced industrial counties—than the more obvious political groups of the left that have been so visible for several decades.

To understand the importance of such radicalism, one must look away from traditional political concerns and seek out subtle shifts in the nebulous realms of world views, value systems, and lifestyles. These phenomena have less to do with the forms of society than with allegiance given to institutions. There is a good argument to be made that fundamental change is not the result of revolution but the cause of it. In such a view, revolution occurred in the American colonies in the 1770s, in France two decades later, and in Russia in 1917 because vast numbers of people no longer believed in or gave emotional allegiance to the old regimes. John Adams put this idea into words when he said that long before the struggles on the battlefield, the American revolution had taken place "in the hearts and minds" of his countrymen.

While the label "cultural radicalism" has not been widely used, the notion of a "counter culture" has gained prominence in recent years in intellectual circles and the popular media. It is a term which brings to mind images of long-haired young people, psychedelic rock groups, rural communes, vegetarian diets, erotic motion pictures, scatological newspapers, and students smoking and swallowing a variety of illegal substances. This is only the latest manifestation of cultural radicalism. But because aspects of the "counter culture" are still highly evident in American life, it is easy to look to them as a way of beginning to understand the whole tradition.

The term was first broached by historian Theodore Roszak, who began in 1968 to publish in the *Nation* articles that would become part of *The Making of a Counter Culture*, which appeared in 1969. The following year, sociologist Philip Slater brought out *The Pursuit of Loneliness*, a penetrating study of modern America that accepted "counter culture" as an established part of the scholarly vocabulary. By 1971 psychologist Kenneth Keniston, in *Youth and Dissent: The Rise of a New Opposition*, could flatly state: "No issue today divides the public or intellectual community so deeply as does the 'counter culture.' "[1]

This quick acceptance does not mean the phrase has ever indicated anything very precise. Roszak himself has never come up with a clear definition. Describing the "generational transition" of the late sixties—what other people were calling the "generation gap"—he calls it unprecedented in both "the scale on which it is taking place and the depth of antagonism it reveals. Indeed, it would hardly seem an exaggeration to call what we see arising among the young a 'counter culture.' Meaning: a culture so radically disaffiliated from the mainstream assumptions of our society that it scarcely looks to many as a culture at all, but takes on the alarming appearance of a barbaric intrusion." Elsewhere he more succinctly defines it as "essentially, an exploration of the politics of consciousness."[2]

If the definition is vague, at least this cultural radicalism can be described. Roszak's subtitle, "Reflections of the Technocratic Society and its Youthful Opposition," gives a partial insight into the phenomenon. Some chapters in his work are devoted to youthful dissent, not political protest but dissent in lifestyles, value systems, and views of reality. They are an exploration of the philosophy and consciousness of the people then called "hippies." A larger section of the book deals with a group of mature men, philosophers, intellectuals, and academics, whose doctrines seem to support the extreme actions of young people in the late sixties. Included are classicist Norman O. Brown, poet Allen Ginsberg, gestalt psychologist Paul Goodman and philosopher Alan Watts. What holds the two groups together is Roszak's own vision, his attack on technocracy and the technological thinking that would like to rationalize all human activities. His is a polemic against what he calls the "myth of objective consciousness," the key to the Western intellectual tradition, that stance by which the self is separated from the world studied. For Roszak, this separation is at the center of virtually everything inhuman in modern society. The subjects of his book, young and old alike, either reject the idea of objective consciousness, attack it, undermine it, or somehow live outside it. In his view, they are the forerunners of a new society in which human needs will presumably take precedence over attempts to make life rational.

Philip Slater has described the values of the counter culture by contrasting them with more traditional views: "The old culture, when forced to choose, tends to give preference to property rights over personal rights, technological requirements over human needs, competition over cooperation, violence over sexuality, concentration over distribution, the producer over the consumer, means over ends, secrecy over openness, social forms over personal expression, striving over gratification, Oedipal love over communal love . . . . The new counter culture tends to reverse all these priorities."[3] This idealized portrait plays off nicely against Slater's subtitle, "American Culture at the Breaking Point." His argument is that technological civilization imposes increasingly painful and con- tradictory demands upon human beings. Since people are not infinitely malleable, he expects great social changes and thinks the counter culture may contain the seeds for making American society more humane.

Whatever its definition, this latest form of cultural radicalism sur- faced in the sixties, a decade of dissent and protest. There is no way to neatly categorize the many-sided movements of those years, but the counter culture may be distinguished from other kinds of radical activity. It had little to do with the powerful waves of ethnic consciousness that moved disadvantaged minorities into action. Nor did it have much connection with the traditional leftist politics that grew out of the antiwar movement and moved towards a Marxist social critique. Sometimes hippies might take part in peace marches or student sit-ins, but they did so as entertainers, musicians and jesters. Cultural politics had a flavor all its own. This was shown when young people invaded the New York Stock Exchange and demonstrated contempt for capitalism by flinging dollar bills onto the floor. The same spirit moved Allen Ginsberg and his followers, during the mammoth peace demonstrations in November, 1967, to hold an exorcism ceremony in front of the Pentagon; there they called on the gods of a dozen cultures to help them drive the evil spirits from the building. During the feverish street battles over the Democratic convention in 1968, it was cultural radicals who took time out to an- nounce they were running a pig for President. Surely such actions were less politics than theater.

Perhaps they were also part of the "politics of consciousness." Making a farce of politics was one way to exhibit the belief that changing social structures was less important than changing one's view of reality. As the Beatles, who had far more followers than any political leader, said in a song entitled "Revolution": "You tell me it's the institution, well, you know, you'd better free your mind instead." In such a viewpoint, even revolutionary politics is part of the old social order, a game that is lost as soon as it is begun. Reversing the idea of creating a revolution and then creating a new man, cultural radicals believe that if you create a new man—starting with yourself—the transformation of society will take care of itself.

This idea is at the center of a cluster of attitudes, biases, points of view, and ideas that comprise the counter culture's world view. Central to it is a kind of anarchism, summed up in the popular phrase "Do your own thing." This kind of individualism to the point of egomania is somehow not at war with another chief value, communalism, the idea that the nuclear family must be extended outward to embrace many other families until a kind of tribe has been reborn. Perhaps the opposition between individualism and communalism dissolves in the medium of a third value: mysticism. This aspect most clearly separates cultural from other kinds of radicals. The belief is in the basic experience that underlies all religious traditions, in the mystery that gives birth to formal churches. Reality is viewed as ultimately awesome, ineffable, and beautiful. Such ideas lead directly to the role of drugs, and it is certainly difficult to imagine the counter culture without mind-altering substances. Most important have been the hallucinogens—psilocybin, mescaline, peyote, and the potent LSD. Both the scientific and popular literature have shown that the effect of these drugs is similar to the mystical experiences reported by sages for many centuries. Hallucinogens are capable of providing a new vision of reality and of introducing a kind of knowledge that is neither linear nor rational, but poetic. Like mysticism and religion, the drug experience can help to provide meaning and can approach questions about life and death that normal politics or the scientific mentality never even bother to ask.

If cultural radicals appear to be against both technology and the concerns of politics and government, they show no consistency in this stance. Young adherents have been inclined to use many technological products, and the electric guitar is certainly crucial to their chief art form, popular music. Similarly, many have proved quite willing to accept benefits from the welfare state, especially as recipients of Department of Agriculture food stamps. Such inconsistencies in philosophy and practice can be dissolved in the solution of a most powerful idea: love. As the Beatles once wrote in what could have been a generation's theme song: "All you need is love." This is seen as the power that holds the universe together, that makes the world go around. While simplistic, such an idea is familiar; it is at the heart of more than one religious tradition, including the Christianity which is America's heritage.

From the mid-sixties to the early seventies, the values of the cultural radicals were broadcast through a variety of media. Most important was popular music, and hundreds of hit songs advised millions of listeners to, in Timothy Leary's phrase, "Turn on, tune in, and drop out." The underground press, a network of newspapers that sprang up all over the country, blended drug information, soft-core pornography and revolutionary politics as it disseminated counter-cultural values. A new kind of art form, the love-in or be-in, where thousands of people gathered in the open to celebrate life with drugs, sex, and music, also helped to spread the gospel. In some cases such meetings reached gigantic proportions. The Woodstock Music Festival became a kind of love-in when young people simply refused to pay admission and took over the area; it involved half a million people for three days.

How much such messages cause and how much they simply reflect social change is irrelevant. What is certain is that these values have been embraced by hundreds of thousands, even millions, of students, and many young adults, faculty members, and professional people—many well beyond the age of thirty. Not all such people have left home to search for a new life, but their attitudes towards life and work have changed, as have the texture, feel, and quality of their daily reality. Certain changes have been highly visible. A revival of crafts—pottery, jewelry, stained glass, woodworking—not only gives new integrity to useful products, but provides a livelihood for thousands of people who do not wish to participate in the academic or corporate rat race. Organic food stores and cooperatives, small restaurants and a move back to the farm also provide counter-institutions to support dropouts from universities and corporations. Perhaps the most enduring creation has been the communal movement. This attempt to downplay competition, destroy the isolation and loneliness of the nuclear family, and extend the range of caring human relationships has by now involved hundreds of thousands of Americans. First a product of the urban young and centered in places like San Francisco's Haight-Ashbury district and New York's East Village, communes spread to rural areas of New England, California, Oregon, New Mexico, and Colorado as people retreated from the problems of city life to a more traditional existence on the land. Today the communal movement involves mature people as well as the young, professors, attorneys, and engineers along with students and dropouts, and it is flourishing in both urban and rural America.

Unlike communes, most manifestations of cultural radicalism seem to have suffered some decline in recent years. Both pop music and the underground press were altered by the pressure of financial success. In the press, pornography became more popular than dissent, though even a sexually-oriented newspaper like the *Los Angeles Free Press* continues to publicize cultural change and *Rolling Stone*, a kind of *New York Times* for young people, still promotes counter-cultural values. While mid-seventies pop music tends towards bizarre modes of transvestism and sexual deviance, a surprising number of songs continue to echo radical themes. In 1974 a serious artist like Bob Dylan could make a triumphal tour of the country, and in 1975 and 1976 his informal, unscheduled "Rolling Thunder Review" (including his female counterpart, Joan Baez) was immensely popular wherever it unexpectedly surfaced.

Cultural radicalism has been much less evident in recent years. One reason for this is that the large, urban centers where it first flourished have drastically changed. The Haight-Ashbury district of San Francisco was destroyed by the dual assault of criminality and popularity; tour buses arrived, chic boutiques sprang up, and organized crime moved in to capture the lucrative drug business. Since most of this was caused by heavy media coverage, serious partisans of cultural change learned their lesson and began to shun the press. A typical strategy was a retreat to small-town America. Today, in fact, there are centers such as Santa Cruz, California, where the values and forms of cultural radicalism seem to have become almost community norms.

The notions expressed by the counter culture may have startled many Americans, but they are certainly familiar to historians. Virtually all the counter culture's ideas have been espoused by earlier individuals and groups. The 1840s, with the millennial and communal movements sired by Charles Fourier, Robert Owen, and dozens of religious groups, were rich in denunciations of competition and the nuclear family. Certainly nobody has expressed radical individualism, anarchism, or the virtue of living close to nature better than Henry David Thoreau. Indeed, the Transcendental Movement to which he was connected always insisted that truth is transcendent, something known only to the heart and intuitions and never through the intellect. Ralph Waldo Emerson would no doubt have been shocked by the antics of hippies, but he would have found their ideas congenial.

In the decade before World War I a vigorous kind of cultural radicalism flourished in many parts of the United States. Centering in Greenwich Village, America's bohemia contained a powerful movement of social, political, and artistic liberation, all of which were believed to be intimately related. Communal living, experimentation with some drugs (chiefly peyote), free love, anarchism, and a certain amount of rural longing were some of the doctrines of that era, and they influenced a significant number of visual and literary artists, people like Eugene O'Neill, Marsden Hartley, John Sloan, Max Eastman, Floyd Dell, Alfred Stieglitz, and John Dos Passos. Many of these beliefs, and certainly an emphasis on hedonism and sensuality, were carried into the literary flowering of the twenties and have remained part of the ethos of the American art community ever since. Of course it is the Beat Generation of the fifties—Allen Ginsberg, Jack Kerouac, Gary Snyder, Lawrence Ferlinghetti and associates—who were the direct fathers of the counter culture. Beat has two meanings: "beat up," a down-and-out anarchistic aspect, and "beatific," a religious aspect. Such a mixture of poverty and spirituality is common to cultural radicals across the ages.

Even this brief glance at history should suggest one point—the lifestyle and values of the recent counter culture have much in common with those of artists in the Western world since the Romantic movement. For over one hundred and fifty years, artists have opposed the lack of transcendent vision that is the burden of the linear, instrumental mentality. Since the eighteenth century artists have been the carriers of transcendence, of religion, even if the religion has sometimes been art itself. The Enlightenment defeated a human institution, the Church, but it could not defeat the impulse towards religion. Technology and industrialism paid off in a rising standard of living, but to the artist, matters of the spirit and imagination were always more important than products.

Contemporary Americans are living at the end of a dream of materialism that has been pursued with increasing success since the beginnings of the industrial revolution. We are the payoff generation, the beneficiaries of one hundred and fifty years of economic progress. Yet it is the children of affluent, white, middle-class people who recently were turning their backs on suburbia and going to live in dingy city apartments and primitive rural communes. A moralist might consider this a reaffirmation that man does not live by bread alone. The historian can see that affluence has brought extended years of freedom to more young people. This means time free of economic pressures to experiment with life, while access to drugs produce insights into reality reserved for mystics, vision-

Stock, Boston

aries, and artists. All reports indicate that the hallucinogens make the world seem deeper and more mysterious than mundane reality. To this religious experience must be added a homelier one. The scientific ideal of rationality and technology puts man in the place of god. He can restructure the environment to suit his needs. Yet during the sixties it began to appear that science has its limits, and in a variety of ways the environment began to say no to man. Pollution has become a tangible, worsening, and perhaps uncontrollable concomitant of American life. This gives powerful backing to the old idea that the universe is ultimately mysterious, that man is far less than a god who can shape the world to his will.

There are at least two ways of looking at the cultural critique of modern society. One is to examine its overt doctrines, the other is to regard it as a symptom of social change. Quite explicitly, Roszak has challenged the idea that science and technology are value free. If he never quite demands the abolition of technology, he makes a case that pollution, waste, junk products, competition, neuroses, war, and a lack of transcendence result from approaching reality with the objective consciousness of technocracy. This is holistic thinking. It refuses to accept the glories of supersonic jets, moon shots, and social engineering at their own value and goes on to ask the cost of manipulating not only the environment but also other human beings in the name of some idea of rationality. Ultimately it finds modern society woefully deficient in meeting many basic human needs that more "backward" cultures fulfill—brotherly love, job satisfaction, joy, community, and meaning in life.

It is certainly possible to reject such a viewpoint and argue that what society needs is better science and technology—more objectivity, not less. That leaves the problem of why so many people seem disillusioned with the present social order. Diverse evidence from imaginative literature and the studies of social scientists attest to a growing dissatisfaction with middle-class work and life in this century. So do indices of social disorganization—statistics for crime, alcoholism, mental disorders, divorce, and extramarital sexual relations. The almost utopian promise of benefits from technology has evidently not resulted in happiness, even for those who have gained the most. This does not mean that millions of Americans are ready to rush off to communal farms, but it does suggest that vast numbers of people may be looking for value systems and lifestyles more fulfilling than those depicted as the cultural norm. Surely the vast interest in mysticism and group psychotherapy and the many new movements towards spiritual and psychological liberation that have become national fads give further evidence of a population in search of new faiths by which to live. Ultimately, the question becomes personal and each human being must decide whether the state of the planet today does not make imperative more reverence for life, oneness with nature, and a search for inner spiritual realities.

Such questions have in recent years penetrated to the center of positivism and objective consciousness, the academic world. Here some strange things are happening that parallel the social movement of the counter culture. A number of serious scholars have been quietly leaving behind the old models of reality and have begun a search for others more congenial. This is in no way a movement, yet enough has occurred to make the historian take note. Quite simply, academics from many disciplines are moving beyond objective consciousness to expand the notion of scholarly activity. Norman O. Brown, the distinguished classics professor and philosopher, has become an apocalyptic visionary who in *Love's Body* has proclaimed poetic statement as the ultimate truth. Anthropologist Carlos Castaneda has produced four volumes about a Yaqui Indian shaman which are no less than a chronicle of an intellectual struggle between the author's ideas of objective, consensual reality and the Indian's notions of an animistic world. When the primitive world view proved more powerful than his own, Castaneda gave up academia to become a shaman himself. R. D. Laing, the respected British psychoanalyst, has gone from major studies of schizophrenia like *The Divided Self* to the notion that insanity is a high form of knowledge, an insight into realities obscured by normal consciousness. In *The Politics of Experience*, Laing moves from scholarship to poetry, and in *Knots* he creates a series of paradoxical statements that resemble Zen koans. Both methods seem necessary to convey truths beyond those that normal language can handle. In the field of history, at least two practitioners have gone beyond the prevailing canons of their discipline. Martin Duberman has recently found it necessary to break down traditional objectivity and to insert details about himself into a book-length study of Black Mountain College. William Irwin Thompson, in *At the Edge of History*, has challenged the notion of progress that underlies both capitalist and Marxist historians, evaluating history in terms of the possible truth of such myths as the story of Atlantis.

Pure science itself has not been immune to this new mood. Biologist John Lilly, who gave up research funded by the American Navy on dolphins because he found them equal to human beings in intelligence and imagination, has in *Center of the Cyclone* described his research into mystical phenomena. American philosopher William James also engaged in psychic research early in this century, but his tentative forays into the area are tame compared to Lilly's accounts, which sound very close to science fiction. Psychologist Robert Ornstein is much more sober than Lilly, but his studies may be more revolutionary. In *The Psychology of Consciousness* he relates how experiments have shown the two halves of the brain to have distinct functions; one half is intellectual and logical, the other spatial and intuitive. This implies that the scientific and mystical aspects of man are equally valid. Modern society only rewards one half of what human beings are, shortchanging man's potential.

It is difficult to know exactly what these strange goings-on in academia portend. Perhaps there have always been oddball professors with outlandish theories. Yet taken together with the recent counter culture, added to the fact that among theoretical physicists the subatomic world seems to be dissolving into a mystery of unmanageable and evanescent particles, put alongside the latest astronomical theories which sound like a Hindu cosmogony of universes dying and being reborn, it may in fact mean that some major change in our models of reality is at hand. Marx speaks of the flight of the intellectuals as a stage in the preparation of revolution. What is currently occurring in the academic world may be the beginnings of a similar flight, but with different ends. If enough intellectuals find the old models of reality too confining or outmoded, eventually those models will change. It is possible that the old notions of objectivity make for too narrow a definition of both scientific and social reality. It is possible that technology, which can only answer "more" or "faster" to any problem, is too narrow a straitjacket for the human spirit. It is possible that a stage has been reached in social life where there is a new need for some kind of religion, mystery, or faith to give human life a purpose. Historical periods of religion and mystery have followed rational, empirical periods in the past; there is no reason why they should not do so again.

To speak of such things, however, is to speak of the future, a land where no human, and certainly no historian, can easily tread. Cultural radicalism is a phenomenon of the present and the past. It is not the first movement to raise disturbing questions about life in industrial and technological society, but it is perhaps the most difficult to understand. Americans—Westerners in general—tend to think of society in terms of problems which can be solved. This attitude is fully part of radical movements of the left, which in this assumption are at one with people pursuing mainstream politics. Cultural radicalism is different. While not truly passive, it certainly includes no conscious plans for remolding society. History is seen as made up of countless individual decisions, with its ultimate course unknowable. Rather than seeking to solve social problems or change the world, the cultural radical attempts to free himself from those institutions and values which seem oppressive and inhuman. The idea is to live fully, both for oneself and perhaps as an example to others. In short, to create a loving world, you should not merely preach about love—you should act from the center of your being as a loving person.

It is the sum of all such individual actions that will create the future. If the reaction against technology and rationality is inevitable in the face of the demands of an increasingly impersonal and inhuman social order, then the ramifications of this reaction will be many in America and in other parts of the world in years to come. Cultural radicalism will return in force, not as a fad but as a change in consciousness that will alter social, political, and economic realities. Right now, cultural radicals in the United States go about their daily lives, transforming their own realities. If you are at one with them, gentle reader, the . the next move is up to you.

Radicalism is normally viewed as involving programs to drastically **SUMMARY** change society. But there is a kind of radicalism that has little to do with conscious plans for social reconstruction. Involving alterations in world views, lifestyles, and consciousness, it may be termed "cultural radicalism." In the sixties and early seventies there was much debate over the most recent manifestation of this phenomenon, something originally termed the "counter culture" by historian Theodore Roszak. This article is an introduction to both cultural radicalism and the counter culture. First it focuses on the beliefs and actions of the counter culture, and then it shows how these reflect a movement of long standing in Western history.

The term "counter culture" was brought into prominence by academics, but the phenomena it described were widespread in the latter half of the sixties. Along with movements against the Vietnam war and those supporting ethnic consciousness were some strange goings-on that centered around the young people then called "hippies." These youngsters refused to take regular jobs, indulged in the use of hallucinogenic drugs, and enjoyed loud music and sexual exhibitionism that made parents and educators uneasy and alarmed. The philosophy of the hippies, the central ideas of the counter culture, were carried in the pages of the new underground press and in the lyrics of wildly successful popular songs. They included an odd blend of anarchism, communalism, and mysticism, all dissolved in a solution of brotherly and erotic love.

This counter culture was part of a larger tradition of protest against a society that has been growing increasingly rational, objective, and technological since the beginning of the nineteenth century. As a countertrend, cultural radicalism has asserted that the unconscious, affective, aesthetic, and mystical side of human beings is as important—perhaps more so—as the rational and productive side. Such beliefs first belonged in the nineteenth century to a subculture of romantic artists, including Americans like Henry David Thoreau. In the twentieth century such ideas have spread outward to larger numbers of people, from the Bohemians of Greenwich Village to the beatniks of San Francisco in the fifties and then to the hippies of the sixties. Because the social changes demanded involve no political programs, they are difficult to fully grasp or analyze. But if the trend continues, and if more intellectuals become involved, cultural radicalism may result in a radical restructuring of our envisioned future—for when beliefs about social values and goals alter for large numbers of people, social upheaval is usually on the way.

NOTES   1. Kenneth Keniston, *Youth and Dissent: The Rise of a New Opposition* (New York: Harcourt Brace Jovanovich, 1971), p.

2. Theodore Roszak, *The Making of a Counter Culture* (New York: Anchor Books, 1969), p. 45.

3. Phillip Slater, *The Pursuit of Loneliness* (Boston: Beacon Press, 1970), p. 100.

QUESTIONS

1 Why is "cultural radicalism" difficult to define or analyze?

2 How can you distinguish cultural radicalism from other forms of political and/or social radicalism?

3 What is the "world view" of the counter culture?

4 Do the ideas of the counter culture reflect or create social change?

5 Trace the historical roots of cultural radicalism. Why has it arisen?

6 Why does the counter culture criticize technology? Is such criticism valid?

7 Why should anyone take cultural radicalism seriously?

8 What does the word "hippie" mean to you? To your parents? If there is any difference in your view and that of your parents, how do you account for it?

READINGS   Cowley, Malcolm. *Exile's Return*. New York: Viking, 1951.

Lipton, Lawrence. *The Holy Barbarians*. New York: Julian Messner, 1959.

May, Henry. *The End of American Innocence*. New York: Alfred A. Knopf, 1959.

Reich, Charles. *The Greening of America*. New York: Random House, 1970.

Roszak, Theodore. *Where the Wasteland Ends*. New York: Doubleday, 1972.

Slater, Phillip. *Earthwalk*. New York: Doubleday, 1974.

Tyler, Alice Felt. *Freedom's Ferment*. Minneapolis: University of Minnesota Press, 1944.

CONTRIBUTORS

CHAPTER 1 | M. J. LUNINE

M. J. Lunine is a student of the politics and ideology of such countries as India, Turkey, and the United States. He has taught at the State University of Iowa, the University of Colorado, Fisk University, the University of Istanbul, and Kent State University. He served as Dean of Hampshire College and is presently Professor of Interdisciplinary Studies and Dean of the Western College of Miami University in Ohio.

CHAPTERS 2 and 11 | JOSEPH BOSKIN

Joseph Boskin is Professor of History and Afro-American Studies and Co-Director of the Urban Studies Program at Boston University. He has previously taught at the State University of Iowa and the University of Southern California, and was a visiting professor at the University of California at Los Angeles. He is the author of numerous scholarly and popular articles on racial conflict, slavery, racial humor and urban issues which have appeared in The Annals of The American Academy of Political and Social Science, The New York Times Magazine, Pacific Historical Review, the Journal of Popular Culture, *and others. His books include* Into Slavery: Racial Decisions in the Virginia Colony, Seasons of Rebellion: Protest and Radicalism in Recent America *(with Robert Rosenstone),* Urban Racial Violence in the Twentieth Century, *and* The Oppenheimer Affair: A Political Play in Three Acts *(with Fred Krinsky). At the University of Southern California he was twice selected as the Outstanding Professor. In 1968 he was awarded an Emmy for his NBC Public Affairs series, "The Negro in American Culture." He also served as a major consultant to the Governor's Commission on the Los Angeles Riot in 1965 and 1966.*

CHAPTERS 3 and 4 | DEENA METZGER

Deena Metzger is a writer and a poet. She is director of the writing program of the Feminist Studio Workshop at the Woman's Building in Los Angeles and Professor of English at Los Angeles Valley College. Skin: Shadows/SILENCE, *a novel, was published by West Coast Poetry Review in 1975. She has just completed a novel,* Scars on the Body Politic, *and a monograph,* In Her Image: Woman's Culture. The Book of Hags *was adapted from a novel in progress for Pacifica Radio in 1976. Her poetry and fiction have been widely published, as have her numerous critical articles on women's culture, literature, writing, and education.*

CHAPTER 5 | FLOYD BARBOUR

Floyd Barbour is a graduate of Bowdoin College in Brunswick, Maine. He has written a number of plays which have been performed at Bowdoin College,

the Yale Festival of One-Act Plays, Brandeis University, Howard
University, and M.I.T. Barbour has lectured on Afro-American Studies at
Williams College, Harvard Medical School, Bowdoin College, the University of
Pittsburgh, and Howard University. He is the editor of The Black Power
Revolt and The Black Seventies. An adaptation of his The Bird
Cage appears in Black Scenes, edited by Alice Childress. He is at present
an assistant professor in the department of humanities at the Massachusetts
Institute of Technology, and professor adjunct to the Afro-American
Studies Center at Boston University.

CHAPTER 6 | FRED T. ARNSTEIN

Fred Arnstein grew up in Chicago, where he attended public schools and lived
in both working-class and middle-class neighborhoods. He continued his
education at Antioch College and the University of Michigan.
He has never lived in poverty himself, but has long been concerned
about poverty and other social and political problems. He participated in
a number of political activities during the 1960s, particularly tenants' rights,
and has done some union organizing at Boston University, where he
now works. He has recently written on the relationship between voluntarism
in hospitals and national efforts to consolidate and promote volunteer activities.

CHAPTER 7 | DAVID F. GREENBERG

David F. Greenberg is a research physicist at Carnegie-Mellon University doing
research in theoretical high-energy physics and teaching history and economics.
He is on leave of absence from the staff of CADRE (Chicago Area Draft
Resisters). With Beverly Houghton he has edited Behind Bars:
The Prison Experiences of War Resisters; an anthology of writings by
men and women who have been imprisoned for antiwar activities. He is a
member of an American Friends Service Committee working party on alternatives
to the present system of criminal justice.

CHAPTER 8 | ROBERT ROSS

Robert Ross is Chairperson of the Department of Sociology and Social
Anthropology at Clark University in Worcester, Massachusetts. He spent 1977
as visiting assistant professor at the University of Michigan's Sociology
Department and School of Social Work, and has also worked at the
Institute for Social Research at the University of Michigan. Professor Ross has
studied community planners and the impact of social movements on social
service professions and his articles on these topics have been published
in various scholarly and professional journals. His writing on
politics and social problems has appeared in both professional
journals and political magazines.
Professor Ross has worked as a community organizer, and as a civil rights
and antiwar activist. He was among the founders of Students for a Democratic
Society, and later, the New University Conference. His current interests include
research on the impact and development of the movement against the war
in Vietnam, and on the nature of recent social policy. He also teaches
Marxian and Weberian theory.

CHAPTER 9 | JAY OSTROWER

Jay Ostrower attended Brooklyn College, where he majored in history and political science with a specialty in urbanism. He received a master's degree in city planning from Harvard's Graduate School of Design in 1967. After a summer working for the London County Council, he worked with the Boston Regional Planning Project on a metropolitan transportation plan for Boston, and during the formative years of the antipoverty program worked with Action for Boston Community Development, the local community action agency. From 1966 to 1969 Mr. Ostrower worked with Arthur D. Little, Inc., a major consulting firm, to help cities prepare for the model cities program. A study of community decision making in the northeast gave him the opportunity to study small community policies and problems firsthand. He then helped East Cleveland, Ohio (an example of the new black suburb discussed in the chapter), develop and implement a program to respond to the major social and racial changes the city had undergone. In Glassboro, New Jersey, Mr. Ostrower planned a new housing development, worked on regional and local planning efforts and developed programs in education and health services to link Glassboro State College to the surrounding community.
In 1973, Mr. Ostrower became Director of the Urban Affairs Program at Boston University, where as head of the master's and undergraduate program that provided part-time education to professionals and students interested in urban careers, he added new courses and made the program a major element in the urban university. Now teaching in the Department of Journalism at Boston University, Mr. Ostrower recently completed a study of the CETA program in the State of Rhode Island.

CHAPTER 10 | ROSLYN L. FELDBERG AND JANET KOHEN

Roslyn L. Feldberg teaches sociology (political sociology and women's studies) at Boston University. She previously lived in Scotland and taught at the University of Aberdeen. As a member of the Women's Research Center of Boston, she has been conducting a study of single-parent families. The group is currently writing a book about single parenthood in America and has previously written several articles on the subject, including "Divorce: Chance of a New Lifetime." The study of single-parent families led to analyzing family life more fully, resulting in several papers with Janet Kohen. Among these papers is "Family Life in an Antifamily Setting: A Critique of Marriage and Divorce." She has also analyzed women's experience of and position in the labor force, concentrating on women in clerical work. She is currently continuing research on clerical workers and developing a new interdisciplinary course, "Women, Society, and Culture," with three other feminist professors.

Janet Kohen received her Ph.D. in social psychology from the University of Iowa in 1972 after working for five years as research director on a delinquency prevention project with the Seattle Atlantic Street Center. She has also conducted evaluation research for other social agencies and mental health centers. She has taught sociology, women's studies, and law and justice as an assistant professor of sociology at the University of Massachusetts at Boston. She has also been working with the Women's Research Center of Boston, a feminist, interdisciplinary group who are now finishing a project on how divorced single-parent mothers organize and take care of their families. She has collaborated on several articles analyzing the nature of the contemporary American family, and is writing a book on the social, political, and economic role of children in American society. In the past two years, she has been doing research on jury behavior and selection.

CHAPTER 12 | PAUL NASH

Paul Nash is Professor and Chairman of the Department of Humanistic and Behavioral Studies at Boston University. He is a member of the NTL Institute for Applied Behavioral Science and an accredited member of the International Association of Applied Social Scientists. Past president of the History of Education Society, the American Educational Studies Association, and the New England Philosophy of Education Society, he is also a Fellow and past executive board member of the Philosophy of Education Society. He has served as a member of the editorial board of the Harvard Educational Review, the History of Education Quarterly, and Educational Philosophy and Theory. In addition he has been consulting editor in education for Random House, Inc., Alfred A. Knopf, Inc., and John Wiley and Sons, Inc. He is the author of Authority and Freedom in Education: An Introduction to the Philosophy of Education, Culture and the State: Matthew Arnold and Continental Education, Models of Man: Explorations in the Western Educational Tradition, and A Humanistic Approach to Performance-Based Teacher Education. Coauthor of The Educated Man: Studies in the History of Educational Thought, Mr. Nash has edited over thirty books and written over fifty articles and reviews for scholarly journals in the United States, Canada, England, and Europe, including the most recent edition of the Encyclopaedia Britannica.

CHAPTER 13 | ROBERT N. BUTLER

Robert N. Butler is a practicing psychiatrist and psychoanalyst at the Washington School of Psychiatry. He is also on the faculties of the Washington Psychoanalytic Institute and the Howard and George Washington University schools of medicine in Washington, D.C. Dr. Butler has concentrated in the area of gerontology for several decades and has written widely and consulted in the field of aging. His books include Why Survive? Being Old in America, Aging and Mental Health (with Myrna I. Lewis), and Human Aging (co-authored). Additionally, he has published many articles in professional journals and popular publications. Dr. Butler has served as a consultant for many governmental agencies exploring issues relating to the aged and aging. He was a consultant to the U.S. Senate Committee on Aging and served as chairperson of the Group for the Advancement of Psychiatry's Committee on Aging. He has long been committed to public advocacy and policy in regard to the ways in which the elderly are treated in American society.

CHAPTER 14 | DAVID KUNZLE

David Kunzle received his B.A. and M.A. degrees in French and German literature from the University of Cambridge, and his Ph.D. in the History of Art from the University of London. He has taught History of Art at the National Gallery in London, at the University of Toronto, and (since 1965) at the

University of California. He has published widely in the fields of popular and political art, particularly graphics. He is the author of Posters of Protest. His major book is The Early Comic Strip and he has recently completed Fashion and Fetishism. He has written numerous articles on children's literature, and on the revolutionary art of Cuba and of Chile. Mr. Kunzle also edited, translated, and introduced the best-selling pioneer study in cultural imperialism, How to Read Donald Duck: Imperialist Ideology in the Disney Comic, by \Ariel Dorfman and Armand Mattelart.

CHAPTER 15 | ROBERT A. ROSENSTONE

Robert A. Rosenstone, a Professor of History at the California Institute of Technology, has written extensively in the fields of political, social, and cultural radicalism. His books include Romantic Revolutionary: A Biography of John Reed and Crusade of the Left: The Lincoln Battalion in the Spanish Civil War. He was coeditor (with Joseph Boskin) of the influential anthology Seasons of Rebellion: Protest and Radicalism in Recent America, editor of a seminal collection about the radical right entitled Protest from the Right, and collaborated with Argentine poet Marcel Covian in producing Los cantos de la conmocion: veinte años de rock, the first major work on rock music to appear in Spanish. Mr. Rosenstone has published articles, both scholarly and popular, in the Journal of American History, The New Republic, the South Atlantic Quarterly, Popular Music and Society, The Annals of the American Academy of Political and Social Science, The Progressive, and the Los Angeles Times. One of his articles, "The Times They are A-Changin': The Music of Protest," has been included in more than ten anthologies, and his work has appeared in French, Spanish, Italian, and Japanese translations. In the 1974–75 academic year he was a visiting Fulbright professor at the University of Kyushu, in Japan. Currently he is studying Japanese-American cultural contacts in the nineteenth century in an effort to assess the impact of Japanese culture and values upon American society.